Pro Football Schedules

Pro Football Schedules

A Complete Historical Guide from 1933 to the Present

Ivan Urena

McFarland & Company, Inc., Publishers
Jefferson, North Carolina, and London

LIBRARY OF CONGRESS CATALOGUING-IN-PUBLICATION DATA

Urena, Ivan, 1968–
Pro football schedules : a complete historical guide from 1933 to the present / Ivan Urena.
 p. cm.
Includes bibliographical references and index.

ISBN 978-0-7864-7351-9
softcover : acid free paper ∞

1. Football—Records—United States—History.
2. Football teams—Records—United States—History.
3. National Football League—History. I. Title.

GV955.U74 2014   796.330973—dc23   2013035475

BRITISH LIBRARY CATALOGUING DATA ARE AVAILABLE

© 2014 Ivan Urena. All rights reserved

No part of this book may be reproduced or transmitted in any form or by any means, electronic or mechanical, including photocopying or recording, or by any information storage and retrieval system, without permission in writing from the publisher.

On the cover: NFL Commissioner Pete Rozelle (right) and the league's director of public relations, Jim Kensil, work on the upcoming schedule in New York City on March 18, 1963 (Associated Press); football linemen © 2014 Laurin Rinder

Manufactured in the United States of America

*McFarland & Company, Inc., Publishers
Box 611, Jefferson, North Carolina 28640
www.mcfarlandpub.com*

Acknowledgments

Words cannot express how grateful I am to some very special people who contributed to this book and helped me get across the goal line. First I would like to thank the research staff at the Pro Football Hall of Fame in Canton, Ohio, Pete Fierle, Saleem Choudhry and Jon Kendle, who were a tremendous help, providing me with many of the research materials used for this book.

A special thank you goes to my friends at the Professional Football Researchers Association which is made up of the sport's foremost authors and historians. Executive director Ken Crippen, Mark L. Ford, Andy Piascik and Chris Willis read my original draft and provided feedback and expert advice. I am grateful, as well, to the PFRA Linescore Committee, which provided game summaries and linescores for every game since 1920, and for PFRA president Tod Maher's website, profootballarchives.com, an invaluable tool for examining team-by-team schedules and game-site information going back to the 1920s.

My thanks also go out to Jon Zimmer, NFL information manager and editor of the *NFL Record & Fact Book*. Jon and I worked together to correct a number of tiebreaker explanations contained in the past standings section of the NFL record book, and I will always appreciate his kind words and assistance.

I want to thank my friend and NFL tiebreaker guru Joe Ferreira. Joe has an annual tiebreaker blog on CBSSports.com in which, over the last several weeks of the season, he analyzes the NFL playoff race and posts official NFL playoff scenarios. I have had the pleasure of participating in Joe's blog the last several seasons by contributing tiebreaker tidbits of seasons past and providing historical perspective to the NFL playoff race. Thanks, Joe, for providing insight on the changes to the NFL scheduling formula during the 1990s and the transition to the 2002 scheduling format.

I am also very thankful to Kay Hoaglin and the friendly staff at Mid-Continent Public Library in Independence, Missouri, as well as the New York Public Library for its historical newspaper archives, which were indispensable for this research project.

Finally, this book would not have been possible without the loving support of family and friends. I am deeply grateful to my mother, Nelly, and my father, Rafael; my brothers, Aldo, Armando, Martin, and Juan Carlos; and my sisters, Aura, Loira, Amanda, and Martha, who have always inspired me and have supported me throughout this long process. It has truly been an amazing experience.

Table of Contents

Acknowledgments v
Preface 1
Introduction 3

1933 23
1934 25
1935 27
1936 28
1937–1942 30
1943 32
1944 32
1945 33
1946 (NFL) 35
1947–1949 (NFL) 35
1946–1948 (AAFC) 37
1949 (AAFC) 38
1950 39
1951 40
1952 42
1953–1959 44
1960 (NFL) 45
1961–1965 (NFL) 47
1966 (NFL) 49
1967–1969 (NFL) 50
1960–1965 (AFL) 53
1966–1967 (AFL) 54
1968–1969 (AFL) 55
1970–1975 56
1976 71
1977 80

1978–1987 84
1988–1994 116
1995–1998 135
1999–2001 145
2002–2017 154

Appendix A: Schedule Release Dates (1933–2013) 213
Appendix B: Number of Teams and Games Played by Season (1933–2012) 214
Appendix C: Divisional, Conference and Interconference Games Per Team/Season (1933–2012) 215
Appendix D: Number of Regular Season Games in Pro Football History (1920–2012) 218
Appendix E: Scheduling Facts and Figures 221
Appendix F: Site Priorities for Postseason Games (1933–2012) 235
Chapter Notes 245
Bibliography 249
Index 251

Preface

During the National Football League's 61st season, I picked up a copy of the *1980 NFL Record Manual*, which was jam-packed with results and statistics from the 1979 season and included a list of All-Pro teams, a chronology of professional football, yearly statistical leaders, and much more. There was one section in particular, "Figuring the 1981 Schedule," that really piqued my interest. The first sentence read: "As soon as the final game of the 1980 NFL regular season has been completed, you'll be able to determine each of the 28 NFL teams' 1981 schedule[s]."[1] The four-page section detailed the NFL's scheduling formula, included a blank template of the NFL division standings (for recording the order of finish, which was the reference point in determining each team's schedule), and contained a table that listed each team's opponents depending on where it finished in the standings.

As the 1980 season progressed, I used the manual to keep track of when each team clinched a specific position in the standings. After the final Monday night game of the season, in which San Diego defeated Pittsburgh to clinch the AFC Western division title, each team's 1981 opponents were set. (See the chapter that covers 1978–1987, which includes the 1980 final standings as well as each team's 1981 non-divisional home and away matchups.) The end of each regular season thus provided a first look at the schedules — or, anyway, the competition — each team faced the following year. The NFL then released its official schedule, with playing dates and times, in the spring.

It was during the 1980 season, then, in my earliest of schedule-figuring efforts, that the idea for this book originated as I began to keep a record and create charts of each team's opponents for every season. The introduction includes a brief history on the evolution of the pro football schedule from the loose scheduling practices of the 1920s and the 1931 controversy between Green Bay and Portsmouth which led to the NFL producing an official playing schedule to today's intricate schedule-making process. The heart of the book explains how the NFL, AFL and AAFC determined each team's opponents for every season, exploring all of the scheduling formats used in pro football history from the 1933 season, when the NFL was divided into two divisions, to the current scheduling formula which was instituted in 2002. Each year or period of years (if the same format was used) is broken down into three parts: the league's alignment, an in-depth look at the scheduling format, and an exhaustive home-and-away breakdown chart of non-division opponents. Round-robin games within a division are not included in the breakdown charts as these are automatically scheduled on a home-and-away basis.

A clear explanation of the 1970–1977 scheduling formula is given which includes an enlightening discussion on how interconference matchups were determined. Additionally, beginning with the 1978–1987 section, since a team's schedule was then based on where it finished in its division the year before, the final divisional standings for each season are included for reference along with the home and away non-divisional breakdown chart. The 2002 section lists each team's rotation of non-divisional opponents through the 2017 season. As of this book's publication, opponents for 2014 and beyond are unofficial but are based on the assumption that the NFL will continue its current scheduling policy, barring future expansion or a change to the 16-game schedule. For the 2013–2017 seasons, 14 out of each team's 16 opponents are provided. The final two opponents for each season will be determined at the end of the previous regular season.

There are six appendices which include official schedule release dates, the number of teams and games played per team, and a breakdown of divisional, conference, and interconference games for each season since 1933. A chart with the number of regular season games played in NFL, AFL, and AAFC history is also provided.

Furthermore, the appendix "Site Priorities for Postseason Games (1933-2012)" provides a detailed explanation of how playoff game sites have been determined since the 1933 NFL Championship game. It also presents the different playoff formats that have been used. Particular attention is given to the 1970–1974 era which in my opinion has yet to be explained thoroughly in any online or published source. The rotation that was used for the Divisional Playoffs and Conference Championship games is provided which will explain oddities such as why the undefeated Miami Dolphins had to play at Pittsburgh in the 1972 AFC Championship game as well as why the Cowboys hosted both the Rams and Vikings in 1973 NFC playoffs. While sites for league and conference championship games alternated by division from 1934 to 1974, beginning in 1975 the NFL began seeding teams based on best won-lost-tied record to determine homefield advantage.

Finally, whether you want to figure out the makeup of the schedule for the 1966 Packers, 1975 Steelers, 1984 49ers, 1992 Cowboys, 2004 Patriots or your favorite team for any season, or want a historical year-by-year breakdown, this book includes all of the pro football scheduling formulas complete with non-divisional opponent charts for every team since 1933 — all in a single volume. A thorough examination of all changes to regular season and postseason scheduling methods in pro football history has been made by carefully reviewing NFL, AFL, and AAFC team and league media guides, NFL press releases, league bylaws, and the official minutes of NFL owners' meetings. It is my hope that this book will be a useful resource for all pro football fans, researchers and historians.

Introduction

Schedule release! Those two words reverberate every April across the football world as teams and their fans gather across the country and eagerly await the release of the National Football League schedule. What was once a brief press release issued by the league commissioner and usually found hidden in a small column in the following day's newspaper has grown into a spectacle filled with lots of buzz and speculation as fans create mock schedules and peer at television listings weeks in advance in anticipation of the schedule's release. The countdown to what has become one of the most anticipated dates on the NFL calendar reaches its climax as the schedule for the upcoming season is finally unveiled in a primetime event shown nationally on the NFL Network, ESPN and NFL.com. But with regards to the playing schedule, how has the NFL determined which clubs play each other? What methods have been used to come up with an equitable schedule? And what changes have been made and how has the scheduling of opponents evolved throughout pro football history?

On September 26, 1920, in the first game featuring a team from the American Professional Football Association (which would be renamed the National Football League in 1922), the Rock Island Independents defeated the St. Paul Ideals 48–0. The following week, the new league would have its first full weekend slate of games which included the first matchup featuring two APFA clubs with the Dayton Triangles defeating the Columbus Panhandles 14–0. These contests would become the first of 14,000 regular season games in pro football history. But unlike today's systematic approach to designing the playing schedule with opponents determined years in advance and the dates, times and sequence of games meticulously arranged, this was far from the case in early days of the NFL. During the 1920s, schedules varied greatly from one team to another as individual team managers arranged their own schedules. Traveling expenses and local ordinances also contributed in the wide disparity of schedules. There was also no requirement that teams even play the same number of games. For example, the 1923 league champion Canton Bulldogs played a total of 12 games, while the Louisville Brecks played just three. In 1927, the New York Giants played 13 games on their way to their first NFL championship, while the Buffalo Bisons only played five games that year. This haphazard method of scheduling games in the league's early years led to much confusion and several disputes as to what constituted a league game which should be counted in the league standings, what games were actually exhibitions, and the official end of the season. But this would all change with the events that occurred during the 1931 season.

The Game That Wasn't (1931) and the Indoor Championship Game (1932)

As the 1931 NFL season was reaching its climax, a controversy would arise which would change NFL scheduling forever. On November 29, the Green Bay Packers beat the Brooklyn Dodgers 7–0 and improved their record to 12–1 atop the league standings. That same day, the Portsmouth Spartans (who in 1934 became the Detroit Lions) defeated the Chicago Bears 3–0 and were in second place with an 11–3 record, just a game and a half behind the Packers. The following week, Portsmouth had a bye and needed a Green Bay loss to the Bears to stay alive for the league championship. In a hard fought matchup, the Bears pulled off an upset and defeated the first-place Packers 7–6 at Wrigley Field dropping Green Bay's record to 12–2. The stage was now set — a season-ending matchup between the top two teams in the league. The Spartans, now only a game behind Green Bay, would have a chance to defeat the Packers at home on December 13 and thus force a playoff the following week for the NFL championship. Or so they thought.

What the Spartans believed to be an official home game versus Green Bay to end the season and decide the league title turned out to be a game that was not set in stone but was scheduled "tentatively." Packers head coach Curly Lambeau declared that since the game against Portsmouth was scheduled as "tentative," either team could choose to call off the game. The Spartans argued that when both clubs scheduled the game as "tentative," it could only be canceled due to inclement weather.

NFL President Joe F. Carr weighed in on the dispute and ruled in favor of the Packers stating that the "Green Bay–Portsmouth arrangement was made after the regular schedule had been drawn up." He added that since the game was "tentatively scheduled," based on league bylaws "he had no power to force Green Bay to play the game, or that he could not forfeit the game to Portsmouth, if Green Bay did not play."[1] The Packers, unwilling to put their league championship at risk, decided to call off the game against Portsmouth. Green Bay's reluctance to play the Spartans led Robert Hooey, a longtime sports editor of the *Ohio State Journal*, to proclaim the Packers as "cheese champions."

With Carr's decision, the Packers won an unprecedented third consecutive title, beating out the Spartans by one game in the standings. But the aftermath of the 1931 scheduling fiasco embittered not just Portsmouth fans, but all fans of the pro game. Carr and the owners took notice and realized that for the league to grow and be successful something had to be done with the schedule. Club owners "hereafter became more careful in scheduling, defining clearly games that were on the league [schedule] and had to be played. Giving greater formality to their task, they adopted a measure in 1933 turning scheduling over to a three-member committee appointed by the league president. They then had to ratify the committee's proposed schedule by at least a three-fourth's vote. Never again was there a dispute over whether a scheduled game was tentative or official and had to be played."[2] With this action, the NFL "finally junked its primitive, every-man-for-himself scheduling practice." There would be no more "tentatives." Once the league approved the committee's schedule, all games were official.[3]

Another pivotal moment in the league's early years that would change the face of pro football forever occurred in 1932, also involving the Portsmouth Spartans. The Chicago Bears and Portsmouth finished the 1932 regular season tied atop the league standings. The Bears were 6–1–6 and the Spartans had a record of 6–1–4, both with a .857 winning percentage. In 1932, tie games were not calculated in a team's winning percentage. In previous seasons, the league awarded the championship to the team that finished with the best overall record. But with the Bears and Spartans deadlocked, the league arranged to have a playoff game that would count in the regular season standings to determine the champion. The extra game, played indoors at Chicago Stadium due to blizzard conditions outside, brought about a number of rule changes the following season which included moving the goal posts to the goal line, moving the hashmarks ten yards in from the sideline, as well as legalizing a forward pass from any point behind the line of scrimmage. But another significant change came about for the 1933 season.

New Divisional Format and Standardized Schedule

On July 8, 1933, club owners, seeking to capitalize on the interest created by having a playoff game determine the league champion, passed a proposal spearheaded by Redskins owner George Preston Marshall and backed by Chicago Bears owner George Halas to divide the league into two divisions. This would result in two separate races, keeping more teams in contention longer and creating an annual championship game. Furthermore, the move led to a standardized league schedule for each club.

In 1933, the NFL grew to ten teams with the addition of the Philadelphia Eagles, Pittsburgh Pirates and Cincinnati Reds. There was still a huge disparity in schedules as teams played from nine games (Eagles) to 14 games (Giants). The following year, a fundamental concept was established in determining a team's schedule — a home-and-home series against each division opponent. By 1936, for the first time all teams played the same number of games (12). As noted in the league bylaws: "Each club in each respective division must schedule at least one game at home and abroad with every other club in its division, and intersectional games may be played by clubs in the different divisions. Each club in each division must play the same number of games."[4]

For the next several years (1937–1942), with the addition of a tenth club (Cleveland Rams), a pattern was set in teams' schedules. Each club played its four divisional opponents home and away and three games against teams from the other division for an 11-game schedule. By 1943, with many players taking part in World War II, the Rams suspended operations for one year and the Eagles and Steelers merged for the 1943 season and were known as the "Steagles." With the league down to eight clubs, each club played their division rivals home and away, and played each team from the other division once. In 1944, the Rams resumed operations and the Cardinals and Steelers merged for one year and were known as "Card-Pitt." For the rest of the 1940s, the league would field ten teams. Teams played 10 games each in both 1944 and 1945 and the number of games increased to 11 in 1946. From 1947 to 1949, the league implemented a 12-game schedule. Aside from the eight games played within the division, each club faced four out of the five clubs from the other division.

During this period, team owners would meet for days at league meetings to try to iron out an equitable schedule which satisfied all teams. Well before the huge TV contracts that arose in the decades to follow, home game ticket sales were the primary source of income. The owners sparred over getting attractive home opponents like the Bears, Packers, and Giants while also playing inferior teams to pad their team's record. To get a glimpse of what would transpire during owners' meetings, author Robert S. Lyons in his book, *On Any Given Sunday: A Life of Bert Bell*, noted how Pittsburgh Steelers owner Art Rooney recounted the marathon sessions:

The owners with the most staying power, who were willing to remain in the meeting rooms day and night arguing, were the ones who came away with the best schedules, [Rooney] explained. The guys who got tired and snuck out to get some sleep or go nightclubbing wound up getting murdered the next season, because when they weren't there to defend themselves, we'd give them all the dates we didn't want.

One year, the owners debated for two or three days over the schedule. Just as it was about to be completed and most of it written on a blackboard, George Preston Marshall exploded because he hadn't been given some of the choice home days he coveted. The Washington Redskins owner stormed up to the blackboard and erased the entire slate as his colleagues screamed and yelled because no one had written any of it down. It took two more days to reformulate the schedule.[5]

After much deliberation and unable to come to an agreement, the owners left the schedule making process in the hands of NFL Commissioner Bert Bell. Bell, trying to accommodate each team's wishes, spent hundreds of hours each offseason formulating the league's playing schedule using his kids' dominoes set. To devise the schedule, Bell used a huge cardboard "laid out in a grid fashion, with team names running along the top and game dates running down the side. Next to the board would be dozens of dominoes, borrowed from his sons, Bert Jr. and Upton, each with a team name Scotch-taped on the back, along with several books of paper matches. When Bell wanted Philadelphia to play Washington on a certain date, he'd find the date on the left-hand side of the board, and on that line he'd place a domino with Philadelphia's name on it into the two-inch-square box below Washington's heading. On the same line, he'd then place a match into the box under Philadelphia's heading, to indicate the Eagles had been assigned a road game that week."[6]

When it came to creating the schedule, Bell realized that for the league to be successful and for it to be popular among fans of all teams, the competitive balance needed to be addressed. From 1933 to 1946, the same few teams dominated their divisions — the Giants and Redskins in the East, and the Bears and Packers in the West. In fact, during this period either the Giants or Redskins won the Eastern Division every year. And the Bears and Packers represented the Western Division in the NFL title game in 12 out of 14 years. The 1935 Detroit Lions and the 1945 Cleveland Rams were the only other teams to win the West during this period.

Bell had proposed back in 1935 for the league to hold an annual draft of college players with teams selecting in reverse standings order. The following year, the NFL adopted Bell's proposal and by the mid to late 1940s, the balance of power began to shift as teams usually at the bottom of the standings began to contend. As commissioner, Bell came up with a simple yet effective philosophy with regards to scheduling. His recipe for success was to have the strong play the strong and the weak play the weak early in the season. This was done to keep more teams in contention longer into the season. In contrast to the previous 14 seasons, from 1947 to 1959, more interest was created as division races were tight down the stretch. During this 13-year period, with the exception of 1954 and 1956, each season had at least one division or conference championship decided in the final week of the season and on six occasions a special playoff was needed to determine the division or conference champion. Also, perennial losers such as the Cardinals and Eagles won their respective divisions and met in the NFL championship game in consecutive seasons in 1947 and 1948. It was the first appearance in a title game for both teams since the championship game was created in 1933. The NFL now had the competitive balance Bell had sought. To quote a phrase made popular by Bell, "On any given Sunday, any team in our league can beat any other team."

As Bert Bell began his tenure as NFL commissioner in 1946, the rival All-America Football Conference began play with eight teams — the Brooklyn Dodgers, Buffalo Bisons (renamed the Bills in 1947), Chicago Rockets, Cleveland Browns, Miami Seahawks, New York Yankees, Los Angeles Dons and San Francisco 49ers. Miami would be replaced by the Baltimore Colts the following year to maintain an eight-team league. For its first three seasons, the AAFC adopted a 14-game schedule, more than a decade before the NFL, to be played over 15 weeks with each team getting a bye week. James H. Crowley, who served as AAFC commissioner in its inaugural season, pronounced the slate "a perfect schedule — the best professional football ever has seen, since it brings each of our eight clubs in competition with each other club twice."[7] The following year, the AAFC would again play a double round-robin schedule, with each team playing every other team home and away. Admiral Jonas H. Ingram, AAFC commissioner in 1947 and 1948, said of the perfectly balanced schedule, "This guarantees a logical champion and means that the fans in each of our eight cities will be able to see every other team and all the star players of the Conference."[8] In its fourth and final season in 1949, the AAFC played a 12-game schedule over 14 weeks in a one-division, seven-team format. Similar to its first three seasons, each club played a home-and-away round-robin against all other teams. The AAFC's "perfect schedule" format would later be adopted by the American Football League in 1960.

In 1950, a merger agreement was made between the NFL and the All-America Football Conference to have three of the AAFC's clubs — the Cleveland Browns, San Francisco 49ers, and Baltimore Colts — join the NFL to create a 13-team league. The NFL renamed the Eastern and Western divisions, the American and National Conferences, respectively. Due to the odd number of teams, one club — Baltimore — was designated as the "swing" team which played a league round-robin schedule with one exception. In order to play a home-and-home series with their regional rival, the Washington Redskins, the Colts did not play the Bears. The Chicago Cardinals, who switched to the American Conference, continued to play a home-and-home series with their former division rival Chicago Bears. When the Colts were disbanded after the 1950 season, the league consisted of 12 teams playing a 12-game schedule. The Dallas Texans replaced the New York Yanks in 1952, however, the Texans franchise folded at the end of the season, the last NFL team to fail.

In January 1953, the holdings of the defunct Dallas Texans were awarded to a Baltimore group headed by Carroll Rosenbloom with the franchise being named the Baltimore Colts — keeping the league at 12 teams. At the league meeting, the NFL decided to change the names of each conference back to the Eastern and Western conferences. Also, the owners agreed, by an 11–1 vote, on a new scheduling pattern that would continue through the 1959 season. With every team's schedule determined by the same formula, Bell called the new system "foolproof," and said: "It's the greatest thing that has ever happened to our system of scheduling."[9]

The new format consisted of each team playing its five division foes home and away, as well as two games against teams from the other conference for a total of 12 games. The Baltimore Colts were placed in the Western Conference with the agreement that they would play the Washington Redskins every year. This resulted in both clubs facing only one other interconference opponent during this period. The same would be true of the Bears and Cardinals who would continue their crosstown rivalry each year until the Cardinals moved to St. Louis in 1960.[10]

Expansion and the American Football League

The Dallas Cowboys entered the league in 1960 to create a 13-team league. The Cowboys played the other 12 clubs once. The following year, the Minnesota Vikings became the league's fourteenth franchise. The NFL was then comprised of two conferences with seven teams each and for the first time, the league adopted a 14-game schedule. For the next five seasons, each team played its six divisional opponents home and away, and played two games against teams from the other conference.

In keeping with tradition, Dan Rooney, son of Pittsburgh Steelers founder Art Rooney, worked on the 1960 schedule using a familiar method utilized by Bert Bell. To help create the schedule, Rooney shuffled around 13 dominoes, one representing each team, and because of the odd number of teams he used a match stick to signify a team's bye week. He worked with former Steelers coach Walt Kiesling, Bert Bell, Jr., and NFL Commissioner Pete Rozelle in making the 78-game schedule. According to Rooney, "We actually did the schedule in one night. The commissioner came and we worked on the dominoes." In 1962, for the first time in pro football history, the NFL created the schedule with the help of an IBM 704 data processing system — an electronic computer capable of calculating roughly 40,000 operations per second — which formulated a dozen different schedules in just eight minutes. The following year, the league utilized a checkerboard filled with colored discs representing each team. Squares were marked off with an "X" whenever a site was unavailable on a particular date. The NFL took into account such factors as stadium availability during the baseball season as 10 out of the 14 teams shared stadiums with baseball clubs, scheduling one interconference game per week because of the odd number of teams (seven) in each conference, and avoiding to schedule games in Cleveland, Green Bay, Minnesota, and Pittsburgh in the final two weeks of the season due to the cold weather.[11]

In 1966, the schedule was modified to include the expansion Atlanta Falcons, who like the 1960 Cowboys, were the "swing" team which played each of the other 14 clubs once. The following year, the New Orleans Saints joined the NFL to bring the total number of franchises to 16. On November 30, 1966, club owners reached a realignment agreement to have the 16 clubs divided into four divisions of four teams each. The Eastern Conference would consist of the Capitol and Century divisions, while the Western Conference would include the Central and Coastal divisions. Each team played its three division rivals home and away, and the four clubs from the other division within the conference to bring the total to 10 games. The remaining four games were played against the four clubs from one of the divisions of the other conference to complete the 14-game schedule. As part of the agreement, the New York Giants were placed in the Century Division and the Saints in the Capitol Division. The two clubs would then switch divisions in 1968. The shuffling of the Giants from one division to the other was a major compromise as the other Eastern conference teams, which had long-standing rivalries with New York, all wanted to schedule a home-and-home series with the Giants and get a share of the Yankee Stadium gate in one of the two years.[12] In addition, the Eastern clubs would also have the opportunity to play the expansion Saints home and away once over the two years. Both New York and New Orleans then returned to the original 1967 alignment in 1969. This scheduling format continued through the 1969 season, with interconference matchups rotating each year.

As the NFL expanded in 1960 with the Dallas Cowboys, the rival American Football league was formed and in its first six seasons from 1960 to 1965, each AFL club played the other seven teams in the league home and away for a 14-game schedule, the same format used by the All-America Football Conference from 1946 to 1948. With the addition of the Miami Dolphins in 1966, the AFL schedule was modified to support nine teams. Teams played six clubs in the league home and away and would play the two other remaining clubs once each. When the AFL added a tenth franchise—Cincinnati in 1968—each club played its four division opponents home and away for eight games. Each club was then matched with one club from the other division for a home and home matchup for two games. The remaining four games on the schedule were played against the other four clubs from the other division.

A New Rotation Scheduling System—"Only when you get the cake do you have the recipe"

While the two leagues formed a merger agreement in 1966, it would be four years later that the 16 NFL clubs and 10 AFL clubs would comprise of a single 26-team league. The 26 teams were divided into two 13-team conferences consisting of three divisions each. In establishing a playing schedule beginning in 1970, a rotation scheduling system was devised. This new preset rotation formula would have each team in a four-team division play a 6–5–3 schedule—six games against its division opponents, five games against teams of the other two divisions within the conference, and three games against teams from the other conference. Teams in a five-team division (AFC East and NFC East), would play an 8–3–3 schedule with eight division games (its four rivals home and away), as well as three games with teams from the other two divisions within the conference, and three interconference games.[13]

When Baltimore, Cleveland and Pittsburgh agreed to join the original ten AFL teams to form a new 13-team American Football Conference in May 1969, Denver was designated as the "wild card" team in terms of future interconference scheduling. While all other AFC clubs would play three interconference games, the Broncos would get a fourth interconference game for five consecutive seasons (1970–1974) since a total of 40 interconference games were needed to balance the schedule. As a concession, Denver was "given the option of deciding which interconference games to play at home and which to play on enemy grounds."[14] For playing an additional interconference game, the Broncos would play only one AFC East club every season, playing a different AFC East team each year. Denver would therefore play a 6–4–4 schedule consisting of six division games, four other games within the conference, and four games against the other conference. To accommodate the Broncos, one NFC club from either the NFC Central or NFC West (with each division alternating each year), would also have to play four interconference games. To determine interconference games, as pointed out on pp. 60–61, all clubs were arranged in two parallel columns, one column listing all AFC clubs and the other all NFC clubs, with the list of teams rotating each year.

Jim Kensil, former executive director of the NFL, designed the new scheduling plan in which each of the 26 teams was assigned a different letter of the alphabet in order to set up both the intraconference and interconference rotations. He used "a large piece of plywood with a grid of tiny nails and multicolored tags" to determine matchups and home sites. With 26 teams each playing 14 games for a 182-game schedule, the possibilities totaled 1,656,200. Kensil compared creating the schedule to "baking a cake knowing which ingredients have to go in but not having the recipe. The only way you can do it is to make cake after cake until the ingredients are in the right proportion. Only when you get the cake do you have the recipe."[15]

In the inaugural season of the new scheduling system, the matchups in 1970 included a Super Bowl rematch between Kansas City and Minnesota and also introduced new natural or regional rivalries such as:

- New York Giants vs. New York Jets
- Houston Oilers vs. Dallas Cowboys
- Kansas City Chiefs vs. St. Louis Cardinals
- Oakland Raiders vs. San Francisco 49ers
- Los Angeles Rams vs. San Diego Chargers
- Atlanta Falcons vs. Miami Dolphins

Shortly after the release of the 1970 schedule, several teams had complained about their difficult schedule for the upcoming season. For example, while other clubs had weaker teams on their schedule, the Jets were given a schedule that included four division champions from the year before — the Rams, Vikings, Browns, and Raiders, and they now had to face the Colts twice, who had just moved to the AFC East. Jets head coach Weeb Ewbank, whose team would open the 1970 campaign at Cleveland in ABC's first *Monday Night Football* game, voiced his displeasure by stating, "They don't want us to win." (The Jets would eventually finish the season with a 4–10 record.) To deflect criticism of the new schedule, the NFL released the full rotation of opponents for the next eight years from 1971 to 1978 to illustrate that every team would have the chance to play the same opponents over a period of years, and by the end of the 1978 season, all teams would have played all others home and away.[16]

While all teams would meet on a rotating basis, one of the drawbacks of the schedule, however, was that meetings between regional rivals and other matchups between teams from different conferences would be rare as interconference matchups would take place approximately once every $4\frac{1}{3}$ years. For instance, after 1970 the Jets and Giants would not meet again until 1974, and then again in 1979.[17] The Rams and Chargers would play again only twice in nine years (1975 and 1979). Among other interconference matchups, Dallas and Oakland, two of the most successful franchises of the 1970s, would have the longest wait. Their first meeting would not come until the final week of the 1974 regular season — at the very end of the rotation's fifth year. It would be the last of the 169 AFC-NFC matchups to take place.[18] Originally, both clubs were not set to meet again until 1978, meaning that the Cowboys and Raiders would only meet twice in the decade. But with the new formula that would be introduced in 1978, both clubs would actually not meet again until the 1980 season.

This preset rotation from 1970 to 1978 would get a slight revision, however, as the NFL expanded to 28 teams in 1976 with the addition of Tampa Bay and Seattle. The Buccaneers and Seahawks were placed in the AFC West and NFC West, respectively. Both clubs played conference round-robin schedules and played each other. All other clubs played similar schedules to the 1970–1975 formula, however, one interconference game was substituted to accommodate each club playing Seattle or Tampa Bay. The exception to this rule was that one club from each conference, Oakland and New Orleans, played a third interconference game in lieu of one game against an Eastern division club in their conference.

The following year, Seattle and Tampa Bay switched conferences. The Seahawks moved to the AFC West and the Buccaneers to the NFC Central. Again, both clubs faced all other

13 clubs in their conference once and played one game against each other. For all other clubs, the setup was similar to 1976 except that Cincinnati and Green Bay played a third interconference game against each other and played just one team from the Eastern division in their conference, instead of two.

Expanded 16-Game Schedule and Common Opponent Formula — A New Cake in the Oven

Since 1961, the NFL had played a 14-game schedule each season. At league meetings in 1977, NFL owners approved an expanded 16-game regular season schedule and a brand new scheduling format for the 1978 season.[19] The league had sought for years a competitive and fair system of determining opponents. During the 1970s, with opponents being preset many years in advance, many competitive imbalances and wide disparity in strength of schedules occurred. For example, the New York Giants, who finished last in the NFC East in 1975, played the most difficult schedule in 1976. Their opponents' combined record was 118–76–2, a .607 percentage. On the other hand, the Minnesota Vikings, champions of the NFC Central in 1975, played the easiest. Their strength of schedule was just 83–112–1 (.426).[20] As mentioned in the *1978 NFL Media Information Book*:

"For years the NFL has been seeking an easily understood, balanced schedule that would provide for both competitive equality and a variety of opponents.... The new approach to scheduling gives the fans the best of both systems, a neat competitive format and variety at the same time. It also reduces inequities in the strength of schedules that popped up too often in the past under the system of rotating opponents over a period of years."[21]

Kensil authored a new "common opponent" formula. With regards to the new format, Michael MacCambridge, in his book *America's Game: The Epic Story of How Pro Football Captured a Nation*, writes:

> Whereas the league had previously made do with a pure rotation formula — home-and-home within the division, plus a cycle of conference and nonconference foes that would rotate each year — Kensil envisioned something else, a way that would not only increase the league's desire for premium match-ups but further the vision first put forth by Bert Bell in the late '40s.
>
> Instead of merely playing other excellent teams when the rotation called for it, Kensil's schedule envisioned that the league's division winners from one season would play every other division winner the following season.[22]

The new schedule format and expanded schedule with its attractive matchups was instrumental in the league securing a new four-year, $576 million contract with CBS, NBC and ABC which at the time was considered the largest TV package ever negotiated.

Val Pinchbeck, Jr., a former NFL director of broadcasting, was a key figure in several contract negotiations between the television networks and the league for broadcast rights. Besides working as a liaison between the TV networks and the 28 teams, beginning in 1971 and for more than 30 years Pinchbeck was responsible for preparing the league schedule. He manually drew up the schedule using a pegboard and meticulously chose the marquee matchups to be set aside for ABC's *Monday Night Football* and also carefully selected attractive doubleheader games for Sunday afternoons on CBS and NBC. Pinchbeck also had to juggle with the potential conflicts that existed with the September and postseason baseball schedule as many teams played in dual purpose stadiums. One famous example was in 1973 when the New York Jets started the season with six consecutive road games, which included four straight road games at each of their AFC East division rivals and also their Week 6 game against Pittsburgh which was moved from Shea Stadium to Three Rivers Stadium, because the Mets advanced to the World Series. "Val was the expert," said Kevin O'Malley, a former CBS Sports vice president. "The balancing act he had to pull off was truly monumental."[23] Dennis Lewin, who later succeeded Pinchbeck as NFL director of broadcasting in 1998, stated: "To do the schedule, Val would literally work seven days a week 10 to 12 hours a day, from mid February until the middle of May. And he was a genius at it."[24]

Schedules for all 28 NFL teams were determined by one of three formulas. Sixteen teams, those that finished among the top four teams in a five-team division, would play an 8–4–4 schedule (eight division games, four other games within the conference, and four interconference games). A total of eight teams, those clubs from the two four-team divisions—the AFC Central and NFC West, played a 6–6–4 schedule with six divisional games, six other conference games, and four interconference games. The remaining four teams, those that finished in fifth-place, played an 8–6–2 schedule. Whereas the other 24 clubs played 12 conference games and four games against the other conference, fifth-place teams played a total of 14 conference games and only two interconference games.

The new scheduling system emphasized the number of common opponents division teams would have. Teams that finished first and fourth in a division the previous season played the other first- and fourth-place teams from the other two divisions in the conference and would thus face 16 common opponents. Similarly, teams that finished second and third in a division would also have 16 common opponents as they were matched with the other second- and third-place teams in the conference. All teams in a division would thus face at least 12 common opponents.

Another facet of the new scheduling formula, as described in the *1977 NFL Record Manual*, was that of "instant" scheduling. To introduce the new schedule, during the 1977 season the league published in an issue of the league's official magazine *Pro!*, a series of articles including "Figure Your Favorite Team's 1978 Schedule," with a home-and-away breakdown chart. Each year, the league continued to publish a helpful chart to figure a team's schedule for the following year in the annual *NFL Record Manual* and *NFL Media Information Book* (which were later combined into the *NFL Record & Fact Book*). The attractiveness of the new schedule format, as opposed to the 1970–1977 formula, was that as soon as the regular season was over, a fan could simply look at the final standings and be able to figure who their favorite team will play the following season and where. If there were any ties within a division, the tiebreaking procedures in effect would be used to determine the order of finish.

Regarding the new format, NFL Commissioner Pete Rozelle stated: "The key ingredient of any format or structure under which an organized sports league operates is that it be easily understood by the fans. Its essence must be simplicity. In our opinion, that's what the NFL now has." As for the balanced scheduling aspect, Rozelle noted that "we like the fact that no longer will a team in a four-team division be at an apparent disadvantage in gaining a wildcard spot because now the clubs in four-team divisions play two games with a fifth-place team just like the teams in the larger divisions."[25]

At NFL owners' meetings in March 1986, NFL clubs voted unanimously to make changes to site locations for interconference games of teams that finish first through fourth in their division so that for the 1987, 1988, and 1989 seasons, teams would not play a second consecutive home or road game with an interconference opponent it played in 1984, 1985, and 1986. The same rule would also apply, if possible, to teams that finish in fifth place.[26]

In March 1990, the owners voted 28–0 to extend the policy of rotating interconference game sites where possible through the 1995 season.[27]

In March 1987, NFL owners passed two bylaw proposals which modified the common opponent formula. The first bylaw, which passed by a 26–2 vote and would take effect in 1988, changed the scheduling pattern of non-divisional games within the conference of teams that finish one through four the previous season in their respective divisions. Schedules for fifth-place teams remained unchanged. The second bylaw, which the owners voted 28–0, specified that "site locations for non-division intraconference games ... will be assigned so that, where possible by formula, teams do not play a second consecutive regular season home or road game with an opponent.... The NFL has also used this philosophy in the determination of site locations for interconference games (AFC vs. NFC), avoiding a team playing two consecutive home or road games with an opponent, where possible by formula."[28] For example, in the 1989 schedule, sites for intraconference games in the NFC were altered so that Green Bay would play at San Francisco, since the Packers had hosted the 49ers six consecutive times since 1976. Similarly, site locations were shuffled in 1990 so that Detroit would host Washington, the two teams having played five straight regular-season games in Washington.

In 1991, however, by unanimous vote, the league eliminated site rotation for non-division intraconference opponents. Teams would play home and away games based on what the scheduling formula dictated, and not where two opponents had played most recently. The Competition Committee reviewed the previous system and concluded that changing sites for non-division intraconference games was ineffective "since only a few sites could be switched and occasionally created competitive inequities."[29]

In 1995, with the addition of Jacksonville and Carolina, the league increased to 30 teams which were divided into six divisions of five teams each. The bylaws that were approved in 1987 required further changes. Fifth-place teams would now be included in the common opponent scheduling format and all teams in the same division would now play at least 11 common opponents. All 30 clubs would play an 8–4–4 schedule which included eight division games against its four division rivals and four other conference games. The non-division games played within the conference by first- and second-place teams remained the same as the 1988–1994 format, however, matchups for teams that finished third, fourth, and fifth-place were modified. For each team's four interconference games, a 15-year rotation was devised in which each team would play all teams from the opposing conference four times (twice home and twice away) from 1995 to 2009.[30] This would later be revised when the NFL realigned in 2002.

The 1995–1998 scheduling plan was further modified with the Cleveland Browns rejoining the league in 1999. With Cleveland added as the thirty-first franchise, further changes were needed to accommodate the six-team AFC Central. At an NFL meeting in Kansas City on October 28, 1998, a 31-team scheduling formula was approved which maintained the league's common opponent scheduling policy.[31] Each team played four non-division conference opponents, except for teams in the AFC Central. In the AFC Central with each club playing 10 divisional games, teams that finished first and second the previous year played only two non-division conference games, while those who finished third through sixth played three. Each team played four interconference games. The only exception being those teams that finished third through sixth the previous season in the AFC Central who played only three interconference games.

In just a few years, from the mid to late 1990s, a number of modifications were made.

And more was to come. In a comment posted to "Ask Tiebreaker Expert Joe Ferreira" on CBSSports.com on December 21, 2008, Joe Ferreira, who configured the schedule stated: "We actually had to work out going from 28-team to 30-team schedules (1995–1998), then the addition of the Cleveland Browns to make a 31-team schedule (from 1999 to 2001), then the existing 32-team scheduling formula and rotation which we devised.... So we went through a lot of changes in a relatively short period of time."[32]

2002 Realignment and New Scheduling Formula

At the NFL Spring Meeting on May 22, 2001, in Rosemont, Illinois, with the addition of the Houston Texans as the league's 32nd franchise, NFL owners unanimously approved a new realignment plan dividing the 32 teams into eight divisions of four teams each.[33] The league also adopted, by a 32–0 vote, a brand new scheduling formula which would guarantee that every team would play every other team on a regular, rotating basis. The new format would have fourteen of each team's 16 games set years in advance by rotation, while the remaining two games would be determined at the end of the regular season.[34] Each team's schedule would be based on the following formula:

- Home and away against its three division rivals.
- Four games against teams from another division within the conference.
- Four games against teams from one of the divisions of the other conference.
- Two games against teams from the other two divisions within the conference that finished in the same position in the previous year's standings.

In August 2001, the NFL released the 2002–2009 schedule rotation with matchups outlined for the next eight seasons. Ferreira, who designed the new scheduling format, added:

> The reference to a rotation is to guarantee that each team will play every other team in the League at least once at home and once away. Each team obviously plays home and home with divisional opponents every year. They play every team in their conference every 3 years with divisional rotations and every team home and home every 6 years.
>
> We then ensured that every team plays every team of the other conference every 4 years and home and home every 8 years. Thus, the 2002–2009 eight year rotation where every team will play every other team in the League at least twice, once at home and once away.[35]

In determining how to begin the divisional rotation for 2002, "the displacement of teams from their old divisions in the new alignment was taken into account. Preference was given to scheduling games with former division rivals and other regional opponents for clubs realigned from otherwise intact divisions."[36] Here's how the matchups between divisions of former rivals, as well as regional rivals, were set early on in the rotation:

2002
NFC West vs. AFC West:
   Seattle played their old AFC West rivals (Denver, Kansas City, Oakland and San Diego).
NFC West vs. NFC East:
   Arizona played their old NFC East rivals (Dallas, New York Giants, Philadelphia, and Washington).
AFC South vs. AFC North:
   Jacksonville and Tennessee met their former rivals from the old AFC Central (Baltimore, Cincinnati, Cleveland, and Pittsburgh).

NFC South vs. NFC North:
  Tampa Bay played its former NFC Central rivals (Chicago, Detroit, Green Bay and Minnesota).

  Regional rivals scheduled in 2002 included Dallas at Houston (NFC East vs. AFC South), and San Francisco at Oakland (NFC West vs. AFC West).

2003
AFC South vs. AFC East:
  Indianapolis played its former AFC East rivals (Buffalo, Miami, New England and the New York Jets).

  Regional rivals included the New York Giants at New York Jets (NFC East vs. AFC East) in 2003.

2004
NFC West vs. NFC South:
  San Francisco and St. Louis met their former NFC West rivals (Atlanta, Carolina and New Orleans).

  Former NFL Commissioner Paul Tagliabue noted regarding the new scheduling formula: "The new formula guarantees that NFL fans will see every team play each other on a regular, rotating basis. The formula will eliminate the many schedule aberrations of the past in which teams either did not play for long periods of time or did not play in another team's stadium for many years."[37] Here are just some of the many scheduling quirks that occurred over the years where teams went at least 20 years without visiting another club (regular season only):

32 years:
- Minnesota at Indianapolis, 2000 — first meeting at Baltimore/Indianapolis since 1968

28 years:
- New York Jets at Dallas, 1999 — first meeting at Dallas since 1971, after meeting five consecutive times at New York

27 years:
- New York Giants at Indianapolis, 1990 — first meeting at Baltimore/Indianapolis since 1963

25 years:
- Green Bay at Washington, 2004 — first meeting at Washington since 1979 (both teams did not play each other from 1989 to 2000)
- New York Jets at Arizona, 1996 — first meeting at St. Louis/Phoenix/Arizona since 1971
- New York Jets at Philadelphia, 2003 — first meeting at Philadelphia since 1978
- Oakland at Arizona, 1998 — first meeting at St. Louis/Phoenix/Arizona since 1973
- Oakland at Indianapolis, 2000 — first meeting at Baltimore/Indianapolis since 1975

23 years:
- Denver at Miami, 1998 — first meeting at Miami since 1975 (both teams played each other only once between 1983 and 1997 when both Dan Marino and John Elway were in their primes)
- Tampa Bay at Pittsburgh, 2006 — first meeting at Pittsburgh since 1983
- Washington at New York Jets, 1999 — first meeting at New York since 1976

Introduction • 16 •

22 years:
- Kansas City at Atlanta, 1994 — first meeting at Atlanta since 1972
- Minnesota at San Diego, 2003 — first meeting at San Diego since 1981
- New England at Kansas City, 1992 — first meeting at Kansas City since 1970
- New England at Washington, 2003 — first meeting at Washington since 1981
- Tampa Bay at Kansas City, 2008 — first meeting at Kansas City since 1986

21 years:
- Arizona at New York Jets, 1999 — first meeting at New York since 1978
- Buffalo at Minnesota, 2000 — first meeting at Minnesota since 1979
- Detroit at Miami, 1994 — first meeting at Miami since 1973
- New York Giants at Cleveland, 1994 — first meeting at Cleveland since 1973
- San Diego at Detroit, 1999 — first meeting at Detroit since 1978
- Washington at Kansas City, 1992 — first meeting at Kansas City since 1971

20 years:
- Atlanta at Indianapolis, 1989 — first meeting at Baltimore/Indianapolis since 1969
- Buffalo at New York Giants, 1990 — first meeting at New York since 1970
- Indianapolis at New Orleans, 1989 — first meeting at New Orleans since 1969
- Minnesota at Cleveland, 2009 — first meeting at Cleveland since 1989
- New York Giants at New England, 1990 — first meeting at New England since 1970
- New York Giants at Pittsburgh, 1991 — first meeting at Pittsburgh since 1971
- Oakland at Pittsburgh, 2000 — first meeting at Pittsburgh since 1980
- Philadelphia at Detroit, 2004 — first meeting at Detroit since 1984
- Philadelphia at Kansas City, 1992 — first meeting at Kansas City since 1972
- Philadelphia at New England, 2007 — first meeting at New England since 1987
- Pittsburgh at Washington, 1988 — first meeting at Washington since 1968
- Pittsburgh at Washington, 2008 — first meeting at Washington since 1988
- San Francisco at Indianapolis, 1989 — first meeting at Baltimore/Indianapolis since 1969
- Seattle at Tampa Bay, 1996 — first meeting at Tampa Bay since 1976

Other notable cases where one team had not visited another team for an extended period of time:

- Atlanta at Kansas City, 1985 — first ever meeting at Kansas City (in the 16th season after the merger)
- Buffalo at Philadelphia, 1985 — first ever meeting at Philadelphia (in the 16th season after the merger)
- Chicago at New York Jets, 1985 — first ever meeting at New York (in the 16th season after the merger)
- Cincinnati at Arizona (St. Louis Cardinals), 1985 — first ever meeting at St. Louis/Arizona (in the 16th season after the merger)
- Dallas at Cincinnati, 1985 — first ever meeting at Cincinnati (in the 16th season after the merger)
- New York Giants at Tennessee, 1985 — first ever meeting at Houston/Tennessee (in the 16th season after the merger)
- Chicago at Cincinnati, 1986 — first ever meeting at Cincinnati (in the 17th season after the merger)

- San Diego at Philadelphia, 1986 — first ever meeting at Philadelphia (in the 17th season after the merger)
- Tennessee (Houston Oilers) at Detroit, 1986 — first ever meeting at Detroit (in the 17th season after the merger)
- Philadelphia at New York Jets, 1987 — first ever meeting at New York (in the 18th season since the merger)
- Chicago at New England, 1988 — first ever meeting at New England (in the 19th season since the merger)
- San Diego at Atlanta, 1988 — first ever meeting at Atlanta (in the 19th season since the merger)
- Dallas at Tampa Bay, 1990 — first ever meeting at Tampa Bay (during the Buccaneers' 15th season; both teams played their first five regular season meetings at Dallas)
- Tampa Bay at San Diego, 1990 — first ever meeting at San Diego (during the Buccaneers' 15th season)
- New York Giants at Miami, 1993 — first ever meeting at Miami (in the 24th season since the merger)
- Cincinnati at New York Giants, 1994 — first ever meeting at New York (in the 25th season after the merger)
- Seattle at Indianapolis, 1994 — first ever meeting at Baltimore/Indianapolis (during the Seahawks' 19th season)
- Seattle at Buffalo, 1995 — first ever meeting at Buffalo (during the Seahawks' 20th season)
- Oakland at Tampa Bay, 1996 — first ever meeting at Tampa Bay (during the Buccaneers' 21st season)
- Kansas City at Philadelphia, 1998 — first ever meeting at Philadelphia (in the 29th season since the merger)
- Tampa Bay at Buffalo, 2009 — first ever meeting at Buffalo (during the Buccaneers' 34th season; both teams played their first eight meetings at Tampa Bay)

The previous scheduling method also produced some instances were teams played several consecutive games at the same site. For example, from 1981 to 1995, New England played at Pittsburgh nine consecutive times. From 1979 to 1994, Denver played at Buffalo eight consecutive times in the regular season. Also, Pittsburgh played seven straight regular season meetings at Kansas City between 1992 and 2003. Also, there were some extreme cases where teams went many years without meeting at all. On four occasions, two teams from the same conference went 13 seasons without playing each other: Broncos vs. Dolphins (played in 1985, did not meet again until 1998); Bills vs. Chargers (1985, 1998); Colts vs. Seahawks (1978, 1991); and Packers vs. Redskins (1988, 2001). Among interconference teams, after their 1972 matchup during the Dolphins' perfect season, it took 18 years for Miami and the New York Giants to meet again in 1990. Their 1976 meeting, which was originally part of the 1970–1978 rotation, were among the interconference games that were eliminated to make room for games against Seattle and Tampa Bay. Then the Dolphins and Giants did not meet in 1978, 1981, or 1984 because on each occasion the Giants finished fifth in the NFC East the year before. Furthermore, their 1987 scheduled matchup was among the only week of games that was canceled due to the players' strike. Finally, Miami and the Giants met during the 1990 season. Also, the New York Jets did not play the Cardinals for 18 years. After their 1978 meeting at New York, they didn't meet again until the 1996 season. During this period, each time the AFC East would play the NFC East every three seasons by rotation, either the Jets or Cardinals finished in fifth place the year before so they would continue to miss each other.

But perhaps one of the strangest quirks on the above list was the rare meetings between Kansas City and Philadelphia. After their 1972 game at Kansas City, the Chiefs and Eagles were originally set to meet in 1977, however, that game was substituted for their games against Seattle and Tampa Bay, respectively. How an entire two decades would then pass without both clubs meeting really shows the drawback of the common opponent scheduling format that was introduced in 1978. Since each team's schedule of non-division opponents would be determined exclusively on where a team finished in the standings, the Philadelphia-Kansas City example illustrates what happened when either club repeatedly finished in fifth place the year before the rotation called for the AFC West and NFC East to play each other. The Eagles and Chiefs did not play in 1980 since Kansas City finished fifth in 1979. In 1983, the teams did not play because Philadelphia had the worst record among NFC East clubs in 1982 and was assigned the fifth-place schedule. In 1986, again the Eagles and Chiefs did not meet since Kansas City finished fifth in 1985. Similarly in 1989, they did not play because once again, Kansas City finished fifth in 1988. Then finally since Kansas City and Philadelphia finished second and third, respectively, in their divisions in 1991, both clubs met at Kansas City in 1992 — their first meeting in 20 years!

The new 2002 scheduling format would eliminate these bizarre scenarios that occurred over the years and were prolonged by the scheduling formula which began in 1978. Now every team would play every other team in the league at least once every four years, and with the exception of international games played in London and Toronto, each team would visit every other team's stadium once every eight years. With teams now meeting consistently on a rotating basis, as opposed to the previous system, the current scheduling formula would provide more variety of attractive games. By the end of the 2009 season, after the initial eight years of the rotation, the last of these obscure scheduling quirks would end. These included the Vikings visiting the Browns for the first time in two decades and Tampa Bay playing their first regular season game at Buffalo since coming into the league in 1976.

While the NFL for many years had moved Sunday games between the early and late afternoon time slots, starting in 2006 the league has utilized "flexible scheduling"— the ability to switch a Sunday afternoon game to primetime — to ensure quality matchups on NBC's *Sunday Night Football* in the last several weeks of the season. After the 2008 season, the NFL decided to continue with the same scheduling rotation for 2010 and beyond.[38] A slight modification was then made to the existing scheduling format at 2009 owners' meetings. Owners voted to modify the West Coast pairings of teams beginning in 2010. After the Patriots and Jets played four games on the West Coast (Oakland, San Diego, San Francisco and Seattle) during the 2008 season, the owners agreed to ease the burden of traveling multiple times out West. ESPN.com reported: "Under the new plan, teams wouldn't have to visit two West Coast teams, just one, along with a team closer to the Midwest. Specifically, Oakland will be paired with Denver, and San Diego will be paired with [Kansas City]. In the NFC, Arizona and San Francisco will be paired as will St. Louis and Seattle."[39]

At the 2010 Annual Meeting, additional scheduling changes were discussed. On the issue of teams resting their starters at the end of the season, NFL Commissioner Roger Goodell said: "We are trying to schedule it so that potentially Week 17 will be all division opponents and maybe even a large part of Week 16 games. We think that will address this to some extent. It will not necessarily eliminate the issue but ... we need to continue to look at this because it's important for the quality of what we do and for the integrity of the game."[40]

As a result, beginning with the 2010 season, all 16 games scheduled in Week 17 were divisional matchups. That same year, the final three weeks of the season included 28 divisional games, up from 15 during the same period in 2009. In 2012, for the third consecutive season, to increase the potential for more games with playoff ramifications and possible divisional titles on the line, all 16 games scheduled for the final weekend of the regular season were division contests.

Creating a Schedule with Trillions of Possibilities — "It's almost like a bake-off"

Once the regular season ends, each team knows *who* they will face the following year and *where*. The question now becomes, *when* will they play?

The scheduling process begins in January when teams "submit lists of requests detailing stadium availability and preferences for scheduling order." In 2012, "more than 70 blocked-out dates" for stadiums were submitted. During the week of the Super Bowl, Howard Katz, the NFL's scheduling guru, meets with representatives from Fox, CBS, NBC, ESPN and NFL Network who present their own wish-lists of games they want on their schedule for the following season.[41]

Now how do you put together the 256-game schedule and balance the needs of each of the NFL's TV partners who want many of the same marquee matchups on their schedule and at the same time produce a fair schedule to all 32 teams and their fans?

Creating the playing schedule has many challenges. Just imagine that there are 824 trillion possible NFL schedules in any given season. The goal is to present attractive matchups for each of the league's broadcast partners in order to increase TV viewership in all time slots and provide a fair and equitable schedule for all NFL teams. Besides specific requests made by the networks and stadium conflicts provided by teams, the league must also consider travel logistics, clubs sharing stadium or parking facilities with baseball teams, and figuring bye weeks. Potential conflicts with the postseason baseball schedule must also be taken into account.

This daunting task of laying out the schedule is handled by Katz and Michael North, NFL director of broadcast planning & scheduling. Computers have immensely aided in streamlining the process. As opposed to Bert Bell's dominoes some six decades earlier to the league drawing up the schedule by hand with a peg board and little tags just 10 years ago, Katz commented in a 2009 *Philadelphia Daily News* article: "The process has improved so dramatically ... a decade ago, we played schedules that we wouldn't even consider today. Eight years ago, we were still playing schedules that we wouldn't consider today."

"We consider more things now than ever before. We look at teams playing road games coming off their byes. How many times teams have consecutive road games," Katz said. "A few years ago, it wasn't uncommon to see a schedule where 10 teams had three-game road trips. Now, that number is usually less than five."

Katz added that in years past, former NFL director of broadcasting, Val Pinchbeck, "started building [the schedule] from the top down. By the time he'd get to Week 6, it was a matter of, 'OK, we just need to finish it.' It's far more sophisticated now than it ever was."

To meet the rigorous scheduling demands with thousands of different variables and constraints, the NFL turned to Rick Stone, a Canadian manufacturing engineer. Stone, president of Optimal Planning Solutions, developed a specialized optimization software that provides scheduling solutions for professional sports leagues.

When the 2009 schedule was created, for example, Stone's software generated roughly 1.3 million schedules which were then narrowed down to 3,500. "Of the 3,500 schedules we actually finished, we probably took 50 of them and read them all the way through," Katz said. "What I mean by that is, once we get what we think is a playable schedule, we'll post that and say, 'Here's our leader. This is a schedule we're prepared to play.'"

"We won't look at another schedule until we think it's better," he went on. "This year [2009], we went through probably another 50 finished schedules. So, once we got a finished schedule, we probably improved it roughly 50 times, where we said, 'OK, this one is better.'"[42]

In 2010, out of an estimated 500,000 schedules that were generated, Katz and his team reviewed "5,000" playable schedules. According to Katz, "Then we keep generating more and more schedules, trying to find something that's better than the one that we've got. We probably went through 50 finished, completed schedules that we wanted to see if they were better than the schedule that we had. It's almost like a bake-off."[43]

In making the 2012 schedule, the computer program, which has been in use since 2004, provided "400,000 complete or partial schedules," and "generated 14,000 playable schedules, which were reduced to 150 with an eyeball test."[44]

In a 2008 CIO.com article, Stone mentioned that there are some 6,000 factors that are considered in creating the 256-game schedule. Stone said: "Say you're going to buy a lottery ticket, and you're trying to pick six numbers out of 50. That's like 15 million combinations, or something like that. So if picking six out of 50 is so difficult, imagine the number of combinations of picking 256 out of 6,000. It's astronomical."

North said in the same article: "Any factor you can think of has to be factored into this decision." He added: "Frankly, it's staggering that the National Football League, a multibillion-dollar company, was taking arguably its most important asset — the schedule — and building it by hand only about 10 years ago. It's remarkable to think where we were not that long ago.... Now we get to look through thousands and thousands and thousands of [schedules] and pick the ones that are fairest overall to everybody as opposed to being able to get one done."

The software has allowed Katz and North to work more efficiently. "We can see the opportunity costs of some of our decisions," North commented. "Whereas in the old days, once you put Cincinnati and Cleveland in week five, that decision was made. You have to just go down that path...."

"The beauty of the software is that we can go into every single game, every single week, every single team, every single place where we could be playing a game and we put some parameters around it," North said. "You can say to the software: Mix and match these any way you want to, just know that each game comes with a certain set of parameters. I don't want to play this game any earlier than week three or this game any later than week 14. That game should fall in sweeps week, somewhere between 9 and 12. That game should be in Pittsburgh instead of in Cleveland. That game needs to be on a Thursday night, which means that both teams need to be playing a home game the week prior. The software," he adds, "can do what we were only dreaming of doing 10 years ago."[45]

According to Katz, "The whole scheduling process is far more sophisticated than it's ever been, and it's a combination of manual input and allowing the software to solve the rest of the puzzle.... It was successful because it helped us ensure there weren't any really bad television windows anywhere. Even our weakest weeks were better than our prior years had been."[46]

And indeed it's been tremendously successful. The brilliant work by Katz and the scheduling department has led to record ratings among all five of the NFL's TV partners. In 2011, according to The Nielsen Company, more than 200 million unique viewers tuned in to NFL games. NFL games were watched by an average of 17.5 million viewers — the NFL's second highest viewership average since 1989. Also, 23 of the 25 most-watched TV shows among all programming in 2011 were NFL games, and the 16 most-watched shows of the fall TV season on cable were NFL games with ESPN's *Monday Night Football* being the most-watched series on cable for the sixth straight year. NFL Network's *Thursday Night Football* also posted its most-watched season ever. Among the broadcast networks, in 2011 FOX posted its most-watched NFL season ever, CBS had its second-most watched NFL season since acquiring the AFC package in 1998, and NBC's *Sunday Night Football* was the most-watched show in primetime for the second consecutive fall TV season and became the first sports series to finish the full fall-spring TV season as the most-watched show in primetime.[47]

In April, after 10 weeks of careful planning, Katz and his team finally have their winner. The official schedule is then unveiled on NFL Network's signature show, *NFL Total Access*, and also on ESPN and online at NFL.com as fans can get to see for the first time when their favorite team will be playing and how many primetime games are on their schedule. Among the many highlights of the schedule include the opening kickoff game involving the Super Bowl Champions, the first Sunday night game, the *Monday Night Football* doubleheader to cap off Kickoff Weekend, as well as the Thanksgiving Day tripleheader and the culminating Week 17 divisional matchups. The annual "Schedule Release Show," which expanded to three hours in 2012, is shown in primetime — a testament to the league's popularity. For NFL fans it has become an unofficial holiday and one of the most anticipated dates in the offseason.

From rule changes to today's players performing at the highest levels to game planning and strategy, pro football continues to evolve. The same can be said of the NFL schedule from its loose scheduling policy of the 1920s and the emergence of a standardized schedule in the 1930s to today's scheduling formula. Much like using trial and error to find exactly the precise measurements needed for each ingredient to create the perfect cake mix, the makeup of the pro football schedule has gone through many changes over the years.

The current formula established in 2002 includes the perfect mixture of ingredients that celebrates the league's past. With the new 8x4 setup, eight divisions with four teams each, a beautiful symmetry was revived. It was 35 years earlier that the NFL had a perfect 4x4, 16-team league. Back in 1967, each NFL team played a 6-4-4 14-game schedule — six division games, four games against teams from another division within the conference, and four games against the other conference. Today, that's precisely how 14 of each team's 16 games are determined. Since 2002, now twice the number of teams, each team plays a 6-6-4 schedule for a total of 16 games. The two additional games, compared to the 1967-1969 era, consists of where a team finished in the standings the year before — a concept that was introduced in 1978.

The existing format also incorporates the best features of the previous two systems, the 1970-1977 rotation system and the 1978-2001 common opponent formula, each of which had its own flaws. The former created competitive imbalances as teams had a great disparity in strength of schedules and the latter produced many scheduling aberrations over the years as certain teams did not meet for long periods of time. The current arrangement includes the perfect mix of both. It ensures the main principle of the 1970-1977 format in which every team faces every other team over a period of years so fans can have a chance to see the stars of the other 31 clubs and it also provides a variety of matchups. Also, today's scheduling plan improves on the 1978 common opponent element as all teams in a division face the same opponents each year, with the exception of the two standings-based matchups, providing for better competitive balance.

Yes, like the art and science of baking a cake in which a recipe's success depends on careful preparation, using the right equipment and ensuring all of the ingredients are in the right proportion, many factors go into the process of creating the schedule. From Bert Bell's dominoes to Jim Kensil's schedule board to today's computers which spit out thousands upon thousands out of trillions of possible schedules, the NFL continues to move ever forward in producing the most anticipated schedule each year in all of professional sports. The art and science of today's schedule-making process has led to NFL programming on Sundays, Mondays, and Thursdays becoming must see television which has resulted not only in increased viewership and record ratings much to the delight of TV executives and fans all over, it has also decorated the NFL as *the* most popular programming on television — just the icing on the cake!

1933

EASTERN DIVISION	WESTERN DIVISION
Boston Redskins	Chicago Bears
Brooklyn Dodgers	Chicago Cardinals
New York Giants	Cincinnati Reds
Philadelphia Eagles	Green Bay Packers
Pittsburgh Pirates	Portsmouth Spartans

Teams played varied schedules and played an uneven number of games. Here is a breakdown of each team's schedule followed by the non-division opponent chart:

EASTERN DIVISION

Boston Redskins:
- Home and away against two clubs (NY Giants and Pittsburgh), and one game with one other club (Brooklyn) within the division.
- Home and away against three clubs (Chicago Bears, Chicago Cardinals and Green Bay) and one game with one other club (Portsmouth) from the other division.

Brooklyn Dodgers:
- Home and away against two clubs (NY Giants and Pittsburgh), and one game with one other club (Boston) within the division.
- Home and away against two clubs (Chicago Cardinals and Cincinnati) and one game with one other club (Chicago Bears) from the other division.

New York Giants:
- Home and away against all other clubs within the division.
- Home and away against three clubs (Chicago Bears, Green Bay and Portsmouth) from the other division.

Philadelphia Eagles:
- Home and away against one club (NY Giants), and one game with one other club (Pittsburgh) within the division.
- Home and away against two clubs (Cincinnati and Green Bay) and one game each with two other clubs (Chicago Bears and Portsmouth) from the other division.

Pittsburgh Pirates:
- Home and away against three clubs (Boston, Brooklyn and NY Giants), and one game with the other club (Philadelphia) within the division.
- Home and away against one club (Cincinnati), and one game each with two other clubs (Chicago Cardinals and Green Bay) from the other division.

Western Division

Chicago Bears:
- Home and away against three clubs (Chicago Cardinals, Green Bay and Portsmouth), within the division. Played Green Bay three times, twice at home.
- Home and away against two clubs (Boston and NY Giants), and one game each with two other clubs (Brooklyn and Philadelphia) from the other division.

Chicago Cardinals:
- Home and away against two clubs (Chicago Bears and Cincinnati), and one game each with the other two other clubs (Green Bay and Portsmouth) within the division.
- Home and away against two clubs (Boston and Brooklyn) and one game with one other club (Pittsburgh) from the other division.

Cincinnati Reds:
- Home and away against two clubs (Chicago Cardinals and Portsmouth), within the division.
- Home and away against three clubs (Brooklyn, Philadelphia and Pittsburgh), from the other division.

Green Bay Packers:
- Home and away against two clubs (Chicago Bears and Portsmouth), and one game with one other club (Chicago Cardinals) within the division. Played the Chicago Bears three times, twice away.
- Home and away against three clubs (Boston, NY Giants and Philadelphia), and one game with one other club (Pittsburgh) from the other division.

Portsmouth Spartans:
- Home and away against three clubs (Chicago Bears, Cincinnati and Green Bay), and one game with the other club (Chicago Cardinals) within the division.
- Home and away against one club (NY Giants), and one game each with two other clubs (Boston and Philadelphia) from the other division.

1933 Non-Divisional Opponents

Eastern Division

BOSTON		BROOKLYN		NY GIANTS		PHILADELPHIA		PITTSBURGH	
Home	*Away*	*Home*	*Away*	*Home*	*Away*	*Home*	*Away*	*Home*	*Away*
ChiB	ChiB	ChiC	ChiC	ChiB	ChiB	CIN	CIN	CIN	CIN
ChiC	ChiC	CIN	CIN	GB	GB[a]	GB	GB	ChiC	GB
GB	GB	ChiB		POR	POR	ChiB			
POR						POR			

Western Division

CHI BEARS		CHI CARDINALS		CINCINNATI		GREEN BAY		PORTSMOUTH	
Home	*Away*	*Home*	*Away*	*Home*	*Away*	*Home*	*Away*	*Home*	*Away*
BOS	BOS	BOS	BOS	BKN	BKN	BOS	BOS	NYG	NYG
NYG	NYG	BKN	BKN	PHI	PHI	NYG[a]	NYG		BOS
	BKN		PIT	PIT	PIT	PHI	PHI		PHI
	PHI					PIT			

[a]Played at Milwaukee.

1934

EASTERN DIVISION	WESTERN DIVISION
Boston Redskins	Chicago Bears
Brooklyn Dodgers	Chicago Cardinals
New York Giants	Cincinnati Reds
Philadelphia Eagles	Detroit Lions*
Pittsburgh Pirates	Green Bay Packers
	St. Louis Gunners

Portsmouth Spartans moved to Detroit and became the Detroit Lions

EASTERN DIVISION

A. Boston Redskins and Pittsburgh Pirates.
1. Home and away round-robin within the division (8 games).
2. One game against four clubs from the other division (4 games).

B. Brooklyn Dodgers and Philadelphia Eagles.
1. Home and away round-robin within the division (8 games).
2. One game against three clubs from the other division (3 games).

C. New York Giants.
1. Home and away round-robin within the division (8 games).
2. Home and away against two clubs (Chicago Bears and Green Bay) from the other division (4 games).
3. One game against one other club (Detroit) from the other division (1 game).

WESTERN DIVISION

D. Chicago Bears.
1. Home and away round-robin against four clubs within the division, except the St. Louis Gunners (8 games).
2. Home and away against one club (New York Giants) from the other division (2 games).
3. One game against three clubs from the other division (3 games).

E. Chicago Cardinals.
1. Home and away against two clubs (Chicago Bears and Detroit) within the division (4 games).
2. Three games against Green Bay (3 games). Games played at Chicago, Green Bay and Milwaukee.
3. Two games at Cincinnati (2 games).
4. One game against two clubs (Boston and Brooklyn) from the other division (2 games).

F. Detroit Lions.
1. Home and away round-robin against three clubs within the division (6 games).
2. One game at Cincinnati and one game vs. St. Louis Gunners (2 games).
3. One game each against all clubs from the other division (5 games).

G. Green Bay Packers.
1. Home and away against two clubs (Chicago Bears and Detroit) within the division (4 games).

2. Three games against Chicago Cardinals (3 games). Games played at Chicago, Green Bay and Milwaukee.
3. One game vs. Cincinnati and one game at St. Louis Gunners (2 games).
4. Home and away against one club (New York Giants) from the other division (2 games).
5. One game against two clubs (Boston and Philadelphia) from the other division (2 games).

H. Cincinnati Reds.
1. Home and away against one club (Chicago Bears) within the division (2 games).
2. One game each against two other clubs (Detroit and Green Bay) within the division (2 games).
3. Two games at home vs. Chicago Cardinals (2 games).
4. One game each against two clubs (Philadelphia and Pittsburgh) from the other division (2 games).
   Note: The Cincinnati Reds disbanded after eight games. The St. Louis Gunners played the remaining games on Cincinnati's schedule.

I. St. Louis Gunners.
1. One game each against two clubs (Detroit and Green Bay) within the division (2 games).
2. One game against a club (Pittsburgh) from the other division (1 game).

1934 Non-Divisional Opponents

Eastern Division

BOSTON		BROOKLYN		NY GIANTS		PHILADELPHIA		PITTSBURGH	
Home	Away	Home	Away	Home	Away	Home	Away	Home	Away
ChiB	DET	ChiB	DET	ChiB	ChiB	CIN	GB	ChiB	DET
ChiC		ChiC		GB	GB[a]	DET		CIN	STL
GB					DET				

Western Division

CHI BEARS		CHI CARDINALS		DETROIT		GREEN BAY		CINCINNATI	
Home	Away	Home	Away	Home	Away	Home	Away	Home	Away
NYG	NYG		BOS	BOS	PHI	NYG[a]	NYG		PHI
	BOS		BKN	BKN		PHI	BOS		PIT
	BKN			NYG					
	PIT			PIT					

ST. LOUIS	
Home	Away
	PIT

[a]Played at Milwaukee.

1935

EASTERN DIVISION	WESTERN DIVISION
Boston Redskins	Chicago Bears
Brooklyn Dodgers	Chicago Cardinals
New York Giants	Detroit Lions
Philadelphia Eagles	Green Bay Packers
Pittsburgh Pirates	

EASTERN DIVISION

A. Brooklyn Dodgers, New York Giants and Pittsburgh Steelers.
1. Home and away round-robin within the division (8 games).
2. Home and away against one club from the other division (2 games).
3. One game against two other clubs from the other division (2 games).

B. Boston Redskins.
1. Home and away round-robin within the division (7 games). Note: One game, Boston at Philadelphia was canceled.
2. Home and away against one club (Detroit) from the other division (2 games).
3. One game against two other clubs (Bears and Cardinals) from the other division (2 games).

C. Philadelphia Eagles.
1. Home and away round-robin within the division (7 games). Note: One game, Boston at Philadelphia was canceled.
2. One game against each club from the Western division (4 games).

WESTERN DIVISION

D. Chicago Bears.
1. Home and away round-robin within the division (6 games).
2. Home and away against the New York Giants (2 games).
3. One game each against the remaining four clubs in the other division (4 games).

E. Chicago Cardinals.
1. Home and away against the Chicago Bears and Detroit Lions (4 games).
2. Three games against Green Bay (3 games). Games played at Chicago, Green Bay and Milwaukee.
3. One game against each club from the other division (5 games).

F. Detroit Lions.
1. Home and away against the Chicago Bears and Chicago Cardinals (4 games).
2. Three games against Green Bay (3 games). Games played at Detroit, Green Bay and Milwaukee.
3. Home and away against both the Boston Redskins and Brooklyn Dodgers (4 games).
4. One game against one other team (Philadelphia) from the other division (1 game).

G. Green Bay.
1. Three games against both the Chicago Cardinals and Detroit Lions. In each set of games, two games were played at home, one game at Green Bay and one game at Milwaukee (6 games).

2. Home and away against the Chicago Bears (2 games).
3. Home and away against Pittsburgh (2 games).
4. One game against two other clubs from the other division (2 games).

1935 Non-Divisional Opponents

Eastern Division

BOSTON		BROOKLYN		NY GIANTS		PHILADELPHIA		PITTSBURGH	
Home	*Away*	*Home*	*Away*	*Home*	*Away*	*Home*	*Away*	*Home*	*Away*
DET	DET	DET	DET	ChiB	ChiB	ChiB	ChiC	GB	GB
ChiB		ChiC	ChiB	ChiC	GB	GB	DET	ChiB	
ChiC								ChiC	

Western Division

CHI BEARS		CHI CARDINALS		DETROIT		GREEN BAY	
Home	*Away*	*Home*	*Away*	*Home*	*Away*	*Home*	*Away*
NYG	NYG	PHI	BOS	BOS	BOS	PIT	PIT
BKN	BOS		BKN	BKN	BKN	NYG	PHI
	PHI		NYG	PHI			
	PIT		PIT				

1936

Eastern Division	Western Division
Boston Redskins	Chicago Bears
Brooklyn Dodgers	Chicago Cardinals
New York Giants	Detroit Lions
Philadelphia Eagles	Green Bay Packers
Pittsburgh Pirates	

Eastern Division

A. Boston Redskins, Brooklyn Dodgers and Philadelphia Eagles.
  1. Home and away round-robin within the division (8 games). Note: The Eagles played the Pittsburgh Pirates once at Pittsburgh and once at Johnstown, PA.
  2. Two games against one club from the other division (2 games). Boston would play home and away vs. Green Bay; Brooklyn would play home and away vs. Detroit; and Philadelphia would host the Chicago Bears twice.
  3. One game against two other clubs from the other division (2 games).
    This completes the 12-game schedule.

B. New York Giants and Pittsburgh Pirates.
  1. Home and away against Boston, Brooklyn and Philadelphia within the division (6 games). Note: The Pirates played the Eagles once at Pittsburgh and once at Johnstown, PA.
  2. One game against each other at Pittsburgh (1 game).
  3. Home and away against one club from the other division (2 games).
  4. One game against the other three clubs in the other division (3 games).
    This completes the 12-game schedule.

Western Division

C. Chicago Bears.
1. Home and away round-robin within the division (6 games).
2. Home and away against one club (Pittsburgh) from the other division (2 games).
3. Two games against the Philadelphia Eagles (2 games). Both games played at Philadelphia.
4. One game against two other clubs from the other division (2 games).
   This completes the 12-game schedule.

D. Chicago Cardinals.
1. Home and away against both the Chicago Bears and Detroit within the division (4 games).
2. Three games against Green Bay (3 games). Games played at Chicago, Green Bay and Milwaukee.
3. One game against each club from the other division (5 games).
   This completes the 12-game schedule.

E. Detroit Lions.
1. Home and away round-robin within the division (6 games).
2. Home and away against two clubs from the other division (4 games).
3. One game against two other clubs from the other division (2 games).
   This completes the 12-game schedule.

F. Green Bay.
1. Home and away against both the Chicago Bears and Detroit within the division (4 games).
2. Three games against the Chicago Cardinals (3 games). Games played at Chicago, Green Bay and Milwaukee.
3. Home and away against one club (Boston) from the other division (2 games).
4. One game against three other clubs from the other division (3 games).
   This completes the 12-game schedule.

1936 Non-Divisional Opponents

Eastern Division

BOSTON		BROOKLYN		NY GIANTS		PHILADELPHIA		PITTSBURGH	
Home	*Away*	*Home*	*Away*	*Home*	*Away*	*Home*	*Away*	*Home*	*Away*
GB	GB	DET	DET	DET	DET	ChiB (2)	ChiC	ChiB	ChiB
ChiB		ChiC		ChiB		DET			ChiC
ChiC		GB		ChiC					DET
				GB					GB[a]

Western Division

CHI BEARS		CHI CARDINALS		DETROIT		GREEN BAY	
Home	*Away*	*Home*	*Away*	*Home*	*Away*	*Home*	*Away*
PIT	PIT	PHI	BOS	BKN	BKN	BOS	BOS
	BOS	PIT	BKN	NYG	NYG	PIT[a]	BKN
	NYG		NYG	PIT	PHI		NYG
	PHI (2)						

[a] Played at Milwaukee.

1937–1942

EASTERN DIVISION	WESTERN DIVISION
Brooklyn Dodgers	Chicago Bears
New York Giants	Chicago Cardinals
Philadelphia Eagles	Cleveland Rams
Pittsburgh Pirates*	Detroit Lions
Washington Redskins	Green Bay Packers

Franchise changed name to Steelers in 1940.

The 11-game regular season schedule of all NFL teams is determined by the following formula:

- Home and away round-robin within the division (8 games). (Note: In 1937, Philadelphia played at Pittsburgh twice; in 1938, the two meetings between the Eagles and Pittsburgh Pirates were played at Buffalo and Charleston, WV; in 1937, 1939 and 1941, the Cardinals played at the Packers twice, once at Green Bay and once at Milwaukee; in 1938, the Cardinals and Packers played one game at Milwaukee and once at Buffalo; in 1939, Brooklyn and Pittsburgh played both of their matchups at Brooklyn; in 1940, the Cardinals played the Lions once at Chicago and once at Buffalo; in 1942, the Cardinals and Rams played once at Cleveland and once at Buffalo, and the Eagles played the Brooklyn Dodgers once at Brooklyn and once at Buffalo).
- One game against three clubs from the other division (3 games).
This completes the 11-game schedule.

1937–1942 Non-Divisional Opponents

Eastern Division

BROOKLYN DODGERS

1937		1938		1939		1940		1941		1942	
Home	Away	Home	Away	Home	Away	Home	Away	Home	Away	Home	Away
CLE	ChiB	ChiB	GBª	CLE	DET	ChiC	ChiB	ChiC	GBª	ChiB	DET
	DET		ChiC	GB			CLE		DET		CLE

ªPlayed at Milwaukee.

NEW YORK GIANTS

1937		1938		1939		1940		1941		1942	
Home	Away	Home	Away	Home	Away	Home	Away	Home	Away	Home	Away
ChiB			ChiC	ChiB	DET	ChiB			ChiC	ChiB	ChiB
DET			CLE		ChiC		CLE		CLE		GB
GB			GB				GB		DET		

PHILADELPHIA EAGLES

1937		1938		1939		1940		1941		1942	
Home	Away	Home	Away	Home	Away	Home	Away	Home	Away	Home	Away
ChiC	GBª	ChiB	DET	GB	ChiB	DET	CLE	ChiB	DET	GB	ChiB
CLE			ChiCᵇ		CLEᶜ		GB		ChiC		CLEᵈ

ªPlayed at Milwaukee.
ᵇPlayed at Erie, PA.
ᶜPlayed at Colorado Springs, CO.
ᵈPlayed at Akron, OH.

PITTSBURGH PIRATES/STEELERS

1937		1938		1939		1940		1941		1942	
Home	Away	Home	Away	Home	Away	Home	Away	Home	Away	Home	Away
ChiB	DET		CLE[a]	ChiB	CLE	ChiC	DET	GB	ChiB	ChiC	DET
ChiC			DET	ChiC			GB[b]		CLE[c]		GB[b]
			GB								

[a]Played at New Orleans, LA.
[b]Played at Milwaukee.
[c]Played at Akron, OH.

WASHINGTON REDSKINS

1937		1938		1939		1940		1941		1942	
Home	Away	Home	Away	Home	Away	Home	Away	Home	Away	Home	Away
ChiC	CLE	CLE	ChiB	ChiC	GB[a]	ChiB	DET	CLE	ChiB	ChiC	DET
GB			DET		DET	ChiC		GB			CLE

[a]Played at Milwaukee.

Western Division

CHICAGO BEARS

1937		1938		1939		1940		1941		1942	
Home	Away	Home	Away	Home	Away	Home	Away	Home	Away	Home	Away
BKN	NYG	WAS	BKN	PHI	NYG	BKN	NYG	PIT	PHI	NYG	BKN
	PIT		PHI		PIT		WAS	WAS		PHI	

CHICAGO CARDINALS

1937		1938		1939		1940		1941		1942	
Home	Away	Home	Away	Home	Away	Home	Away	Home	Away	Home	Away
	PHI		BKN		NYG		BKN		BKN		NYG
	PIT		NYG		PIT		PIT		NYG		PIT
	WAS		PHI[a]		WAS		WAS		PHI		WAS

[a]Played at Erie, PA.

CLEVELAND RAMS

1937		1938		1939		1940		1941		1942	
Home	Away	Home	Away	Home	Away	Home	Away	Home	Away	Home	Away
WAS	BKN	PIT[a]	NYG	PHI[b]	BKN	PHI	BKN	PIT[c]	NYG	PHI[c]	BKN
	PHI		WAS		PIT		NYG		WAS		WAS

[a]Played at New Orleans, LA.
[b]Played at Colorado Springs, CO.
[c]Played at Akron, OH.

DETROIT LIONS

1937		1938		1939		1940		1941		1942	
Home	Away	Home	Away	Home	Away	Home	Away	Home	Away	Home	Away
BKN	NYG	PHI		BKN	WAS	PIT	PHI	PHI	BKN	BKN	
PIT		PIT		NYG		WAS			NYG	PIT	
		WAS								WAS	

GREEN BAY PACKERS

1937		1938		1939		1940		1941		1942	
Home	Away	Home	Away	Home	Away	Home	Away	Home	Away	Home	Away
PHI[a]	NYG	BKN[a]	NYG	WAS[a]	BKN	PHI	NYG	BKN[a]	PIT	PIT[a]	NYG
	WAS		PIT		PHI	PIT[a]			WAS		PHI

[a]Played at Milwaukee.

1943

EASTERN DIVISION	WESTERN DIVISION
Brooklyn Dodgers	Chicago Bears
New York Giants	Chicago Cardinals
Phil-Pitt "Steagles"	Detroit Lions
Washington Redskins	Green Bay

The 10-game regular season schedule of all NFL teams is determined by the following formula:

- Home and away round-robin within the division (6 games). Note: The Cardinals and Lions played once at Detroit and once at Buffalo.
- One game against all clubs from the other division (4 games).

This completes the 10-game schedule.

1943 Non-Divisional Opponents

Eastern Division

BROOKLYN		NY GIANTS		PHIL-PITT		WASHINGTON	
Home	*Away*	*Home*	*Away*	*Home*	*Away*	*Home*	*Away*
ChiC	ChiB	ChiB	DET	ChiC[a]	ChiB	ChiB	GB[c]
GB	DET	ChiC		DET[a]		ChiC	
		GB		GB[b]		DET	

Western Division

CHI BEARS		CHI CARDINALS		DETROIT		GREEN BAY	
Home	*Away*	*Home*	*Away*	*Home*	*Away*	*Home*	*Away*
BKN	NYG	BKN		BKN	Phil-Pitt[a]	WAS[c]	BKN
Phil-Pitt	WAS	NYG		NYG	WAS		NYG
		Phil-Pitt[a]					Phil-Pitt[b]
		WAS					

[a]Played at Pittsburgh.
[b]Played at Philadelphia.
[c]Played at Milwaukee.

1944

EASTERN DIVISION	WESTERN DIVISION
Boston Yanks	Card-Pitt "Carpets"
Brooklyn Tigers*	Chicago Bears
New York Giants	Cleveland Rams
Philadelphia Eagles	Detroit Lions
Washington Redskins	Green Bay Packers

Brooklyn Dodgers changed name to Tigers in 1944.

The 10-game regular season schedule of all NFL teams is determined by the following formula:

- Home and away round-robin within the division (8 games). Note: Cleveland Rams played twice at Card-Pitt, one game at Chicago and one game at Pittsburgh.
- One game against two clubs from the other division (2 games).

This completes the 10-game schedule.

1944 Non-Divisional Opponents

Eastern Division

BOSTON YANKS		BROOKLYN		NEW YORK		PHILADELPHIA		WASHINGTON	
Home	*Away*	*Home*	*Away*	*Home*	*Away*	*Home*	*Away*	*Home*	*Away*
	ChiB		DET	Card-Pitt		ChiB		Card-Pitt	
	DET		GB[a]	GB		CLE		CLE	

Western Division

CHI BEARS		CARD-PITT		CLEVELAND RAMS		DETROIT		GREEN BAY	
Home	*Away*	*Home*	*Away*	*Home*	*Away*	*Home*	*Away*	*Home*	*Away*
BOS	PHI	NYG		PHI		BOS		BKN[a]	NYG
		WAS		WAS		BKN			

[a]Played at Milwaukee.

1945

EASTERN DIVISION	WESTERN DIVISION
Boston Yanks	Chicago Bears
New York Giants	Chicago Cardinals
Philadelphia Eagles	Cleveland Rams
Pittsburgh Steelers	Detroit Lions
Washington Redskins	Green Bay Packers

EASTERN DIVISION

A. New York Giants and Philadelphia Eagles.
1. Home and away round-robin within the division, except the Boston Yanks (6 games).
2. One game at home vs. Boston Yanks (1 game).
3. One game against three clubs from the other division (3 games).
   This completes the 10-game schedule.

B. Pittsburgh Steelers and Washington Redskins.
1. Home and away round-robin within the division (8 games).
2. One game against two clubs from the other division (2 games).
   This completes the 10-game schedule.

C. Boston Yanks.
1. Home and away vs. Pittsburgh and Washington within the division (4 games).
2. One game at both the New York Giants and Philadelphia Eagles (2 games).

3. Home and away against one club (Green Bay) from the other division (2 games).
4. One game against two other clubs from the other division (2 games).
   This completes the 10-game schedule.

WESTERN DIVISION

D. Chicago Bears.
1. Home and away round-robin within the division (8 games).
2. One game against two clubs from the other division (2 games).
   This completes the 10-game schedule.

E. Chicago Cardinals.
1. Home and away round-robin within the division, except Green Bay (6 games). Note: The Cardinals played the Lions once at Detroit and once at Milwaukee.
2. One game played at Green Bay (1 game).
3. One game against three clubs from the division (3 games).
   This completes the 10-game schedule.

F. Cleveland Rams and Detroit Lions.
1. Home and away vs. the Chicago Bears, Chicago Cardinals and Green Bay within the division (6 games). Note: The Lions played the Cardinals once at Detroit and once at Milwaukee.
2. One game vs. each other, played at Detroit (1 game).
3. One game against three clubs from the other division (3 games).
   This completes the 10-game schedule.

G. Green Bay.
1. Home and away round-robin within the division, except the Chicago Cardinals (6 games).
2. One game played vs. the Chicago Cardinals at home (1 game).
3. Home and away against one club (Boston Yanks) from the other division (2 games).
4. One game against one other club (NY Giants) from the other division (1 game).
   This completes the 10-game schedule.

1945 Non-Divisional Opponents

Eastern Division

BOSTON YANKS		NEW YORK		PHILADELPHIA		PITTSBURGH		WASHINGTON	
Home	Away	Home	Away	Home	Away	Home	Away	Home	Away
GB	GB[a]	CLE		ChiC	DET	ChiC	ChiB	ChiB	
DET	CLE	DET		CLE				ChiC	
		GB							

Western Division

CHI BEARS		CHI CARDINALS		CLEVELAND RAMS		DETROIT		GREEN BAY	
Home	Away	Home	Away	Home	Away	Home	Away	Home	Away
PIT	WAS		PHI	BOS	NYG	PHI	BOS	BOS[a]	BOS
			PIT		PHI		NYG		NYG
			WAS						

[a]Played at Milwaukee.

1946 (NFL)

EASTERN DIVISION	WESTERN DIVISION
Boston Yanks	Chicago Bears
New York Giants	Chicago Cardinals
Philadelphia Eagles	Detroit Lions
Pittsburgh Steelers	Green Bay Packers
Washington Redskins	Los Angeles Rams[a]

[a]*Cleveland Rams moved to Los Angeles in 1946.*

The 11-game regular season schedule of all NFL teams is determined by the following formula:

- Home and away round-robin within the division (8 games).
- One game against three clubs from the other division (3 games).

This completes the 11-game schedule.

1946 NFL Non-Divisional Opponents

Eastern Division

BOSTON YANKS		NEW YORK		PHILADELPHIA		PITTSBURGH		WASHINGTON	
Home	*Away*	*Home*	*Away*	*Home*	*Away*	*Home*	*Away*	*Home*	*Away*
ChiC	DET	ChiB		GB	ChiB	ChiC	DET	DET	ChiB
LA		ChiC			LA		GB	GB	
		LA							

Western Division

CHI BEARS		CHI CARDINALS		DETROIT		GREEN BAY		LOS ANGELES	
Home	*Away*	*Home*	*Away*	*Home*	*Away*	*Home*	*Away*	*Home*	*Away*
PHI	NYG		BOS	BOS	WAS	PIT	PHI	PHI	BOS
WAS			NYG	PIT			WAS		NYG
			PIT						

1947–1949 (NFL)

1947 & 1948 ALIGNMENT

EASTERN DIVISION	WESTERN DIVISION
Boston Yanks	Chicago Bears
New York Giants	Chicago Cardinals
Philadelphia Eagles	Detroit Lions
Pittsburgh Steelers	Green Bay Packers
Washington Redskins	Los Angeles Rams

1949 Alignment

Eastern Division	Western Division
New York Bulldogs	Chicago Bears
New York Giants	Chicago Cardinals
Philadelphia Eagles	Detroit Lions
Pittsburgh Steelers	Green Bay Packers
Washington Redskins	Los Angeles Rams

1947–1949 (NFL)

The 12-game regular season schedule of all NFL teams is determined by the following formula:

- Home and away round-robin within the division (8 games).
- One game each against four of the five clubs from the other division (4 games). Two of such games would be played at home and two of such games played away. (Note: In 1947, the Chicago Cardinals played one of their non–division games at home and three away, and the Eagles played three games at home and one away against teams from the other division).

This completes the 12-game schedule.

1947–1949 NFL Non-Divisional Opponents

Eastern Division

BOSTON YANKS

1947		1948	
Home	Away	Home	Away
ChiB	ChiC	ChiB	ChiC
DET	LA	GB	DET

NY BULLDOGS

1949	
Home	Away
ChiC	DET
GB	LA

NEW YORK GIANTS

1947		1948		1949	
Home	Away	Home	Away	Home	Away
ChiC	DET	ChiC	ChiB	ChiB	ChiC
GB	LA	LA	GB[a]	DET	GB

[a]Played at Milwaukee.

PHILADELPHIA EAGLES

1947		1948		1949	
Home	Away	Home	Away	Home	Away
ChiC	ChiB	ChiB	ChiC	ChiC	ChiB
GB		DET	LA	LA	DET
LA					

PITTSBURGH STEELERS

1947		1948		1949	
Home	Away	Home	Away	Home	Away
DET	ChiB	ChiC	DET	DET	ChiB
LA	GB[a]	GB	LA	LA	GB[a]

[a]Played at Milwaukee.

WASHINGTON REDSKINS

1947		1948		1949	
Home	Away	Home	Away	Home	Away
ChiB	DET	DET	ChiB	ChiB	ChiC
ChiC	GB[a]	LA	GB[a]	GB	LA

[a]Played at Milwaukee.

Western Division

CHICAGO BEARS

1947		1948		1949	
Home	*Away*	*Home*	*Away*	*Home*	*Away*
PHI	BOS	NYG	BOS	PHI	NYG
PIT	WAS	WAS	PHI	PIT	WAS

CHICAGO CARDINALS

1947		1948		1949	
Home	*Away*	*Home*	*Away*	*Home*	*Away*
BOS	NYG	BOS	NYG	NYG	NYB
	PHI	PHI	PIT	WAS	PHI
	WAS				

DETROIT LIONS

1947		1948		1949	
Home	*Away*	*Home*	*Away*	*Home*	*Away*
NYG	BOS	BOS	PHI	NYB	NYG
WAS	PIT	PIT	WAS	PHI	PIT

GREEN BAY PACKERS

1947		1948		1949	
Home	*Away*	*Home*	*Away*	*Home*	*Away*
PIT[a]	NYG	NYG[a]	BOS	NYG	NYB
WAS[a]	PHI	WAS[a]	PIT	PIT[a]	WAS

[a] Played at Milwaukee.

LOS ANGELES RAMS

1947		1948		1949	
Home	*Away*	*Home*	*Away*	*Home*	*Away*
BOS	PHI	PHI	NYG	NYB	PHI
NYG	PIT	PIT	WAS	WAS	PIT

1946–1948 (AAFC)

1946 Alignment

Eastern Division	**Western Division**
Brooklyn Dodgers	Chicago Rockets
Buffalo Bisons	Cleveland Browns
Miami Seahawks	Los Angeles Dons
New York Yankees	San Francisco 49ers

1947–1948 Alignment

Eastern Division	**Western Division**
Baltimore Colts	Chicago Rockets
Brooklyn Dodgers	Cleveland Browns
Buffalo Bills	Los Angeles Dons
New York Yankees	San Francisco 49ers

1946–1948 (AAFC)

The 14-game regular season schedule of all AAFC teams is determined by the following formula:

- Home and away round-robin against the other seven teams in the league (14 games).

This completes the 14-game schedule.

1946–1948 AAFC Non-Divisional Opponents

Each AAFC team played all other teams twice, once at home and once away. Listed below are games against teams from the other division.

1946				1947–1948			
ALL EASTERN DIVISION TEAMS		ALL WESTERN DIVISION TEAMS		ALL EASTERN DIVISION TEAMS		ALL WESTERN DIVISION TEAMS	
Home	*Away*	*Home*	*Away*	*Home*	*Away*	*Home*	*Away*
ChiR	ChiR	BKN	BKN	ChiR	ChiR	BAL	BAL
CLE	CLE	BUF	BUF	CLE	CLE	BKN	BKN
LAD	LAD	MIA	MIA	LAD	LAD	BUF	BUF
SF	SF	NYY	NYY	SF	SF	NYY	NYY

1949 (AAFC)

Baltimore Colts
Brooklyn–New York Yankees
Buffalo Bills
Chicago Hornets
Cleveland Browns
Los Angeles Dons
San Francisco 49ers

1949 (AAFC)

The 12-game regular season schedule of all AAFC teams is determined by the following formula:

- Home and away round-robin against the other six teams in the league (12 games).

This completes the 12-game schedule.

1949 AAFC Opponents

Each AAFC team played all other six teams twice, once at home and once away.

BALTIMORE		BKN–NY YANKEES		BUFFALO		CHICAGO	
Home	*Away*	*Home*	*Away*	*Home*	*Away*	*Home*	*Away*
Bkn-NYY	Bkn-NYY	BAL	BAL	BAL	BAL	BAL	BAL
BUF	BUF	BUF	BUF	Bkn-NYY	Bkn-NYY	Bkn-NYY	Bkn-NYY
ChiH	ChiH	ChiH	ChiH	ChiH	ChiH	BUF	BUF
CLE	CLE	CLE	CLE	CLE	CLE	CLE	CLE
LAD	LAD	LAD	LAD	LAD	LAD	LAD	LAD
SF	SF	SF	SF	SF	SF	SF	SF

CLEVELAND		LOS ANGELES		SAN FRANCISCO	
Home	*Away*	*Home*	*Away*	*Home*	*Away*
BAL	BAL	BAL	BAL	BAL	BAL
Bkn-NYY	Bkn-NYY	Bkn-NYY	Bkn-NYY	Bkn-NYY	Bkn-NYY
BUF	BUF	BUF	BUF	BUF	BUF
ChiH	ChiH	ChiH	ChiH	ChiH	ChiH
LAD	LAD	CLE	CLE	CLE	CLE
SF	SF	SF	SF	LAD	LAD

1950

AMERICAN CONFERENCE	NATIONAL CONFERENCE
Chicago Cardinals	Baltimore Colts
Cleveland Browns	Chicago Bears
New York Giants	Detroit Lions
Philadelphia Eagles	Green Bay Packers
Pittsburgh Steelers	Los Angeles Rams
Washington Redskins	New York Yanks
	San Francisco 49ers

American Conference

A. Cleveland Browns, NY Giants, Philadelphia Eagles, and Pittsburgh Steelers.
  1. Home and away round-robin within the conference (10 games).
  2. One game against two clubs from the National Conference (2 games).
  This completes the 12 game schedule.

B. Chicago Cardinals and Washington Redskins.
  1. Home and away round-robin with the four teams within the conference in section 'A' (8 games).
  2. One game against each other (1 game). Chicago Cardinals play at the Washington Redskins.
  3. Home and away against one team from the National Conference (2 games). The Chicago Cardinals will play the Chicago Bears and Washington will play Baltimore twice, home and away.
  4. One game against one other club from the National Conference (1 game). The Cardinals will play the Baltimore Colts once, and the Washington Redskins will play the Green Bay Packers once.
  This completes the 12-game schedule.

National Conference

C. Detroit Lions, Green Bay Packers, Los Angeles Rams, New York Yanks and San Francisco 49ers.
  1. Home and away round-robin with all teams within the conference, with the exception of Baltimore (10 games).
  2. One game against the Baltimore Colts (1 game).
  3. One game against one team from the American Conference (1 game).
  This completes the 12-game schedule.

D. Chicago Bears.
  1. Home and away round-robin with all teams within the conference, with the exception of Baltimore (10 games).
  2. Home and away against the Chicago Cardinals (2 games).
  This completes the 12-game schedule.

E. Baltimore Colts.
  1. One game against all teams in the National Conference, except the Chicago Bears (5 games).

2. Home and away against the Washington Redskins (2 games).
3. One game against the other five clubs from the American Conference (5 games). This completes the 12-game schedule.

1950 Non-Conference Opponents

AMERICAN CONFERENCE

CHI CARDS		CLEVELAND		NY GIANTS		PHILADELPHIA		PITTSBURGH		WASHINGTON	
Home	*Away*	*Home*	*Away*	*Home*	*Away*	*Home*	*Away*	*Home*	*Away*	*Home*	*Away*
ChiB	ChiB	SF	BAL	NYY	BAL	LA	BAL	BAL	DET	BAL	BAL
BAL											GB[1]

NATIONAL CONFERENCE

CHI BEARS		DETROIT		GREEN BAY		LOS ANGELES		NY YANKS		SAN FRANCISCO	
Home	*Away*	*Home*	*Away*	*Home*	*Away*	*Home*	*Away*	*Home*	*Away*	*Home*	*Away*
ChiC	ChiC	PIT	BAL[a]	WAS[1]	BAL[a]	BAL[a]	PHI	BAL[a]	NYG	BAL[a]	CLE

BALTIMORE	
Home	*Away*

National	DET	NYY
	GB	LA
		SF
American	WAS	WAS
	CLE	ChiC
	NYG	PIT
	PHI	

[a]Played conference opponent Baltimore once.
[1]Played at Milwaukee.

1951

AMERICAN CONFERENCE	NATIONAL CONFERENCE
Chicago Cardinals	Chicago Bears
Cleveland Browns	Detroit Lions
New York Giants	Green Bay Packers
Philadelphia Eagles	Los Angeles Rams
Pittsburgh Steelers	New York Yanks
Washington Redskins	San Francisco 49ers

AMERICAN CONFERENCE

A. Cleveland Browns, Philadelphia Eagles, Pittsburgh Steelers and Washington Redskins.

1. Home and away round-robin with four of the five other clubs within the conference (8 games).

2. One game against the other club within the conference (1 game). Washington played at Cleveland. Both Philadelphia and Pittsburgh played the Cardinals once (at Chicago).
   3. Three games against teams from the National Conference (3 games). Pittsburgh played Green Bay home and away, and also played San Francisco.
   This completes the 12-game schedule.

B. Chicago Cardinals.
   1. Home and away round-robin with three (Cleveland, NY Giants and Washington) of the five other clubs within the conference (6 games).
   2. One game against two other clubs within the conference, Philadelphia and Pittsburgh (2 games).
   3. Home and away against the Chicago Bears (2 games).
   4. One game against two other clubs (Los Angeles and San Francisco) from the National Conference (2 games).
   This completes the 12-game schedule.

C. New York Giants.
   1. Home and away round-robin against all other clubs within the conference (10 games).
   2. Home and away against the New York Yanks (2 games).
   This completes the 12-game schedule.

NATIONAL CONFERENCE

D. Chicago Bears and San Francisco 49ers.
   1. Home and away round-robin with three of the five other clubs within the conference (6 games).
   2. One game each against two other clubs within the conference (2 games). The Chicago Bears will play Los Angeles and San Francisco. The San Francisco 49ers will play the Chicago Bears and Green Bay.
   3. Four games against teams from the American Conference (4 games). The Chicago Bears will play the Chicago Cardinals twice, home and away, and Cleveland and Washington once. The San Francisco 49ers will play the Chicago Cardinals, Cleveland, Philadelphia and Pittsburgh.
   This completes the 12-game schedule.

E. Detroit Lions and New York Yanks.
   1. Home and away round-robin against all other clubs within the conference (10 games). Note: Both games between Detroit and the NY Yanks played at Detroit. Also, both games between NY Yanks and the LA Rams played at Los Angeles.
   2. Two games against teams from the American Conference (2 games). The New York Yanks will play the New York Giants twice, home and away. Detroit will play Philadelphia and Washington once.
   This completes the 12-game schedule.

F. Green Bay and Los Angeles.
   1. Home and away round-robin with four of the five other clubs within the conference (8 games). Note: Both games between NY Yanks and the LA Rams played at Los Angeles.

2. One game against the other club within the conference (1 game). Green Bay played San Francisco once, and Los Angeles played the Chicago Bears once.
3. Three games against teams from the American Conference (3 games). Green Bay played Pittsburgh home and away, and also played Philadelphia.
This completes the 12-game schedule.

1951 Non-Conference Opponents

AMERICAN CONFERENCE

CHI CARDS		CLEVELAND		NY GIANTS		PHILADELPHIA		PITTSBURGH		WASHINGTON	
Home	Away	Home	Away	Home	Away	Home	Away	Home	Away	Home	Away
ChiB	ChiB	ChiB	LA	NYY	NYY	DET	GB	GB	GB[a]	ChiB	DET
LA			SF			SF		SF		LA	
SF											

NATIONAL CONFERENCE

CHI BEARS		DETROIT		GREEN BAY		LOS ANGELES		NY YANKS		SAN FRANCISCO	
Home	Away	Home	Away	Home	Away	Home	Away	Home	Away	Home	Away
ChiC	ChiC	WAS	PHI	PIT[a]	PIT	ChiC	WAS	NYG	NYG	ChiC	PHI
	CLE			PHI		CLE				CLE	PIT
	WAS										

[a]Played at Milwaukee.

1952

AMERICAN CONFERENCE	NATIONAL CONFERENCE
Chicago Cardinals	Chicago Bears
Cleveland Browns	Dallas Texans
New York Giants	Detroit Lions
Philadelphia Eagles	Green Bay Packers
Pittsburgh Steelers	Los Angeles Rams
Washington Redskins	San Francisco 49ers

AMERICAN CONFERENCE

A. Chicago Cardinals, Cleveland Browns, Philadelphia Eagles and Washington Redskins.
1. Home and away round-robin within the conference (10 games).
2. Two games against teams from the National Conference (2 games). The Chicago Cardinals will play the Chicago Bears twice, home and away. Cleveland, Philadelphia and Washington will play one National Conference club at home and another club away.
This completes the 12-game schedule.

B. **New York Giants and Pittsburgh Steelers.**
  1. Home and away round-robin with the four teams within the conference in section 'A' (8 games).
  2. One game against each other (1 game). The New York Giants will play at Pittsburgh.
  3. Three games against teams from the National Conference (3 games).
     This completes the 12-game schedule.

NATIONAL CONFERENCE

C. **Chicago Bears, Dallas Texans, Detroit Lions and Los Angeles Rams.**
  1. Home and away round-robin within the conference (10 games). Note: The Chicago Bears and Dallas Texans would play one game at Chicago and one game at Akron, Ohio. The Dallas Texans would play both their games vs. the Lions at Detroit.
  2. Two games against teams from the American Conference (2 games). The Chicago Bears will play the Chicago Cardinals twice, home and away. The Dallas Texans, Detroit and Los Angeles will play one American Conference club at home and another club away.
     This completes the 12-game schedule.

D. **Green Bay Packers and San Francisco 49ers.**
  1. Home and away round-robin with the four teams within the conference in section 'C' (8 games).
  2. One game against each other (1 game). Green Bay will play at San Francisco.
  3. Three games against teams from the American Conference (3 games).
     This completes the 12-game schedule.

1952 Non-Conference Opponents

AMERICAN CONFERENCE

CHI CARDS		CLEVELAND		NY GIANTS		PHILADELPHIA		PITTSBURGH		WASHINGTON	
Home	*Away*	*Home*	*Away*	*Home*	*Away*	*Home*	*Away*	*Home*	*Away*	*Home*	*Away*
ChiB	ChiB	LA	DET	GB	DAL	DAL	GB[a]	DET	LA	SF	GB[a]
				SF					SF		

NATIONAL CONFERENCE

CHI BEARS		DALLAS TEXANS		DETROIT		GREEN BAY		LOS ANGELES		SAN FRANCISCO	
Home	*Away*	*Home*	*Away*	*Home*	*Away*	*Home*	*Away*	*Home*	*Away*	*Home*	*Away*
ChiC	ChiC	NYG	PHI	CLE	PIT	PHI[a]	NYG	PIT	CLE	PIT	NYG
						WAS[a]					WAS

[a] Played at Milwaukee

1953–1959

EASTERN CONFERENCE	WESTERN CONFERENCE
Chicago Cardinals	Baltimore Colts
Cleveland Browns	Chicago Bears
New York Giants	Detroit Lions
Philadelphia Eagles	Green Bay Packers
Pittsburgh Steelers	Los Angeles Rams
Washington Redskins	San Francisco 49ers

The 12-game regular season schedule of all NFL teams is determined by the following formula:

- Home and away round-robin within the conference (10 games). Note: in 1958, the Cardinals and Giants played once at New York and once at Buffalo; in 1959, the Cardinals and Giants played once at New York and once at Minneapolis, and also the Cardinals and Eagles played once at Philadelphia and once at Minneapolis.
- One game each against two clubs from the other conference (2 games). One game played at home, and one game played away.

This completes the 12-game schedule.

1953–1959 Non-Conference Opponents

EASTERN CONFERENCE

CHICAGO CARDINALS

1953		1954		1955		1956		1957		1958		1959	
Home	*Away*	*Home*	*Away*	*Home*	*Away*	*Home*	*Away*	*Home*	*Away*	*Home*	*Away*	*Home*	*Away*
LA	ChiB	ChiB	LA	ChiB	GB	GB	ChiB	ChiB	SF	LA	ChiB	ChiB	DET

CLEVELAND BROWNS

1953		1954		1955		1956		1957		1958		1959	
Home	*Away*	*Home*	*Away*	*Home*	*Away*	*Home*	*Away*	*Home*	*Away*	*Home*	*Away*	*Home*	*Away*
SF	GBª	DET	ChiB	GB	SF	BAL	GBª	LA	DET	DET	LA	SF	BAL

ªPlayed at Milwaukee.

NEW YORK GIANTS

1953		1954		1955		1956		1957		1958		1959	
Home	*Away*	*Home*	*Away*	*Home*	*Away*	*Home*	*Away*	*Home*	*Away*	*Home*	*Away*	*Home*	*Away*
DET	LA	LA	BAL	BAL	DET	ChiB	SF	SF	GB	BAL	DET	GB	LA

PHILADELPHIA EAGLES

1953		1954		1955		1956		1957		1958		1959	
Home	*Away*	*Home*	*Away*	*Home*	*Away*	*Home*	*Away*	*Home*	*Away*	*Home*	*Away*	*Home*	*Away*
BAL	SF	GB	DET	LA	ChiB	SF	LA	DET	LA	SF	GB	LA	SF

PITTSBURGH STEELERS

1953		1954		1955		1956		1957		1958		1959	
Home	*Away*	*Home*	*Away*	*Home*	*Away*	*Home*	*Away*	*Home*	*Away*	*Home*	*Away*	*Home*	*Away*
GB	DET	SF	GB	DET	LA	LA	DET	GB	BAL	ChiB	SF	DET	ChiB

WASHINGTON REDSKINS

1953		1954		1955		1956		1957		1958		1959	
Home	*Away*	*Home*	*Away*	*Home*	*Away*	*Home*	*Away*	*Home*	*Away*	*Home*	*Away*	*Home*	*Away*
ChiB	BAL	BAL	SF	SF	BAL	DET	BAL	BAL	ChiB	GB	BAL	BAL	GB

WESTERN CONFERENCE

BALTIMORE COLTS

1953		1954		1955		1956		1957		1958		1959	
Home	*Away*	*Home*	*Away*	*Home*	*Away*	*Home*	*Away*	*Home*	*Away*	*Home*	*Away*	*Home*	*Away*
WAS	PHI	NYG	WAS	WAS	NYG	WAS	CLE	PIT	WAS	WAS	NYG	CLE	WAS

CHICAGO BEARS

1953		1954		1955		1956		1957		1958		1959	
Home	*Away*	*Home*	*Away*	*Home*	*Away*	*Home*	*Away*	*Home*	*Away*	*Home*	*Away*	*Home*	*Away*
ChiC	WAS	CLE	ChiC	PHI	ChiC	ChiC	NYG	WAS	ChiC	ChiC	PIT	PIT	ChiC

DETROIT LIONS

1953		1954		1955		1956		1957		1958		1959	
Home	*Away*	*Home*	*Away*	*Home*	*Away*	*Home*	*Away*	*Home*	*Away*	*Home*	*Away*	*Home*	*Away*
PIT	NYG	PHI	CLE	NYG	PIT	PIT	WAS	CLE	PHI	NYG	CLE	ChiC	PIT

GREEN BAY PACKERS

1953		1954		1955		1956		1957		1958		1959	
Home	*Away*	*Home*	*Away*	*Home*	*Away*	*Home*	*Away*	*Home*	*Away*	*Home*	*Away*	*Home*	*Away*
CLE[a]	PIT	PIT	PHI	ChiC	CLE	CLE[a]	ChiC	NYG	PIT	PHI	WAS	WAS	NYG

[a]Played at Milwaukee.

LOS ANGELES RAMS

1953		1954		1955		1956		1957		1958		1959	
Home	*Away*	*Home*	*Away*	*Home*	*Away*	*Home*	*Away*	*Home*	*Away*	*Home*	*Away*	*Home*	*Away*
NYG	ChiC	ChiC	NYG	PIT	PHI	PHI	PIT	PHI	CLE	CLE	ChiC	NYG	PHI

SAN FRANCISCO 49ERS

1953		1954		1955		1956		1957		1958		1959	
Home	*Away*	*Home*	*Away*	*Home*	*Away*	*Home*	*Away*	*Home*	*Away*	*Home*	*Away*	*Home*	*Away*
PHI	CLE	WAS	PIT	CLE	WAS	NYG	PHI	ChiC	NYG	PIT	PHI	PHI	CLE

1960 (NFL)

EASTERN CONFERENCE	WESTERN CONFERENCE
Cleveland Browns	Baltimore Colts
New York Giants	Chicago Bears
Philadelphia Eagles	Dallas Cowboys
Pittsburgh Steelers	Detroit Lions
St. Louis Cardinals	Green Bay Packers
Washington Redskins	Los Angeles Rams
	San Francisco 49ers

1960 (NFL)

The 12-game regular season schedule of any NFL team is determined by one of the following formulas:

A. Eastern Conference teams.
1. Home and away round-robin within the conference (10 games).
2. One game against two teams from the Western Conference, including one game against the expansion Dallas Cowboys (2 games).
This completes the 12-game schedule.

B. Western Conference teams (except Dallas).
1. Home and away round-robin with five clubs within the conference (10 games).
2. One game against the expansion Dallas Cowboys (1 game).
3. One game against one club from the Eastern Conference (1 game).
This completes the 12-game schedule.

C. Dallas Cowboys.
1. One game against all other 12 clubs in the league (12 games).
This completes the 12-game schedule.

1960 NFL Non-Conference Opponents

EASTERN CONFERENCE

CLEVELAND		NY GIANTS		PHILADELPHIA		PITTSBURGH		ST. LOUIS		WASHINGTON	
Home	*Away*	*Home*	*Away*	*Home*	*Away*	*Home*	*Away*	*Home*	*Away*	*Home*	*Away*
CHI	DAL	DAL	SF	DET	DAL	GB	DAL	DAL	LA	DAL	BAL

WESTERN CONFERENCE

BALTIMORE		CHICAGO		DETROIT		GREEN BAY		LOS ANGELES		SAN FRANCISCO	
Home	*Away*	*Home*	*Away*	*Home*	*Away*	*Home*	*Away*	*Home*	*Away*	*Home*	*Away*
WAS	DAL[a]	DAL[a]	CLE	DAL[a]	PHI	DAL[a]	PIT	STL	DAL[a]	NYG	DAL[a]

	DALLAS	
	Home	*Away*
West	BAL	CHI
	LA	DET
	SF	GB
East	CLE	NYG
	PHI	STL
	PIT	WAS

[a]Played conference opponent Dallas once.

1961–1965 (NFL)

EASTERN CONFERENCE
Cleveland Browns
Dallas Cowboys
New York Giants
Philadelphia Eagles
Pittsburgh Steelers
St. Louis Cardinals
Washington Redskins

WESTERN CONFERENCE
Baltimore Colts
Chicago Bears
Detroit Lions
Green Bay Packers
Los Angeles Rams
Minnesota Vikings
San Francisco 49ers

1961–1965 (NFL)

The 14-game regular season schedule of all NFL teams is determined by the following formula:

- Home and away round-robin within the conference (12 games).
- Two games (one home, one away) against teams from the other conference (2 games). Note: In 1961, Dallas and Minnesota played each other twice, home and away.

This completes the 14-game schedule.

1961–1965 NFL Non-Conference Opponents

EASTERN CONFERENCE

CLEVELAND BROWNS

1961		1962		1963		1964		1965	
Home	Away	Home	Away	Home	Away	Home	Away	Home	Away
GB	CHI	BAL	SF	LA	DET	DET	GB[a]	MIN	LA

[a] Played at Milwaukee.

DALLAS COWBOYS

1961		1962		1963		1964		1965	
Home	Away	Home	Away	Home	Away	Home	Away	Home	Away
MIN[a]	MIN[a]	CHI	LA	DET	SF	GB	CHI	SF	GB[b]

[a] Dallas played Minnesota twice, home and away.
[b] Played at Milwaukee.

NEW YORK GIANTS

1961		1962		1963		1964		1965	
Home	Away	Home	Away	Home	Away	Home	Away	Home	Away
LA	GB[a]	DET	CHI	SF	BAL	MIN	DET	CHI	MIN

[a] Played at Milwaukee.

PHILADELPHIA EAGLES

1961		1962		1963		1964		1965	
Home	Away	Home	Away	Home	Away	Home	Away	Home	Away
CHI	DET	GB	MIN	MIN	CHI	SF	LA	DET	BAL

1961–1965 (NFL)

PITTSBURGH STEELERS

1961		1962		1963		1964		1965	
Home	*Away*	*Home*	*Away*	*Home*	*Away*	*Home*	*Away*	*Home*	*Away*
SF	LA	MIN	DET	CHI	GB[a]	LA	MIN	GB	SF

[a] Played at Milwaukee.

ST. LOUIS CARDINALS

1961		1962		1963		1964		1965	
Home	*Away*	*Home*	*Away*	*Home*	*Away*	*Home*	*Away*	*Home*	*Away*
DET	BAL	SF	GB[a]	GB	MIN	BAL[b]	SF	LA	CHI

[a] Played at Milwaukee.
[b] Game originally scheduled to be played in St. Louis; moved to Baltimore due to World Series.

WASHINGTON REDSKINS

1961		1962		1963		1964		1965	
Home	*Away*	*Home*	*Away*	*Home*	*Away*	*Home*	*Away*	*Home*	*Away*
BAL	SF	LA	BAL	BAL	LA	CHI	BAL	BAL	DET

Western Conference

BALTIMORE COLTS

1961		1962		1963		1964		1965	
Home	*Away*	*Home*	*Away*	*Home*	*Away*	*Home*	*Away*	*Home*	*Away*
STL	WAS	WAS	CLE	NYG	WAS	WAS	STL[a]	PHI	WAS

[a] Game originally scheduled to be played in St. Louis; moved to Baltimore due to World Series.

CHICAGO BEARS

1961		1962		1963		1964		1965	
Home	*Away*	*Home*	*Away*	*Home*	*Away*	*Home*	*Away*	*Home*	*Away*
CLE	PHI	NYG	DAL	PHI	PIT	DAL	WAS	STL	NYG

DETROIT LIONS

1961		1962		1963		1964		1965	
Home	*Away*	*Home*	*Away*	*Home*	*Away*	*Home*	*Away*	*Home*	*Away*
PHI	STL	PIT	NYG	CLE	DAL	NYG	CLE	WAS	PHI

GREEN BAY PACKERS

1961		1962		1963		1964		1965	
Home	*Away*	*Home*	*Away*	*Home*	*Away*	*Home*	*Away*	*Home*	*Away*
NYG[a]	CLE	STL[a]	PHI	PIT[a]	STL	CLE[a]	DAL	DAL[a]	PIT

[a] Played at Milwaukee.

LOS ANGELES RAMS

1961		1962		1963		1964		1965	
Home	*Away*	*Home*	*Away*	*Home*	*Away*	*Home*	*Away*	*Home*	*Away*
PIT	NYG	DAL	WAS	WAS	CLE	PHI	PIT	CLE	STL

MINNESOTA VIKINGS

1961		1962		1963		1964		1965	
Home	*Away*	*Home*	*Away*	*Home*	*Away*	*Home*	*Away*	*Home*	*Away*
DAL[a]	DAL[a]	PHI	PIT	STL	PHI	PIT	NYG	NYG	CLE

[a] Minnesota played Dallas twice, home and away.

SAN FRANCISCO 49ERS

1961		1962		1963		1964		1965	
Home	*Away*	*Home*	*Away*	*Home*	*Away*	*Home*	*Away*	*Home*	*Away*
WAS	PIT	CLE	STL	DAL	NYG	STL	PHI	PIT	DAL

1966 (NFL)

EASTERN CONFERENCE	WESTERN CONFERENCE
Atlanta Falcons	Baltimore Colts
Cleveland Browns	Chicago Bears
Dallas Cowboys	Detroit Lions
New York Giants	Green Bay Packers
Philadelphia Eagles	Los Angeles Rams
Pittsburgh Steelers	Minnesota Vikings
St. Louis Cardinals	San Francisco 49ers
Washington Redskins	

1966 (NFL)

The 14-game regular season schedule of any NFL team is determined by one of the following formulas:

A. Eastern Conference teams (except Atlanta).
1. Home and away round-robin within the conference, except Atlanta (12 games).
2. One game against the expansion Atlanta Falcons (1 game).
3. One game against one club from the Western Conference (1 game).
This completes the 14-game schedule.

B. Western Conference teams.
1. Home and away round-robin within the conference (12 games).
2. Two games (one home, one away) against teams from the Eastern Conference, including one game against the expansion Atlanta Falcons (2 games).
This completes the 14-game schedule.

C. Atlanta Falcons.
1. One game against all other 14 clubs in the league (14 games).
This completes the 14-game schedule.

1966 NFL Non-Conference Opponents

EASTERN CONFERENCE

CLEVELAND		DALLAS		NY GIANTS		PHILADELPHIA		PITTSBURGH		ST. LOUIS	
Home	*Away*	*Home*	*Away*	*Home*	*Away*	*Home*	*Away*	*Home*	*Away*	*Home*	*Away*
GB	ATL[a]	MIN	ATL[a]	ATL[a]	LA	ATL[a]	SF	DET	ATL[a]	CHI	ATL[a]

1967–1969 (NFL)

WASHINGTON			ATLANTA	
Home	*Away*		*Home*	*Away*
ATL[a]	BAL	*East*	CLE	NYG
			DAL	PHI
			PIT	WAS
			STL	
		West	BAL	CHI
			LA	DET
			SF	GB[b]
				MIN

[a]Played conference opponent Atlanta once.

WESTERN CONFERENCE

BALTIMORE		CHICAGO		DETROIT		GREEN BAY		LOS ANGELES		MINNESOTA	
Home	*Away*	*Home*	*Away*	*Home*	*Away*	*Home*	*Away*	*Home*	*Away*	*Home*	*Away*
WAS	ATL	ATL	STL	ATL	PIT	ATL[b]	CLE	NYG	ATL	ATL	DAL

SAN FRANCISCO	
Home	*Away*
PHI	ATL

[b]Played at Milwaukee.

1967–1969 (NFL)

1967 & 1969 ALIGNMENT

EASTERN CONFERENCE	WESTERN CONFERENCE
Capitol Division	**Coastal Division**
Dallas Cowboys	Atlanta Falcons
New Orleans Saints	Baltimore Colts
Philadelphia Eagles	Los Angeles Rams
Washington Redskins	San Francisco 49ers
Century Division	**Central Division**
Cleveland Browns	Chicago Bears
New York Giants	Detroit Lions
Pittsburgh Steelers	Green Bay Packers
St. Louis Cardinals	Minnesota Vikings

1968 ALIGNMENT

EASTERN CONFERENCE	WESTERN CONFERENCE
Capitol Division	**Coastal Division**
Dallas Cowboys	Atlanta Falcons
New York Giants	Baltimore Colts
Philadelphia Eagles	Los Angeles Rams
Washington Redskins	San Francisco 49ers

Century Division	Central Division
Cleveland Browns	Chicago Bears
New Orleans Saints	Detroit Lions
Pittsburgh Steelers	Green Bay Packers
St. Louis Cardinals	Minnesota Vikings

1967–1969 (NFL)

The 14-game regular season schedule of all NFL teams is determined by the following formula[1]:

- Home and away round-robin within the division (6 games).
- Four games (two home, two away) against each team from the other division within the conference (4 games).
- Four games (two home, two away) against each team from one of the divisions of the other conference (4 games).

This completes the 14-game schedule.

NOTE: The New Orleans Saints and New York Giants switched divisions in 1968, and returned to the 1967 alignment in 1969.

Interconference Rotation

	1967	1968	1969
Capitol Division[a]	Coastal	Central	Coastal
Century Division[b]	Central	Coastal	Central
Central Division	Century	Capitol[a]	Century
Coastal Division	Capitol	Century[b]	Capitol

[a]Dallas, New Orleans, Philadelphia and Washington. The New Orleans Saints followed the Capitol Division interconference rotation in 1968, despite being in the Century Division.
[b]Cleveland, New York Giants, Pittsburgh and St. Louis. The New York Giants followed the Century Division interconference rotation in 1968, despite being in the Capitol Division.

1967 NFL Non-Divisional Opponents

EASTERN CONFERENCE

Capitol		Century	
DALLAS		**CLEVELAND**	
Home	Away	Home	Away
NYG	CLE	DAL	NO
STL	PIT	WAS	PHI
W ATL	W BAL	W CHI	W DET
LA	SF	MIN	GB[a]
NEW ORLEANS		**NY GIANTS**	
Home	Away	Home	Away
CLE	NYG	NO	DAL
PIT	STL	PHI	WAS
W ATL	W BAL	W DET	W CHI
LA	SF	GB	MIN

WESTERN CONFERENCE

Central		Coastal	
CHICAGO		**ATLANTA**	
Home	Away	Home	Away
BAL	ATL	CHI	DET
LA	SF	MIN	GB[a]
E NYG	E CLE	E PHI	E DAL
STL	PIT	WAS	NO
DETROIT		**BALTIMORE**	
Home	Away	Home	Away
ATL	BAL	DET	CHI
LA	SF	GB	MIN
E CLE	E NYG	E DAL	E PHI
PIT	STL	NO	WAS

	PHILADELPHIA				PITTSBURGH				GREEN BAY				LOS ANGELES	
	Home		*Away*		*Home*		*Away*		*Home*		*Away*		*Home*	*Away*
	CLE		NYG		DAL		NO		ATL[a]		BAL		GB	CHI
	PIT		STL		WAS		PHI		SF		LA		MIN	DET
W	BAL	W	ATL	W	CHI	W	DET	E	CLE[a]	E	NYG	E	PHI	E DAL
	SF		LA		MIN		GB		PIT		STL		WAS	NO

	WASHINGTON				ST. LOUIS				MINNESOTA				SAN FRANCISCO	
	Home		*Away*		*Home*		*Away*		*Home*		*Away*		*Home*	*Away*
	NYG		CLE		NO		DAL		BAL		ATL		CHI	GB
	STL		PIT		PHI		WAS		SF		LA		DET	MIN
W	BAL	W	ATL	W	DET	W	CHI	E	NYG	E	CLE	E	DAL	E PHI
	SF		LA		GB		MIN		STL		PIT		NO	WAS

[a] Played at Milwaukee.

1968 NFL Non-Divisional Opponents

Eastern Conference

	Capitol				Century		
	DALLAS				**CLEVELAND**		
	Home		*Away*		*Home*		*Away*
	CLE		NO		NYG		DAL
	PIT		STL		PHI		WAS
W	DET	W	CHI	W	ATL	W	BAL
	GB		MIN		LA		SF

	NY GIANTS				NEW ORLEANS		
	Home		*Away*		*Home*		*Away*
	NO		CLE		DAL		NYG
	STL		PIT		WAS		PHI
W	BAL	W	ATL	W	CHI	W	DET
	SF		LA		MIN		GB[a]

	PHILADELPHIA				PITTSBURGH		
	Home		*Away*		*Home*		*Away*
	NO		CLE		NYG		DAL
	STL		PIT		PHI		WAS
W	CHI	W	DET	W	BAL	W	ATL
	MIN		GB		SF		LA

	WASHINGTON				ST. LOUIS		
	Home		*Away*		*Home*		*Away*
	CLE		NO		DAL		NYG
	PIT		STL		WAS		PHI
W	DET	W	CHI	W	ATL	W	BAL
	GB		MIN		LA		SF

Western Conference

	Central				Coastal		
	CHICAGO				**ATLANTA**		
	Home		*Away*		*Home*		*Away*
	ATL		BAL		DET		CHI
	SF		LA		GB		MIN
E	DAL	E	NO	E	NYG	E	CLE
	WAS		PHI		PIT		STL

	DETROIT				BALTIMORE		
	Home		*Away*		*Home*		*Away*
	BAL		ATL		CHI		DET
	SF		LA		MIN		GB
E	NO	E	DAL	E	CLE	E	NYG
	PHI		WAS		STL		PIT

	GREEN BAY				LOS ANGELES		
	Home		*Away*		*Home*		*Away*
	BAL		ATL		CHI		GB[a]
	LA[a]		SF		DET		MIN
E	NO[a]	E	DAL	E	NYG	E	CLE
	PHI		WAS		PIT		STL

	MINNESOTA				SAN FRANCISCO		
	Home		*Away*		*Home*		*Away*
	ATL		BAL		GB		CHI
	LA		SF		MIN		DET
E	DAL	E	NO	E	CLE	E	NYG
	WAS		PHI		STL		PIT

[a] Played at Milwaukee.

1969 NFL Non-Divisional Opponents

EASTERN CONFERENCE

Capitol

Home	Away		
	NYG		CLE
	STL		PIT
W	BAL	W	ATL
	SF		LA

DALLAS

Home	Away		
	CLE		NYG
	PIT		STL
W	BAL	W	ATL
	SF		LA

NEW ORLEANS

Home	Away		
	CLE		NYG
	PIT		STL
W	ATL	W	BAL
	LA		SF

PHILADELPHIA

Home	Away		
	NYG		CLE
	STL		PIT
W	ATL	W	BAL
	LA		SF

WASHINGTON

Century

CLEVELAND

Home	Away		
	DAL		NO
	WAS		PHI
W	DET	W	CHI
	GB		MIN

NY GIANTS

Home	Away		
	NO		DAL
	PHI		WAS
W	CHI	W	DET
	MIN		GB^a

PITTSBURGH

Home	Away		
	DAL		NO
	WAS		PHI
W	DET	W	CHI
	GB		MIN

ST. LOUIS

Home	Away		
	NO		DAL
	PHI		WAS
W	CHI	W	DET
	MIN		GB

WESTERN CONFERENCE

Central

CHICAGO

Home	Away		
	BAL		ATL
	LA		SF
E	CLE	E	NYG
	PIT		STL

DETROIT

Home	Away		
	ATL		BAL
	LA		SF
E	NYG	E	CLE
	STL		PIT

GREEN BAY

Home	Away		
	ATL		BAL
	SF^a		LA
E	NYG^a	E	CLE
	STL		PIT

MINNESOTA

Home	Away		
	BAL		ATL
	SF		LA
E	CLE	E	NYG
	PIT		STL

Coastal

ATLANTA

Home	Away		
	CHI		DET
	MIN		GB
E	DAL	E	PHI
	NO		WAS

BALTIMORE

Home	Away		
	DET		CHI
	GB		MIN
E	PHI	E	DAL
	WAS		NO

LOS ANGELES

Home	Away		
	GB		CHI
	MIN		DET
E	DAL	E	PHI
	NO		WAS

SAN FRANCISCO

Home	Away		
	CHI		GB^a
	DET		MIN
E	PHI	E	DAL
	WAS		NO

^{a}Played at Milwaukee.

1960–1965 (AFL)

EASTERN DIVISION
Boston Patriots
Buffalo Bills
Houston Oilers
New York Jets^a

WESTERN DIVISION
Denver Broncos
Kansas City Chiefs^b
Oakland Raiders
San Diego Chargers^c

^{a}Franchise known as New York Titans, 1960–1962
^{b}Franchise known as the Dallas Texans, 1960–1962
^{c}Franchise known as the Los Angeles Chargers in 1960

1960–1965 (AFL)

The 14-game regular season schedule of all AFL teams is determined by the following formula:

- Home and away round-robin against the other seven teams in the league (14 games).

This completes the 14-game schedule.

1960–1965 AFL Non-Divisional Opponents

Each AFL team played all other teams twice, once at home and once away. Listed below are games against teams from the other division.[a]

All Eastern Division Teams						*All Western Division Teams*					
1960		1961–1962		1963–1965		1960		1961–1962		1963–1965	
Home	Away	Home	Away	Home	Away	Home	Away	Home	Away	Home	Away
DalT	DalT	DalT	DalT	DEN	DEN	BOS	BOS	BOS	BOS	BOS	BOS
DEN	DEN	DEN	DEN	KC	KC	BUF	BUF	BUF	BUF	BUF	BUF
LAC	LAC	OAK	OAK	OAK	OAK	HOU	HOU	HOU	HOU	HOU	HOU
OAK	OAK	SD	SD	SD	SD	NYT	NYT	NYT	NYT	NYJ	NYJ

[a]The Kansas City Chiefs were known as the Dallas Texans (DalT) from 1960 to 1962, the San Diego Chargers were known as the Los Angeles Chargers (LAC) in 1960, and the New York Jets were known as the New York Titans (NYT) from 1960–1962.

1966–1967 (AFL)

EASTERN DIVISION	WESTERN DIVISION
Boston Patriots	Denver Broncos
Buffalo Bills	Kansas City Chiefs
Houston Oilers	Oakland Raiders
Miami Dolphins	San Diego Chargers
New York Jets	

1966–1967 (AFL)

The 14-game regular season schedule of all AFL teams is determined by the following formula:

- Home and away round-robin against six of the other eight clubs in the league (12 games). Note: In 1967, Boston and San Diego played both games at San Diego. Their second matchup, originally scheduled to be played at Boston, was moved to San Diego due to the World Series.
- One game each against the other two clubs in the league (2 games).

This completes the 14-game schedule.

1966–1967 AFL Opponents

NOTE: The following lists opponents played only once. All other opponents scheduled home and away.

Eastern Division

BOSTON PATRIOTS				BUFFALO BILLS				HOUSTON OILERS			
1966		1967		1966		1967		1966		1967	
Home	*Away*	*Home*	*Away*	*Home*	*Away*	*Home*	*Away*	*Home*	*Away*	*Home*	*Away*
OAK	MIA	KC	DEN	DEN	OAK	SD	KC	SD	KC	OAK	NYJ

MIAMI DOLPHINS				NEW YORK JETS			
1966		1967		1966		1967	
Home	*Away*	*Home*	*Away*	*Home*	*Away*	*Home*	*Away*
BOS	SD	DEN	OAK	KC	DEN	HOU	SD

Western Division

DENVER BRONCOS				KANSAS CITY CHIEFS				OAKLAND RAIDERS			
1966		1967		1966		1967		1966		1967	
Home	*Away*	*Home*	*Away*	*Home*	*Away*	*Home*	*Away*	*Home*	*Away*	*Home*	*Away*
NYJ	BUF	BOS	MIA	HOU	NYJ	BUF	BOS	BUF	BOS	MIA	HOU

SAN DIEGO CHARGERS			
1966		1967	
Home	*Away*	*Home*	*Away*
MIA	HOU	NYJ	BUF

1968–1969 (AFL)

Eastern Division	Western Division
Boston Patriots	Cincinnati Bengals
Buffalo Bills	Denver Broncos
Houston Oilers	Kansas City Chiefs
Miami Dolphins	Oakland Raiders
New York Jets	San Diego Chargers

1968–1969 (AFL)

The 14-game regular season schedule of all AFL teams is determined by the following formula:

- Home and away round-robin within the division (8 games). Note: In 1968, the Boston Patriots and NY Jets played one game at Birmingham, Alabama and one game at New York. In 1969, Boston and Miami played one game at Boston and one game at Tampa, FL.
- Home and away against one club from the other division (2 games).
- One game each against the remaining four clubs from the other division (4 games). Two games played at home, and two games played away.

This completes the 14-game schedule.

1968–1969 AFL Non-Divisional Opponents

Eastern Division

BOSTON PATRIOTS				BUFFALO BILLS				HOUSTON OILERS			
1968		1969		1968		1969		1968		1969	
Home	Away	Home	Away	Home	Away	Home	Away	Home	Away	Home	Away
DEN	DEN	SD	SD	OAK	OAK	KC	KC	KC	KC	DEN	DEN
CIN	KC	KC	CIN	KC	CIN	CIN	OAK	DEN	CIN	CIN	KC
SD	OAK	OAK	DEN	SD	DEN	DEN	SD	OAK	SD	SD	OAK

MIAMI DOLPHINS				NEW YORK JETS			
1968		1969		1968		1969	
Home	Away	Home	Away	Home	Away	Home	Away
CIN	CIN	OAK	OAK	SD	SD	CIN	CIN
KC	DEN	DEN	CIN	CIN	KC	KC	DEN
OAK	SD	SD	KC	DEN	OAK	OAK	SD

Western Division

CINCINNATI BENGALS				DENVER BRONCOS				KANSAS CITY CHIEFS			
1968		1969		1968		1969		1968		1969	
Home	Away	Home	Away	Home	Away	Home	Away	Home	Away	Home	Away
MIA	MIA	NYJ	NYJ	BOS	BOS	HOU	HOU	HOU	HOU	BUF	BUF
BUF	BOS	BOS	BUF	BUF	HOU	BOS	BUF	BOS	BUF	HOU	BOS
HOU	NYJ	MIA	HOU	MIA	NYJ	NYJ	MIA	NYJ	MIA	MIA	NYJ

OAKLAND RAIDERS				SAN DIEGO CHARGERS			
1968		1969		1968		1969	
Home	Away	Home	Away	Home	Away	Home	Away
BUF	BUF	MIA	MIA	NYJ	NYJ	BOS	BOS
BOS	HOU	BUF	BOS	HOU	BOS	BUF	HOU
NYJ	MIA	HOU	NYJ	MIA	BUF	NYJ	MIA

1970–1975

AMERICAN CONFERENCE

Eastern Division
Baltimore Colts
Buffalo Bills
Miami Dolphins
New England Patriots[a]
New York Jets

Central Division
Cincinnati Bengals
Cleveland Browns
Houston Oilers
Pittsburgh Steelers

Western Division
Denver Broncos
Kansas City Chiefs
Oakland Raiders
San Diego Chargers

NATIONAL CONFERENCE

Eastern Division
Dallas Cowboys
New York Giants
Philadelphia Eagles
St. Louis Cardinals
Washington Redskins

Central Division
Chicago Bears
Detroit Lions
Green Bay Packers
Minnesota Vikings

Western Division
Atlanta Falcons
Los Angeles Rams
New Orleans Saints
San Francisco 49ers

[a]*Boston Patriots (1970)*

1970–1975

The 14-game regular season schedule of any NFL team is determined by one of the following three formulas:[1]

A. Teams in a five-team division (AFC East, NFC East).
1. Home and away round-robin within the division (8 games).
2. One game against two clubs from one of the four-team divisions within the conference and one game with one club from the other four-team division within the conference (3 games).
3. Three games against teams from the other conference (3 games).
This completes the 14-game schedule.

B. Teams in a four-team division (AFC Central, AFC West, NFC Central, NFC West), with the exception of one club in each conference listed in Section C.
1. Home and away round-robin within the division (6 games).
2. One game against three out of the four clubs from the other four-team division within the conference (3 games).
3. One game against two clubs from the five-team division (East) within the conference (2 games).
4. Three games against teams from the other conference (3 games).
This completes the 14-game schedule.

C. One team from one of the four-team divisions in each conference will be assigned to play an additional interconference game in lieu of one game against an Eastern division club within the conference. As part of the realignment agreement, beginning in 1970 and for a period of five years, Denver would play four games against teams from the other conference. Here are the teams to play four interconference games from 1970 to 1975:

	AFC	NFC
1970	Denver	San Francisco
1971	Denver	Detroit
1972	Denver	Atlanta
1973	Denver	Chicago
1974	Denver	Los Angeles
1975	Cleveland	Minnesota

1. Home and away round-robin within the division (6 games).
2. One game against three out of the four clubs from the other four-team division within the conference (3 games).
3. One game against one club from the five-team division (East) within the conference (1 game).
4. Four games against teams from the other conference (4 games). This includes the AFC-NFC matchup against the team from the other conference assigned to play an additional interconference game.
This completes the 14-game schedule.

Note: In the 1970–1975 section, teams followed with a superscript a (ª) played four interconference games instead of three.

1970–1975 Intraconference Rotation

AFC East

VS. CENTRAL/WEST (3 GAMES)

1970	1971	1972	1973	1974	1975	OPPONENTS
BAL	BUF	MIA	NE	NYJ		HOU-KC-SD
NYJ	BAL	BUF	MIA	NE		CLE-PIT-OAK
NE	NYJ	BAL	BUF	MIA		CIN-KC-SD
MIA	NE	NYJ	BAL	BUF		CLE-HOU-OAK
BUF	MIA	NE	NYJ	BAL		
					BUF	CIN-PIT-DEN
					BAL	CLE-KC-OAK
					NYJ	PIT-KC-SD
					NE	CIN-HOU-SD
					MIA	HOU-DEN-OAK

AFC Central

VS. EAST (CENTRAL TEAMS PLAYED 2 OF THE 5 EAST CLUBS)

1970	1971	1972	1973	1974	1975	OPPONENTS
CIN	HOU	PIT		CLE	CIN	BUF-NE
CLE	CIN	HOU	PIT			MIA-NYJ
PIT		CLE	CIN	HOU	PIT	BUF-NYJ
HOU	PIT		CLE	CIN		BAL-MIA
	CLE	CIN	HOU	PIT		BAL-NE
					HOU	MIA-NE
					CLE[a]	BAL

VS. WEST (CENTRAL TEAMS PLAYED 3 OF THE 4 WEST CLUBS)

1970	1971	1972	1973	1974	1975	OPPONENTS
CIN	HOU	PIT	CLE	CIN	HOU	KC-OAK-SD
CLE	CIN	HOU	PIT	CLE	CIN	DEN-OAK-SD
PIT	CLE	CIN	HOU	PIT	CLE	DEN-KC-OAK
HOU	PIT	CLE	CIN	HOU	PIT	DEN-KC-SD

AFC West

VS. EAST (WEST TEAMS PLAYED 2 OF THE 5 EAST CLUBS)

1970	1971	1972	1973	1974	1975	OPPONENTS
OAK				KC/SD		MIA-NYJ
KC/SD	OAK					BAL-NE
	KC/SD	OAK				BUF-NYJ
		KC/SD	OAK		OAK	BAL-MIA
			KC/SD	OAK		BUF-NE
					KC	BAL-NYJ
					DEN	BUF-MIA
					SD	NE-NYJ
DEN[a]						BUF
	DEN[a]					MIA
		DEN[a]				NE
			DEN[a]			NYJ
				DEN[a]		BAL

VS. CENTRAL (WEST TEAMS PLAYED 3 OF THE 4 CENTRAL CLUBS)

1970	1971	1972	1973	1974	1975	OPPONENTS
OAK	DEN	KC	SD	OAK	DEN	CIN-CLE-PIT
SD	OAK	DEN	KC	SD	OAK	CIN-CLE-HOU
KC	SD	OAK	DEN	KC	SD	CIN-HOU-PIT
DEN	KC	SD	OAK	DEN	KC	CLE-HOU-PIT

NFC East

VS. CENTRAL/WEST (3 GAMES)

1970	1971	1972	1973	1974	1975	OPPONENTS
DAL	NYG	WAS				GB-MIN-ATL
NYG	DAL/WAS	PHI	DAL			CHI-LA-NO
PHI						CHI-GB-ATL
STL						DET-LA-NO
WAS	PHI					DET-MIN-SF
	STL					GB-ATL-SF
		DAL				DET-GB-SF
		NYG	WAS			DET-NO-SF
		STL				CHI-MIN-LA
			NYG			GB-MIN-LA
			PHI	DAL		MIN-ATL-SF
			STL			DET-GB-ATL
				NYG	STL	CHI-DET-ATL
				PHI		DET-GB-NO
				STL		MIN-NO-SF
				WAS		CHI-GB-LA
					DAL	DET-GB-LA
					NYG	GB-NO-SF
					PHI	CHI-LA-SF
					WAS	MIN-ATL-NO

NFC Central

VS. EAST (CENTRAL TEAMS PLAYED 2 OF THE 5 EAST CLUBS)

1970	1971	1972	1973	1974	1975	OPPONENTS
CHI	MIN		MIN	DET		NYG-PHI
DET		MIN	DET			STL-WAS
GB						DAL-PHI
MIN	CHI	GB				DAL-WAS
	GB		GB			NYG-STL
			CHI		CHI	PHI-STL
			DET		GB	DAL-NYG
				CHI		NYG-WAS
				GB		PHI-WAS
				MIN	DET	DAL-STL
	DET[a]					PHI
			CHI[a]			DAL
				MIN[a]		WAS

VS. WEST (CENTRAL TEAMS PLAYED 3 OF THE 4 WEST CLUBS)

1970	1971	1972	1973	1974	1975	OPPONENTS
CHI	MIN	GB	DET	CHI	MIN	ATL-NO-SF
DET	CHI	MIN	GB	DET	CHI	LA-NO-SF
GB	DET	CHI	MIN	GB	DET	ATL-LA-SF
MIN	GB	DET	CHI	MIN	GB	ATL-LA-NO

NFC West

VS. EAST (WEST TEAMS PLAYED 2 OF THE 5 EAST CLUBS)

1970	1971	1972	1973	1974	1975	OPPONENTS
ATL					LA	DAL-PHI
LA/NO	ATL					NYG-STL
	LA/NO		NO			DAL-WAS
	SF	LA	ATL	NO		PHI-STL
		NO			SF	NYG-PHI
		SF	LA	ATL		DAL-NYG
			SF			PHI-WAS
				SF		DAL-STL
					ATL	STL-WAS
					NO	NYG-WAS
SF[a]		ATL[a]		LA[a]		WAS

VS. CENTRAL (WEST TEAMS PLAYED 3 OF THE 4 CENTRAL CLUBS)

1970	1971	1972	1973	1974	1975	OPPONENTS
SF	LA	ATL	NO	SF	LA	CHI-DET-GB
NO	SF	LA	ATL	NO	SF	CHI-DET-MIN
ATL	NO	SF	LA	ATL	NO	CHI-GB-MIN
LA	ATL	NO	SF	LA	ATL	DET-GB-MIN

1970–1975 Interconference Rotation

Beginning with the 1970 season, an established regular pattern of games between the two conferences was implemented in which each club would face three interconference opponents, with the exception of one club in each conference, as denoted by a superscript a ([a]), which would play an additional interconference matchup against such team from the opposite conference.

The 13 clubs in each conference were placed in parallel columns (as shown below):

1970		1971		1972		1973		1974		1975	
AFC	NFC	AFC	NFC	AFC	NFC	AFC	NFC	AFC	NFC	AFC	NFC
NYJ	NYG	BAL	NYG	DEN[a]	NYG	CLE	NYG	NE	NYG	SD	NYG
BUF	LA	PIT	LA	CIN	LA	HOU	LA	NYJ	LA[a]	BAL	LA
SD	CHI	MIA	CHI	OAK	CHI	KC	CHI[a]	BUF	CHI	PIT	CHI
BAL	GB	DEN[a]	GB	CLE	GB	NE	GB	SD	GB	MIA	GB
PIT	PHI	CIN	PHI	HOU	PHI	NYJ	PHI	BAL	PHI	DEN	PHI
MIA	ATL	OAK	ATL	KC	ATL[a]	BUF	ATL	PIT	ATL	CIN	ATL
DEN[a]	NO	CLE	NO	NE	NO	SD	NO	MIA	NO	OAK	NO
CIN	WAS	HOU	WAS	NYJ	WAS	BAL	WAS	DEN[a]	WAS	CLE[a]	WAS
OAK	DET	KC	DET[a]	BUF	DET	PIT	DET	CIN	DET	HOU	DET
CLE	SF[a]	NE	SF	SD	SF	MIA	SF	OAK	SF	KC	SF
HOU	DAL	NYJ	DAL	BAL	DAL	DEN[a]	DAL	CLE	DAL	NE	DAL
KC	STL	BUF	STL	PIT	STL	CIN	STL	HOU	STL	NYJ	STL
BOS	MIN	SD	MIN	MIA	MIN	OAK	MIN	KC	MIN	BUF	MIN[a]

Each of the 13 clubs in one conference would play the clubs from the other conference in the following manner:

Each team's three interconference opponents would consist of the teams that are listed directly opposite, directly above it, and directly below it in the parallel column of the opposing conference. For example, in 1970, the New York Jets played the team directly opposite in the NFC column (New York Giants), the team directly 'above' it (Minnesota), and directly below it (Los Angeles). Buffalo played Los Angeles, New York Giants and Chicago; San Diego played Chicago, Los Angeles and Green Bay, etc. In the NFC, the New York Giants played the New York Jets, the Boston Patriots and Buffalo Bills; the Los Angeles Rams played Buffalo, the New York Jets and San Diego, etc.

In 1971, the teams in the AFC column would be rotated by removing the three teams originally listed at the top of the column (New York Jets, Buffalo and San Diego), and placing those three teams at the bottom of the AFC column. The remaining 10 clubs in the AFC column would be moved up three positions in the column. Then the same method as described above for determining each team's interconference opponents would be applied. This rotation would be repeated annually with the AFC column rotated each year in the same manner.[2]

Based on the chart on page 60, the following set of interconference opponents were formed. Each year, teams played one of 13 groups of three teams each on a rotating basis.

In the chart below, read horizontally to figure which team played a particular set of opponents in a given year. For example, in 1970 the New York Jets played Los Angeles, Minnesota and the New York Giants. Baltimore played the same three clubs in 1971, Denver in 1972, etc. Read vertically to figure which set of teams each club faced in a given year. For example, in 1970, the New York Giants played the Bills, Patriots and Jets; Green Bay played Baltimore, Pittsburgh and San Diego; New Orleans played Cincinnati, Denver and Miami, etc. Teams with a superscript a ([a]) in each conference in a given year played each other for a fourth interconference game.

AFC

	1970	1971	1972	1973	1974	1975	OPPONENTS
Team A	NYJ	BAL	DEN[a]	CLE	NE	SD	LA-MIN-NYG
Team B	HOU	NYJ	BAL	DEN[a]	CLE	NE	DAL-STL-SF
Team C	CIN	HOU	NYJ	BAL	DEN[a]	CLE[a]	DET-NO-WAS
Team D	PIT	CIN	HOU	NYJ	BAL	DEN	ATL-GB-PHI
Team E	BUF	PIT	CIN	HOU	NYJ	BAL	CHI-LA-NYG
Team F	KC	BUF	PIT	CIN	HOU	NYJ	DAL-MIN-STL
Team G	OAK	KC	BUF	PIT	CIN	HOU	DET-SF-WAS
Team H	MIA	OAK	KC	BUF	PIT	CIN	ATL-NO-PHI
Team I	SD	MIA	OAK	KC	BUF	PIT	CHI-GB-LA
Team J	NE	SD	MIA	OAK	KC	BUF	MIN-NYG-STL
Team K	CLE	NE	SD	MIA	OAK	KC	DAL-DET-SF
Team L	DEN[a]	CLE	NE	SD	MIA	OAK	ATL-NO-WAS
Team M	BAL	DEN[a]	CLE	NE	SD	MIA	CHI-GB-PHI

NFC

	1970	1971	1972	1973	1974	1975	OPPONENTS
Team A	NYG	DAL	WAS	PHI	LA[a]	STL	BUF-NE-NYJ
Team B	GB	NYG	DAL	WAS	PHI	LA	BAL-PIT-SD
Team C	NO	GB	NYG	DAL	WAS	PHI	CIN-DEN-MIA
Team D	SF[a]	NO	GB	NYG	DAL	WAS	CLE-HOU-OAK
Team E	MIN	SF	NO	GB	NYG	DAL	KC-NE-NYJ
Team F	CHI	MIN	SF	NO	GB	NYG	BAL-BUF-SD
Team G	ATL	CHI	MIN	SF	NO	GB	DEN-MIA-PIT
Team H	DET	ATL	CHI	MIN	SF	NO	CIN-CLE-OAK
Team I	STL	DET[a]	ATL[a]	CHI[a]	MIN	SF	HOU-KC-NE

Team J	LA	STL	DET	ATL	CHI	MIN[a]	BUF-NYJ-SD
Team K	PHI	LA	STL	DET	ATL	CHI	BAL-MIA-PIT
Team L	WAS	PHI	LA	STL	DET	ATL	CIN-DEN-OAK
Team M	DAL	WAS	PHI	LA	STL	DET	CLE-HOU-KC

1970–1975 NON-DIVISIONAL OPPONENTS

AFC East

BALTIMORE COLTS

1970		1971		1972	
Home	Away	Home	Away	Home	Away
	AC HOU	AC CLE			AC CIN
AW KC	AW SD	AC PIT		AW SD	AW KC
NFC CHI	NFC GB[1]		AW OAK	NFC DAL	NFC SF
PHI		NFC LA	NFC MIN	STL	
			NYG		

1973		1974		1975	
Home	Away	Home	Away	Home	Away
AC HOU	AC CLE	AC CIN	AC PIT	AC CLE	
AW OAK		AW DEN		AW KC	
NFC NO	NFC DET	NFC GB	NFC ATL	AW OAK	
	WAS		PHI		NFC CHI
					LA
					NYG[2]

[1]Played at Milwaukee.
[2]Played at Shea Stadium, Flushing, NY.

BUFFALO BILLS

1970		1971		1972	
Home	Away	Home	Away	Home	Away
AC CIN	AC PIT	AC HOU		AC PIT	AC CLE
AW DEN			AW KC		AW OAK
NFC LA	NFC CHI		AW SD	NFC DET	NFC WAS
	NYG	NFC DAL	NFC MIN	SF	
		STL			

1973		1974		1975	
Home	Away	Home	Away	Home	Away
AC CIN		AC HOU	AC CLE		AC CIN
AW KC	AW SD	AW OAK			AC PIT
NFC PHI	NFC ATL	NFC CHI	NFC GB	AW DEN	
	NO		LA	NFC MIN	NFC STL
				NYG	

MIAMI DOLPHINS

1970		1971		1972	
Home	Away	Home	Away	Home	Away
AC CLE	AC HOU	AC PIT	AC CIN	AC HOU	
AW OAK			AW DEN	AW SD	AW KC
NFC NO	NFC ATL	NFC CHI	NFC LA	NFC STL	NFC MIN
	PHI	GB			NYG

	1973				1974				1975		
Home		*Away*		*Home*		*Away*		*Home*		*Away*	
AC	PIT	AC	CLE	AC	CIN					AC	HOU
		AW	OAK[1]	AW	KC	AW	SD	AW	DEN		
NFC	DET	NFC	DAL	NFC	ATL	NFC	NO	AW	OAK		
	SF						WAS	NFC	PHI	NFC	CHI
											GB

[1]Played at Berkeley, CA.

NEW ENGLAND PATRIOTS

	1970				1971				1972		
Home		*Away*		*Home*		*Away*		*Home*		*Away*	
		AC	CIN	AC	HOU	AC	CLE	AC	CIN	AC	PIT
AW	SD	AW	KC	AW	OAK					AW	DEN
NFC	MIN	NFC	STL	NFC	DET	NFC	DAL	NFC	ATL	NFC	NO
	NYG						SF		WAS		

	1973				1974				1975		
Home		*Away*		*Home*		*Away*		*Home*		*Away*	
		AC	HOU	AC	CLE			AC	HOU	AC	CIN
AW	KC			AC	PIT					AW	SD
AW	SD					AW	OAK	NFC	DAL	NFC	STL
NFC	GB	NFC	CHI	NFC	LA	NFC	MIN		SF		
			PHI				NYG[1]				

[1]Played at New Haven, CT.

NEW YORK JETS

	1970				1971				1972		
Home		*Away*		*Home*		*Away*		*Home*		*Away*	
		AC	CLE	AC	CIN			AC	CLE	AC	HOU
		AC	PIT	AW	KC	AW	SD			AW	OAK
AW	OAK			NFC	SF	NFC	DAL	NFC	NO	NFC	DET
NFC	MIN	NFC	LA				STL		WAS		
	NYG										

	1973				1974				1975		
Home		*Away*		*Home*		*Away*		*Home*		*Away*	
		AC	CIN	AC	HOU			AC	PIT		
		AC	PIT[a]	AW	SD	AW	KC			AW	KC
AW	DEN			NFC	LA	NFC	CHI			AW	SD
NFC	ATL	NFC	GB[1]				NYG[2]	NFC	DAL	NFC	MIN
			PHI						STL		

[1]Played at Milwaukee.
[2]Played at New Haven, CT.
[a]Game originally scheduled to be played in New York but moved to Pittsburgh due to World Series.

AFC CENTRAL

CINCINNATI BENGALS

	1970				1971				1972		
Home		*Away*		*Home*		*Away*		*Home*		*Away*	
AE	BOS	AE	BUF	AE	MIA	AE	NYJ	AE	BAL	AE	NE
AW	KC	AW	SD	AW	SD	AW	DEN	AW	DEN	AW	KC
AW	OAK					AW	OAK	AW	OAK		
NFC	NO	NFC	DET	NFC	ATL	NFC	GB	NFC	NYG	NFC	CHI
			WAS		PHI						LA

1970–1975

	1973				1974				1975		
	Home		*Away*		*Home*		*Away*		*Home*		*Away*
AE	NYJ	AE	BUF			AE	BAL	AE	BUF		
AW	KC	AW	DEN			AE	MIA	AE	NE		
		AW	SD	AW	KC	AW	OAK	AW	OAK	AW	DEN
NFC	MIN	NFC	DAL	AW	SD			AW	SD		
	STL			NFC	DET	NFC	SF			NFC	ATL
					WAS						NO
											PHI

CLEVELAND BROWNS

	1970				1971				1972		
	Home		*Away*		*Home*		*Away*		*Home*		*Away*
AE	NYJ	AE	MIA	AE	NE	AE	BAL	AE	BUF	AE	NYJ
AW	SD	AW	DEN	AW	DEN	AW	KC	AW	KC	AW	DEN
		AW	OAK	AW	OAK					AW	SD
NFC	DAL	NFC	SF	NFC	ATL	NFC	NO	NFC	CHI	NFC	PHI
	DET						WAS		GB		

	1973				1974				1975[a]		
	Home		*Away*		*Home*		*Away*		*Home*		*Away*
AE	BAL			AE	BUF	AE	NE			AE	BAL
AE	MIA			AW	DEN	AW	SD	AW	KC	AW	DEN
AW	SD	AW	KC	AW	OAK					AW	OAK
		AW	OAK	NFC	SF	NFC	DAL	NFC	MIN[a]	NFC	DET
NFC	NYG	NFC	LA				STL		NO		
			MIN						WAS		

[a] Played additional interconference game.

HOUSTON OILERS

	1970				1971				1972		
	Home		*Away*		*Home*		*Away*		*Home*		*Away*
AE	BAL					AE	BUF	AE	NYJ	AE	MIA
AE	MIA					AE	NE	AW	OAK	AW	DEN
AW	DEN	AW	KC	AW	KC	AW	OAK			AW	SD
		AW	SD	AW	SD			NFC	GB	NFC	ATL
NFC	SF	NFC	DAL	NFC	DET	NFC	WAS		PHI		
			STL		NO						

	1973				1974				1975		
	Home		*Away*		*Home*		*Away*		*Home*		*Away*
AE	NE	AE	BAL			AE	BUF	AE	MIA	AE	NE
AW	DEN	AW	KC			AE	NYJ	AW	SD	AW	KC
AW	OAK			AW	KC	AW	DEN			AW	OAK
NFC	LA	NFC	CHI	AW	SD			NFC	DET	NFC	SF
			NYG	NFC	DAL	NFC	MIN		WAS		
					STL						

PITTSBURGH STEELERS

	1970				1971				1972		
	Home		*Away*		*Home*		*Away*		*Home*		*Away*
AE	BUF					AE	BAL	AE	NE	AE	BUF
AE	NYJ					AE	MIA	AW	KC	AW	SD
AW	KC	AW	DEN	AW	DEN	AW	KC	AW	OAK		
		AW	OAK	AW	SD			NFC	MIN	NFC	DAL
NFC	GB	NFC	ATL	NFC	LA	NFC	CHI				STL
			PHI		NYG						

1973		1974		1975	
Home	Away	Home	Away	Home	Away
AE NYJ[a]	AE MIA	AE BAL	AE NE	AE BUF	AE NYJ
AW DEN	AW OAK	AW OAK	AW DEN	AW DEN	AW SD
AW SD			AW KC	AW KC	
NFC DET	NFC SF	NFC ATL	NFC NO	NFC CHI	NFC GB[1]
WAS		PHI			LA

[1] Played at Milwaukee.
[a] Game originally scheduled to be played in New York but moved to Pittsburgh due to World Series.

AFC WEST

DENVER BRONCOS

1970[A]		1971[A]		1972[A]	
Home	Away	Home	Away	Home	Away
	AE BUF	AE MIA		AE NE	
AC CLE	AC HOU	AC CIN	AC CLE	AC CLE	AC CIN
AC PIT			AC PIT	AC HOU	
NFC ATL	NFC NO	NFC CHI	NFC GB[1]	NFC MIN	NFC ATL[a]
WAS	SF[a]	DET[a]	PHI		LA
					NYG

1973[A]		1974[A]		1975	
Home	Away	Home	Away	Home	Away
	AE NYJ		AE BAL		AE BUF
AC CIN	AC HOU	AC HOU	AC CLE		AE MIA
	AC PIT	AC PIT		AC CIN	AC PIT
NFC CHI[a]	NFC STL	NFC LA[a]	NFC DET	AC CLE	
DAL		NO	WAS	NFC GB	NFC ATL
SF				PHI	

[1] Played at Milwaukee.
[a] Played additional interconference game.

KANSAS CITY CHIEFS

1970		1971		1972	
Home	Away	Home	Away	Home	Away
AE BOS	AE BAL	AE BUF	AE NYJ	AE BAL	
AC HOU	AC CIN	AC CLE	AC HOU	AE MIA	
	AC PIT	AC PIT		AC CIN	AC CLE
NFC DAL	NFC MIN	NFC WAS	NFC DET		AC PIT
STL			SF	NFC PHI	NFC ATL
					NO

1973		1974		1975	
Home	Away	Home	Away	Home	Away
	AE BUF	AE NYJ	AE MIA	AE NYJ	AE BAL
	AE NE	AC PIT	AC CIN	AC HOU	AC CLE
AC CLE	AC CIN		AC HOU		AC PIT
AC HOU		NFC MIN	NFC STL	NFC DET	NFC DAL
NFC CHI	NFC GB[1]	NYG		SF	
LA					

[1] Played at Milwaukee.

OAKLAND RAIDERS

1970
Home	Away
	AE MIA
	AE NYJ
AC CLE	AC CIN
AC PIT	
NFC SF	NFC DET
WAS	

1971
Home	Away
AE BAL	AE NE
AC CIN	AC CLE
AC HOU	
NFC PHI	NFC ATL
	NO

1972
Home	Away
AE BUF	
AE NYJ	
	AC CIN
	AC HOU
	AC PIT
NFC CHI	NFC GB
LA	

1973
Home	Away
AE MIA[1]	AE BAL
AC CLE	AC HOU
AC PIT	
NFC NYG	NFC MIN
	STL

1974
Home	Away
AE NE	AE BUF
AC CIN	AC CLE
	AC PIT
NFC DAL	NFC SF
DET	

1975
Home	Away
	AE BAL
	AE MIA
AC CLE	AC CIN
AC HOU	
NFC ATL	NFC WAS
NO	

[1] Played at Berkeley, CA.

SAN DIEGO CHARGERS

1970
Home	Away
AE BAL	AE BOS
AC CIN	AC CLE
AC HOU	
NFC GB	NFC CHI
	LA

1971
Home	Away
AE BUF	
AE NYJ	
AC CIN	AC CLE
AC HOU	AC HOU
AC PIT	AC PIT
NFC MIN	NFC NYG
STL	

1972
Home	Away
	AE BAL
	AE MIA
AC CLE	
AC HOU	
AC PIT	
NFC DAL	NFC DET
	SF

1973
Home	Away
AE BUF	AE NE
AC CIN	AC CLE
	AC PIT
NFC ATL	NFC WAS
NO	

1974
Home	Away
AE MIA	AE NYJ
AC CLE	AC CIN
	AC HOU
NFC CHI	NFC GB
PHI	

1975
Home	Away
AE NE	
AE NYJ	
AC PIT	AC CIN
	AC HOU
NFC LA	NFC MIN
	NYG[1]

[1] Played at Shea Stadium, Flushing, NY.

NFC EAST

DALLAS COWBOYS

1970
Home	Away
NC GB	NC MIN
NW ATL	
AFC HOU	AFC CLE
	KC

1971
Home	Away
	NC CHI
NW LA	NW NO
AFC NE	AFC BUF
NYJ	

1972
Home	Away
NC DET	NC GB[1]
NW SF	
AFC PIT	AFC BAL
	SD

	1973				1974				1975		
Home		Away		Home		Away		Home		Away	
		NC	CHI	NC	MIN			NC	GB	NC	DET
NW	NO	NW	LA	NW	SF			NW	LA		
AFC	CIN	AFC	DEN	AFC	CLE	AFC	HOU	AFC	KC	AFC	NE
	MIA						OAK				NYJ

¹Played at Milwaukee.

NEW YORK GIANTS

	1970				1971				1972		
Home		Away		Home		Away		Home		Away	
NC	CHI			NC	MIN	NC	GB			NC	DET
NW	LA	NW	NO			NW	ATL	NW	NO	NW	SF
AFC	BUF	AFC	BOS	AFC	BAL	AFC	PIT	AFC	DEN	AFC	CIN
			NYJ		SD				MIA		

	1973				1974				1975		
Home		Away		Home		Away		Home		Away	
NC	GB¹					NC	CHI			NC	GB³
NC	MIN¹					NC	DET	NW	NO²	NW	SF
		NW	LA	NW	ATL¹			AFC	BAL²	AFC	BUF
AFC	HOU	AFC	CLE	AFC	NE¹	AFC	KC		SD²		
			OAK		NYJ¹						

¹Played at New Haven, CT.
²Played at Shea Stadium, Flushing, NY.
³Played at Milwaukee.

PHILADELPHIA EAGLES

	1970				1971				1972		
Home		Away		Home		Away		Home		Away	
		NC	CHI¹	NC	MIN	NC	DET	NC	CHI		
		NC	GB²	NW	SF			NW	LA	NW	NO
NW	ATL			AFC	DEN	AFC	CIN	AFC	CLE	AFC	HOU
AFC	MIA	AFC	BAL				OAK				KC
	PIT										

	1973				1974				1975		
Home		Away		Home		Away		Home		Away	
		NC	MIN	NC	DET					NC	CHI
NW	ATL	NW	SF	NC	GB			NW	LA		
AFC	NE	AFC	BUF			NW	NO	NW	SF		
	NYJ			AFC	BAL	AFC	PIT	AFC	CIN	AFC	DEN
							SD				MIA

¹Played at Evanston, IL.
²Played at Milwaukee.

ST. LOUIS CARDINALS

	1970				1971				1972		
Home		Away		Home		Away		Home		Away	
		NC	DET	NC	GB			NC	CHI	NC	MIN
NW	NO	NW	LA	NW	SF	NW	ATL	NW	LA		
AFC	BOS	AFC	KC	AFC	NYJ	AFC	BUF	AFC	PIT	AFC	BAL
	HOU						SD				MIA

1970–1975

	1973			1974			1975	
Home		Away	Home		Away	Home		Away
NC	DET	NC GB	NC	MIN				NC CHI
		NW ATL			NW NO	NW	ATL	NC DET
AFC	DEN	AFC CIN			NW SF	AFC	BUF	AFC NYJ
	OAK		AFC	CLE	AFC HOU		NE	
				KC				

WASHINGTON REDSKINS

	1970			1971			1972	
Home		Away	Home		Away	Home		Away
NC	DET				NC CHI	NC	GB	NC MIN
NC	MIN		NW	NO	NW LA	NW	ATL	
		NW SF	AFC	CLE	AFC KC	AFC	BUF	AFC NE
AFC	CIN	AFC DEN		HOU				NYJ
		OAK						

	1973			1974			1975	
Home		Away	Home		Away	Home		Away
		NC DET	NC	CHI	NC GB	NC	MIN	
NW	SF	NW NO			NW LA	NW	NO	NW ATL
AFC	BAL	AFC PIT	AFC	DEN	AFC CIN	AFC	OAK	AFC CLE
	SD			MIA				HOU

NFC Central

CHICAGO BEARS

	1970			1971			1972	
Home		Away	Home		Away	Home		Away
NE	PHI[1]	NE NYG	NE	DAL				NE PHI
NW	SF	NW ATL	NE	WAS				NE STL
		NO	NW	NO	NW LA	NW	ATL	
AFC	BUF	AFC BAL			NW SF	NW	LA	
	SD		AFC	PIT	AFC DEN	NW	SF	
					MIA	AFC	CIN	AFC CLE
								OAK

	1973[A]			1974			1975	
Home		Away	Home		Away	Home		Away
NE	DAL		NE	NYG	NE WAS	NE	PHI	
NW	LA	NW ATL	NW	NO	NW ATL	NE	STL	
		NW NO	NW	SF				NW LA
AFC	HOU	AFC DEN[a]	AFC	NYJ	AFC BUF			NW NO
	NE	KC			SD			NW SF
						AFC	BAL	AFC PIT
							MIA	

[1]Played at Evanston, IL.
[a]Played additional interconference game.

DETROIT LIONS

	1970			1971[A]			1972	
Home		Away	Home		Away	Home		Away
NE	STL	NE WAS	NE	PHI		NE	NYG	NE DAL
NW	SF	NW LA	NW	ATL	NW SF	NW	NO	NW ATL
		NW NO	NW	LA				NW LA
AFC	CIN	AFC CLE	AFC	KC	AFC DEN[a]	AFC	NYJ	AFC BUF
	OAK				HOU		SD	
					NE			

1973		1974		1975	
Home	*Away*	*Home*	*Away*	*Home*	*Away*
NE WAS	NE STL	NE NYG	NE PHI	NE DAL	
NW ATL	NW NO	NW NO	NW LA	NE STL	
NW SF		NW SF		NW LA	NW ATL
AFC BAL	AFC MIA	AFC DEN	AFC CIN		NW SF
	PIT		OAK	AFC CLE	AFC HOU
					KC

ᵃPlayed additional interconference game.

GREEN BAY PACKERS

1970		1971		1972	
Home	*Away*	*Home*	*Away*	*Home*	*Away*
NE PHI[1]	NE DAL	NE NYG	NE STL	NE DAL[1]	NE WAS
NW ATL	NW SF	NW NO[1]	NW ATL	NW ATL[1]	NW NO
NW LA			NW LA	NW SF[1]	
AFC BAL[1]	AFC PIT	AFC CIN	AFC MIA	AFC OAK	AFC CLE
	SD		DEN[1]		HOU

1973		1974		1975	
Home	*Away*	*Home*	*Away*	*Home*	*Away*
NE STL	NE NYG[2]	NE WAS	NE PHI	NE NYG[1]	NE DAL
NW NO[1]	NW LA	NW LA[1]	NW ATL	NW ATL	NW LA
	NW SF		NW SF		NW NO
AFC KC[1]	AFC NE	AFC BUF	AFC BAL	AFC MIA	AFC DEN
NYJ[1]		SD		PIT[1]	

[1]Played at Milwaukee.
[2]Played at New Haven, CT.

MINNESOTA VIKINGS

1970		1971		1972	
Home	*Away*	*Home*	*Away*	*Home*	*Away*
NE DAL	NE WAS		NE NYG	NE STL	
NW LA	NW ATL		NE PHI	NE WAS	
NW NO		NW ATL	NW NO	NW NO	NW LA
AFC KC	AFC BOS	NW SF			NW SF
	NYJ	AFC BAL	AFC SD	AFC MIA	AFC DEN
		BUF			PIT

1973		1974		1975ᴬ	
Home	*Away*	*Home*	*Away*	*Home*	*Away*
NE PHI	NE NYG[1]		NE DAL		NE WAS
NW LA	NW ATL		NE STL	NW ATL	NW NO
	NW SF	NW ATL	NW LA	NW SF	
AFC CLE	AFC CIN	NW NO		AFC NYJ	AFC BUF
OAK		AFC HOU	AFC KC	SD	CLEᵃ
		NE			

[1]Played at New Haven, CT.
ᵃPlayed additional interconference game.

NFC WEST

ATLANTA FALCONS

1970		1971		1972ᴬ	
Home	*Away*	*Home*	*Away*	*Home*	*Away*
NE DAL		NE NYG			NE WAS
NE PHI		NE STL		NC DET	NC CHI
NC CHI	NC GB	NC GB	NC DET		NC GB¹
NC MIN			NC MIN	AFC DENᵃ	AFC NE
AFC MIA	AFC DEN	AFC OAK	AFC CIN	HOU	
PIT			CLE	KC	

1973		1974		1975	
Home	*Away*	*Home*	*Away*	*Home*	*Away*
NE STL	NE PHI	NE DAL	NE NYG²	NE WAS	NE STL
NC CHI	NC DET	NC CHI	NC MIN	NC DET	NC GB
NC MIN		NC GB			NC MIN
AFC BUF	AFC NYJ	AFC BAL	AFC MIA	AFC CIN	AFC OAK
	SD		PIT	DEN	

¹Played at Milwaukee.
²Played at New Haven, CT.
ᵃPlayed additional interconference game.

LOS ANGELES RAMS

1970		1971		1972	
Home	*Away*	*Home*	*Away*	*Home*	*Away*
NE STL	NE NYG	NE WAS	NE DAL		NE PHI
NC DET	NC GB	NC CHI	NC DET		NE STL
	NC MIN	NC GB		NC DET	NC CHI
AFC NYJ	AFC BUF	AFC MIA	AFC BAL	NC MIN	
SD			PIT	AFC CIN	AFC OAK
				DEN	

1973		1974ᴬ		1975	
Home	*Away*	*Home*	*Away*	*Home*	*Away*
NE DAL		NE WAS			NE DAL
NE NYG		NC DET	NC GB¹		NE PHI
NC GB	NC CHI	NC MIN		NC CHI	NC DET
	NC MIN	AFC BUF	AFC DENᵃ	NC GB	
AFC CLE	AFC HOU		NE	AFC BAL	AFC SD
	KC		NYJ	PIT	

¹Played at Milwaukee.
ᵃPlayed additional interconference game.

NEW ORLEANS SAINTS

1970		1971		1972	
Home	*Away*	*Home*	*Away*	*Home*	*Away*
NE NYG	NE STL	NE DAL	NE WAS	NE PHI	NE NYG
NC CHI	NC MIN	NC MIN	NC CHI	NC GB	NC DET
NC DET			NC GB¹		NC MIN
AFC DEN	AFC CIN	AFC CLE	AFC HOU	AFC KC	AFC NYJ
	MIA	OAK		NE	

	1973			1974			1975	
Home		**Away**		**Home**		**Away**		
NE	WAS	NE	DAL	NE	PHI			NE	NYG[2]
NC	CHI	NC	GB[1]	NE	STL			NE	WAS
NC	DET					NC	CHI	NC	CHI
AFC	BUF	AFC	BAL			NC	DET	NC	GB
		SD				NC	MIN	NC	MIN
				AFC	MIA	AFC	DEN	AFC	CIN	AFC	CLE
				PIT						OAK

[1]Played at Milwaukee.
[2]Played at Shea Stadium, Flushing, NY.

SAN FRANCISCO 49ERS

	1970[A]			1971			1972	
Home		**Away**		**Home**		**Away**		
NE	WAS					NE	PHI	NE	NYG	NE	DAL
NC	GB	NC	CHI			NE	STL	NC	MIN	NC	CHI
		NC	DET	NC	CHI	NC	MIN			NC	GB[1]
AFC	CLE	AFC	HOU	NC	DET			AFC	BAL	AFC	BUF
DEN[a]		OAK		AFC	KC	AFC	NYJ	SD			
				NE							

	1973			1974			1975	
Home		**Away**		**Home**		**Away**		
NE	PHI	NE	WAS	NE	STL	NE	DAL	NE	NYG	NE	PHI
NC	GB	NC	DET	NC	GB	NC	CHI	NC	CHI	NC	MIN
NC	MIN					NC	DET	NC	DET		
AFC	PIT	AFC	DEN	AFC	CIN	AFC	CLE	AFC	HOU	AFC	KC
		MIA		OAK						NE	

[1]Played at Milwaukee.
[a]Played additional interconference game.

1976

AMERICAN CONFERENCE	NATIONAL CONFERENCE
Eastern Division	**Eastern Division**
Baltimore Colts	Dallas Cowboys
Buffalo Bills	New York Giants
Miami Dolphins	Philadelphia Eagles
New England Patriots	St. Louis Cardinals
New York Jets	Washington Redskins
Central Division	**Central Division**
Cincinnati Bengals	Chicago Bears
Cleveland Browns	Detroit Lions
Houston Oilers	Green Bay Packers
Pittsburgh Steelers	Minnesota Vikings

Western Division	Western Division
Denver Broncos	Atlanta Falcons
Kansas City Chiefs	Los Angeles Rams
Oakland Raiders	New Orleans Saints
San Diego Chargers	San Francisco 49ers
Tampa Bay Buccaneers	Seattle Seahawks

1976

The 14-game regular season schedule of any NFL team is determined by one of the following formulas:

A. Teams in the AFC East and NFC East.
1. Home and away round-robin within the division (8 games).
2. One game against two clubs from one of the divisions within the conference and one game against one club from the other division within the conference (3 games).
3. One game against the expansion club within the conference (1 game). All AFC teams play Tampa Bay once and all NFC teams play Seattle once.
4. Two games against teams from the other conference (2 games).
   This completes the 14-game schedule.

B. Teams in the AFC Central and NFC Central.
1. Home and away round-robin within the division (6 games).
2. One game against four out of the five clubs from the Western division within the conference (4 games). This includes one game against the expansion club within the conference.
3. One game against two clubs from the Eastern division within the conference (2 games).
4. Two games against teams from the other conference (2 games).
   This completes the 14-game schedule.

C. Teams in the AFC West and NFC West (except Oakland, New Orleans, Tampa Bay and Seattle).
1. Home and away round-robin within the division, with the exception of only playing one game against the expansion club in their division (7 games).
2. One game against three out of the four clubs from the Central division within the conference (3 games).
3. One game against two clubs from the Eastern division within the conference (2 games).
4. Two games against teams from the other conference (2 games).
   This completes the 14-game schedule.

D. Oakland and New Orleans. Both teams assigned to play an additional interconference game in lieu of one game against an Eastern division club within the conference.
1. Home and away round-robin within the division, with the exception of only playing one game against the expansion club (7 games).
2. One game against three out of the four clubs from the Central division within the conference (3 games).
3. One game against one club from the Eastern division within the conference (1 game).
4. Three games against teams from the other conference (3 games).
   This completes the 14-game schedule.

E. Seattle and Tampa Bay.
1. One game against all other 13 clubs within the conference (13 games). Tampa Bay will play in the AFC West and will play each AFC team. Seattle will play in the NFC West and will play each NFC team.
2. One game against the other expansion club (1 game). Seattle will play at Tampa Bay. This completes the 14-game schedule.

1976–1977 INTRACONFERENCE ROTATION

AFC East

VS. CENTRAL/WEST (4 GAMES)

1976	1977	Opponents
BAL		CIN-HOU-SD-TB
NYJ		CIN-CLE-DEN-TB
NE		PIT-DEN-OAK-TB
MIA		CLE-PIT-KC-TB
BUF		HOU-KC-SD-TB
	BAL	PIT-DEN-KC-SEA
	NYJ	HOU-PIT-OAK-SEA
	NE	CLE-KC-SD-SEA
	MIA	CIN-HOU-SD-SEA
	BUF	CLE-DEN-OAK-SEA

AFC Central

VS. EAST (CENTRAL TEAMS PLAYED 2 OF THE 5 EAST CLUBS)

1976	1977	Opponents
	CLE	BUF-NE
CLE	HOU	MIA-NYJ
PIT		MIA-NE
CIN	PIT	BAL-NYJ
HOU		BAL-BUF
	CIN[a]	MIA

VS. WEST (CENTRAL TEAMS PLAYED 4 OF THE 5 WEST CLUBS)

1976	1977	Opponents
PIT		KC-OAK-SD-TB
HOU		DEN-OAK-SD-TB
CIN		DEN-KC-OAK-TB
CLE		DEN-KC-SD-TB
	CLE	KC-OAK-SD-SEA
	PIT	DEN-OAK-SD-SEA
	HOU	DEN-KC-OAK-SEA
	CIN	DEN-KC-SD-SEA

AFC West

VS. EAST (WEST TEAMS PLAYED 2 OF THE 5 EAST CLUBS)

1976	1977	Opponents
	KC	BAL-NE
	OAK	BUF-NYJ
KC		BUF-MIA
DEN		NE-NYJ
SD	DEN	BAL-BUF
	SD	MIA-NE
OAK[a]		NE

VS. CENTRAL (WEST TEAMS PLAYED 3 OF THE 4 CENTRAL CLUBS)

1976	1977	Opponents
KC	SD	CIN-CLE-PIT
DEN	KC	CIN-CLE-HOU
OAK	DEN	CIN-HOU-PIT
SD	OAK	CLE-HOU-PIT

NFC East

VS. CENTRAL/WEST (4 GAMES)

1976	1977	Opponents
DAL		CHI-ATL-NO-SEA
NYG		DET-MIN-LA-SEA
PHI		GB-MIN-ATL-SEA
STL		GB-LA-SF-SEA
WAS		CHI-DET-SF-SEA
	DAL	DET-MIN-TB-SF
	NYG	CHI-TB-ATL-SF
	PHI	DET-TB-LA-NO
	STL	CHI-MIN-TB-NO
	WAS	GB-TB-ATL-LA

NFC Central

VS. EAST (CENTRAL TEAMS PLAYED 2 OF THE 5 EAST CLUBS)

1976	1977	Opponents
MIN		NYG-PHI
	DET	DAL-PHI
CHI		DAL-WAS
	CHI	NYG-STL
GB		PHI-STL
DET		NYG-WAS
	MIN	DAL-STL
	GB[a]	WAS

VS. WEST (CENTRAL TEAMS PLAYED 3 WEST CLUBS PLUS SEA IN 1976)

1976	1977	Opponents
GB		ATL-NO-SF-SEA
MIN		LA-NO-SF-SEA
CHI		ATL-LA-SF-SEA
DET		ATL-LA-NO-SEA
	DET	ATL-NO-SF
	GB	LA-NO-SF
	MIN	ATL-LA-SF
	CHI	ATL-LA-NO

NFC West

VS. EAST (WEST TEAMS PLAYED 2 OF THE 5 EAST CLUBS)

1976	1977	Opponents
ATL		DAL-PHI
LA		NYG-STL
	NO	PHI-STL
	SF	DAL-NYG
	LA	PHI-WAS
SF		STL-WAS
	ATL	NYG-WAS
NO[a]		DAL

VS. CENTRAL (WEST TEAMS PLAYED 3 CENTRAL CLUBS PLUS TB IN 1977)

1976	1977	Opponents
ATL		CHI-DET-GB
LA		CHI-DET-MIN
SF		CHI-GB-MIN
NO		DET-GB-MIN
	NO	CHI-DET-GB-TB
	ATL	CHI-DET-MIN-TB
	LA	CHI-GB-MIN-TB
	SF	DET-GB-MIN-TB

1976–1977 INTERCONFERENCE ROTATION

On November 4, 1975, NFL owners voted unanimously to adopt a scheduling format for the expansion Seattle Seahawks and Tampa Bay Buccaneers in which both clubs would play a conference round-robin schedule during their first two seasons. Both the Seahawks and Buccaneers would play each other plus the other 13 teams in its conference. By draw, Seattle was placed in the NFC West and Tampa Bay in the AFC West for the 1976 season. In 1977, the two expansion teams would then switch conferences and divisions — Seattle to the AFC West and Tampa Bay to the NFC Central, utilizing the same scheduling formula.

As part of the agreement, for the 1976 and 1977 seasons, "member clubs empowered the Commissioner's office to delete from the regular season schedule rotation in effect since 1970 a total of 13 interconference games [one interconference game per team] in both '76 and '77 based on least gate and TV potential in order to clear the way for each team's games with Seattle and Tampa Bay."[1] To balance the schedule, for each season one club in each conference (Oakland and New Orleans in 1976, and Cincinnati and Green Bay in 1977), would play a total of three interconference games, instead of two.

Also, in 1976 and 1977 the rotation that was established in 1970 in which a team from one of the four-team divisions in each conference would play an additional interconference game was continued. In the NFC, one team alternated each year from the two four-team divisions. This allowed all eight clubs in the NFC Central and NFC Western divisions an extra game vs. an AFC opponent once during the eight-year period from 1970 to 1977:

1970 San Francisco (Western)
1971 Detroit (Central)
1972 Atlanta (Western)
1973 Chicago (Central)
1974 Los Angeles (Western)
1975 Minnesota (Central)
1976 New Orleans (Western)
1977 Green Bay (Central)

In the AFC, Denver was designated to play an additional interconference game each year for five consecutive seasons against the assigned NFC team listed above from 1970 to 1974. Thereafter, one club from one of the two four-team divisions, which alternated each year, played an additional game vs. an NFC opponent:

1970–1974 Denver (Western)
1975 Cleveland (Central)
1976 Oakland (Western)
1977 Cincinnati (Central)

Here is the original 1976 and 1977 chart, based on the 1970–1975 interconference rotation, in which each team's interconference opponents would consist of the teams that are listed directly opposite, directly above it, and directly below it in the parallel column of the opposing conference.

	1976		1977
AFC	NFC	AFC	NFC
MIA	NYG	OAK	NYG
DEN	LA	CLE	LA
CIN	CHI	HOU	CHI
OAK[a]	GB	KC	GB[a]
CLE	PHI	NE	PHI
HOU	ATL	NYJ	ATL
KC	NO[a]	BUF	NO
NE	WAS	SD	WAS
NYJ	DET	BAL	DET
BUF	SF	PIT	SF
SD	DAL	MIA	DAL
BAL	STL	DEN	STL
PIT	MIN	CIN[a]	MIN

Based on the above chart, each team's three original interconference opponents are shown below. The opponents that are bolded were the games that were replaced by one game vs. Seattle or Tampa Bay:

AFC

1976 vs. Tampa Bay

	1976	OPPONENTS
Team A	MIA	LA-MIN-**NYG**
Team B	SD	**DAL**-STL-SF
Team C	NE	DET-NO-**WAS**
Team D	CLE	ATL-**GB**-PHI

1977 vs. Seattle

	1977	OPPONENTS
Team A	OAK	LA-MIN-**NYG**
Team B	MIA	**DAL**-STL-SF
Team C	SD	DET-NO-**WAS**
Team D	NE	ATL-**GB**-PHI

Team E	DEN	CHI-**LA**-NYG	Team E	CLE	CHI-**LA**-NYG
Team F	BAL	DAL-**MIN**-STL	Team F	DEN	DAL-**MIN**-STL
Team G	NYJ	DET-**SF**-WAS	Team G	BAL	DET-**SF**-WAS
Team H	HOU	ATL-NO-**PHI**	Team H	NYJ	ATL-NO-**PHI**
Team I	CIN	CHI-GB-**LA**	Team I	HOU	CHI-GB-**LA**
Team J	PIT	MIN-NYG-**STL**	Team J	CIN[b]	MIN-NYG-**STL**
Team K	BUF	DAL-**DET**-SF	Team K	PIT	DAL-**DET**-SF
Team L	KC	ATL-**NO**-WAS	Team L	BUF	ATL-**NO**-WAS
Team M	OAK[a]	CHI-GB-**PHI**	Team M	KC	CHI-GB-**PHI**

NFC

1976 vs. Seattle   1977 vs. Tampa Bay

1976		OPPONENTS		1977	OPPONENTS
Team A	DET	BUF-NE-**NYJ**	Team A	ATL	BUF-NE-**NYJ**
Team B	STL	BAL-**PIT**-SD	Team B	DET	BAL-**PIT**-SD
Team C	LA	CIN-**DEN**-MIA	Team C	STL	CIN-**DEN**-MIA
Team D	PHI	CLE-**HOU**-OAK	Team D	LA	CLE-**HOU**-OAK
Team E	WAS	KC-**NE**-NYJ	Team E	PHI	KC-**NE**-NYJ
Team F	DAL	BAL-BUF-**SD**	Team F	WAS	BAL-BUF-**SD**
Team G	NYG	DEN-**MIA**-PIT	Team G	DAL	DEN-**MIA**-PIT
Team H	GB	CIN-**CLE**-OAK	Team H	NYG	CIN-CLE-**OAK**
Team I	NO[a]	HOU-KC-NE	Team I	GB[b]	HOU-KC-**NE**
Team J	SF	**BUF**-NYJ-SD	Team J	NO	**BUF**-NYJ-SD
Team K	MIN	**BAL**-MIA-PIT	Team K	SF	**BAL**-MIA-PIT
Team L	CHI	CIN-**DEN**-OAK	Team L	MIN	CIN-**DEN**-OAK
Team M	ATL	CLE-HOU-**KC**	Team M	CHI	CLE-HOU-KC

[a]In 1976, Oakland and New Orleans played three interconference games.
[b]In 1977, Cincinnati and Green Bay also played each other and had three interconference games.

Here is the list of interconference games that were tentatively scheduled for 1976 and 1977, based on the interconference rotation that was introduced in 1970, that were deleted to make room for each team's game against Seattle and Tampa Bay:

1976[A]

Baltimore vs. Minnesota
Buffalo vs. San Francisco
Cincinnati vs. Chicago
Cleveland vs. Green Bay
Denver vs. Los Angeles
Houston vs. Philadelphia
Kansas City vs. Atlanta
Miami vs. New York Giants
New England vs. Washington
New York Jets vs. Detroit
Pittsburgh vs. St. Louis
San Diego vs. Dallas

[a]Oakland and New Orleans (not listed above) played all of three of their interconference opponents based on the original schedule rotation established in 1970.

1977

Baltimore vs. San Francisco
Buffalo vs. New Orleans
Cincinnati[b] vs. St. Louis
Cleveland vs. Chicago
Denver vs. Minnesota
Houston vs. Los Angeles
Kansas City vs. Philadelphia
Miami vs. Dallas
New England vs. Green Bay[b]
New York Jets vs. Atlanta
Oakland vs. New York Giants
Pittsburgh vs. Detroit
San Diego vs. Washington

[b]Cincinnati and Green Bay's games against St. Louis and New England, respectively, were removed from the schedule. Cincinnati and Green Bay played each other for their third interconference game.

1976 NON-DIVISIONAL OPPONENTS (AFC)

AFC East
AE

BALTIMORE

Home		Away	
AC	CIN		
AC	HOU		
AW	TB	AW	SD
		NFC	DAL
			STL

BUFFALO

Home		Away	
AC	HOU		
AW	KC	AW	TB
AW	SD		
		NFC	DAL
			DET

MIAMI

Home		Away	
		AC	CLE
		AC	PIT
AW	KC	AW	TB
NFC	LA		
	MIN		

AFC Central
AC

CINCINNATI

Home		Away	
		AE	BAL
		AE	NYJ
AW	DEN	AW	KC
AW	TB	AW	OAK
NFC	GB		
	LA		

CLEVELAND

Home		Away	
AE	MIA		
AE	NYJ		
AW	SD	AW	DEN
		AW	KC
		AW	TB
NFC	PHI	NFC	ATL

HOUSTON

Home		Away	
		AE	BAL
		AE	BUF
AW	DEN	AW	SD
AW	OAK		
AW	TB		
NFC	ATL	NFC	NO

AFC West
AW

DENVER

Home		Away	
AE	NYJ	AE	NE
AC	CLE	AC	CIN
		AC	HOU
AW	TB[a]		
NFC	NYG	NFC	CHI

KANSAS CITY

Home		Away	
		AE	BUF
		AE	MIA
AC	CIN		
AC	CLE		
AC	PIT		
		AW	TB[a]
NFC	NO	NFC	WAS

OAKLAND[B]

Home		Away	
		AE	NE
AC	CIN	AC	HOU
AC	PIT		
AW	TB[a]		
NFC	GB	NFC	CHI
			PHI

1976

NEW ENGLAND				PITTSBURGH				SAN DIEGO			
Home		*Away*		*Home*		*Away*		*Home*		*Away*	
		AC	PIT	AE	MIA			AE	BAL	AE	BUF
AW	DEN	AW	TB	AE	NE			AC	HOU	AC	CLE
AW	OAK			AW	SD	AW	KC			AC	PIT
NFC	NO	NFC	DET	AW	TB	AW	OAK			AW	TB[a]
						NFC	MIN	NFC	STL		
							NYG		SF		

NY JETS								TAMPA BAY			
Home		*Away*						*Home*		*Away*	
AC	CIN	AC	CLE					AE	BUF	AE	BAL
AW	TB	AW	DEN					AE	MIA	AE	NYJ
NFC	WAS	NFC	SF					AE	NE		
								AC	CLE	AC	CIN
										AC	HOU
										AC	PIT
								AW	KC	AW	DEN
								AW	SD	AW	OAK
								NFC	SEA		

[a] Played division opponent Tampa Bay once.
[b] Played extra interconference game.

1976 NON-DIVISIONAL OPPONENTS (NFC)

NFC East
NE

NFC Central
NC

NFC West
NW

DALLAS				CHICAGO				ATLANTA			
Home		*Away*		*Home*		*Away*		*Home*		*Away*	
NC	CHI			NE	WAS	NE	DAL	NE	DAL		
		NW	ATL	NW	ATL	NW	LA	NE	PHI		
		NW	NO			NW	SF	NC	GB	NC	CHI
		NW	SEA			NW	SEA			NC	DET
AFC	BAL			AFC	DEN					NW	SEA[a]
	BUF				OAK			AFC	CLE	AFC	HOU

NY GIANTS				DETROIT				LOS ANGELES			
Home		*Away*		*Home*		*Away*		*Home*		*Away*	
NC	DET	NC	MIN			NE	NYG	NE	NYG		
NW	SEA	NW	LA			NE	WAS	NE	STL		
AFC	PIT	AFC	DEN	NW	ATL	NW	NO	NC	CHI	NC	DET
				NW	LA	NW	SEA			NC	MIN
				AFC	BUF			NW	SEA[a]		
					NE					AFC	CIN
											MIA

PHILADELPHIA				GREEN BAY				NEW ORLEANS[B]			
Home		*Away*		*Home*		*Away*		*Home*		*Away*	
NC	MIN	NC	GB	NE	PHI	NE	STL	NE	DAL		
NW	SEA	NW	ATL	NW	NO[1]	NW	ATL	NC	DET	NC	GB[1]
AFC	OAK	AFC	CLE	NW	SF			NC	MIN		
				NW	SEA[1]					NW	SEA[a]
						AFC	CIN	AFC	HOU	AFC	KC
							OAK				NE

ST. LOUIS			
Home		*Away*	
NC	GB		
NW	SF	NW	LA
		NW	SEA
AFC	BAL	AFC	SD

MINNESOTA			
Home		*Away*	
NE	NYG	NE	PHI
NW	LA	NW	NO
NW	SEA	NW	SF
AFC	PIT	AFC	MIA

SAN FRANCISCO			
Home		*Away*	
NE	WAS	NE	STL
NC	CHI	NC	GB
NC	MIN		
		NW	SEA[a]
AFC	NYJ	AFC	SD

WASHINGTON			
Home		*Away*	
NC	DET	NC	CHI
NW	SEA	NW	SF
AFC	KC	AFC	NYJ

SEATTLE			
Home		*Away*	
NE	DAL	NE	NYG
NE	STL	NE	PHI
		NE	WAS
NC	CHI	NC	GB[1]
NC	DET	NC	MIN
NW	ATL	NW	LA
NW	NO		
NW	SF		
		AFC	TB

[1]Played at Milwaukee.
[a]Played division opponent Seattle once.
[b]Played extra interconference game.

1977

American Conference

Eastern Division
Baltimore Colts
Buffalo Bills
Miami Dolphins
New England Patriots
New York Jets

Central Division
Cincinnati Bengals
Cleveland Browns
Houston Oilers
Pittsburgh Steelers

Western Division
Denver Broncos
Kansas City Chiefs
Oakland Raiders
San Diego Chargers
Seattle Seahawks

National Conference

Eastern Division
Dallas Cowboys
New York Giants
Philadelphia Eagles
St. Louis Cardinals
Washington Redskins

Central Division
Chicago Bears
Detroit Lions
Green Bay Packers
Minnesota Vikings
Tampa Bay Buccaneers

Western Division
Atlanta Falcons
Los Angeles Rams
New Orleans Saints
San Francisco 49ers

1977

The 14-game regular season schedule of any NFL team is determined by one of the following formulas:

A. Teams in the AFC East and NFC East.
1. Home and away round-robin within the division (8 games).
2. One game against two clubs from one of the divisions within the conference and one game against one club from the other division within the conference (3 games).
3. One game against the expansion club within the conference (1 game). All AFC teams play Seattle once and all NFC teams play Tampa Bay once.
4. Two games against teams from the other conference (2 games).
This completes the 14-game schedule.

B. Teams in the AFC Central, except Cincinnati.
1. Home and away round-robin within the division (6 games).
2. One game against four out of the five clubs from the Western division within the conference (4 games). This includes one game against Seattle.
3. One game against two clubs from the Eastern division within the conference (2 games).
4. Two games against teams from the other conference (2 games).
This completes the 14-game schedule.

C. Teams in the AFC West and NFC Central (except Green Bay, Tampa Bay and Seattle).
1. Home and away round-robin within the division, with the exception of only playing one game against the expansion club in their division (7 games).
2. One game against three out of the four clubs from the four-team division within the conference (3 games).
3. One game against two clubs from the Eastern division within the conference (2 games).
4. Two games against teams from the other conference (2 games).
This completes the 14-game schedule.

D. Teams in the NFC West.
1. Home and away round-robin within the division (6 games).
2. One game against four out of the five clubs from the Central division within the conference (4 games). This includes one game against Tampa Bay.
3. One game against two clubs from the Eastern division within the conference (2 games).
4. Two games against teams from the other conference (2 games).
This completes the 14-game schedule.

E. Cincinnati. Assigned to play an additional interconference game in lieu of one game against an Eastern division club within the conference.
1. Home and away round-robin within the division (6 games).
2. One game against four out of the five clubs from the Western division within the conference (4 games). This includes one game against Seattle.
3. One game against one club from the Eastern division within the conference (1 game).
4. Three games against teams from the other conference (3 games).
This completes the 14-game schedule.

F. Green Bay. Assigned to play additional interconference game in lieu of one Eastern division club within the conference.
1. Home and away round-robin within the division, with the exception of only playing one game against Tampa Bay (7 games).
2. One game against three out of the four clubs from the Western division within the conference (3 games).

3. One game against one club from the Eastern division within the conference (1 game).
4. Three games against teams from the other conference (3 games).
   This completes the 14-game schedule.

G. Seattle and Tampa Bay.
   1. One game against all other 13 clubs within the conference (13 games). Seattle will play in the AFC West and will play each AFC team. Tampa Bay will play in the NFC Central and will play each NFC team.
   2. One game against each other (1 game). Tampa Bay will play at Seattle.
      This completes the 14-game schedule.

Note: Please see pp. 73–78 for the 1977 intraconference and interconference rotation chart.

1977 Non-Divisional Opponents (AFC)

AFC East AE		AFC Central AC		AFC West AW	
BALTIMORE		**CINCINNATI**[B]		**DENVER**	
Home	*Away*	*Home*	*Away*	*Home*	*Away*
AC PIT		AE MIA		AE BAL	
	AW DEN	AW DEN	AW KC	AE BUF	
	AW KC	AW SEA	AW SD	AC PIT	AC CIN
	AW SEA	NFC NYG	NFC GB[1b]		AC HOU
NFC DET			MIN		AW SEA[a]
	WAS			NFC STL	NFC DAL
BUFFALO		**CLEVELAND**		**KANSAS CITY**	
Home	*Away*	*Home*	*Away*	*Home*	*Away*
AC CLE		AE NE	AE BUF	AE BAL	AE NE
	AW DEN	AW KC	AW SD	AC CIN	AC CLE
	AW OAK	AW OAK	AW SEA		AC HOU
	AW SEA	NFC LA	NFC NYG	AW SEA[a]	
NFC ATL				NFC GB	NFC CHI
	WAS				
MIAMI		**HOUSTON**		**OAKLAND**	
Home	*Away*	*Home*	*Away*	*Home*	*Away*
AC HOU	AC CIN	AE NYJ	AE MIA	AE BUF	AE NYJ
AW SD		AW DEN	AW OAK	AC HOU	AC CLE
AW SEA		AW KC	AW SEA		AC PIT
	NFC STL	NFC CHI	NFC GB	AW SEA[a]	
	SF			NFC MIN	NFC LA
NEW ENGLAND		**PITTSBURGH**		**SAN DIEGO**	
Home	*Away*	*Home*	*Away*	*Home*	*Away*
	AC CLE		AE BAL	AE NE	AE MIA
AW KC	AW SD		AE NYJ	AC CIN	
AW SEA		AW OAK	AW DEN	AC CLE	
NFC PHI	NFC ATL	AW SEA	AW SD	AC PIT	
		NFC DAL			AW SEA[a]
		SF			NFC DET
					NO

NY JETS

Home		Away	
AC	PIT	AC	HOU
AW	OAK		
AW	SEA		
		NFC	NO
			PHI

SEATTLE

Home		Away	
AE	BAL	AE	MIA
AE	BUF	AE	NE
		AE	NYJ
AC	CLE	AC	CIN
AC	HOU	AC	PIT
AW	DEN	AW	KC
AW	SD	AW	OAK
NFC	TB		

[1]Played at Milwaukee.
[a]Played division opponent Seattle once.
[b]Played extra interconference game.

1977 Non-Divisional Opponents (NFC)

NFC East — NE
NFC Central — NC
NFC West — NW

DALLAS

Home		Away	
NC	DET	NC	MIN
NC	TB		
		NW	SF
AFC	DEN	AFC	PIT

CHICAGO

Home		Away	
		NE	NYG
		NE	STL
		NC	TB[a]
NW	ATL		
NW	LA		
NW	NO		
AFC	KC	AFC	HOU

ATLANTA

Home		Away	
NE	NYG	NE	WAS
NC	DET	NC	CHI
NC	MIN	NC	TB
AFC	NE	AFC	BUF

NY GIANTS

Home		Away	
NC	CHI	NC	TB
NW	SF	NW	ATL
AFC	CLE	AFC	CIN

DETROIT

Home		Away	
NE	PHI	NE	DAL
NC	TB[a]		
NW	NO	NW	ATL
		NW	SF
AFC	SD	AFC	BAL

LOS ANGELES

Home		Away	
NE	PHI	NE	WAS
NC	MIN	NC	CHI
NC	TB	NC	GB[1]
AFC	OAK	AFC	CLE

PHILADELPHIA

Home		Away	
NC	TB	NC	DET
NW	NO	NW	LA
AFC	NYJ	AFC	NE

GREEN BAY[b]

Home		Away	
		NE	WAS
		NC	TB[a]
NW	LA[1]	NW	NO
NW	SF[1]		
AFC	CIN[1b]	AFC	KC
	HOU		

NEW ORLEANS

Home		Away	
		NE	PHI
		NE	STL
NC	GB	NC	CHI
NC	TB	NC	DET
AFC	NYJ		
	SD		

ST. LOUIS

Home		Away	
NC	CHI	NC	MIN
		NC	TB
NW	NO		
AFC	MIA	AFC	DEN

MINNESOTA

Home		Away	
NE	DAL		
NE	STL		
		NC	TB[a]
NW	SF	NW	ATL
		NW	LA
AFC	CIN	AFC	OAK

SAN FRANCISCO

Home		Away	
NE	DAL	NE	NYG
NC	DET	NC	GB[1]
NC	TB	NC	MIN
AFC	MIA	AFC	PIT

	WASHINGTON				TAMPA BAY		
Home		*Away*		*Home*		*Away*	
NC	GB	NC	TB	NE	NYG	NE	DAL
NW	ATL			NE	STL	NE	PHI
NW	LA			NE	WAS		
		AFC	BAL	NC	CHI	NC	DET
			BUF	NC	GB		
				NC	MIN		
				NW	ATL	NW	LA
						NW	NO
						NW	SF
						AFC	SEA

[1]Played at Milwaukee.
[a]Played division opponent Tampa Bay once.
[b]Played extra interconference game.

1978–1987

AMERICAN CONFERENCE	NATIONAL CONFERENCE
Eastern Division	**Eastern Division**
Baltimore Colts[a]	Dallas Cowboys
Buffalo Bills	New York Giants
Miami Dolphins	Philadelphia Eagles
New England Patriots	St. Louis Cardinals
New York Jets	Washington Redskins
Central Division	**Central Division**
Cincinnati Bengals	Chicago Bears
Cleveland Browns	Detroit Lions
Houston Oilers	Green Bay Packers
Pittsburgh Steelers	Minnesota Vikings
	Tampa Bay Buccaneers
Western Division	**Western Division**
Denver Broncos	Atlanta Falcons
Kansas City Chiefs	Los Angeles Rams
Oakland Raiders[b]	New Orleans Saints
San Diego Chargers	San Francisco 49ers
Seattle Seahawks	

[a]*Indianapolis Colts (1984–)*
[b]*Los Angeles Raiders (1982–1994)*

1978–1987

Source: 1978 NFL Media Information Book, p. 8

The 16-game regular season schedule of any NFL team is determined by one of the following three formulas. (The reference point for figuring is the team's final division standing):[1]

A. First- through fourth-place teams in a five-team division (AFC East, AFC West, NFC East, NFC Central).
   1. Home and away against its four division opponents (8 games).
   2. Four games against teams from the other two divisions within the conference (4 games).

   1st place: plays the other two 1st-place teams and the other two 4th-place teams
   2nd place: plays the other two 2nd-place teams and the other two 3rd-place teams
   3rd place: plays the other two 3rd-place teams and the other two 2nd-place teams
   4th place: plays the other two 4th-place teams and the other two 1st-place teams

Prior Year's Finish in Division	Pairings in Non-Division Games Within Conference 1978–1987
1	1–1–4–4
2	2–2–3–3
3	2–2–3–3
4	1–1–4–4

   3. One game each with the first- through fourth-place teams in a division of the other conference (4 games).
   This completes the 16-game schedule.

B. First- through fourth-place teams in a four-team division (AFC Central, NFC West).
   1. Home and away against its three division opponents (6 games).
   2. Four games against teams from the other two divisions within the conference (4 games).

   1st place: plays the other two 1st-place teams and the other two 4th-place teams
   2nd place: plays the other two 2nd-place teams and the other two 3rd-place teams
   3rd place: plays the other two 3rd-place teams and the other two 2nd-place teams
   4th place: plays the other two 4th-place teams and the other two 1st-place teams

   3. One game with each of the fifth-place teams in the conference (2 games).
   4. One game each with the first- through fourth-place teams in a division of the other conference (4 games).
   This completes the 16-game schedule.

C. The fifth-place teams in a division (AFC East, AFC West, NFC East, NFC Central).
   1. Home and away against its four division opponents (8 games).
   2. Home and away with the other fifth-place team in the conference (2 games).
   3. One game with each team in the four-team division of the conference (4 games).
   4. One game each with the fifth-place teams of the other conference (2 games).
   This completes the 16-game schedule.

1978–1987 Scheduling Formula by Position

In a Five-Team Division
(AFC East, AFC West, NFC East, NFC Central)

1st Place:
1. Home and away with the other four teams within the division (8 games).
2. One game each with the two other first-place teams and the two other fourth-place teams in the conference (4 games).
3. One game each with teams 1 through 4 in a division of the other conference (4 games).

2nd Place:
1. Home and away with the other four teams within the division (8 games).
2. One game each with the two other second-place teams and the two other third-place teams in the conference (4 games).
3. One game each with teams 1 through 4 in a division of the other conference (4 games).

3rd Place:
1. Home and away with the other four teams within the division (8 games).
2. One game each with the two other third-place teams and the two other second-place teams in the conference (4 games).
3. One game each with teams 1 through 4 in a division of the other conference (4 games).

4th Place:
1. Home and away with the other four teams within the division (8 games).
2. One game each with the two other fourth-place teams and the two other first-place teams in the conference (4 games).
3. One game each with teams 1 through 4 in a division of the other conference (4 games).

5th Place:
1. Home and away with the other four teams within the division (8 games).
2. One game each with all teams in the four-team division in the conference (4 games).
3. Home and away with the other fifth-place team in the conference (2 games).
4. One game with each of the fifth-place teams of the other conference (2 games).

In a Four-Team Division
(AFC Central, NFC West)

1st Place:
1. Home and away with the other three teams within the division (6 games).
2. One game each with the two other first-place teams and the two other fourth-place teams in the conference (4 games).
3. One game with each of the fifth-place teams in the conference (2 games).
4. One game each with teams 1 through 4 in a division of the other conference (4 games).

2nd Place:

1. Home and away with the other three teams within the division (6 games).
2. One game each with the two other second-place teams and the two other third-place teams in the conference (4 games).
3. One game with each of the fifth-place teams in the conference (2 games).
4. One game each with teams 1 through 4 in a division of the other conference (4 games).

3rd Place:

1. Home and away with the other three teams within the division (6 games).
2. One game each with the two other third-place teams and the two other second-place teams in the conference (4 games).
3. One game with each of the fifth-place teams in the conference (2 games).
4. One game each with teams 1 through 4 in a division of the other conference (4 games).

4th Place:

1. Home and away with the other three teams within the division (6 games).
2. One game each with the two other fourth-place teams and the two other first-place teams in the conference (4 games).
3. One game with each of the fifth-place teams in the conference (2 games).
4. One game each with teams 1 through 4 in a division of the other conference (4 games).

In March 1977, NFL owners agreed unanimously to utilize the following division designations for scheduling purposes:[2]

> A — AFC East
> B — AFC Central
> C — AFC West
> D — NFC East
> E — NFC West
> F — NFC Central

To determine home and away opponents for AFC-NFC interconference games, teams 1 through 4 in each division would play teams 1 through 4 in a division of the other conference on a rotating three-year basis as follows:

> First year (1978)   A vs. D,   B vs. E,   C vs. F
> Second year (1979) B vs. D,   C vs. E,   A vs. F
> Third year (1980)   C vs. D,   A vs. E,   B vs. F

The initial pairings for 1978 home sites were then determined on a left to right basis: Team A-1 at Team D-1; B-1 at E-1; C-1 at F-1; etc. For example, Baltimore, who finished in first place in the AFC East the year before, was team "A-1." The Colts then would play at "D-1," Dallas (who finished in first place in the NFC East in 1977). Sites would then alternate based on alphanumeric designation: A-1 hosts D-2 (Baltimore hosts Washington), A-1 at D-3 (Baltimore at St. Louis), A-1 hosts D-4 (Baltimore hosts Philadelphia), etc. The same formula would be applied to the other two sets of matchups, B vs. E (AFC Central vs. NFC West), and C vs. F (AFC West vs. NFC Central). The divisions would then rotate each year as shown above.

After the initial three-year cycle, based on the final standings the 1981 matchups would revert back to the 1978 pairings, but with the sites reversed. After 1983, the pairings were then recycled with the 1984 matchups and home and away designations being the same as 1978, 1985 the same as 1979, etc.[3]

In this section, beginning with the 1978 non–divisional opponent breakdown chart on page 89, instead of using the original A–F listings for each division, the following division designations will be used:

AE — AFC East
AC — AFC Central
AW — AFC West
NE — NFC East
NC — NFC Central
NW — NFC West

Interconference Rotation (1978–2001)

	1978	1979	1980	1981	1982	1983	1984	1985
AFC EAST	NFCE	NFCC	NFCW	NFCE	NFCC	NFCW	NFCE	NFCC
AFC CENTRAL	NFCW	NFCE	NFCC	NFCW	NFCE	NFCC	NFCW	NFCE
AFC WEST	NFCC	NFCW	NFCE	NFCC	NFCW	NFCE	NFCC	NFCW
NFC EAST	AFCE	AFCC	AFCW	AFCE	AFCC	AFCW	AFCE	AFCC
NFC CENTRAL	AFCW	AFCE	AFCC	AFCW	AFCE	AFCC	AFCW	AFCE
NFC WEST	AFCC	AFCW	AFCE	AFCC	AFCW	AFCE	AFCC	AFCW

	1986	1987	1988	1989	1990	1991	1992	1993
AFC EAST	NFCW	NFCE	NFCC	NFCW	NFCE	NFCC	NFCW	NFCE
AFC CENTRAL	NFCC	NFCW	NFCE	NFCC	NFCW	NFCE	NFCC	NFCW
AFC WEST	NFCE	NFCC	NFCW	NFCE	NFCC	NFCW	NFCE	NFCC
NFC EAST	AFCW	AFCE	AFCC	AFCW	AFCE	AFCC	AFCW	AFCE
NFC CENTRAL	AFCC	AFCW	AFCE	AFCC	AFCW	AFCE	AFCC	AFCW
NFC WEST	AFCE	AFCC	AFCW	AFCE	AFCC	AFCW	AFCE	AFCC

	1994	1995	1996	1997	1998	1999	2000	2001
AFC EAST	NFCC	NFCW	NFCE	NFCC	NFCW	NFCE	NFCC	NFCW
AFC CENTRAL	NFCE	NFCC	NFCW	NFCE	NFCC	NFCW	NFCE	NFCC
AFC WEST	NFCW	NFCE	NFCC	NFCW	NFCE	NFCC	NFCW	NFCE
NFC EAST	AFCC	AFCW	AFCE	AFCC	AFCW	AFCE	AFCC	AFCW
NFC CENTRAL	AFCE	AFCC	AFCW	AFCE	AFCC	AFCW	AFCE	AFCC
NFC WEST	AFCW	AFCE	AFCC	AFCW	AFCE	AFCC	AFCW	AFCE

1977 Final Standings
(To Determine 1978 Opponents)

AFC East AE	AFC Central AC	AFC West AW
1 BALTIMORE	1 PITTSBURGH	1 DENVER
2 MIAMI	2 HOUSTON	2 OAKLAND
3 NEW ENGLAND	3 CINCINNATI	3 SAN DIEGO
4 NY JETS	4 CLEVELAND	4 SEATTLE
5 BUFFALO		5 KANSAS CITY

NFC East	NFC Central	NFC West
NE	**NC**	**NW**
1 DALLAS	1 MINNESOTA	1 LOS ANGELES
2 WASHINGTON	2 CHICAGO	2 ATLANTA
3 ST. LOUIS	3 DETROIT	3 SAN FRANCISCO
4 PHILADELPHIA	4 GREEN BAY	4 NEW ORLEANS
5 NY GIANTS	5 TAMPA BAY	

1978 NON-DIVISIONAL OPPONENTS (AFC)

AFC East		AFC Central		AFC West	
AE		**AC**		**AW**	

1 BAL

Home		Away	
AW1	DEN	AC1	PIT
AC4	CLE	AW4	SEA
NE2	WAS	NE1	DAL
NE4	PHI	NE3	STL

1 PIT

Home		Away	
AE1	BAL	AW1	DEN
AW4	SEA	AE4	NYJ
AW5	KC	AE5	BUF
NW2	ATL	NW1	LA
NW4	NO	NW3	SF

1 DEN

Home		Away	
AC1	PIT	AE1	BAL
AE4	NYJ	AC4	CLE
NC2	CHI	NC1	MIN
NC4	GB	NC3	DET

2 MIA

Home		Away	
AW2	OAK	AC2	HOU
AC3	CIN	AW3	SD
NE1	DAL	NE2	WAS
NE3	STL	NE4	PHI

2 HOU

Home		Away	
AE2	MIA	AW2	OAK
AW3	SD	AE3	NE
AE5	BUF	AW5	KC
NW1	LA	NW2	ATL
NW3	SF	NW4	NO

2 OAK

Home		Away	
AC2	HOU	AE2	MIA
AE3	NE	AC3	CIN
NC1	MIN	NC2	CHI
NC3	DET	NC4	GB

3 NE

Home		Away	
AW3	SD	AC3	CIN
AC2	HOU	AW2	OAK
NE2	WAS	NE1	DAL
NE4	PHI	NE3	STL

3 CIN

Home		Away	
AE3	NE	AW3	SD
AW2	OAK	AE2	MIA
AW5	KC	AE5	BUF
NW2	ATL	NW1	LA
NW4	NO	NW3	SF

3 SD

Home		Away	
AC3	CIN	AE3	NE
AE2	MIA	AC2	HOU
NC2	CHI	NC1	MIN
NC4	GB	NC3	DET

4 NYJ

Home		Away	
AW4	SEA	AC4	CLE
AC1	PIT	AW1	DEN
NE1	DAL	NE2	WAS
NE3	STL	NE4	PHI

4 CLE

Home		Away	
AE4	NYJ	AW4	SEA
AW1	DEN	AE1	BAL
AE5	BUF	AW5	KC
NW1	LA	NW2	ATL
NW3	SF	NW4	NO

4 SEA

Home		Away	
AC4	CLE	AE4	NYJ
AE1	BAL	AC1	PIT
NC1	MIN	NC2	CHI
NC3	DET	NC4	GB[1]

5 BUF

Home		Away	
AW5	KC	AW5	KC
AC1	PIT	AC2	HOU
AC3	CIN	AC4	CLE
NE5	NYG	NC5	TB

5 KC

Home		Away	
AE5	BUF	AE5	BUF
AC2	HOU	AC1	PIT
AC4	CLE	AC3	CIN
NC5	TB	NE5	NYG

[1]Played at Milwaukee.

1978 NON-DIVISIONAL OPPONENTS (NFC)

NFC East — NE | NFC Central — NC | NFC West — NW

1 DAL

Home		Away	
NC1	MIN	NW1	LA
NW4	NO	NC4	GB[1]
AE1	BAL	AE2	MIA
AE3	NE	AE4	NYJ

1 MIN

Home		Away	
NW1	LA	NE1	DAL
NE4	PHI	NW4	NO
AW1	DEN	AW2	OAK
AW3	SD	AW4	SEA

1 LA

Home		Away	
NE1	DAL	NC1	MIN
NC4	GB	NE4	PHI
NC5	TB	NE5	NYG
AC1	PIT	AC2	HOU
AC3	CIN	AC4	CLE

2 WAS

Home		Away	
NC2	CHI	NW2	ATL
NW3	SF	NC3	DET
AE2	MIA	AE1	BAL
AE4	NYJ	AE3	NE

2 CHI

Home		Away	
NW2	ATL	NE2	WAS
NE3	STL	NW3	SF
AW2	OAK	AW1	DEN
AW4	SEA	AW3	SD

2 ATL

Home		Away	
NE2	WAS	NC2	CHI
NC3	DET	NE3	STL
NE5	NYG	NC5	TB
AC2	HOU	AC1	PIT
AC4	CLE	AC3	CIN

3 STL

Home		Away	
NC3	DET	NW3	SF
NW2	ATL	NC2	CHI
AE1	BAL	AE2	MIA
AE3	NE	AE4	NYJ

3 DET

Home		Away	
NW3	SF	NE3	STL
NE2	WAS	NW2	ATL
AW1	DEN	AW2	OAK
AW3	SD	AW4	SEA

3 SF

Home		Away	
NE3	STL	NC3	DET
NC2	CHI	NE2	WAS
NC5	TB	NE5	NYG
AC1	PIT	AC2	HOU
AC3	CIN	AC4	CLE

4 PHI

Home		Away	
NC4	GB	NW4	NO
NW1	LA	NC1	MIN
AE2	MIA	AE1	BAL
AE4	NYJ	AE3	NE

4 GB

Home		Away	
NW4	NO[1]	NE4	PHI
NE1	DAL[1]	NW1	LA
AW2	OAK	AW1	DEN
AW4	SEA[1]	AW3	SD

4 NO

Home		Away	
NE4	PHI	NC4	GB[1]
NC1	MIN	NE1	DAL
NE5	NYG	NC5	TB
AC2	HOU	AC1	PIT
AC4	CLE	AC3	CIN

5 NYG

Home		Away	
NC5	TB	NC5	TB
NW1	LA	NW2	ATL
NW3	SF	NW4	NO
AW5	KC	AE5	BUF

5 TB

Home		Away	
NE5	NYG	NE5	NYG
NW2	ATL	NW1	LA
NW4	NO	NW3	SF
AE5	BUF	AW5	KC

[1]Played at Milwaukee.

1978 Final Standings
(To Determine 1979 Opponents)

AFC East AE	AFC Central AC	AFC West AW
1 NEW ENGLAND	1 PITTSBURGH	1 DENVER
2 MIAMI	2 HOUSTON	2 OAKLAND
3 NY JETS	3 CLEVELAND	3 SEATTLE
4 BUFFALO	4 CINCINNATI	4 SAN DIEGO
5 BALTIMORE		5 KANSAS CITY

NFC East NE	NFC Central NC	NFC West NW
1 DALLAS	1 MINNESOTA	1 LOS ANGELES
2 PHILADELPHIA	2 GREEN BAY	2 ATLANTA
3 WASHINGTON	3 DETROIT	3 NEW ORLEANS
4 ST. LOUIS	4 CHICAGO	4 SAN FRANCISCO
5 NY GIANTS	5 TAMPA BAY	

1979 NON-DIVISIONAL OPPONENTS (AFC)

AFC East — AE

1 NE

Home		Away	
AC1	PIT	AW1	DEN
AW4	SD	AC4	CIN
NC1	MIN	NC2	GB
NC3	DET	NC4	CHI

2 MIA

Home		Away	
AC2	HOU	AW2	OAK
AW3	SEA	AC3	CLE
NC2	GB	NC1	MIN
NC4	CHI	NC3	DET

3 NYJ

Home		Away	
AC3	CLE	AW3	SEA
AW2	OAK	AC2	HOU
NC1	MIN	NC2	GB
NC3	DET	NC4	CHI

AFC Central — AC

1 PIT

Home		Away	
AW1	DEN	AE1	NE
AE4	BUF	AW4	SD
AE5	BAL	AW5	KC
NE1	DAL	NE2	PHI
NE3	WAS	NE4	STL

2 HOU

Home		Away	
AW2	OAK	AE2	MIA
AE3	NYJ	AW3	SEA
AW5	KC	AE5	BAL
NE2	PHI	NE1	DAL
NE4	STL	NE3	WAS

3 CLE

Home		Away	
AW3	SEA	AE3	NYJ
AE2	MIA	AW2	OAK
AE5	BAL	AW5	KC
NE1	DAL	NE2	PHI
NE3	WAS	NE4	STL

AFC West — AW

1 DEN

Home		Away	
AE1	NE	AC1	PIT
AC4	CIN	AE4	BUF
NW1	LA	NW2	ATL
NW3	NO	NW4	SF

2 OAK

Home		Away	
AE2	MIA	AC2	HOU
AC3	CLE	AE3	NYJ
NW2	ATL	NW1	LA
NW4	SF	NW3	NO

3 SEA

Home		Away	
AE3	NYJ	AC3	CLE
AC2	HOU	AE2	MIA
NW1	LA	NW2	ATL
NW3	NO	NW4	SF

4	BUF			4	CIN			4	SD		
Home		*Away*		*Home*		*Away*		*Home*		*Away*	
AC4	CIN	AW4	SD	AW4	SD	AE4	BUF	AE4	BUF	AC4	CIN
AW1	DEN	AC1	PIT	AE1	NE	AW1	DEN	AC1	PIT	AE1	NE
NC2	GB	NC1	MIN	AW5	KC	AE5	BAL	NW2	ATL	NW1	LA
NC4	CHI	NC3	DET	NE2	PHI	NE1	DAL	NW4	SF	NW3	NO
				NE4	STL	NE3	WAS				

5	BAL							5	KC		
Home		*Away*						*Home*		*Away*	
AW5	KC	AW5	KC					AE5	BAL	AE5	BAL
AC2	HOU	AC1	PIT					AC1	PIT	AC2	HOU
AC4	CIN	AC3	CLE					AC3	CLE	AC4	CIN
NC5	TB	NE5	NYG					NE5	NYG	NC5	TB

1979 NON-DIVISIONAL OPPONENTS (NFC)

NFC East — NE   NFC Central — NC   NFC West — NW

1	DAL			1	MIN			1	LA		
Home		*Away*		*Home*		*Away*		*Home*		*Away*	
NW1	LA	NC1	MIN	NE1	DAL	NW1	LA	NC1	MIN	NE1	DAL
NC4	CHI	NW4	SF	NW4	SF	NE4	STL	NE4	STL	NC4	CHI
AC2	HOU	AC1	PIT	AE2	MIA	AE1	NE	NE5	NYG	NC5	TB
AC4	CIN	AC3	CLE	AE4	BUF	AE3	NYJ	AW2	OAK	AW1	DEN
								AW4	SD	AW3	SEA

2	PHI			2	GB			2	ATL		
Home		*Away*		*Home*		*Away*		*Home*		*Away*	
NW2	ATL	NC2	GB	NE2	PHI	NW2	ATL	NC2	GB	NE2	PHI
NC3	DET	NW3	NO	NW3	NO[1]	NE3	WAS	NE3	WAS	NC3	DET
AC1	PIT	AC2	HOU	AE1	NE	AE2	MIA	NC5	TB	NE5	NYG
AC3	CLE	AC4	CIN	AE3	NYJ	AE4	BUF	AW1	DEN	AW2	OAK
								AW3	SEA	AW4	SD

3	WAS			3	DET			3	NO		
Home		*Away*		*Home*		*Away*		*Home*		*Away*	
NW3	NO	NC3	DET	NE3	WAS	NW3	NO	NC3	DET	NE3	WAS
NC2	GB	NW2	ATL	NW2	ATL	NE2	PHI	NE2	PHI	NC2	GB[1]
AC2	HOU	AC1	PIT	AE2	MIA	AE1	NE	NE5	NYG	NC5	TB
AC4	CIN	AC3	CLE	AE4	BUF	AE3	NYJ	AW2	OAK	AW1	DEN
								AW4	SD	AW3	SEA

4	STL			4	CHI			4	SF		
Home		*Away*		*Home*		*Away*		*Home*		*Away*	
NW4	SF	NC4	CHI	NE4	STL	NW4	SF	NC4	CHI	NE4	STL
NC1	MIN	NW1	LA	NW1	LA	NE1	DAL	NE1	DAL	NC1	MIN
AC1	PIT	AC2	HOU	AE1	NE	AE2	MIA	NC5	TB	NE5	NYG
AC3	CLE	AC4	CIN	AE3	NYJ	AE4	BUF	AW1	DEN	AW2	OAK
								AW3	SEA	AW4	SD

5	NYG			5	TB		
Home		*Away*		*Home*		*Away*	
NC5	TB	NC5	TB	NE5	NYG	NE5	NYG
NW2	ATL	NW1	LA	NW1	LA	NW2	ATL
NW4	SF	NW3	NO	NW3	NO	NW4	SF
AE5	BAL	AW5	KC	AW5	KC	AE5	BAL

[1] Played at Milwaukee.

1979 Final Standings
(To Determine 1980 Opponents)

AFC East AE	AFC Central AC	AFC West AW
1 MIAMI	1 PITTSBURGH	1 SAN DIEGO
2 NEW ENGLAND	2 HOUSTON	2 DENVER
3 NY JETS	3 CLEVELAND	3 SEATTLE
4 BUFFALO	4 CINCINNATI	4 OAKLAND
5 BALTIMORE		5 KANSAS CITY

NFC East NE	NFC Central NC	NFC West NW
1 DALLAS	1 TAMPA BAY	1 LOS ANGELES
2 PHILADELPHIA	2 CHICAGO	2 NEW ORLEANS
3 WASHINGTON	3 MINNESOTA	3 ATLANTA
4 NY GIANTS	4 GREEN BAY	4 SAN FRANCISCO
5 ST. LOUIS	5 DETROIT	

1980 NON-DIVISIONAL OPPONENTS (AFC)

AFC East — AE

1	MIA		
Home		*Away*	
AW1	SD	AC1	PIT
AC4	CIN	AW4	OAK
NW2	NO	NW1	LA
NW4	SF	NW3	ATL

2	NE		
Home		*Away*	
AW2	DEN	AC2	HOU
AC3	CLE	AW3	SEA
NW1	LA	NW2	NO
NW3	ATL	NW4	SF

AFC Central — AC

1	PIT		
Home		*Away*	
AE1	MIA	AW1	SD
AW4	OAK	AE4	BUF
AW5	KC	AE5	BAL
NC2	CHI	NC1	TB
NC4	GB	NC3	MIN

2	HOU		
Home		*Away*	
AE2	NE	AW2	DEN
AW3	SEA	AE3	NYJ
AE5	BAL	AW5	KC
NC1	TB	NC2	CHI
NC3	MIN	NC4	GB

AFC West — AW

1	SD		
Home		*Away*	
AC1	PIT	AE1	MIA
AE4	BUF	AC4	CIN
NE2	PHI	NE1	DAL
NE4	NYG	NE3	WAS

2	DEN		
Home		*Away*	
AC2	HOU	AE2	NE
AE3	NYJ	AC3	CLE
NE1	DAL	NE2	PHI
NE3	WAS	NE4	NYG

3	NYJ			3	CLE			3	SEA		
Home		*Away*		*Home*		*Away*		*Home*		*Away*	
AW3	SEA	AC3	CLE	AE3	NYJ	AW3	SEA	AC3	CLE	AE3	NYJ
AC2	HOU	AW2	DEN	AW2	DEN	AE2	NE	AE2	NE	AC2	HOU
NW2	NO	NW1	LA	AW5	KC	AE5	BAL	NE2	PHI	NE1	DAL
NW4	SF	NW3	ATL	NC2	CHI	NC1	TB	NE4	NYG	NE3	WAS
				NC4	GB	NC3	MIN				

4	BUF			4	CIN			4	OAK		
Home		*Away*		*Home*		*Away*		*Home*		*Away*	
AW4	OAK	AC4	CIN	AE4	BUF	AW4	OAK	AC4	CIN	AE4	BUF
AC1	PIT	AW1	SD	AW1	SD	AE1	MIA	AE1	MIA	AC1	PIT
NW1	LA	NW2	NO	AE5	BAL	AW5	KC	NE1	DAL	NE2	PHI
NW3	ATL	NW4	SF	NC1	TB	NC2	CHI	NE3	WAS	NE4	NYG
				NC3	MIN	NC4	GB				

5	BAL							5	KC		
Home		*Away*						*Home*		*Away*	
AW5	KC	AW5	KC					AE5	BAL	AE5	BAL
AC1	PIT	AC2	HOU					AC2	HOU	AC1	PIT
AC3	CLE	AC4	CIN					AC4	CIN	AC3	CLE
NE5	STL	NC5	DET					NC5	DET	NE5	STL

1980 NON-DIVISIONAL OPPONENTS (NFC)

NFC East				NFC Central				NFC West			
NE				**NC**				**NW**			

1	DAL			1	TB			1	LA		
Home		*Away*		*Home*		*Away*		*Home*		*Away*	
NC1	TB	NW1	LA	NW1	LA	NE1	DAL	NE1	DAL	NC1	TB
NW4	SF	NC4	GB[1]	NE4	NYG	NW4	SF	NC4	GB	NE4	NYG
AW1	SD	AW2	DEN	AC1	PIT	AC2	HOU	NC5	DET	NE5	STL
AW3	SEA	AW4	OAK	AC3	CLE	AC4	CIN	AE1	MIA	AE2	NE
								AE3	NYJ	AE4	BUF

2	PHI			2	CHI			2	NO		
Home		*Away*		*Home*		*Away*		*Home*		*Away*	
NC2	CHI	NW2	NO	NW2	NO	NE2	PHI	NE2	PHI	NC2	CHI
NW3	ATL	NC3	MIN	NE3	WAS	NW3	ATL	NC3	MIN	NE3	WAS
AW2	DEN	AW1	SD	AC2	HOU	AC1	PIT	NE5	STL	NC5	DET
AW4	OAK	AW3	SEA	AC4	CIN	AC3	CLE	AE2	NE	AE1	MIA
								AE4	BUF	AE3	NYJ

3	WAS			3	MIN			3	ATL		
Home		*Away*		*Home*		*Away*		*Home*		*Away*	
NC3	MIN	NW3	ATL	NW3	ATL	NE3	WAS	NE3	WAS	NC3	MIN
NW2	NO	NC2	CHI	NE2	PHI	NW2	NO	NC2	CHI	NE2	PHI
AW1	SD	AW2	DEN	AC1	PIT	AC2	HOU	NC5	DET	NE5	STL
AW3	SEA	AW4	OAK	AC3	CLE	AC4	CIN	AE1	MIA	AE2	NE
								AE3	NYJ	AE4	BUF

4	NYG			4	GB			4	SF		
Home		*Away*		*Home*		*Away*		*Home*		*Away*	
NC4	GB	NW4	SF	NW4	SF[1]	NE4	NYG	NE4	NYG	NC4	GB[1]
NW1	LA	NC1	TB	NE1	DAL[1]	NW1	LA	NC1	TB	NE1	DAL
AW2	DEN	AW1	SD	AC2	HOU	AC1	PIT	NE5	STL	NC5	DET
AW4	OAK	AW3	SEA	AC4	CIN	AC3	CLE	AE2	NE	AE1	MIA
								AE4	BUF	AE3	NYJ

5	STL			5	DET		
Home		*Away*		*Home*		*Away*	
NC5	DET	NC5	DET	NE5	STL	NE5	STL
NW1	LA	NW2	NO	NW2	NO	NW1	LA
NW3	ATL	NW4	SF	NW4	SF	NW3	ATL
AW5	KC	AE5	BAL	AE5	BAL	AW5	KC

[1]Played at Milwaukee.

1980 Final Standings
(To Determine 1981 Opponents)

AFC EAST AE	AFC CENTRAL AC	AFC WEST AW
1 BUFFALO	1 CLEVELAND	1 SAN DIEGO
2 NEW ENGLAND	2 HOUSTON	2 OAKLAND
3 MIAMI	3 PITTSBURGH	3 KANSAS CITY
4 BALTIMORE	4 CINCINNATI	4 DENVER
5 NY JETS		5 SEATTLE

NFC EAST NE	NFC CENTRAL NC	NFC WEST NW
1 PHILADELPHIA	1 MINNESOTA	1 ATLANTA
2 DALLAS	2 DETROIT	2 LOS ANGELES
3 WASHINGTON	3 CHICAGO	3 SAN FRANCISCO
4 ST. LOUIS	4 TAMPA BAY	4 NEW ORLEANS
5 NY GIANTS	5 GREEN BAY	

1981 NON-DIVISIONAL OPPONENTS (AFC)

AFC EAST				AFC CENTRAL				AFC WEST			
AE				AC				AW			
1	BUF			1	CLE			1	SD		
Home		*Away*		*Home*		*Away*		*Home*		*Away*	
AC1	CLE	AW1	SD	AW1	SD	AE1	BUF	AE1	BUF	AC1	CLE
AW4	DEN	AC4	CIN	AE4	BAL	AW4	DEN	AC4	CIN	AE4	BAL
NE1	PHI	NE2	DAL	AE5	NYJ	AW5	SEA	NC1	MIN	NC3	CHI
NE3	WAS	NE4	STL	NW1	ATL	NW2	LA	NC2	DET	NC4	TB
				NW4	NO	NW3	SF				

2 NE				2 HOU				2 OAK			
Home		Away		Home		Away		Home		Away	
AC2	HOU	AW2	OAK	AW2	OAK	AE2	NE	AE2	NE	AC2	HOU
AW3	KC	AC3	PIT	AE3	MIA	AW3	KC	AC3	PIT	AE3	MIA
NE2	DAL	NE1	PHI	AW5	SEA	AE5	NYJ	NC3	CHI	NC1	MIN
NE4	STL	NE3	WAS	NW1	ATL	NW2	LA	NC4	TB	NC2	DET
				NW4	NO	NW3	SF				

3 MIA				3 PIT				3 KC			
Home		Away		Home		Away		Home		Away	
AC3	PIT	AW3	KC	AW3	KC	AE3	MIA	AE3	MIA	AC3	PIT
AW2	OAK	AC2	HOU	AE2	NE	AW2	OAK	AC2	HOU	AE2	NE
NE1	PHI	NE2	DAL	AE5	NYJ	AW5	SEA	NC3	CHI	NC1	MIN
NE3	WAS	NE4	STL	NW2	LA	NW1	ATL	NC4	TB	NC2	DET
				NW3	SF	NW4	NO				

4 BAL				4 CIN				4 DEN			
Home		Away		Home		Away		Home		Away	
AC4	CIN	AW4	DEN	AW4	DEN	AE4	BAL	AE4	BAL	AC4	CIN
AW1	SD	AC1	CLE	AE1	BUF	AW1	SD	AC1	CLE	AE1	BUF
NE2	DAL	NE1	PHI	AW5	SEA	AE5	NYJ	NC1	MIN	NC3	CHI
NE4	STL	NE3	WAS	NW2	LA	NW1	ATL	NC2	DET	NC4	TB
				NW3	SF	NW4	NO				

5 NYJ								5 SEA			
Home		Away						Home		Away	
AW5	SEA	AW5	SEA					AE5	NYJ	AE5	NYJ
AC2	HOU	AC1	CLE					AC1	CLE	AC2	HOU
AC4	CIN	AC3	PIT					AC3	PIT	AC4	CIN
NC5	GB	NE5	NYG					NE5	NYG	NC5	GB

1981 NON-DIVISIONAL OPPONENTS (NFC)

NFC East				NFC Central				NFC West			
NE				NC				NW			

1 PHI				1 MIN				1 ATL			
Home		Away		Home		Away		Home		Away	
NW1	ATL	NC1	MIN	NE1	PHI	NW1	ATL	NC1	MIN	NE1	PHI
NC4	TB	NW4	NO	NW4	NO	NE4	STL	NE4	STL	NC4	TB
AE2	NE	AE1	BUF	AW2	OAK	AW1	SD	NE5	NYG	NC5	GB
AE4	BAL	AE3	MIA	AW3	KC	AW4	DEN	AC3	PIT	AC1	CLE
								AC4	CIN	AC2	HOU

2 DAL				2 DET				2 LA			
Home		Away		Home		Away		Home		Away	
NW2	LA	NC2	DET	NE2	DAL	NW2	LA	NC2	DET	NE2	DAL
NC3	CHI	NW3	SF	NW3	SF	NE3	WAS	NE3	WAS	NC3	CHI
AE1	BUF	AE2	NE	AW2	OAK	AW1	SD	NC5	GB	NE5	NYG
AE3	MIA	AE4	BAL	AW3	KC	AW4	DEN	AC1	CLE	AC3	PIT
								AC2	HOU	AC4	CIN

3	WAS			3	CHI			3	SF		
Home		Away		Home		Away		Home		Away	
NW3	SF	NC3	CHI	NE3	WAS	NW3	SF	NC3	CHI	NE3	WAS
NC2	DET	NW2	LA	NW2	LA	NE2	DAL	NE2	DAL	NC2	DET
AE2	NE	AE1	BUF	AW1	SD	AW2	OAK	NE5	NYG	NC5	GB[1]
AE4	BAL	AE3	MIA	AW4	DEN	AW3	KC	AC1	CLE	AC3	PIT
								AC2	HOU	AC4	CIN

4	STL			4	TB			4	NO		
Home		Away		Home		Away		Home		Away	
NW4	NO	NC4	TB	NE4	STL	NW4	NO	NC4	TB	NE4	STL
NC1	MIN	NW1	ATL	NW1	ATL	NE1	PHI	NE1	PHI	NC1	MIN
AE1	BUF	AE2	NE	AW1	SD	AW2	OAK	NC5	GB	NE5	NYG
AE3	MIA	AE4	BAL	AW4	DEN	AW3	KC	AC3	PIT	AC1	CLE
								AC4	CIN	AC2	HOU

5	NYG			5	GB		
Home		Away		Home		Away	
NC5	GB	NC5	GB[1]	NE5	NYG[1]	NE5	NYG
NW2	LA	NW1	ATL	NW1	ATL	NW2	LA
NW4	NO	NW3	SF	NW3	SF[1]	NW4	NO
AE5	NYJ	AW5	SEA	AW5	SEA	AE5	NYJ

[1]Played at Milwaukee.

1981 Final Standings
(To Determine 1982 Opponents)

AFC East
AE

1. MIAMI
2. NY JETS
3. BUFFALO
4. BALTIMORE
5. NEW ENGLAND

AFC Central
AC

1. CINCINNATI
2. PITTSBURGH
3. HOUSTON
4. CLEVELAND

AFC West
AW

1. SAN DIEGO
2. DENVER
3. KANSAS CITY
4. OAKLAND[a]
5. SEATTLE

NFC East
NE

1. DALLAS
2. PHILADELPHIA
3. NY GIANTS
4. WASHINGTON
5. ST. LOUIS

NFC Central
NC

1. TAMPA BAY
2. DETROIT
3. GREEN BAY
4. MINNESOTA
5. CHICAGO

NFC West
NW

1. SAN FRANCISCO
2. ATLANTA
3. LOS ANGELES
4. NEW ORLEANS

[a]In 1982, Oakland moved to Los Angeles and became the Los Angeles Raiders.

1982 NON-DIVISIONAL OPPONENTS (AFC)

AFC East
AE

1	MIA		
Home		*Away*	
AW1	SD[a]	AC1	CIN[a]
AC4	CLE[a]	AW4	LARd[a]
NC2	DET[a]	NC1	TB
NC4	MIN	NC3	GB[a]

2	NYJ		
Home		*Away*	
AW2	DEN[a]	AC2	PIT[a]
AC3	HOU[a]	AW3	KC
NC1	TB	NC2	DET
NC3	GB	NC4	MIN

3	BUF		
Home		*Away*	
AW3	KC	AC3	HOU[a]
AC2	PIT	AW2	DEN[a]
NC2	DET[a]	NC1	TB
NC4	MIN	NC3	GB[1]

4	BAL		
Home		*Away*	
AW4	LARd[a]	AC4	CLE[a]
AC1	CIN	AW1	SD
NC1	TB[a]	NC2	DET[a]
NC3	GB	NC4	MIN

5	NE		
Home		*Away*	
AW5	SEA[a]	AW5	SEA
AC1	CIN[a]	AC2	PIT
AC3	HOU	AC4	CLE
NE5	STL[a]	NC5	CHI

AFC Central
AC

1	CIN		
Home		*Away*	
AE1	MIA[a]	AW1	SD
AW4	LARd	AE4	BAL
AW5	SEA	AE5	NE[a]
NE1	DAL[a]	NE2	PHI
NE4	WAS[a]	NE3	NYG[a]

2	PIT		
Home		*Away*	
AE2	NYJ[a]	AW2	DEN[a]
AW3	KC	AE3	BUF
AE5	NE	AW5	SEA
NE2	PHI[a]	NE1	DAL
NE3	NYG[a]	NE4	WAS[a]

3	HOU		
Home		*Away*	
AE3	BUF[a]	AW3	KC[a]
AW2	DEN[a]	AE2	NYJ[a]
AW5	SEA	AE5	NE
NE1	DAL	NE2	PHI
NE4	WAS[a]	NE3	NYG

4	CLE		
Home		*Away*	
AE4	BAL[a]	AW4	LARd[a]
AW1	SD	AE1	MIA[a]
AE5	NE	AW5	SEA
NE2	PHI	NE1	DAL
NE3	NYG[a]	NE4	WAS[a]

AFC West
AW

1	SD		
Home		*Away*	
AC1	CIN	AE1	MIA[a]
AE4	BAL	AC4	CLE
NW3	LARm[a]	NW1	SF
NW4	NO[a]	NW2	ATL[a]

2	DEN		
Home		*Away*	
AC2	PIT[a]	AE2	NYJ[a]
AE3	BUF[a]	AC3	HOU[a]
NW1	SF	NW3	LARm
NW2	ATL	NW4	NO[a]

3	KC		
Home		*Away*	
AC3	HOU[a]	AE3	BUF
AE2	NYJ	AC2	PIT
NW1	SF	NW3	LARm
NW2	ATL[a]	NW4	NO

4	LARd		
Home		*Away*	
AC4	CLE[a]	AE4	BAL[a]
AE1	MIA[a]	AC1	CIN
NW3	LARm	NW1	SF
NW4	NO[a]	NW2	ATL

5	SEA		
Home		*Away*	
AE5	NE	AE5	NE[a]
AC2	PIT	AC1	CIN
AC4	CLE	AC3	HOU
NC5	CHI	NE5	STL[a]

[a]Game canceled due to the 57-day players' strike. The regular season was reduced from 16 weeks to 9.
[1]Played at Milwaukee.

1982 NON-DIVISIONAL OPPONENTS (NFC)

NFC East — NE

1 DAL

Home		Away	
NC1	TB	NW1	SF[a]
NW4	NO	NC4	MIN
AC2	PIT	AC1	CIN[a]
AC4	CLE	AC3	HOU

2 PHI

Home		Away	
NC2	DET[a]	NW2	ATL[a]
NW3	LARm[a]	NC3	GB[1a]
AC1	CIN	AC2	PIT[a]
AC3	HOU	AC4	CLE

3 NYG

Home		Away	
NC3	GB	NW3	LARm[a]
NW2	ATL	NC2	DET
AC1	CIN[a]	AC2	PIT[a]
AC3	HOU	AC4	CLE[a]

4 WAS

Home		Away	
NC4	MIN[a]	NW4	NO
NW1	SF[a]	NC1	TB
AC2	PIT[a]	AC1	CIN[a]
AC4	CLE[a]	AC3	HOU[a]

5 STL

Home		Away	
NC5	CHI[a]	NC5	CHI
NW1	SF	NW2	ATL
NW3	LARm[a]	NW4	NO
AW5	SEA[a]	AE5	NE[a]

NFC Central — NC

1 TB

Home		Away	
NW1	SF[a]	NE1	DAL
NE4	WAS	NW4	NO
AE1	MIA	AE2	NYJ
AE3	BUF	AE4	BAL[a]

2 DET

Home		Away	
NW2	ATL[a]	NE2	PHI[a]
NE3	NYG	NW3	LARm
AE2	NYJ	AE1	MIA[a]
AE4	BAL[a]	AE3	BUF[a]

3 GB

Home		Away	
NW3	LARm[1]	NE3	NYG
NE2	PHI[1a]	NW2	ATL
AE1	MIA[a]	AE2	NYJ
AE3	BUF[1]	AE4	BAL

4 MIN

Home		Away	
NW4	NO[a]	NE4	WAS[a]
NE1	DAL	NW1	SF[a]
AE2	NYJ	AE1	MIA
AE4	BAL	AE3	BUF

5 CHI

Home		Away	
NE5	STL	NE5	STL[a]
NW2	ATL[a]	NW1	SF[a]
NW4	NO	NW3	LARm
AE5	NE	AW5	SEA

NFC West — NW

1 SF

Home		Away	
NE1	DAL[a]	NC1	TB[a]
NC4	MIN[a]	NE4	WAS[a]
NC5	CHI[a]	NE5	STL
AW1	SD	AW2	DEN
AW4	LARd	AW3	KC

2 ATL

Home		Away	
NE2	PHI[a]	NC2	DET[a]
NC3	GB	NE3	NYG
NE5	STL	NC5	CHI[a]
AW1	SD[a]	AW2	DEN
AW4	LARd	AW3	KC[a]

3 LARm

Home		Away	
NE3	NYG[a]	NC3	GB[1]
NC2	DET	NE2	PHI[a]
NC5	CHI	NE5	STL[a]
AW2	DEN	AW1	SD[a]
AW3	KC	AW4	LARd

4 NO

Home		Away	
NE4	WAS	NC4	MIN[a]
NC1	TB	NE1	DAL
NE5	STL	NC5	CHI
AW2	DEN[a]	AW1	SD[a]
AW3	KC	AW4	LARd[a]

[a] Game canceled due to the 57-day players' strike. The regular season was reduced from 16 weeks to 9.
[1] Played at Milwaukee.

1982 GAMES CANCELED BY STRIKE

As a result of the 57-day players' strike that began after the second week of the 1982 season, the regular-season schedule was reduced from 16 games to nine. The season resumed on Sunday, November 21 with the originally scheduled games for that weekend. Only one of the eight weeks missed (Weeks 3 through 10) during the strike would be made up the weekend of Jan. 2–3. Here's a look at how the schedule was revised:

ORIGINAL SCHEDULE		REVISED SCHEDULE
Week 1	→	Played as scheduled
Week 2	→	Played as scheduled
Week 3–10	→	Canceled*
Weeks 11–16	→	Weeks 3–8
*One game for each team selected from Weeks 3–10	→	Week 9

The games that were selected to be played on the final weekend (Jan. 2–3) were not from one specific week from the original schedule, but rather were handpicked to make sure that each team would end up playing at least four of their nine games at home. Here are the games that were rescheduled (in **bold**), for the final week (Week 9) with their new date and time:[4]

WEEK 3

Thursday, September 23, 1982
Atlanta Falcons at Kansas City Chiefs, 8:30 (ABC)
Sunday, September 26, 1982 (NBC-TV Doubleheader)
Tampa Bay Buccaneers at Detroit Lions, 1:00 (CBS)
Miami Dolphins at Green Bay Packers, 1:00 (NBC)
Buffalo Bills at Houston Oilers, 1:00 (NBC)
Dallas Cowboys at Minnesota Vikings, 1:00 (CBS) → **Monday, January 3, 9:00 (ABC)**
Seattle Seahawks at New England Patriots, 1:00 (NBC)
Denver Broncos at New Orleans Saints, 1:00 (NBC)
Los Angeles Rams at Philadelphia Eagles, 1:00 (CBS)
New York Giants at Pittsburgh Steelers, 1:00 (CBS)
St. Louis Cardinals at Washington Redskins, 1:00 (CBS) → **Sunday, January 2, 1:00 (CBS)**
New York Jets at Baltimore Colts, 4:00 (NBC)
Los Angeles Raiders at San Diego Chargers, 4:00 (NBC) → **Sunday, January 2, 4:00 (NBC)**
Chicago Bears at San Francisco 49ers, 4:00 (CBS)
Monday, September 27, 1982
Cincinnati Bengals at Cleveland Browns, 9:00 (ABC)

WEEK 4

Sunday, October 3, 1982 (CBS-TV Doubleheader)
San Diego Chargers at Atlanta Falcons, 1:00 (NBC)
New England Patriots at Buffalo Bills, 1:00 (NBC)
Minnesota Vikings at Chicago Bears, 1:00 (CBS)
Miami Dolphins at Cincinnati Bengals, 1:00 (NBC)
Baltimore Colts at Detroit Lions, 1:00 (NBC)
Philadelphia Eagles vs. Green Bay Packers at Milwaukee, 1:00 (CBS)
Houston Oilers at New York Jets, 1:00 (NBC)
Los Angeles Rams at St. Louis Cardinals, 1:00 (CBS)
Cleveland Browns at Washington Redskins, 1:00 (NBC)
New York Giants at Dallas Cowboys, 4:00 (CBS)
Pittsburgh Steelers at Denver Broncos, 4:00 (NBC)

New Orleans Saints at Los Angeles Raiders, 4:00 (CBS)
Kansas City Chiefs at Seattle Seahawks, 4:00 (NBC)
Monday, October 4, 1982
San Francisco 49ers at Tampa Bay Buccaneers, 9:00 (ABC)

WEEK 5
Sunday, October 10, 1982 (NBC-TV Doubleheader)
Green Bay Packers at Chicago Bears, 1:00 (CBS)
Washington Redskins at Dallas Cowboys, 1:00 (CBS)
Houston Oilers at Kansas City Chiefs, 1:00 (NBC)
Cincinnati Bengals at New England Patriots, 1:00 (NBC)
San Francisco 49ers at New Orleans Saints, 1:00 (CBS)
St. Louis Cardinals at New York Giants, 1:00 (CBS)
Minnesota Vikings at Tampa Bay Buccaneers, 1:00 (CBS)
Buffalo Bills at Baltimore Colts, 2:00 (NBC)
Cleveland Browns at Los Angeles Raiders, 4:00 (NBC)
Atlanta Falcons at Los Angeles Rams, 4:00 (CBS)
Detroit Lions at Miami Dolphins, 4:00 (CBS)
Denver Broncos at New York Jets, 4:00 (NBC)
Seattle Seahawks at San Diego Chargers, 4:00 (NBC)
Monday, October 11, 1982
Philadelphia Eagles at Pittsburgh Steelers, 9:00 (ABC)

WEEK 6
Sunday, October 17, 1982 (CBS-TV Doubleheader)
Baltimore Colts at Cleveland Browns, 1:00 (NBC)
Atlanta Falcons at Detroit Lions, 1:00 (CBS)
Tampa Bay Buccaneers at Green Bay Packers, 1:00 (CBS)
Denver Broncos at Houston Oilers, 1:00 (NBC)
New England Patriots at Miami Dolphins, 1:00 (NBC)
New Orleans Saints at Minnesota Vikings, 1:00 (CBS)
Cincinnati Bengals at New York Giants, 1:00 (NBC)
Chicago Bears at St. Louis Cardinals, 1:00 (CBS)
Pittsburgh Steelers at Washington Redskins, 1:00 (NBC)
Dallas Cowboys at Philadelphia Eagles, 4:00 (CBS)
Kansas City Chiefs at San Diego Chargers, 4:00 (NBC)
Los Angeles Rams at San Francisco 49ers, 4:00 (CBS) → Sunday, January 2, 4:00 (CBS)
Los Angeles Raiders at Seattle Seahawks, 4:00 (NBC)
Monday, October 18, 1982
Buffalo Bills at New York Jets, 9:00 (ABC)

WEEK 7
Sunday, October 24, 1982 (NBC-TV Doubleheader)
San Francisco 49ers at Atlanta Falcons, 1:00 (CBS)
Detroit Lions at Buffalo Bills, 1:00 (CBS)
Tampa Bay Buccaneers at Chicago Bears, 1:00 (CBS)
Washington Redskins at Houston Oilers, 1:00 (CBS)

New York Jets at Kansas City Chiefs, 1:00 (NBC) → Sunday, January 2, 1:00 (NBC)
Green Bay Packers at Minnesota Vikings, 1:00 (CBS)
St. Louis Cardinals at New England Patriots, 1:00 (CBS)
Cleveland Browns at Pittsburgh Steelers, 1:00 (NBC) → Sunday, January 2, 1:00 (NBC)
Miami Dolphins at Baltimore Colts, 2:00 (NBC) → Sunday, January 2, 2:00 (NBC)
Los Angeles Raiders at Denver Broncos, 4:00 (NBC)
New Orleans Saints at Los Angeles Rams, 4:00 (CBS)
San Diego Chargers at Seattle Seahawks, 4:00 (NBC)
Dallas Cowboys at Cincinnati Bengals, 9:00 (ABC)
Monday, October 25, 1982
New York Giants at Philadelphia Eagles, 9:00 (ABC) → Sunday, January 2, 1:00 (CBS)

WEEK 8
Sunday, October 31, 1982 (CBS-TV Doubleheader)
Pittsburgh Steelers at Cincinnati Bengals, 1:00 (NBC)
Houston Oilers at Cleveland Browns, 1:00 (NBC)
Chicago Bears at Green Bay Packers, 1:00 (CBS)
Seattle Seahawks at Kansas City Chiefs, 1:00 (NBC)
Atlanta Falcons at New Orleans Saints, 1:00 (CBS) → Sunday, January 2, 4:00 (CBS)
New England Patriots at New York Jets, 1:00 (NBC)
Philadelphia Eagles at St. Louis Cardinals, 1:00 (CBS)
San Francisco 49ers at Washington Redskins, 1:00 (CBS)
Tampa Bay Buccaneers at Baltimore Colts, 2:00 (CBS)
Buffalo Bills at Denver Broncos, 4:00 (NBC)
Miami Dolphins at Los Angeles Raiders, 4:00 (NBC)
Dallas Cowboys at New York Giants, 4:00 (CBS)
Los Angeles Rams at San Diego Chargers, 4:00 (CBS)
Monday, November 1, 1982
Detroit Lions at Minnesota Vikings, 9:00 (ABC)

WEEK 9
Sunday, November 7, 1982 (NBC-TV Doubleheader)
Atlanta Falcons at Chicago Bears, 1:00 (CBS)
Washington Redskins at Cincinnati Bengals, 1:00 (CBS)
New York Giants at Cleveland Browns, 1:00 (CBS)
St. Louis Cardinals at Dallas Cowboys, 1:00 (CBS)
Baltimore Colts at New England Patriots, 1:00 (NBC)
Los Angeles Rams at New Orleans Saints, 1:00 (CBS)
Detroit Lions at Philadelphia Eagles, 1:00 (CBS)
Houston Oilers at Pittsburgh Steelers, 1:00 (NBC)
Green Bay Packers at Tampa Bay Buccaneers, 1:00 (CBS)
New York Jets at Buffalo Bills, 4:00 (NBC)
Kansas City Chiefs at Los Angeles Raiders, 4:00 (NBC)

Minnesota Vikings at San Francisco 49ers, 4:00 (CBS)
Denver Broncos at Seattle Seahawks, 4:00 (NBC) → Sunday, January 2, 4:00 (NBC)
Monday, November 8, 1982
San Diego Chargers at Miami Dolphins, 9:00 (ABC)

WEEK 10
Sunday, November 14, 1982 (CBS-TV Doubleheader)
Green Bay Packers at Detroit Lions, 1:00 (CBS) → Sunday, January 2, 4:00 (CBS)
Cincinnati Bengals at Houston Oilers, 1:00 (NBC) → Sunday, January 2, 1:00 (NBC)
Denver Broncos at Kansas City Chiefs, 1:00 (NBC)
Buffalo Bills at New England Patriots, 1:00 (NBC) → Sunday, January 2, 1:00 (NBC)
New York Jets at Pittsburgh Steelers, 1:00 (NBC)
Seattle Seahawks at St. Louis Cardinals, 1:00 (NBC)
Chicago Bears at Tampa Bay Buccaneers, 1:00 (CBS) → Sunday, January 2, 1:00 (CBS)
Minnesota Vikings at Washington Redskins, 1:00 (CBS)
Los Angeles Raiders at Baltimore Colts, 2:00 (NBC)
New York Giants at Los Angeles Rams, 4:00 (CBS)
Cleveland Browns at Miami Dolphins, 4:00 (NBC)
New Orleans Saints at San Diego Chargers, 4:00 (CBS)
Dallas Cowboys at San Francisco 49ers, 4:00 (CBS)
Monday, November 15, 1982
Philadelphia Eagles at Atlanta Falcons, 9:00 (ABC)

The following is a list of the 43 divisional games that were among the 98 games that were wiped out by the strike:

AFC

East (8)	*Central (4)*	*West (9)*
Bal at NE	Cin at Cle	Den at KC
Buf at Bal	Hou at Cle	KC at LARd
Buf at NYJ	Hou at Pit	KC at SD
NE at Buf	Pit at Cin	KC at Sea
NE at Mia		LARd at Den
NE at NYJ		LARd at Sea
NYJ at Bal		SD at Sea
NYJ at Buf		Sea at KC
		Sea at SD

NFC

East (7)	*Central (10)*	*West (5)*
Dal at NYG	Chi at GB	Atl at LARm
Dal at Phi	Det at Min	LARm at NO
NYG at Dal	GB at Chi	NO at LARm
Phi at StL	GB at Min	SF at Atl
StL at Dal	GB at TB	SF at NO
StL at NYG	Min at Chi	
Was at Dal	Min at TB	
	TB at Chi	
	TB at Det	
	TB at GB	

1982 Final Standings
(To Determine 1983 Opponents)

NOTE: Due to the strike-shortened 1982 season, the NFL conducted a 16-team postseason tournament in which teams were ranked 1–8 by conference. The final division standings provided below are for scheduling purposes *only* to determine 1983 opponents.

AFC East AE	AFC Central AC	AFC West AW
1 MIAMI	1 CINCINNATI	1 LA RAIDERS
2 NY JETS	2 PITTSBURGH	2 SAN DIEGO
3 NEW ENGLAND	3 CLEVELAND	3 SEATTLE
4 BUFFALO	4 HOUSTON	4 KANSAS CITY
5 BALTIMORE		5 DENVER

NFC East NE	NFC Central NC	NFC West NW
1 WASHINGTON	1 GREEN BAY	1 ATLANTA
2 DALLAS	2 MINNESOTA	2 NEW ORLEANS
3 ST. LOUIS	3 TAMPA BAY	3 SAN FRANCISCO
4 NY GIANTS	4 DETROIT	4 LA RAMS
5 PHILADELPHIA	5 CHICAGO	

1983 NON-DIVISIONAL OPPONENTS (AFC)

AFC East AE				AFC Central AC				AFC West AW			
1 MIA				**1 CIN**				**1 LARd**			
Home		Away		Home		Away		Home		Away	
AC1	CIN	AW1	LARd	AW1	LARd	AE1	MIA	AE1	MIA	AC1	CIN
AW4	KC	AC4	HOU	AE4	BUF	AW4	KC	AC4	HOU	AE4	BUF
NW1	ATL	NW2	NO	AE5	BAL	AW5	DEN	NE3	STL	NE1	WAS
NW4	LARm	NW3	SF	NC1	GB	NC2	MIN	NE4	NYG	NE2	DAL
				NC4	DET	NC3	TB				
2 NYJ				**2 PIT**				**2 SD**			
Home		Away		Home		Away		Home		Away	
AC2	PIT	AW2	SD	AW2	SD	AE2	NYJ	AE2	NYJ	AC2	PIT
AW3	SEA	AC3	CLE	AE3	NE	AW3	SEA	AC3	CLE	AE3	NE
NW1	ATL	NW2	NO	AW5	DEN	AE5	BAL	NE1	WAS	NE3	STL
NW4	LARm	NW3	SF	NC2	MIN	NC1	GB	NE2	DAL	NE4	NYG
				NC3	TB	NC4	DET				
3 NE				**3 CLE**				**3 SEA**			
Home		Away		Home		Away		Home		Away	
AC3	CLE	AW3	SEA	AW3	SEA	AE3	NE	AE3	NE	AC3	CLE
AW2	SD	AC2	PIT	AE2	NYJ	AW2	SD	AC2	PIT	AE2	NYJ
NW2	NO	NW1	ATL	AE5	BAL	AW5	DEN	NE1	WAS	NE3	STL
NW3	SF	NW4	LARm	NC2	MIN	NC1	GB[1]	NE2	DAL	NE4	NYG
				NC3	TB	NC4	DET				

4	BUF			4	HOU			4	KC		
Home		*Away*		*Home*		*Away*		*Home*		*Away*	
AC4	HOU	AW4	KC	AW4	KC	AE4	BUF	AE4	BUF	AC4	HOU
AW1	LARd	AC1	CIN	AE1	MIA	AW1	LARd	AC1	CIN	AE1	MIA
NW2	NO	NW1	ATL	AW5	DEN	AE5	BAL	NE3	STL	NE1	WAS
NW3	SF	NW4	LARm	NC1	GB	NC2	MIN	NE4	NYG	NE2	DAL
				NC4	DET	NC3	TB				

5	BAL							5	DEN		
Home		*Away*						*Home*		*Away*	
AW5	DEN	AW5	DEN					AE5	BAL	AE5	BAL
AC2	PIT	AC1	CIN					AC1	CIN	AC2	PIT
AC4	HOU	AC3	CLE					AC3	CLE	AC4	HOU
NC5	CHI	NE5	PHI					NE5	PHI	NC5	CHI

[1]Played at Milwaukee.

1983 NON-DIVISIONAL OPPONENTS (NFC)

NFC East — NE   NFC Central — NC   NFC West — NW

1	WAS			1	GB			1	ATL		
Home		*Away*		*Home*		*Away*		*Home*		*Away*	
NW1	ATL	NC1	GB	NE1	WAS	NW1	ATL	NC1	GB	NE1	WAS
NC4	DET	NW4	LARm	NW4	LARm[1]	NE4	NYG	NE4	NYG	NC4	DET
AW1	LARd	AW2	SD	AC2	PIT	AC1	CIN	NE5	PHI	NC5	CHI
AW4	KC	AW3	SEA	AC3	CLE[1]	AC4	HOU	AE3	NE	AE1	MIA
								AE4	BUF	AE2	NYJ

2	DAL			2	MIN			2	NO		
Home		*Away*		*Home*		*Away*		*Home*		*Away*	
NW2	NO	NC2	MIN	NE2	DAL	NW2	NO	NC2	MIN	NE2	DAL
NC3	TB	NW3	SF	NW3	SF	NE3	STL	NE3	STL	NC3	TB
AW1	LARd	AW2	SD	AC1	CIN	AC2	PIT	NC5	CHI	NE5	PHI
AW4	KC	AW3	SEA	AC4	HOU	AC3	CLE	AE1	MIA	AE3	NE
								AE2	NYJ	AE4	BUF

3	STL			3	TB			3	SF		
Home		*Away*		*Home*		*Away*		*Home*		*Away*	
NW3	SF	NC3	TB	NE3	STL	NW3	SF	NC3	TB	NE3	STL
NC2	MIN	NW2	NO	NW2	NO	NE2	DAL	NE2	DAL	NC2	MIN
AW2	SD	AW1	LARd	AC1	CIN	AC2	PIT	NE5	PHI	NC5	CHI
AW3	SEA	AW4	KC	AC4	HOU	AC3	CLE	AE1	MIA	AE3	NE
								AE2	NYJ	AE4	BUF

4	NYG			4	DET			4	LARm		
Home		*Away*		*Home*		*Away*		*Home*		*Away*	
NW4	LARm	NC4	DET	NE4	NYG	NW4	LARm	NC4	DET	NE4	NYG
NC1	GB	NW1	ATL	NW1	ATL	NE1	WAS	NE1	WAS	NC1	GB[1]
AW2	SD	AW1	LARd	AC2	PIT	AC1	CIN	NC5	CHI	NE5	PHI
AW3	SEA	AW4	KC	AC3	CLE	AC4	HOU	AE3	NE	AE1	MIA
								AE4	BUF	AE2	NYJ

	5	PHI			5	CHI	
	Home		*Away*		*Home*		*Away*
NC5	CHI	NC5	CHI	NE5	PHI	NE5	PHI
NW2	NO	NW1	ATL	NW1	ATL	NW2	NO
NW4	LARm	NW3	SF	NW3	SF	NW4	LARm
AE5	BAL	AW5	DEN	AW5	DEN	AE5	BAL

[1] Played at Milwaukee.

1983 Final Standings
(To Determine 1984 Opponents)

AFC East AE	AFC Central AC	AFC West AW
1 MIAMI	1 PITTSBURGH	1 LA RAIDERS
2 NEW ENGLAND	2 CLEVELAND	2 SEATTLE
3 BUFFALO	3 CINCINNATI	3 DENVER
4 BALTIMORE[a]	4 HOUSTON	4 SAN DIEGO
5 NY JETS		5 KANSAS CITY

NFC East NE	NFC Central NC	NFC West NW
1 WASHINGTON	1 DETROIT	1 SAN FRANCISCO
2 DALLAS	2 GREEN BAY	2 LA RAMS
3 ST. LOUIS	3 CHICAGO	3 NEW ORLEANS
4 PHILADELPHIA	4 MINNESOTA	4 ATLANTA
5 NY GIANTS	5 TAMPA BAY	

[a] In 1984, Baltimore moved to Indianapolis and became the Indianapolis Colts.

1984 NON-DIVISIONAL OPPONENTS (AFC)

AFC East AE				AFC Central AC				AFC West AW			
1	MIA			1	PIT			1	LARd		
Home		*Away*		*Home*		*Away*		*Home*		*Away*	
AW1	LARd	AC1	PIT	AE1	MIA	AW1	LARd	AC1	PIT	AE1	MIA
AC4	HOU	AW4	SD	AW4	SD	AE4	IND	AE4	IND	AC4	HOU
NE2	DAL	NE1	WAS	AW5	KC	AE5	NYJ	NC2	GB	NC1	DET
NE4	PHI	NE3	STL	NW2	LARm	NW1	SF	NC4	MIN	NC3	CHI
				NW4	ATL	NW3	NO				
2	NE			2	CLE			2	SEA		
Home		*Away*		*Home*		*Away*		*Home*		*Away*	
AW2	SEA	AC2	CLE	AE2	NE	AW2	SEA	AC2	CLE	AE2	NE
AC3	CIN	AW3	DEN	AW3	DEN	AE3	BUF	AE3	BUF	AC3	CIN
NE1	WAS	NE2	DAL	AE5	NYJ	AW5	KC	NC1	DET	NC2	GB[1]
NE3	STL	NE4	PHI	NW1	SF	NW2	LARm	NC3	CHI	NC4	MIN
				NW3	NO	NW4	ATL				

3	BUF			3	CIN			3	DEN		
Home		*Away*		*Home*		*Away*		*Home*		*Away*	
AW3	DEN	AC3	CIN	AE3	BUF	AW3	DEN	AC3	CIN	AE3	BUF
AC2	CLE	AW2	SEA	AW2	SEA	AE2	NE	AE2	NE	AC2	CLE
NE2	DAL	NE1	WAS	AW5	KC	AE5	NYJ	NC2	GB	NC1	DET
NE4	PHI	NE3	STL	NW2	LARm	NW1	SF	NC4	MIN	NC3	CHI
				NW4	ATL	NW3	NO				

4	IND			4	HOU			4	SD		
Home		*Away*		*Home*		*Away*		*Home*		*Away*	
AW4	SD	AC4	HOU	AE4	IND	AW4	SD	AC4	HOU	AE4	IND
AC1	PIT	AW1	LARd	AW1	LARd	AE1	MIA	AE1	MIA	AC1	PIT
NE1	WAS	NE2	DAL	AE5	NYJ	AW5	KC	NC1	DET	NC2	GB
NE3	STL	NE4	PHI	NW1	SF	NW2	LARm	NC3	CHI	NC4	MIN
				NW3	NO	NW4	ATL				

5	NYJ							5	KC		
Home		*Away*						*Home*		*Away*	
AW5	KC	AW5	KC					AE5	NYJ	AE5	NYJ
AC1	PIT	AC2	CLE					AC2	CLE	AC1	PIT
AC3	CIN	AC4	HOU					AC4	HOU	AC3	CIN
NE5	NYG	NC5	TB					NC5	TB	NE5	NYG

[1] Played at Milwaukee.

1984 NON-DIVISIONAL OPPONENTS (NFC)

NFC East — NE   NFC Central — NC   NFC West — NW

1	WAS			1	DET			1	SF		
Home		*Away*		*Home*		*Away*		*Home*		*Away*	
NC1	DET	NW1	SF	NW1	SF	NE1	WAS	NE1	WAS	NC1	DET
NW4	ATL	NC4	MIN	NE4	PHI	NW4	ATL	NC4	MIN	NE4	PHI
AE1	MIA	AE2	NE	AW1	LARd	AW2	SEA	NC5	TB	NE5	NYG
AE3	BUF	AE4	IND	AW3	DEN	AW4	SD	AC1	PIT	AC2	CLE
								AC3	CIN	AC4	HOU

2	DAL			2	GB			2	LARm		
Home		*Away*		*Home*		*Away*		*Home*		*Away*	
NC2	GB	NW2	LARm	NW2	LARm[1]	NE2	DAL	NE2	DAL	NC2	GB[1]
NW3	NO	NC3	CHI	NE3	STL	NW3	NO	NC3	CHI	NE3	STL
AE2	NE	AE1	MIA	AW2	SEA[1]	AW1	LARd	NE5	NYG	NC5	TB
AE4	IND	AE3	BUF	AW4	SD	AW3	DEN	AC2	CLE	AC1	PIT
								AC4	HOU	AC3	CIN

3	STL			3	CHI			3	NO		
Home		*Away*		*Home*		*Away*		*Home*		*Away*	
NC3	CHI	NW3	NO	NW3	NO	NE3	STL	NE3	STL	NC3	CHI
NW2	LARm	NC2	GB	NE2	DAL	NW2	LARm	NC2	GB	NE2	DAL
AE1	MIA	AE2	NE	AW1	LARd	AW2	SEA	NC5	TB	NE5	NYG
AE3	BUF	AE4	IND	AW3	DEN	AW4	SD	AC1	PIT	AC2	CLE
								AC3	CIN	AC4	HOU

4	PHI			4	MIN			4	ATL		
Home		*Away*		*Home*		*Away*		*Home*		*Away*	
NC4	MIN	NW4	ATL	NW4	ATL	NE4	PHI	NE4	PHI	NC4	MIN
NW1	SF	NC1	DET	NE1	WAS	NW1	SF	NC1	DET	NE1	WAS
AE2	NE	AE1	MIA	AW2	SEA	AW1	LARd	NE5	NYG	NC5	TB
AE4	IND	AE3	BUF	AW4	SD	AW3	DEN	AC2	CLE	AC1	PIT
								AC4	HOU	AC3	CIN

5	NYG			5	TB		
Home		*Away*		*Home*		*Away*	
NC5	TB	NC5	TB	NE5	NYG	NE5	NYG
NW1	SF	NW2	LARm	NW2	LARm	NW1	SF
NW3	NO	NW4	ATL	NW4	ATL	NW3	NO
AW5	KC	AE5	NYJ	AE5	NYJ	AW5	KC

¹Played at Milwaukee.

1984 Final Standings
(To Determine 1985 Opponents)

AFC East AE	AFC Central AC	AFC West AW
1 MIAMI	1 PITTSBURGH	1 DENVER
2 NEW ENGLAND	2 CINCINNATI	2 SEATTLE
3 NY JETS	3 CLEVELAND	3 LA RAIDERS
4 INDIANAPOLIS	4 HOUSTON	4 KANSAS CITY
5 BUFFALO		5 SAN DIEGO

NFC East NE	NFC Central NC	NFC West NW
1 WASHINGTON	1 CHICAGO	1 SAN FRANCISCO
2 NY GIANTS	2 GREEN BAY	2 LA RAMS
3 ST. LOUIS	3 TAMPA BAY	3 NEW ORLEANS
4 DALLAS	4 DETROIT	4 ATLANTA
5 PHILADELPHIA	5 MINNESOTA	

1985 NON-DIVISIONAL OPPONENTS (AFC)

AFC East				AFC Central				AFC West			
AE				AC				AW			
1	MIA			1	PIT			1	DEN		
Home		*Away*		*Home*		*Away*		*Home*		*Away*	
AC1	PIT	AW1	DEN	AW1	DEN	AE1	MIA	AE1	MIA	AC1	PIT
AW4	KC	AC4	HOU	AE4	IND	AW4	KC	AC4	HOU	AE4	IND
NC1	CHI	NC2	GB	AE5	BUF	AW5	SD	NW1	SF	NW2	LARm
NC3	TB	NC4	DET	NE1	WAS	NE2	NYG	NW3	NO	NW4	ATL
				NE3	STL	NE4	DAL				

2	NE			2	CIN			2	SEA		
Home		*Away*		*Home*		*Away*		*Home*		*Away*	
AC2	CIN	AW2	SEA	AW2	SEA	AE2	NE	AE2	NE	AC2	CIN
AW3	LARd	AC3	CLE	AE3	NYJ	AW3	LARd	AC3	CLE	AE3	NYJ
NC2	GB	NC1	CHI	AW5	SD	AE5	BUF	NW2	LARm	NW1	SF
NC4	DET	NC3	TB	NE2	NYG	NE1	WAS	NW4	ATL	NW3	NO
				NE4	DAL	NE3	STL				

3	NYJ			3	CLE			3	LARd		
Home		*Away*		*Home*		*Away*		*Home*		*Away*	
AC3	CLE	AW3	LARd	AW3	LARd	AE3	NYJ	AE3	NYJ	AC3	CLE
AW2	SEA	AC2	CIN	AE2	NE	AW2	SEA	AC2	CIN	AE2	NE
NC1	CHI	NC2	GB[1]	AE5	BUF	AW5	SD	NW1	SF	NW2	LARm
NC3	TB	NC4	DET	NE1	WAS	NE2	NYG	NW3	NO	NW4	ATL
				NE3	STL	NE4	DAL				

4	IND			4	HOU			4	KC		
Home		*Away*		*Home*		*Away*		*Home*		*Away*	
AC4	HOU	AW4	KC	AW4	KC	AE4	IND	AE4	IND	AC4	HOU
AW1	DEN	AC1	PIT	AE1	MIA	AW1	DEN	AC1	PIT	AE1	MIA
NC2	GB	NC1	CHI	AW5	SD	AE5	BUF	NW2	LARm	NW1	SF
NC4	DET	NC3	TB	NE2	NYG	NE1	WAS	NW4	ATL	NW3	NO
				NE4	DAL	NE3	STL				

5	BUF							5	SD		
Home		*Away*						*Home*		*Away*	
AW5	SD	AW5	SD					AE5	BUF	AE5	BUF
AC2	CIN	AC1	PIT					AC1	PIT	AC2	CIN
AC4	HOU	AC3	CLE					AC3	CLE	AC4	HOU
NC5	MIN	NE5	PHI					NE5	PHI	NC5	MIN

[1]Played at Milwaukee.

1985 NON-DIVISIONAL OPPONENTS (NFC)

NFC East — NE
NFC Central — NC
NFC West — NW

1	WAS			1	CHI			1	SF		
Home		*Away*		*Home*		*Away*		*Home*		*Away*	
NW1	SF	NC1	CHI	NE1	WAS	NW1	SF	NC1	CHI	NE1	WAS
NC4	DET	NW4	ATL	NW4	ATL	NE4	DAL	NE4	DAL	NC4	DET
AC2	CIN	AC1	PIT	AE2	NE	AE1	MIA	NE5	PHI	NC5	MIN
AC4	HOU	AC3	CLE	AE4	IND	AE3	NYJ	AW2	SEA	AW1	DEN
								AW4	KC	AW3	LARd

2	NYG			2	GB			2	LARm		
Home		*Away*		*Home*		*Away*		*Home*		*Away*	
NW2	LARm	NC2	GB	NE2	NYG	NW2	LARm	NC2	GB	NE2	NYG
NC3	TB	NW3	NO	NW3	NO[1]	NE3	STL	NE3	STL	NC3	TB
AC1	PIT	AC2	CIN	AE1	MIA	AE2	NE	NC5	MIN	NE5	PHI
AC3	CLE	AC4	HOU	AE3	NYJ[1]	AE4	IND	AW1	DEN	AW2	SEA
								AW3	LARd	AW4	KC

3	STL			3	TB			3	NO		
Home		*Away*		*Home*		*Away*		*Home*		*Away*	
NW3	NO	NC3	TB	NE3	STL	NW3	NO	NC3	TB	NE3	STL
NC2	GB	NW2	LARm	NW2	LARm	NE2	NYG	NE2	NYG	NC2	GB[1]
AC2	CIN	AC1	PIT	AE2	NE	AE1	MIA	NE5	PHI	NC5	MIN
AC4	HOU	AC3	CLE	AE4	IND	AE3	NYJ	AW2	SEA	AW1	DEN
								AW4	KC	AW3	LARd

4	DAL			4	DET			4	ATL		
Home		*Away*		*Home*		*Away*		*Home*		*Away*	
NW4	ATL	NC4	DET	NE4	DAL	NW4	ATL	NC4	DET	NE4	DAL
NC1	CHI	NW1	SF	NW1	SF	NE1	WAS	NE1	WAS	NC1	CHI
AC1	PIT	AC2	CIN	AE1	MIA	AE2	NE	NC5	MIN	NE5	PHI
AC3	CLE	AC4	HOU	AE3	NYJ	AE4	IND	AW1	DEN	AW2	SEA
								AW3	LARd	AW4	KC

5	PHI			5	MIN		
Home		*Away*		*Home*		*Away*	
NC5	MIN	NC5	MIN	NE5	PHI	NE5	PHI
NW2	LARm	NW1	SF	NW1	SF	NW2	LARm
NW4	ATL	NW3	NO	NW3	NO	NW4	ATL
AE5	BUF	AW5	SD	AW5	SD	AE5	BUF

[1]Played at Milwaukee.

1985 Final Standings
(To Determine 1986 Opponents)

AFC EAST
AE

1. MIAMI
2. NY JETS
3. NEW ENGLAND
4. INDIANAPOLIS
5. BUFFALO

AFC CENTRAL
AC

1. CLEVELAND
2. CINCINNATI
3. PITTSBURGH
4. HOUSTON

AFC WEST
AW

1. LA RAIDERS
2. DENVER
3. SEATTLE
4. SAN DIEGO
5. KANSAS CITY

NFC EAST
NE

1. DALLAS
2. NY GIANTS
3. WASHINGTON
4. PHILADELPHIA
5. ST. LOUIS

NFC CENTRAL
NC

1. CHICAGO
2. GREEN BAY
3. MINNESOTA
4. DETROIT
5. TAMPA BAY

NFC WEST
NW

1. LA RAMS
2. SAN FRANCISCO
3. NEW ORLEANS
4. ATLANTA

1986 NON-DIVISIONAL OPPONENTS (AFC)

AFC East — AE

1 MIA

Home		Away	
AW1	LARd	AC1	CLE
AC4	HOU	AW4	SD
NW2	SF	NW1	LARm
NW4	ATL	NW3	NO

2 NYJ

Home		Away	
AW2	DEN	AC2	CIN
AC3	PIT	AW3	SEA
NW1	LARm	NW2	SF
NW3	NO	NW4	ATL

3 NE

Home		Away	
AW3	SEA	AC3	PIT
AC2	CIN	AW2	DEN
NW2	SF	NW1	LARm
NW4	ATL	NW3	NO

4 IND

Home		Away	
AW4	SD	AC4	HOU
AC1	CLE	AW1	LARd
NW1	LARm	NW2	SF
NW3	NO	NW4	ATL

5 BUF

Home		Away	
AW5	KC	AW5	KC
AC1	CLE	AC2	CIN
AC3	PIT	AC4	HOU
NE5	STL	NC5	TB

AFC Central — AC

1 CLE

Home		Away	
AE1	MIA	AW1	LARd
AW4	SD	AE4	IND
AW5	KC	AE5	BUF
NC2	GB	NC1	CHI
NC4	DET	NC3	MIN

2 CIN

Home		Away	
AE2	NYJ	AW2	DEN
AW3	SEA	AE3	NE
AE5	BUF	AW5	KC
NC1	CHI	NC2	GB[1]
NC3	MIN	NC4	DET

3 PIT

Home		Away	
AE3	NE	AW3	SEA
AW2	DEN	AE2	NYJ
AW5	KC	AE5	BUF
NC2	GB	NC1	CHI
NC4	DET	NC3	MIN

4 HOU

Home		Away	
AE4	IND	AW4	SD
AW1	LARd	AE1	MIA
AE5	BUF	AW5	KC
NC1	CHI	NC2	GB
NC3	MIN	NC4	DET

AFC West — AW

1 LARd

Home		Away	
AC1	CLE	AE1	MIA
AE4	IND	AC4	HOU
NE2	NYG	NE1	DAL
NE4	PHI	NE3	WAS

2 DEN

Home		Away	
AC2	CIN	AE2	NYJ
AE3	NE	AC3	PIT
NE1	DAL	NE2	NYG
NE3	WAS	NE4	PHI

3 SEA

Home		Away	
AC3	PIT	AE3	NE
AE2	NYJ	AC2	CIN
NE2	NYG	NE1	DAL
NE4	PHI	NE3	WAS

4 SD

Home		Away	
AC4	HOU	AE4	IND
AE1	MIA	AC1	CLE
NE1	DAL	NE2	NYG
NE3	WAS	NE4	PHI

5 KC

Home		Away	
AE5	BUF	AE5	BUF
AC2	CIN	AC1	CLE
AC4	HOU	AC3	PIT
NC5	TB	NE5	STL

[1]Played at Milwaukee.

1986 NON-DIVISIONAL OPPONENTS (NFC)

NFC East
NE

1 DAL

Home		Away	
NC1	CHI	NW1	LARm
NW4	ATL	NC4	DET
AW1	LARd	AW2	DEN
AW3	SEA	AW4	SD

2 NYG

Home		Away	
NC2	GB	NW2	SF
NW3	NO	NC3	MIN
AW2	DEN	AW1	LARd
AW4	SD	AW3	SEA

3 WAS

Home		Away	
NC3	MIN	NW3	NO
NW2	SF	NC2	GB
AW1	LARd	AW2	DEN
AW3	SEA	AW4	SD

4 PHI

Home		Away	
NC4	DET	NW4	ATL
NW1	LARm	NC1	CHI
AW2	DEN	AW1	LARd
AW4	SD	AW3	SEA

5 STL

Home		Away	
NC5	TB	NC5	TB
NW1	LARm	NW2	SF
NW3	NO	NW4	ATL
AW5	KC	AE5	BUF

NFC Central
NC

1 CHI

Home		Away	
NW1	LARm	NE1	DAL
NE4	PHI	NW4	ATL
AC1	CLE	AC2	CIN
AC3	PIT	AC4	HOU

2 GB

Home		Away	
NW2	SF[1]	NE2	NYG
NE3	WAS	NW3	NO
AC2	CIN[1]	AC1	CLE
AC4	HOU	AC3	PIT

3 MIN

Home		Away	
NW3	NO	NE3	WAS
NE2	NYG	NW2	SF
AC1	CLE	AC2	CIN
AC3	PIT	AC4	HOU

4 DET

Home		Away	
NW4	ATL	NE4	PHI
NE1	DAL	NW1	LARm
AC2	CIN	AC1	CLE
AC4	HOU	AC3	PIT

5 TB

Home		Away	
NE5	STL	NE5	STL
NW2	SF	NW1	LARm
NW4	ATL	NW3	NO
AE5	BUF	AW5	KC

NFC West
NW

1 LARm

Home		Away	
NE1	DAL	NC1	CHI
NC4	DET	NE4	PHI
NC5	TB	NE5	STL
AE1	MIA	AE2	NYJ
AE3	NE	AE4	IND

2 SF

Home		Away	
NE2	NYG	NC2	GB[1]
NC3	MIN	NE3	WAS
NE5	STL	NC5	TB
AE2	NYJ	AE1	MIA
AE4	IND	AE3	NE

3 NO

Home		Away	
NE3	WAS	NC3	MIN
NC2	GB	NE2	NYG
NC5	TB	NE5	STL
AE1	MIA	AE2	NYJ
AE3	NE	AE4	IND

4 ATL

Home		Away	
NE4	PHI	NC4	DET
NC1	CHI	NE1	DAL
NE5	STL	NC5	TB
AE2	NYJ	AE1	MIA
AE4	IND	AE3	NE

[1]Played at Milwaukee.

1986 Final Standings
(To Determine 1987 Opponents)

AFC East AE	AFC Central AC	AFC West AW
1 NEW ENGLAND	1 CLEVELAND	1 DENVER
2 NY JETS	2 CINCINNATI	2 KANSAS CITY
3 MIAMI	3 PITTSBURGH	3 SEATTLE
4 BUFFALO	4 HOUSTON	4 LA RAIDERS
5 INDIANAPOLIS		5 SAN DIEGO

NFC East NE	NFC Central NC	NFC West NW
1 NY GIANTS	1 CHICAGO	1 SAN FRANCISCO
2 WASHINGTON	2 MINNESOTA	2 LA RAMS
3 DALLAS	3 DETROIT	3 ATLANTA
4 PHILADELPHIA	4 GREEN BAY	4 NEW ORLEANS
5 ST. LOUIS	5 TAMPA BAY	

1987 NON-DIVISIONAL OPPONENTS (AFC)

AFC East — AE

1 NE

Home		Away	
AC1	CLE	AW1	DEN
AW4	LARd	AC4	HOU
NE3	DAL	NE1	NYG
NE4	PHI	NE2	WAS[a]

2 NYJ

Home		Away	
AC2	CIN	AW2	KC
AW3	SEA	AC3	PIT[a]
NE3	DAL	NE1	NYG
NE4	PHI	NE2	WAS

3 MIA

Home		Away	
AC3	PIT	AW3	SEA
AW2	KC	AC2	CIN
NE1	NYG[a]	NE3	DAL
NE2	WAS	NE4	PHI

AFC Central — AC

1 CLE

Home		Away	
AW1	DEN[a]	AE1	NE
AE4	BUF	AW4	LARd
AE5	IND	AW5	SD
NW2	LARm	NW1	SF
NW3	ATL	NW4	NO

2 CIN

Home		Away	
AW2	KC	AE2	NYJ
AE3	MIA	AW3	SEA
AE5	SD	AE5	IND
NW1	SF	NW2	LARm[a]
NW4	NO	NW3	ATL

3 PIT

Home		Away	
AW3	SEA	AE3	MIA
AE2	NYJ[a]	AW2	KC
AE5	IND	AW5	SD
NW1	SF	NW2	LARm
NW4	NO	NW3	ATL

AFC West — AW

1 DEN

Home		Away	
AE1	NE	AC1	CLE[a]
AC4	HOU	AE4	BUF
NC1	CHI	NC2	MIN
NC3	DET	NC4	GB[1]

2 KC

Home		Away	
AE2	NYJ	AC2	CIN
AC3	PIT	AE3	MIA
NC2	MIN[a]	NC1	CHI
NC4	GB	NC3	DET

3 SEA[A]

Home		Away	
AE3	MIA	AC3	PIT
AC2	CIN	AE2	NYJ
NC2	MIN	NC1	CHI
NC4	GB	NC3	DET

4	BUF			4	HOU			4	LARd		
Home		Away		Home		Away		Home		Away	
AC4	HOU	AW4	LARd	AW4	LARd[a]	AE4	BUF	AE4	BUF	AC4	HOU[a]
AW1	DEN	AC1	CLE	AE1	NE	AW1	DEN	AC1	CLE	AE1	NE
NE1	NYG	NE3	DAL[a]	AW5	SD	AE5	IND	NC1	CHI	NC2	MIN
NE2	WAS	NE4	PHI	NW2	LARm	NW1	SF	NC3	DET	NC4	GB
				NW3	ATL	NW4	NO				

5	IND							5	SD[A]		
Home		Away						Home		Away	
AW5	SD	AW5	SD					AE5	IND	AE5	IND
AC2	CIN	AC1	CLE					AC1	CLE	AC2	CIN
AC4	HOU	AC3	PIT					AC3	PIT	AC4	HOU
NC5	TB	NE5	STL[a]					NE5	STL	NC5	TB

[a]Game canceled due to players' strike, including divisional game SEA at SD.
[1]Played at Milwaukee.

1987 NON-DIVISIONAL OPPONENTS (NFC)

NFC East — NE   NFC Central — NC   NFC West — NW

1	NYG			1	CHI[A]			1	SF		
Home		Away		Home		Away		Home		Away	
NW1	SF	NC1	CHI	NE1	NYG	NW1	SF	NC1	CHI	NE1	NYG
NC4	GB	NW4	NO	NW4	NO	NE4	PHI	NE4	PHI[a]	NC4	GB
AE1	NE	AE3	MIA[a]	AW2	KC	AW1	DEN	NE5	STL	NC5	TB
AE2	NYJ	AE4	BUF	AW3	SEA	AW4	LARd	AC1	CLE	AC2	CIN
								AC4	HOU	AC3	PIT

2	WAS			2	MIN			2	LARm		
Home		Away		Home		Away		Home		Away	
NW2	LARm	NC2	MIN	NE2	WAS	NW2	LARm	NC2	MIN	NE2	WAS
NC3	DET	NW3	ATL	NW3	ATL	NE3	DAL	NE3	DAL	NC3	DET
AE1	NE[a]	AE3	MIA	AW1	DEN	AW2	KC[a]	NC5	TB	NE5	STL
AE2	NYJ	AE4	BUF	AW4	LARd	AW3	SEA	AC2	CIN[a]	AC1	CLE
								AC3	PIT	AC4	HOU

3	DAL			3	DET[A]			3	ATL[A]		
Home		Away		Home		Away		Home		Away	
NW3	ATL	NC3	DET	NE3	DAL	NW3	ATL	NC3	DET	NE3	DAL
NC2	MIN	NW2	LARm	NW2	LARm	NE2	WAS	NE2	WAS	NC2	MIN
AE3	MIA	AE1	NE	AW2	KC	AW1	DEN	NE5	STL	NC5	TB
AE4	BUF[a]	AE2	NYJ	AW3	SEA	AW4	LARd	AC2	CIN	AC1	CLE
								AC3	PIT	AC4	HOU

4	PHI			4	GB[A]			4	NO[A]		
Home		Away		Home		Away		Home		Away	
NW4	NO	NC4	GB	NE4	PHI	NW4	NO	NC4	GB	NE4	PHI
NC1	CHI	NW1	SF[a]	NW1	SF	NE1	NYG	NE1	NYG	NC1	CHI
AE3	MIA	AE1	NE	AW1	DEN[1]	AW2	KC	NC5	TB	NE5	STL
AE4	BUF	AE2	NYJ	AW4	LARd	AW3	SEA	AC1	CLE	AC2	CIN
								AC4	HOU	AC3	PIT

5	STL			5	TB[a]		
Home		*Away*		*Home*		*Away*	
NC5	TB	NC5	TB	NE5	STL	NE5	STL
NW2	LARm	NW1	SF	NW1	SF	NW2	LARm
NW4	NO	NW3	ATL	NW3	ATL	NW4	NO
AE5	IND[a]	AW5	SD	AW5	SD	AE5	IND

[a]Game canceled due to players' strike, including division games for CHI, DET, GB, TB, ATL, NO: (CHI at DET, GB at TB, ATL at NO).
[1]Played at Milwaukee.

1987 GAMES CANCELED BY STRIKE:

As a result of the 24-day players' strike, the 1987 regular season was reduced from 16 games to 15. Games scheduled originally for Week 3 were canceled. Here is the original Week 3 schedule:[5]

WEEK 3
Sunday, September 27, 1987 (NBC-TV Doubleheader)
Buffalo Bills at Dallas Cowboys, 1:00 (NBC)
Chicago Bears at Detroit Lions, 1:00 (CBS)
Los Angeles Raiders at Houston Oilers, 1:00 (NBC)
Minnesota Vikings at Kansas City Chiefs, 1:00 (CBS)
New York Giants at Miami Dolphins, 1:00 (CBS)
Atlanta Falcons at New Orleans Saints, 1:00 (CBS)
Indianapolis Colts at St. Louis Cardinals, 1:00 (NBC)
Green Bay Packers at Tampa Bay Buccaneers, 1:00 (CBS)
New England Patriots at Washington Redskins, 1:00 (NBC)
Cincinnati Bengals at Los Angeles Rams, 4:00 (NBC)
New York Jets at Pittsburgh Steelers, 4:00 (NBC)
Seattle Seahawks at San Diego Chargers, 4:00 (NBC)
Philadelphia Eagles at San Francisco 49ers, 4:00 (CBS)
Monday, September 28, 1987
Denver Broncos at Cleveland Browns, 9:00 (ABC)

Games for Weeks 4 through 6 were played with replacement players, with striking players returning in Week 7.

1988–1994

American Conference	National Conference
Eastern Division	**Eastern Division**
Buffalo Bills	Dallas Cowboys
Indianapolis Colts	New York Giants
Miami Dolphins	Philadelphia Eagles
New England Patriots	Phoenix Cardinals[a]
New York Jets	Washington Redskins
Central Division	**Central Division**
Cincinnati Bengals	Chicago Bears
Cleveland Browns	Detroit Lions
Houston Oilers	Green Bay Packers
Pittsburgh Steelers	Minnesota Vikings
	Tampa Bay Buccaneers
Western Division	**Western Division**
Denver Broncos	Atlanta Falcons
Kansas City Chiefs	Los Angeles Rams
Los Angeles Raiders	New Orleans Saints
San Diego Chargers	San Francisco 49ers
Seattle Seahawks	

[a]Phoenix Cardinals (1988–1993), Arizona Cardinals (1994–)

1988–1994

Source: 1987 NFL Record & Fact Book, p. 14

The 16-game regular season schedule of any NFL team is determined by one of the following three formulas. (The reference point for figuring is the team's final division standing):[1]

A. First- through fourth-place teams in a five-team division (AFC East, AFC West, NFC East, NFC Central).
1. Home and away against its four division opponents (8 games).
2. Four games against teams from the other two divisions within the conference (4 games).

1st place: plays the other two 1st-place teams, a 2nd- and a 3rd-place team
2nd place: plays the other two 2nd-place teams, a 1st- and a 4th-place team
3rd place: plays the other two 3rd-place teams, a 1st- and a 4th-place team
4th place: plays the other two 4th-place teams, a 2nd- and a 3rd-place team

Prior Year's Finish in Division	Pairings in Non-Division Games Within Conference 1988–1994
1	1–1–2–3
2	1–2–2–4
3	1–3–3–4
4	2–3–4–4

3. One game each with the first- through fourth-place teams in a division of the other conference (4 games).
This completes the 16-game schedule.

B. First- through fourth-place teams in a four-team division (AFC Central, NFC West).
1. Home and away against its three division opponents (6 games).
2. Four games against teams from the other two divisions within the conference (4 games).

1st place: plays the other two 1st-place teams, a 2nd- and a 3rd-place team
2nd place: plays the other two 2nd-place teams, a 1st- and a 4th-place team
3rd place: plays the other two 3rd-place teams, a 1st- and a 4th-place team
4th place: plays the other two 4th-place teams, a 2nd- and a 3rd-place team

3. One game with each of the fifth-place teams in the conference (2 games).
4. One game each with the first- through fourth-place teams in a division of the other conference (4 games).
This completes the 16-game schedule.

C. The fifth-place teams in a division (AFC East, AFC West, NFC East, NFC Central).
1. Home and away against its four division opponents (8 games).
2. Home and away with the other fifth-place team in the conference (2 games).
3. One game with each team in the four-team division of the conference (4 games).
4. One game each with the fifth-place teams of the other conference (2 games).
This completes the 16-game schedule.

Comparison Intraconference Chart (1978–1994)

Prior Year's Finish in Division	Pairings in Non-Division Games Within Conference	
	1978–1987	1988–1994
1	1–1–4–4	1–1–2–3
2	2–2–3–3	1–2–2–4
3	2–2–3–3	1–3–3–4
4	1–1–4–4	2–3–4–4

1988–1994 Scheduling Formula by Position

IN A FIVE-TEAM DIVISION
(AFC EAST, AFC WEST, NFC EAST, NFC CENTRAL)

1st Place:
1. Home and away with the other four teams within the division (8 games).
2. One game each with the two other first-place teams, a second-place team and a third-place team in the conference (4 games).
3. One game each with teams 1 through 4 in a division of the other conference (4 games).

2nd Place:

1. Home and away with the other four teams within the division (8 games).
2. One game each with the two other second-place teams, a first-place team and a fourth-place team in the conference (4 games).
3. One game each with teams 1 through 4 in a division of the other conference (4 games).

3rd Place:

1. Home and away with the other four teams within the division (8 games).
2. One game each with the two other third-place teams, a first-place team and a fourth-place team in the conference (4 games).
3. One game each with teams 1 through 4 in a division of the other conference (4 games).

4th Place:

1. Home and away with the other four teams within the division (8 games).
2. One game each with the two other fourth-place teams, a second-place team and a third-place team in the conference (4 games).
3. One game each with teams 1 through 4 in a division of the other conference (4 games).

5th Place:

1. Home and away with the other four teams within the division (8 games).
2. One game each with all teams in the four-team division in the conference (4 games).
3. Home and away with the other fifth-place team in the conference (2 games).
4. One game with each of the fifth-place teams of the other conference (2 games).

IN A FOUR-TEAM DIVISION
(AFC CENTRAL, NFC WEST)

1st Place:

1. Home and away with the other three teams within the division (6 games).
2. One game each with the two other first-place teams, a second-place team and a third-place team in the conference (4 games).
3. One game with each of the fifth-place teams in the conference (2 games).
4. One game each with teams 1 through 4 in a division of the other conference (4 games).

2nd Place:

1. Home and away with the other three teams within the division (6 games).
2. One game each with the two other second-place teams, a first-place team and a fourth-place team in the conference (4 games).
3. One game with each of the fifth-place teams in the conference (2 games).
4. One game each with teams 1 through 4 in a division of the other conference (4 games).

3rd Place:

1. Home and away with the other three teams within the division (6 games).
2. One game each with the two other third-place teams, a first-place team and a fourth-place team in the conference (4 games).

3. One game with each of the fifth-place teams in the conference (2 games).
4. One game each with teams 1 through 4 in a division of the other conference (4 games).

4th Place:

1. Home and away with the other three teams within the division (6 games).
2. One game each with the two other fourth-place teams, a second-place team and a third-place team in the conference (4 games).
3. One game with each of the fifth-place teams in the conference (2 games).
4. One game each with teams 1 through 4 in a division of the other conference (4 games).

1987 Final Standings
(To Determine 1988 Opponents)

AFC East AE	AFC Central AC	AFC West AW
1 INDIANAPOLIS	1 CLEVELAND	1 DENVER
2 NEW ENGLAND	2 HOUSTON	2 SEATTLE
3 MIAMI	3 PITTSBURGH	3 SAN DIEGO
4 BUFFALO	4 CINCINNATI	4 LA RAIDERS
5 NY JETS		5 KANSAS CITY

NFC East NE	NFC Central NC	NFC West NW
1 WASHINGTON	1 CHICAGO	1 SAN FRANCISCO
2 DALLAS	2 MINNESOTA	2 NEW ORLEANS
3 ST. LOUIS[a]	3 GREEN BAY	3 LA RAMS
4 PHILADELPHIA	4 TAMPA BAY	4 ATLANTA
5 NY GIANTS	5 DETROIT	

[a] In 1988, the St. Louis Cardinals moved to Phoenix and became the Phoenix Cardinals.

1988 NON-DIVISIONAL OPPONENTS (AFC)

AFC East — AE

1	IND		
Home		**Away**	
AW1	DEN	AC1	CLE
AC2	HOU	AW3	SD
NC1	CHI	NC2	MIN
NC4	TB	NC3	GB

2	NE		
Home		**Away**	
AW2	SEA	AC2	HOU
AC4	CIN	AW1	DEN
NC1	CHI	NC2	MIN
NC4	TB	NC3	GB[1]

AFC Central — AC

1	CLE		
Home		**Away**	
AE1	IND	AW1	DEN
AW2	SEA	AE3	MIA
AE5	NYJ	AW5	KC
NE2	DAL	NE1	WAS
NE4	PHI	NE3	PHX

2	HOU		
Home		**Away**	
AE2	NE	AW2	SEA
AW4	LARd	AE1	IND
AW5	KC	AE5	NYJ
NE1	WAS	NE2	DAL
NE3	PHX	NE4	PHI

AFC West — AW

1	DEN		
Home		**Away**	
AC1	CLE	AE1	IND
AE2	NE	AC3	PIT
NW3	LARm	NW1	SF
NW4	ATL	NW2	NO

2	SEA		
Home		**Away**	
AC2	HOU	AE2	NE
AE4	BUF	AC1	CLE
NW1	SF	NW3	LARm
NW2	NO	NW4	ATL

	3	MIA			3	PIT			3	SD	
	Home		*Away*		*Home*		*Away*		*Home*		*Away*
AW3	SD	AC3	PIT	AE3	MIA	AW3	SD	AC3	PIT	AE3	MIA
AC1	CLE	AW4	LARd	AW1	DEN	AE4	BUF	AE1	IND	AC4	CIN
NC2	MIN	NC1	CHI	AW5	KC	AE5	NYJ	NW1	SF	NW3	LARm
NC3	GB	NC4	TB	NE2	DAL	NE1	WAS	NW2	NO	NW4	ATL
				NE4	PHI	NE3	PHX				

	4	BUF			4	CIN			4	LARd	
	Home		*Away*		*Home*		*Away*		*Home*		*Away*
AW4	LARd	AC4	CIN	AE4	BUF	AW4	LARd	AC4	CIN	AE4	BUF
AC3	PIT	AW2	SEA	AW3	SD	AE2	NE	AE3	MIA	AC2	HOU
NC2	MIN	NC1	CHI	AE5	NYJ	AW5	KC	NW3	LARm	NW1	SF
NC3	GB	NC4	TB	NE1	WAS	NE2	DAL	NW4	ATL	NW2	NO
				NE3	PHX	NE4	PHI				

	5	NYJ							5	KC	
	Home		*Away*						*Home*		*Away*
AW5	KC	AW5	KC					AE5	NYJ	AE5	NYJ
AC2	HOU	AC1	CLE					AC1	CLE	AC2	HOU
AC3	PIT	AC4	CIN					AC4	CIN	AC3	PIT
NE5	NYG	NC5	DET					NC5	DET	NE5	NYG

[1]Played at Milwaukee.

1988 NON-DIVISIONAL OPPONENTS (NFC)

NFC East
NE

NFC Central
NC

NFC West
NW

	1	WAS			1	CHI			1	SF	
	Home		*Away*		*Home*		*Away*		*Home*		*Away*
NC1	CHI	NW1	SF	NW1	SF	NE1	WAS	NE1	WAS	NC1	CHI
NW2	NO	NC3	GB[1]	NE2	DAL	NW3	LARm	NC2	MIN	NE3	PHX
AC1	CLE	AC2	HOU	AE3	MIA	AE1	IND	NC5	DET	NE5	NYG
AC3	PIT	AC4	CIN	AE4	BUF	AE2	NE	AW1	DEN	AW2	SEA
								AW4	LARd	AW3	SD

	2	DAL			2	MIN			2	NO	
	Home		*Away*		*Home*		*Away*		*Home*		*Away*
NC2	MIN	NW2	NO	NW2	NO	NE2	DAL	NE2	DAL	NC2	MIN
NW4	ATL	NC1	CHI	NE4	PHI	NW1	SF	NC4	TB	NE1	WAS
AC2	HOU	AC1	CLE	AE1	IND	AE3	MIA	NE5	NYG	NC5	DET
AC4	CIN	AC3	PIT	AE2	NE	AE4	BUF	AW1	DEN	AW2	SEA
								AW4	LARd	AW3	SD

	3	PHX			3	GB			3	LARm	
	Home		*Away*		*Home*		*Away*		*Home*		*Away*
NC3	GB	NW3	LARm	NW3	LARm	NE3	PHX	NE3	PHX	NC3	GB
NW1	SF	NC4	TB	NE1	WAS[1]	NW4	ATL	NC1	CHI	NE4	PHI
AC1	CLE	AC2	HOU	AE1	IND	AE3	MIA	NC5	DET	NE5	NYG
AC3	PIT	AC4	CIN	AE2	NE[1]	AE4	BUF	AW2	SEA	AW1	DEN
								AW3	SD	AW4	LARd

4	PHI			4	TB			4	ATL		
Home		*Away*		*Home*		*Away*		*Home*		*Away*	
NW4	ATL	NC4	TB	NE4	PHI	NW4	ATL	NC4	TB	NE4	PHI
NW3	LARm	NC2	MIN	NE3	PHX	NW2	NO	NC3	GB	NE2	DAL
AC2	HOU	AC1	CLE	AE3	MIA	AE1	IND	NE5	NYG	NC5	DET
AC4	CIN	AC3	PIT	AE4	BUF	AE2	NE	AW2	SEA	AW1	DEN
								AW3	SD	AW4	LARd

5	NYG			5	DET		
Home		*Away*		*Home*		*Away*	
NC5	DET	NC5	DET	NE5	NYG	NE5	NYG
NW1	SF	NW2	NO	NW2	NO	NW1	SF
NW3	LARm	NW4	ATL	NW4	ATL	NW3	LARm
AW5	KC	AE5	NYJ	AE5	NYJ	AW5	KC

¹Played at Milwaukee.

1988 Final Standings
(To Determine 1989 Opponents)

AFC East AE	AFC Central AC	AFC West AW
1 BUFFALO	1 CINCINNATI	1 SEATTLE
2 INDIANAPOLIS	2 CLEVELAND	2 DENVER
3 NEW ENGLAND	3 HOUSTON	3 LA RAIDERS
4 NY JETS	4 PITTSBURGH	4 SAN DIEGO
5 MIAMI		5 KANSAS CITY

NFC East NE	NFC Central NC	NFC West NW
1 PHILADELPHIA	1 CHICAGO	1 SAN FRANCISCO
2 NY GIANTS	2 MINNESOTA	2 LA RAMS
3 WASHINGTON	3 TAMPA BAY	3 NEW ORLEANS
4 PHOENIX	4 DETROIT	4 ATLANTA
5 DALLAS	5 GREEN BAY	

1989 NON-DIVISIONAL OPPONENTS (AFC)

AFC East AE	AFC Central AC	AFC West AW
1 BUF	1 CIN	1 SEA

1	BUF			1	CIN			1	SEA		
Home		*Away*		*Home*		*Away*		*Home*		*Away*	
AC1	CIN	AW1	SEA	AW1	SEA	AE1	BUF	AE1	BUF	AC1	CIN
AW2	DEN	AC3	HOU	AE2	IND	AW3	LARd	AC2	CLE	AE3	NE
NW2	LARm	NW1	SF	AE5	MIA	AW5	KC	NE3	WAS	NE1	PHI
NW3	NO	NW4	ATL	NC3	TB	NC1	CHI	NE4	PHX	NE2	NYG
				NC4	DET	NC2	MIN				

2	IND			2	CLE			2	DEN		
Home		*Away*		*Home*		*Away*		*Home*		*Away*	
AC2	CLE	AW2	DEN	AW2	DEN	AE2	IND	AE2	IND	AC2	CLE
AW4	SD	AC1	CIN	AE4	NYJ	AW1	SEA	AC4	PIT	AE1	BUF
NW1	SF	NW2	LARm	AW5	KC	AE5	MIA	NE1	PHI	NE3	WAS
NW4	ATL	NW3	NO	NC1	CHI	NC3	TB	NE2	NYG	NE4	PHX
				NC2	MIN	NC4	DET				

3	NE			3	HOU			3	LARd		
Home		*Away*		*Home*		*Away*		*Home*		*Away*	
AC3	HOU	AW3	LARd	AW3	LARd	AE3	NE	AE3	NE	AC3	HOU
AW1	SEA	AC4	PIT	AE1	BUF	AW4	SD	AC1	CIN	AE4	NYJ
NW2	LARm	NW1	SF[1]	AE5	MIA	AW5	KC	NE3	WAS	NE1	PHI
NW3	NO	NW4	ATL	NC3	TB	NC1	CHI	NE4	PHX	NE2	NYG
				NC4	DET	NC2	MIN				

4	NYJ			4	PIT			4	SD		
Home		*Away*		*Home*		*Away*		*Home*		*Away*	
AC4	PIT	AW4	SD	AW4	SD	AE4	NYJ	AE4	NYJ	AC4	PIT
AW3	LARd	AC2	CLE	AE3	NE	AW2	DEN	AC3	HOU	AE2	IND
NW1	SF	NW2	LARm	AW5	KC	AE5	MIA	NE1	PHI	NE3	WAS
NW4	ATL	NW3	NO	NC1	CHI	NC3	TB	NE2	NYG	NE4	PHX
				NC2	MIN	NC4	DET				

5	MIA							5	KC		
Home		*Away*						*Home*		*Away*	
AW5	KC	AW5	KC					AE5	MIA	AE5	MIA
AC2	CLE	AC1	CIN					AC1	CIN	AC2	CLE
AC4	PIT	AC3	HOU					AC3	HOU	AC4	PIT
NC5	GB	NE5	DAL					NE5	DAL	NC5	GB

[1] Game moved to Palo Alto, CA due to Bay Area Earthquake.

1989 NON-DIVISIONAL OPPONENTS (NFC)

| NFC East | | | | NFC Central | | | | NFC West | | | |
NE				NC				NW			
1	PHI			1	CHI			1	SF		
Home		*Away*		*Home*		*Away*		*Home*		*Away*	
NW1	SF	NC1	CHI	NE1	PHI	NW1	SF	NC1	CHI	NE1	PHI
NC2	MIN	NW3	NO	NW2	LARm	NE3	WAS	NE2	NYG	NC3	TB
AW1	SEA	AW2	DEN	AC1	CIN	AC2	CLE	NC5	GB	NE5	DAL
AW3	LARd	AW4	SD	AC3	HOU	AC4	PIT	AE1	BUF	AE2	IND
								AE3	NE[1]	AE4	NYJ

2	NYG			2	MIN			2	LARm		
Home		*Away*		*Home*		*Away*		*Home*		*Away*	
NC2	MIN	NW2	LARm	NW2	LARm	NE2	NYG	NE2	NYG	NC2	MIN
NC4	DET	NW1	SF	NW4	ATL	NE1	PHI	NE4	PHX	NC1	CHI
AW1	SEA	AW2	DEN	AC1	CIN	AC2	CLE	NC5	GB	NE5	DAL
AW3	LARd	AW4	SD	AC3	HOU	AC4	PIT	AE2	IND	AE1	BUF
								AE4	NYJ	AE3	NE

3	WAS			3	TB			3	NO		
Home		*Away*		*Home*		*Away*		*Home*		*Away*	
NC3	TB	NW3	NO	NW3	NO	NE3	WAS	NE3	WAS	NC3	TB
NC1	CHI	NW4	ATL	NW1	SF	NE4	PHX	NE1	PHI	NC4	DET
AW2	DEN	AW1	SEA	AC2	CLE	AC1	CIN	NE5	DAL	NC5	GB
AW4	SD	AW3	LARd	AC4	PIT	AC3	HOU	AE2	IND	AE1	BUF
								AE4	NYJ	AE3	NE

4	PHX			4	DET			4	ATL		
Home		*Away*		*Home*		*Away*		*Home*		*Away*	
NW4	ATL	NC4	DET	NE4	PHX	NW4	ATL	NC4	DET	NE4	PHX
NC3	TB	NW2	LARm	NW3	NO	NE2	NYG	NE3	WAS	NC2	MIN
AW2	DEN	AW1	SEA	AC2	CLE	AC1	CIN	NE5	DAL	NC5	GB[2]
AW4	SD	AW3	LARd	AC4	PIT	AC3	HOU	AE1	BUF	AE2	IND
								AE3	NE	AE4	NYJ

5	DAL			5	GB		
Home		*Away*		*Home*		*Away*	
NC5	GB	NC5	GB	NE5	DAL	NE5	DAL
NW1	SF	NW3	NO	NW3	NO	NW1	SF
NW2	LARm	NW4	ATL	NW4	ATL[2]	NW2	LARm
AE5	MIA	AW5	KC	AW5	KC	AE5	MIA

[1] Game moved to Palo Alto, CA due to Bay Area Earthquake.
[2] Played at Milwaukee.

1989 Final Standings
(To Determine 1990 Opponents)

AFC East
AE
1 BUFFALO
2 INDIANAPOLIS
3 MIAMI
4 NEW ENGLAND
5 NY JETS

AFC Central
AC
1 CLEVELAND
2 HOUSTON
3 PITTSBURGH
4 CINCINNATI

AFC West
AW
1 DENVER
2 KANSAS CITY
3 LA RAIDERS
4 SEATTLE
5 SAN DIEGO

NFC East
NE
1 NY GIANTS
2 PHILADELPHIA
3 WASHINGTON
4 PHOENIX
5 DALLAS

NFC Central
NC
1 MINNESOTA
2 GREEN BAY
3 DETROIT
4 CHICAGO
5 TAMPA BAY

NFC West
NW
1 SAN FRANCISCO
2 LA RAMS
3 NEW ORLEANS
4 ATLANTA

1990 NON-DIVISIONAL OPPONENTS (AFC)

AFC East
AE

1	BUF		
Home		*Away*	
AW1	DEN	AC1	CLE
AW3	LARd	AC2	HOU
NE2	PHI	NE1	NYG
NE4	PHX	NE3	WAS

2	IND		
Home		*Away*	
AW2	KC	AC2	HOU
AW1	DEN	AC4	CIN
NE1	NYG	NE2	PHI
NE3	WAS	NE4	PHX

3	MIA		
Home		*Away*	
AW3	LARd	AC3	PIT
AW4	SEA	AC1	CLE
NE2	PHI	NE1	NYG
NE4	PHX	NE3	WAS

4	NE		
Home		*Away*	
AW4	SEA	AC4	CIN
AW2	KC	AC3	PIT
NE1	NYG	NE2	PHI
NE3	WAS	NE4	PHX

5	NYJ		
Home		*Away*	
AW5	SD	AW5	SD
AC1	CLE	AC2	HOU
AC3	PIT	AC4	CIN
NE5	DAL	NC5	TB

AFC Central
AC

1	CLE		
Home		*Away*	
AE1	BUF	AW1	DEN
AE3	MIA	AW2	KC
AW5	SD	AE5	NYJ
NW2	LARm	NW1	SF
NW4	ATL	NW3	NO

2	HOU		
Home		*Away*	
AE2	IND	AW2	KC
AE1	BUF	AW4	SEA
AE5	NYJ	AW5	SD
NW1	SF	NW2	LARm
NW3	NO	NW4	ATL

3	PIT		
Home		*Away*	
AE3	MIA	AW3	LARd
AE4	NE	AW1	DEN
AW5	SD	AE5	NYJ
NW2	LARm	NW1	SF
NW4	ATL	NW3	NO

4	CIN		
Home		*Away*	
AE4	NE	AW4	SEA
AE2	IND	AW3	LARd
AE5	NYJ	AW5	SD
NW1	SF	NW2	LARm
NW3	NO	NW4	ATL

AFC West
AW

1	DEN		
Home		*Away*	
AC1	CLE	AE1	BUF
AC3	PIT	AE2	IND
NC2	GB	NC1	MIN
NC4	CHI	NC3	DET

2	KC		
Home		*Away*	
AC2	HOU	AE2	IND
AC1	CLE	AE4	NE
NC1	MIN	NC2	GB
NC3	DET	NC4	CHI

3	LARd		
Home		*Away*	
AC3	PIT	AE3	MIA
AC4	CIN	AE1	BUF
NC2	GB	NC1	MIN
NC4	CHI	NC3	DET

4	SEA		
Home		*Away*	
AC4	CIN	AE4	NE
AC2	HOU	AE3	MIA
NC1	MIN	NC2	GB[1]
NC3	DET	NC4	CHI

5	SD		
Home		*Away*	
AE5	NYJ	AE5	NYJ
AC2	HOU	AC1	CLE
AC4	CIN	AC3	PIT
NC5	TB	NE5	DAL

[1] Played at Milwaukee.

1990 NON-DIVISIONAL OPPONENTS (NFC)

NFC East — NE

1 NYG

Home		Away	
NC1	MIN	NW1	SF
NC3	DET	NW2	LARm
AE1	BUF	AE2	IND
AE3	MIA	AE4	NE

2 PHI

Home		Away	
NC2	GB	NW2	LARm
NC1	MIN	NW4	ATL
AE2	IND	AE1	BUF
AE4	NE	AE3	MIA

3 WAS

Home		Away	
NW3	NO	NC3	DET
NC4	CHI	NW1	SF
AE1	BUF	AE2	IND
AE3	MIA	AE4	NE

4 PHX

Home		Away	
NC4	CHI	NW4	ATL
NC2	GB	NW3	NO
AE2	IND	AE1	BUF
AE4	NE	AE3	MIA

5 DAL

Home		Away	
NC5	TB	NC5	TB
NW1	SF	NW2	LARm
NW3	NO	NW4	ATL
AW5	SD	AE5	NYJ

NFC Central — NC

1 MIN

Home		Away	
NW1	SF	NE1	NYG
NW3	NO	NE2	PHI
AW1	DEN	AW2	KC
AW3	LARd	AW4	SEA

2 GB

Home		Away	
NW2	LARm	NE2	PHI
NW1	SF	NE4	PHX
AW2	KC	AW1	DEN
AW4	SEA[1]	AW3	LARd

3 DET

Home		Away	
NE3	WAS	NW3	NO
NW4	ATL	NE1	NYG
AW1	DEN	AW2	KC
AW3	LARd	AW4	SEA

4 CHI

Home		Away	
NW4	ATL	NE4	PHX
NW2	LARm	NE3	WAS
AW2	KC	AW1	DEN
AW4	SEA	AW3	LARd

5 TB

Home		Away	
NE5	DAL	NE5	DAL
NW2	LARm	NW1	SF
NW4	ATL	NW3	NO
AE5	NYJ	AW5	SD

NFC West — NW

1 SF

Home		Away	
NE1	NYG	NC1	MIN
NE3	WAS	NC2	GB
NC5	TB	NE5	DAL
AC1	CLE	AC2	HOU
AC3	PIT	AC4	CIN

2 LARm

Home		Away	
NE2	PHI	NC2	GB
NE1	NYG	NC4	CHI
NE5	DAL	NC5	TB
AC2	HOU	AC1	CLE
AC4	CIN	AC3	PIT

3 NO

Home		Away	
NC3	DET	NE3	WAS
NE4	PHX	NC1	MIN
NC5	TB	NE5	DAL
AC1	CLE	AC2	HOU
AC3	PIT	AC4	CIN

4 ATL

Home		Away	
NE4	PHX	NC4	CHI
NE2	PHI	NC3	DET
NE5	DAL	NC5	TB
AC2	HOU	AC1	CLE
AC4	CIN	AC3	PIT

[1]Played at Milwaukee.

1990 Final Standings
(To Determine 1991 Opponents)

AFC East AE	AFC Central AC	AFC West AW
1 BUFFALO	1 CINCINNATI	1 LA RAIDERS
2 MIAMI	2 HOUSTON	2 KANSAS CITY
3 INDIANAPOLIS	3 PITTSBURGH	3 SEATTLE
4 NY JETS	4 CLEVELAND	4 SAN DIEGO
5 NEW ENGLAND		5 DENVER

NFC East NE	NFC Central NC	NFC West NW
1 NY GIANTS	1 CHICAGO	1 SAN FRANCISCO
2 PHILADELPHIA	2 TAMPA BAY	2 NEW ORLEANS
3 WASHINGTON	3 DETROIT	3 LA RAMS
4 DALLAS	4 GREEN BAY	4 ATLANTA
5 PHOENIX	5 MINNESOTA	

1991 NON-DIVISIONAL OPPONENTS (AFC)

AFC East — AE

1 BUF

Home		Away	
AC1	CIN	AW1	LARd
AC3	PIT	AW2	KC
NC1	CHI	NC2	TB
NC3	DET	NC4	GB[1]

2 MIA

Home		Away	
AC2	HOU	AW2	KC
AC1	CIN	AW4	SD
NC2	TB	NC1	CHI
NC4	GB	NC3	DET

3 IND

Home		Away	
AC3	PIT	AW3	SEA
AC4	CLE	AW1	LARd
NC1	CHI	NC2	TB
NC3	DET	NC4	GB[1]

AFC Central — AC

1 CIN

Home		Away	
AW1	LARd	AE1	BUF
AW3	SEA	AE2	MIA
AE5	NE	AW5	DEN
NE1	NYG	NE2	PHI
NE3	WAS	NE4	DAL

2 HOU

Home		Away	
AW2	KC	AE2	MIA
AW1	LARd	AE4	NYJ
AW5	DEN	AE5	NE
NE2	PHI	NE1	NYG
NE4	DAL	NE3	WAS

3 PIT

Home		Away	
AW3	SEA	AE3	IND
AW4	SD	AE1	BUF
AE5	NE	AW5	DEN
NE1	NYG	NE2	PHI
NE3	WAS	NE4	DAL

AFC West — AW

1 LARd

Home		Away	
AE1	BUF	AC1	CIN
AE3	IND	AC2	HOU
NW1	SF	NW2	NO
NW3	LARm	NW4	ATL

2 KC

Home		Away	
AE2	MIA	AC2	HOU
AE1	BUF	AC4	CLE
NW2	NO	NW1	SF
NW4	ATL	NW3	LARm

3 SEA

Home		Away	
AE3	IND	AC3	PIT
AE4	NYJ	AC1	CIN
NW1	SF	NW2	NO
NW3	LARm	NW4	ATL

4	NYJ			4	CLE			4	SD		
Home		*Away*		*Home*		*Away*		*Home*		*Away*	
AW4	SD	AC4	CLE	AE4	NYJ	AW4	SD	AC4	CLE	AE4	NYJ
AC2	HOU	AW3	SEA	AW2	KC	AE3	IND	AE2	MIA	AC3	PIT
NC2	TB	NC1	CHI	AW5	DEN	AE5	NE	NW2	NO	NW1	SF
NC4	GB	NC3	DET	NE2	PHI	NE1	NYG	NW4	ATL	NW3	LARm
				NE4	DAL	NE3	WAS				

5	NE							5	DEN		
Home		*Away*						*Home*		*Away*	
AW5	DEN	AW5	DEN					AE5	NE	AE5	NE
AC2	HOU	AC1	CIN					AC1	CIN	AC2	HOU
AC4	CLE	AC3	PIT					AC3	PIT	AC4	CLE
NC5	MIN	NE5	PHX					NE5	PHX	NC5	MIN

[1] Played at Milwaukee.

1991 NON-DIVISIONAL OPPONENTS (NFC)

NFC East NFC Central NFC West
NE NC NW

1	NYG			1	CHI			1	SF		
Home		*Away*		*Home*		*Away*		*Home*		*Away*	
NW1	SF	NC1	CHI	NE1	NYG	NW1	SF	NC1	CHI	NE1	NYG
NW3	LARm	NC2	TB	NE3	WAS	NW2	NO	NC3	DET	NE2	PHI
AC2	HOU	AC1	CIN	AE2	MIA	AE1	BUF	NE5	PHX	NC5	MIN
AC4	CLE	AC3	PIT	AE4	NYJ	AE3	IND	AW2	KC	AW1	LARd
								AW4	SD	AW3	SEA

2	PHI			2	TB			2	NO		
Home		*Away*		*Home*		*Away*		*Home*		*Away*	
NW2	NO	NC2	TB	NE2	PHI	NW2	NO	NC2	TB	NE2	PHI
NW1	SF	NC4	GB	NE1	NYG	NW4	ATL	NC1	CHI	NE4	DAL
AC1	CIN	AC2	HOU	AE1	BUF	AE2	MIA	NC5	MIN	NE5	PHX
AC3	PIT	AC4	CLE	AE3	IND	AE4	NYJ	AW1	LARd	AW2	KC
								AW3	SEA	AW4	SD

3	WAS			3	DET			3	LARm		
Home		*Away*		*Home*		*Away*		*Home*		*Away*	
NC3	DET	NW3	LARm	NW3	LARm	NE3	WAS	NE3	WAS	NC3	DET
NW4	ATL	NC1	CHI	NE4	DAL	NW1	SF	NC4	GB	NE1	NYG
AC2	HOU	AC1	CIN	AE2	MIA	AE1	BUF	NE5	PHX	NC5	MIN
AC4	CLE	AC3	PIT	AE4	NYJ	AE3	IND	AW2	KC	AW1	LARd
								AW4	SD	AW3	SEA

4	DAL			4	GB			4	ATL		
Home		*Away*		*Home*		*Away*		*Home*		*Away*	
NW4	ATL	NC4	GB[1]	NE4	DAL[1]	NW4	ATL	NC4	GB	NE4	DAL
NW2	NO	NC3	DET	NE2	PHI	NW3	LARm	NC2	TB	NE3	WAS
AC1	CIN	AC2	HOU	AE1	BUF[1]	AE2	MIA	NC5	MIN	NE5	PHX
AC3	PIT	AC4	CLE	AE3	IND[1]	AE4	NYJ	AW1	LARd	AW2	KC
								AW3	SEA	AW4	SD

5	PHX			5	MIN		
Home		*Away*		*Home*		*Away*	
NC5	MIN	NC5	MIN	NE5	PHX	NE5	PHX
NW2	NO	NW1	SF	NW1	SF	NW2	NO
NW4	ATL	NW3	LARm	NW3	LARm	NW4	ATL
AE5	NE	AW5	DEN	AW5	DEN	AE5	NE

[1]Played at Milwaukee.

1991 Final Standings
(To Determine 1992 Opponents)

AFC East AE	AFC Central AC	AFC West AW
1 BUFFALO	1 HOUSTON	1 DENVER
2 NY JETS	2 PITTSBURGH	2 KANSAS CITY
3 MIAMI	3 CLEVELAND	3 LA RAIDERS
4 NEW ENGLAND	4 CINCINNATI	4 SEATTLE
5 INDIANAPOLIS		5 SAN DIEGO

NFC East NE	NFC Central NC	NFC West NW
1 WASHINGTON	1 DETROIT	1 NEW ORLEANS
2 DALLAS	2 CHICAGO	2 ATLANTA
3 PHILADELPHIA	3 MINNESOTA	3 SAN FRANCISCO
4 NY GIANTS	4 GREEN BAY	4 LA RAMS
5 PHOENIX	5 TAMPA BAY	

1992 NON-DIVISIONAL OPPONENTS (AFC)

AFC East — AE

1	BUF			2	NYJ		
Home		*Away*		*Home*		*Away*	
AW1	DEN	AC1	HOU	AW2	KC	AC2	PIT
AC2	PIT	AW3	LARd	AC4	CIN	AW1	DEN
NW2	ATL	NW1	NO	NW1	NO	NW2	ATL
NW4	LARm	NW3	SF	NW3	SF	NW4	LARm

AFC Central — AC

1	HOU			2	PIT		
Home		*Away*		*Home*		*Away*	
AE1	BUF	AW1	DEN	AE2	NYJ	AW2	KC
AW2	KC	AE3	MIA	AW4	SEA	AE1	BUF
AW5	SD	AE5	IND	AE5	IND	AW5	SD
NC2	CHI	NC1	DET	NC1	DET	NC2	CHI
NC4	GB	NC3	MIN	NC3	MIN	NC4	GB

AFC West — AW

1	DEN			2	KC		
Home		*Away*		*Home*		*Away*	
AC1	HOU	AE1	BUF	AC2	PIT	AE2	NYJ
AE2	NYJ	AC3	CLE	AE4	NE	AC1	HOU
NE2	DAL	NE1	WAS	NE1	WAS	NE2	DAL
NE4	NYG	NE3	PHI	NE3	PHI	NE4	NYG

3	MIA			3	CLE			3	LARd		
Home		*Away*		*Home*		*Away*		*Home*		*Away*	
AW3	LARd	AC3	CLE	AE3	MIA	AW3	LARd	AC3	CLE	AE3	MIA
AC1	HOU	AW4	SEA	AW1	DEN	AE4	NE	AE1	BUF	AC4	CIN
NW2	ATL	NW1	NO	AW5	SD	AE5	IND	NE2	DAL	NE1	WAS
NW4	LARm	NW3	SF	NC2	CHI	NC1	DET	NE4	NYG	NE3	PHI
				NC4	GB	NC3	MIN				

4	NE			4	CIN			4	SEA		
Home		*Away*		*Home*		*Away*		*Home*		*Away*	
AW4	SEA	AC4	CIN	AE4	NE	AW4	SEA	AC4	CIN	AE4	NE
AC3	CLE	AW2	KC	AW3	LARd	AE2	NYJ	AE3	MIA	AC2	PIT
NW1	NO	NW2	ATL	AE5	IND	AW5	SD	NE1	WAS	NE2	DAL
NW3	SF	NW4	LARm	NC1	DET	NC2	CHI	NE3	PHI	NE4	NYG
				NC3	MIN	NC4	GB				

5	IND							5	SD		
Home		*Away*						*Home*		*Away*	
AW5	SD	AW5	SD					AE5	IND	AE5	IND
AC1	HOU	AC2	PIT					AC2	PIT	AC1	HOU
AC3	CLE	AC4	CIN					AC4	CIN	AC3	CLE
NE5	PHX	NC5	TB					NC5	TB	NE5	PHX

1992 NON-DIVISIONAL OPPONENTS (NFC)

NFC East
NE

NFC Central
NC

NFC West
NW

1	WAS			1	DET			1	NO		
Home		*Away*		*Home*		*Away*		*Home*		*Away*	
NC1	DET	NW1	NO	NW1	NO	NE1	WAS	NE1	WAS	NC1	DET
NW2	ATL	NC3	MIN	NE2	DAL	NW3	SF	NC2	CHI	NE3	PHI
AW1	DEN	AW2	KC	AC1	HOU	AC2	PIT	NC5	TB	NE5	PHX
AW3	LARd	AW4	SEA	AC3	CLE	AC4	CIN	AE1	BUF	AE2	NYJ
								AE3	MIA	AE4	NE

2	DAL			2	CHI			2	ATL		
Home		*Away*		*Home*		*Away*		*Home*		*Away*	
NC2	CHI	NW2	ATL	NW2	ATL	NE2	DAL	NE2	DAL	NC2	CHI
NW4	LARm	NC1	DET	NE4	NYG	NW1	NO	NC4	GB	NE1	WAS
AW2	KC	AW1	DEN	AC2	PIT	AC1	HOU	NE5	PHX	NC5	TB
AW4	SEA	AW3	LARd	AC4	CIN	AC3	CLE	AE2	NYJ	AE1	BUF
								AE4	NE	AE3	MIA

3	PHI			3	MIN			3	SF		
Home		*Away*		*Home*		*Away*		*Home*		*Away*	
NC3	MIN	NW3	SF	NW3	SF	NE3	PHI	NE3	PHI	NC3	MIN
NW1	NO	NC4	GB[1]	NE1	WAS	NW4	LARm	NC1	DET	NE4	NYG
AW1	DEN	AW2	KC	AC1	HOU	AC2	PIT	NC5	TB	NE5	PHX
AW3	LARd	AW4	SEA	AC3	CLE	AC4	CIN	AE1	BUF	AE2	NYJ
								AE3	MIA	AE4	NE

4	NYG			4	GB			4	LARm		
Home		*Away*		*Home*		*Away*		*Home*		*Away*	
NC4	GB	NW4	LARm	NW4	LARm	NE4	NYG	NE4	NYG	NC4	GB
NW3	SF	NC2	CHI	NE3	PHI[1]	NW2	ATL	NC3	MIN	NE2	DAL
AW2	KC	AW1	DEN	AC2	PIT	AC1	HOU	NE5	PHX	NC5	TB
AW4	SEA	AW3	LARd	AC4	CIN	AC3	CLE	AE2	NYJ	AE1	BUF
								AE4	NE	AE3	MIA

5	PHX			5	TB		
Home		*Away*		*Home*		*Away*	
NC5	TB	NC5	TB	NE5	PHX	NE5	PHX
NW1	NO	NW2	ATL	NW2	ATL	NW1	NO
NW3	SF	NW4	LARm	NW4	LARm	NW3	SF
AW5	SD	AE5	IND	AE5	IND	AW5	SD

[1]Played at Milwaukee.

1992 Final Standings
(To Determine 1993 Opponents)

AFC East AE	AFC Central AC	AFC West AW
1 MIAMI	1 PITTSBURGH	1 SAN DIEGO
2 BUFFALO	2 HOUSTON	2 KANSAS CITY
3 INDIANAPOLIS	3 CLEVELAND	3 DENVER
4 NY JETS	4 CINCINNATI	4 LA RAIDERS
5 NEW ENGLAND		5 SEATTLE

NFC East NE	NFC Central NC	NFC West NW
1 DALLAS	1 MINNESOTA	1 SAN FRANCISCO
2 PHILADELPHIA	2 GREEN BAY	2 NEW ORLEANS
3 WASHINGTON	3 TAMPA BAY	3 ATLANTA
4 NY GIANTS	4 CHICAGO	4 LA RAMS
5 PHOENIX	5 DETROIT	

1993 NON-DIVISIONAL OPPONENTS (AFC)

AFC East AE				AFC Central AC				AFC West AW			
1	MIA			1	PIT			1	SD		
Home		*Away*		*Home*		*Away*		*Home*		*Away*	
AC1	PIT	AW1	SD	AW1	SD	AE1	MIA	AE1	MIA	AC1	PIT
AW2	KC	AC3	CLE	AE2	BUF	AW3	DEN	AC2	HOU	AE3	IND
NE3	WAS	NE1	DAL	AE5	NE	AW5	SEA	NC2	GB	NC1	MIN
NE4	NYG	NE2	PHI	NW1	SF	NW3	ATL	NC4	CHI	NC3	TB
				NW2	NO	NW4	LARm				

2	BUF			2	HOU			2	KC		
Home		*Away*		*Home*		*Away*		*Home*		*Away*	
AC2	HOU	AW2	KC	AW2	KC	AE2	BUF	AE2	BUF	AC2	HOU
AW4	LARd	AC1	PIT	AE4	NYJ	AW1	SD	AC4	CIN	AE1	MIA
NE3	WAS	NE1	DAL	AW5	SEA	AE5	NE	NC2	GB	NC1	MIN
NE4	NYG	NE2	PHI	NW3	ATL	NW1	SF	NC4	CHI	NC3	TB
				NW4	LARm	NW2	NO				

3	IND			3	CLE			3	DEN		
Home		*Away*		*Home*		*Away*		*Home*		*Away*	
AC3	CLE	AW3	DEN	AW3	DEN	AE3	IND	AE3	IND	AC3	CLE
AW1	SD	AC4	CIN	AE1	MIA	AW4	LARd	AC1	PIT	AE4	NYJ
NE1	DAL	NE3	WAS	AE5	NE	AW5	SEA	NC1	MIN	NC2	GB
NE2	PHI	NE4	NYG	NW1	SF	NW3	ATL	NC3	TB	NC4	CHI
				NW2	NO	NW4	LARm				

4	NYJ			4	CIN			4	LARd		
Home		*Away*		*Home*		*Away*		*Home*		*Away*	
AC4	CIN	AW4	LARd	AW4	LARd	AE4	NYJ	AE4	NYJ	AC4	CIN
AW3	DEN	AC2	HOU	AE3	IND	AW2	KC	AC3	CLE	AE2	BUF
NE1	DAL	NE3	WAS	AW5	SEA	AE5	NE	NC1	MIN	NC2	GB
NE2	PHI	NE4	NYG	NW3	ATL	NW1	SF	NC3	TB	NC4	CHI
				NW4	LARm	NW2	NO				

5	NE							5	SEA		
Home		*Away*						*Home*		*Away*	
AW5	SEA	AW5	SEA					AE5	NE	AE5	NE
AC2	HOU	AC1	PIT					AC1	PIT	AC2	HOU
AC4	CIN	AC3	CLE					AC3	CLE	AC4	CIN
NC5	DET	NE5	PHX					NE5	PHX	NC5	DET

1993 NON-DIVISIONAL OPPONENTS (NFC)

NFC East
NE

NFC Central
NC

NFC West
NW

1	DAL			1	MIN			1	SF		
Home		*Away*		*Home*		*Away*		*Home*		*Away*	
NW1	SF	NC1	MIN	NE1	DAL	NW1	SF	NC1	MIN	NE1	DAL
NC2	GB	NW3	ATL	NW2	NO	NE3	WAS	NE2	PHI	NC3	TB
AE1	MIA	AE3	IND	AW1	SD	AW3	DEN	NE5	PHX	NC5	DET
AE2	BUF	AE4	NYJ	AW2	KC	AW4	LARd	AC2	HOU	AC1	PIT
								AC4	CIN	AC3	CLE

2	PHI			2	GB			2	NO		
Home		*Away*		*Home*		*Away*		*Home*		*Away*	
NW2	NO	NC2	GB	NE2	PHI	NW2	NO	NC2	GB	NE2	PHI
NC4	CHI	NW1	SF	NW4	LARm[1]	NE1	DAL	NE4	NYG	NC1	MIN
AE1	MIA	AE3	IND	AW3	DEN	AW1	SD	NC5	DET	NE5	PHX
AE2	BUF	AE4	NYJ	AW4	LARd	AW2	KC	AC2	HOU	AC1	PIT
								AC4	CIN	AC3	CLE

3	WAS			3	TB			3	ATL		
Home		*Away*		*Home*		*Away*		*Home*		*Away*	
NW3	ATL	NC3	TB	NE3	WAS	NW3	ATL	NC3	TB	NE3	WAS
NC1	MIN	NW4	LARm	NW1	SF	NE4	NYG	NE1	DAL	NC4	CHI
AE3	IND	AE1	MIA	AW1	SD	AW3	DEN	NE5	PHX	NC5	DET
AE4	NYJ	AE2	BUF	AW2	KC	AW4	LARd	AC1	PIT	AC2	HOU
								AC3	CLE	AC4	CIN

4	NYG			4	CHI			4	LARm		
Home		*Away*		*Home*		*Away*		*Home*		*Away*	
NW4	LARm	NC4	CHI	NE4	NYG	NW4	LARm	NC4	CHI	NE4	NYG
NC3	TB	NW2	NO	NW3	ATL	NE2	PHI	NE3	WAS	NC2	GB[1]
AE3	IND	AE1	MIA	AW3	DEN	AW1	SD	NC5	DET	NE5	PHX
AE4	NYJ	AE2	BUF	AW4	LARd	AW2	KC	AC1	PIT	AC2	HOU
								AC3	CLE	AC4	CIN

5	PHX			5	DET		
Home		*Away*		*Home*		*Away*	
NC5	DET	NC5	DET	NE5	PHX	NE5	PHX
NW2	NO	NW1	SF	NW1	SF	NW2	NO
NW4	LARm	NW3	ATL	NW3	ATL	NW4	LARm
AE5	NE	AW5	SEA	AW5	SEA	AE5	NE

[1]Played at Milwaukee.

1993 Final Standings
(To Determine 1994 Opponents)

AFC East
AE
1 BUFFALO
2 MIAMI
3 NY JETS
4 NEW ENGLAND
5 INDIANAPOLIS

AFC Central
AC
1 HOUSTON
2 PITTSBURGH
3 CLEVELAND
4 CINCINNATI

AFC West
AW
1 KANSAS CITY
2 LA RAIDERS
3 DENVER
4 SAN DIEGO
5 SEATTLE

NFC East
NE
1 DALLAS
2 NY GIANTS
3 PHILADELPHIA
4 PHOENIX[a]
5 WASHINGTON

NFC Central
NC
1 DETROIT
2 MINNESOTA
3 GREEN BAY
4 CHICAGO
5 TAMPA BAY

NFC West
NW
1 SAN FRANCISCO
2 NEW ORLEANS
3 ATLANTA
4 LA RAMS

[a]In 1994, Phoenix Cardinals changed name to Arizona Cardinals.

1994 NON-DIVISIONAL OPPONENTS (AFC)

AFC East — AE

1 BUF

Home		Away	
AW1	KC	AC1	HOU
AW3	DEN	AC2	PIT
NC2	MIN	NC1	DET
NC3	GB	NC4	CHI

2 MIA

Home		Away	
AW2	LARd	AC2	PIT
AW1	KC	AC4	CIN
NC1	DET	NC2	MIN
NC4	CHI	NC3	GB[1]

3 NYJ

Home		Away	
AW3	DEN	AC3	CLE
AW4	SD	AC1	HOU
NC1	DET	NC2	MIN
NC4	CHI	NC3	GB

4 NE

Home		Away	
AW4	SD	AC4	CIN
AW2	LARd	AC3	CLE
NC2	MIN	NC1	DET
NC3	GB	NC4	CHI

5 IND

Home		Away	
AW5	SEA	AW5	SEA
AC1	HOU	AC2	PIT
AC3	CLE	AC4	CIN
NE5	WAS	NC5	TB

AFC Central — AC

1 HOU

Home		Away	
AE1	BUF	AW1	KC
AE3	NYJ	AW2	LARd
AW5	SEA	AE5	IND
NE2	NYG	NE1	DAL
NE4	ARI	NE3	PHI

2 PIT

Home		Away	
AE2	MIA	AW2	LARd
AE1	BUF	AW4	SD
AE5	IND	AW5	SEA
NE1	DAL	NE2	NYG
NE3	PHI	NE4	ARI

3 CLE

Home		Away	
AE3	NYJ	AW3	DEN
AE4	NE	AW1	KC
AW5	SEA	AE5	IND
NE2	NYG	NE1	DAL
NE4	ARI	NE3	PHI

4 CIN

Home		Away	
AE4	NE	AW4	SD
AE2	MIA	AW3	DEN
AE5	IND	AW5	SEA
NE1	DAL	NE2	NYG
NE3	PHI	NE4	ARI

AFC West — AW

1 KC

Home		Away	
AC1	HOU	AE1	BUF
AC3	CLE	AE2	MIA
NW1	SF	NW2	NO
NW4	LARm	NW3	ATL

2 LARd

Home		Away	
AC2	PIT	AE2	MIA
AC1	HOU	AE4	NE
NW2	NO	NW1	SF
NW3	ATL	NW4	LARm

3 DEN

Home		Away	
AC3	CLE	AE3	NYJ
AC4	CIN	AE1	BUF
NW2	NO	NW1	SF
NW3	ATL	NW4	LARm

4 SD

Home		Away	
AC4	CIN	AE4	NE
AC2	PIT	AE3	NYJ
NW1	SF	NW2	NO
NW4	LARm	NW3	ATL

5 SEA

Home		Away	
AE5	IND	AE5	IND
AC2	PIT	AC1	HOU
AC4	CIN	AC3	CLE
NC5	TB	NE5	WAS

[1]Played at Milwaukee.

1994 NON-DIVISIONAL OPPONENTS (NFC)

NFC East
NE

1   DAL

Home		Away	
NC1	DET	NW1	SF
NC3	GB	NW2	NO
AC1	HOU	AC2	PIT
AC3	CLE	AC4	CIN

2   NYG

Home		Away	
NC2	MIN	NW2	NO
NC1	DET	NW4	LARm
AC2	PIT	AC1	HOU
AC4	CIN	AC3	CLE

3   PHI

Home		Away	
NC3	GB	NW3	ATL
NC4	CHI	NW1	SF
AC1	HOU	AC2	PIT
AC3	CLE	AC4	CIN

4   ARI

Home		Away	
NC4	CHI	NW4	LARm
NC2	MIN	NW3	ATL
AC2	PIT	AC1	HOU
AC4	CIN	AC3	CLE

5   WAS

Home		Away	
NC5	TB	NC5	TB
NW1	SF	NW2	NO
NW3	ATL	NW4	LARm
AW5	SEA	AE5	IND

NFC Central
NC

1   DET

Home		Away	
NW1	SF	NE1	DAL
NW3	ATL	NE2	NYG
AE1	BUF	AE2	MIA
AE4	NE	AE3	NYJ

2   MIN

Home		Away	
NW2	NO	NE2	NYG
NW1	SF	NE4	ARI
AE2	MIA	AE1	BUF
AE3	NYJ	AE4	NE

3   GB

Home		Away	
NW3	ATL[1]	NE3	PHI
NW4	LARm	NE1	DAL
AE2	MIA[1]	AE1	BUF
AE3	NYJ	AE4	NE

4   CHI

Home		Away	
NW4	LARm	NE4	ARI
NW2	NO	NE3	PHI
AE1	BUF	AE2	MIA
AE4	NE	AE3	NYJ

5   TB

Home		Away	
NE5	WAS	NE5	WAS
NW2	NO	NW1	SF
NW4	LARm	NW3	ATL
AE5	IND	AW5	SEA

NFC West
NW

1   SF

Home		Away	
NE1	DAL	NC1	DET
NE3	PHI	NC2	MIN
NC5	TB	NE5	WAS
AW2	LARd	AW1	KC
AW3	DEN	AW4	SD

2   NO

Home		Away	
NE2	NYG	NC2	MIN
NE1	DAL	NC4	CHI
NE5	WAS	NC5	TB
AW1	KC	AW2	LARd
AW4	SD	AW3	DEN

3   ATL

Home		Away	
NE3	PHI	NC3	GB[1]
NE4	ARI	NC1	DET
NC5	TB	NE5	WAS
AW1	KC	AW2	LARd
AW4	SD	AW3	DEN

4   LARm

Home		Away	
NE4	ARI	NC4	CHI
NE2	NYG	NC3	GB
NE5	WAS	NC5	TB
AW2	LARd	AW1	KC
AW3	DEN	AW4	SD

[1]Played at Milwaukee.

1995–1998

1995 ALIGNMENT

AMERICAN CONFERENCE	NATIONAL CONFERENCE
Eastern Division	**Eastern Division**
Buffalo Bills	Arizona Cardinals
Indianapolis Colts	Dallas Cowboys
Miami Dolphins	New York Giants
New England Patriots	Philadelphia Eagles
New York Jets	Washington Redskins
Central Division	**Central Division**
Cincinnati Bengals	Chicago Bears
Cleveland Browns	Detroit Lions
Houston Oilers	Green Bay Packers
Jacksonville Jaguars	Minnesota Vikings
Pittsburgh Steelers	Tampa Bay Buccaneers
Western Division	**Western Division**
Denver Broncos	Atlanta Falcons
Kansas City Chiefs	Carolina Panthers
Oakland Raiders	New Orleans Saints
San Diego Chargers	St. Louis Rams
Seattle Seahawks	San Francisco 49ers

1996–1998 ALIGNMENT

AMERICAN CONFERENCE	NATIONAL CONFERENCE
Eastern Division	**Eastern Division**
Buffalo Bills	Arizona Cardinals
Indianapolis Colts	Dallas Cowboys
Miami Dolphins	New York Giants
New England Patriots	Philadelphia Eagles
New York Jets	Washington Redskins
Central Division	**Central Division**
Baltimore Ravens	Chicago Bears
Cincinnati Bengals	Detroit Lions
Houston Oilers[a]	Green Bay Packers
Jacksonville Jaguars	Minnesota Vikings
Pittsburgh Steelers	Tampa Bay Buccaneers
Western Division	**Western Division**
Denver Broncos	Atlanta Falcons
Kansas City Chiefs	Carolina Panthers
Oakland Raiders	New Orleans Saints
San Diego Chargers	St. Louis Rams
Seattle Seahawks	San Francisco 49ers

[a] *Tennessee Oilers (1997–1998)*

1995–1998

Source: 1997 NFL Record & Fact Book, p. 14

The 16-game regular season schedule of all NFL teams is determined by the following formula. (The reference point for figuring is the team's final division standing):[1]

1. *Divisional Games*: Home and away against its four division opponents (8 games).
2. *Intraconference Games*: Four games against teams from the other two divisions within the conference (4 games).

1st place: plays the other two 1st-place teams, a 2nd- and a 3rd-place team
2nd place: plays the other two 2nd-place teams, a 1st- and a 4th-place team
3rd place: plays the other two 3rd-place teams, a 1st- and a 5th-place team
4th place: plays the other two 4th-place teams, a 2nd- and a 5th-place team
5th place: plays the other two 5th-place teams, a 3rd- and a 4th-place team

Prior Year's Finish in Division	Pairings in Non-Division Games Within Conference 1995–1998
1	1–1–2–3
2	1–2–2–4
3	1–3–3–5
4	2–4–4–5
5	3–4–5–5

3. *Interconference Games*: Four games against teams from one of the divisions of the other conference (4 games). During the first cycle of interconference games from 1995 to 1997, matchups would depend on the previous season's final standings (see chart below). Thereafter, interconference matchups would be based on a rotation with each team playing all teams of the other conference four times in 15 seasons (twice at home and twice away) from 1995 to 2009.

Prior Year's Finish in Division	Pairings in Interconference Games 1995–1997
1	1–2–3–4
2	1–2–3–5
3	1–2–4–5
4	1–3–4–5
5	2–3–4–5

This completes the 16-game schedule.

Comparison Intraconference Chart (1978–1998)

Prior Year's Finish in Division	Pairings in Non-Division Games Within Conference		
	1978–1987	1988–1994	1995–1998
1	1–1–4–4	1–1–2–3	1–1–2–3
2	2–2–3–3	1–2–2–4	1–2–2–4
3	2–2–3–3	1–3–3–4	1–3–3–5
4	1–1–4–4	2–3–4–4	2–4–4–5
5			3–4–5–5

1994 Final Standings
(To Determine 1995 Opponents)

	AFC East AE		AFC Central AC		AFC West AW
1	MIAMI	1	PITTSBURGH	1	SAN DIEGO
2	NEW ENGLAND	2	CLEVELAND	2	KANSAS CITY
3	INDIANAPOLIS	3	CINCINNATI	3	LA RAIDERS[a]
4	BUFFALO	4	HOUSTON	4	DENVER
5	NY JETS			5	SEATTLE

	NFC East NE		NFC Central NC		NFC West NW
1	DALLAS	1	MINNESOTA	1	SAN FRANCISCO
2	NY GIANTS	2	GREEN BAY	2	NEW ORLEANS
3	ARIZONA	3	DETROIT	3	ATLANTA
4	PHILADELPHIA	4	CHICAGO	4	LA RAMS[b]
5	WASHINGTON	5	TAMPA BAY		

[a] In 1995, the Los Angeles Raiders moved back to Oakland.
[b] The Los Angeles Rams moved to St. Louis and became the St. Louis Rams.

Note: In determining 1995 opponents, the Jacksonville Jaguars and Carolina Panthers were assigned the fifth-place schedule in the AFC Central and NFC West, respectively.

1995 NON-DIVISIONAL OPPONENTS (AFC)

AFC East AE				AFC Central AC				AFC West AW			
1	MIA			1	PIT			1	SD		
Home		Away		Home		Away		Home		Away	
AC1	PIT	AW1	SD	AW1	SD	AE1	MIA	AE1	MIA	AC1	PIT
AW2	KC	AC3	CIN	AE2	NE	AW3	OAK	AC2	CLE	AE3	IND
NW1	SF	NW2	NO	NC1	MIN	NC2	GB	NE1	DAL	NE2	NYG
NW3	ATL	NW4	STL	NC3	DET	NC4	CHI	NE3	ARI	NE4	PHI
2	NE			2	CLE			2	KC		
Home		Away		Home		Away		Home		Away	
AC2	CLE	AW2	KC	AW2	KC	AE2	NE	AE2	NE	AC2	CLE
AW4	DEN	AC1	PIT	AE4	BUF	AW1	SD	AC4	HOU	AE1	MIA
NW2	NO	NW1	SF	NC2	GB	NC1	MIN	NE2	NYG	NE1	DAL
NW5	CAR	NW3	ATL	NC5	TB	NC3	DET	NE5	WAS	NE3	ARI

3	IND			3	CIN			3	OAK		
Home		*Away*		*Home*		*Away*		*Home*		*Away*	
AC3	CIN	AW3	OAK	AW3	OAK	AE3	IND	AE3	IND	AC3	CIN
AW1	SD	AC5	JAC	AE1	MIA	AW5	SEA	AC1	PIT	AE5	NYJ
NW1	SF	NW2	NO	NC1	MIN	NC2	GB	NE1	DAL	NE2	NYG
NW4	STL	NW5	CAR	NC4	CHI	NC5	TB	NE4	PHI	NE5	WAS
4	BUF			4	HOU			4	DEN		
Home		*Away*		*Home*		*Away*		*Home*		*Away*	
AC4	HOU	AW4	DEN	AW4	DEN	AE4	BUF	AE4	BUF	AC4	HOU
AW5	SEA	AC2	CLE	AE5	NYJ	AW2	KC	AC5	JAC	AE2	NE
NW3	ATL	NW1	SF	NC3	DET	NC1	MIN	NE3	ARI	NE1	DAL
NW5	CAR	NW4	STL	NC5	TB	NC4	CHI	NE5	WAS	NE4	PHI
5	NYJ			5	JAC			5	SEA		
Home		*Away*		*Home*		*Away*		*Home*		*Away*	
AC5	JAC	AW5	SEA	AW5	SEA	AE5	NYJ	AE5	NYJ	AC5	JAC
AW3	OAK	AC4	HOU	AE3	IND	AW4	DEN	AC3	CIN	AE4	BUF
NW2	NO	NW3	ATL	NC2	GB	NC3	DET	NE2	NYG	NE3	ARI
NW4	STL	NW5	CAR	NC4	CHI	NC5	TB	NE4	PHI	NE5	WAS

1995 NON-DIVISIONAL OPPONENTS (NFC)

NFC East				NFC Central				NFC West			
NE				**NC**				**NW**			
1	DAL			1	MIN			1	SF		
Home		*Away*		*Home*		*Away*		*Home*		*Away*	
NW1	SF	NC1	MIN	NE1	DAL	NW1	SF	NC1	MIN	NE1	DAL
NC2	GB	NW3	ATL	NW2	NO	NE3	ARI	NE2	NYG	NC3	DET
AW2	KC	AW1	SD	AC2	CLE	AC1	PIT	AE2	NE	AE1	MIA
AW4	DEN	AW3	OAK	AC4	HOU	AC3	CIN	AE4	BUF	AE3	IND
2	NYG			2	GB			2	NO		
Home		*Away*		*Home*		*Away*		*Home*		*Away*	
NW2	NO	NC2	GB	NE2	NYG	NW2	NO	NC2	GB	NE2	NYG
NC4	CHI	NW1	SF	NW4	STL	NE1	DAL	NE4	PHI	NC1	MIN
AW1	SD	AW2	KC	AC1	PIT	AC2	CLE	AE1	MIA	AE2	NE
AW3	OAK	AW5	SEA	AC3	CIN	AC5	JAC	AE3	IND	AE5	NYJ
3	ARI			3	DET			3	ATL		
Home		*Away*		*Home*		*Away*		*Home*		*Away*	
NW3	ATL	NC3	DET	NE3	ARI	NW3	ATL	NC3	DET	NE3	ARI
NC1	MIN	NW5	CAR	NW1	SF	NE5	WAS	NE1	DAL	NC5	TB
AW2	KC	AW1	SD	AC2	CLE	AC1	PIT	AE2	NE	AE1	MIA
AW5	SEA	AW4	DEN	AC5	JAC	AC4	HOU	AE5	NYJ	AE4	BUF
4	PHI			4	CHI			4	STL		
Home		*Away*		*Home*		*Away*		*Home*		*Away*	
NW4	STL	NC4	CHI	NE4	PHI	NW4	STL	NC4	CHI	NE4	PHI
NC5	TB	NW2	NO	NW5	CAR	NE2	NYG	NE5	WAS	NC2	GB
AW1	SD	AW3	OAK	AC1	PIT	AC3	CIN	AE1	MIA	AE3	IND
AW4	DEN	AW5	SEA	AC4	HOU	AC5	JAC	AE4	BUF	AE5	NYJ

5	WAS			5	TB			5	CAR		
Home		*Away*		*Home*		*Away*		*Home*		*Away*	
NW5	CAR	NC5	TB	NE5	WAS	NW5	CAR	NC5	TB	NE5	WAS
NC3	DET	NW4	STL	NW3	ATL	NE4	PHI	NE3	ARI	NC4	CHI
AW3	OAK	AW2	KC	AC3	CIN	AC2	CLE	AE3	IND	AE2	NE
AW5	SEA	AW4	DEN	AC5	JAC	AC4	HOU	AE5	NYJ	AE4	BUF

1995 Final Standings
(To Determine 1996 Opponents)

AFC East AE	AFC Central AC	AFC West AW
1 BUFFALO	1 PITTSBURGH	1 KANSAS CITY
2 INDIANAPOLIS	2 CINCINNATI	2 SAN DIEGO
3 MIAMI	3 HOUSTON	3 SEATTLE
4 NEW ENGLAND	4 CLEVELAND[a]	4 DENVER
5 NY JETS	5 JACKSONVILLE	5 OAKLAND

NFC East NE	NFC Central NC	NFC West NW
1 DALLAS	1 GREEN BAY	1 SAN FRANCISCO
2 PHILADELPHIA	2 DETROIT	2 ATLANTA
3 WASHINGTON	3 CHICAGO	3 ST. LOUIS
4 NY GIANTS	4 MINNESOTA	4 CAROLINA
5 ARIZONA	5 TAMPA BAY	5 NEW ORLEANS

[a] In 1996, the Baltimore Ravens assumed Cleveland's fourth-place schedule in AFC Central.

1996 NON-DIVISIONAL OPPONENTS (AFC)

AFC East AE				AFC Central AC				AFC West AW			
1	BUF			1	PIT			1	KC		
Home		*Away*		*Home*		*Away*		*Home*		*Away*	
AW1	KC	AC1	PIT	AE1	BUF	AW1	KC	AC1	PIT	AE1	BUF
AC2	CIN	AW3	SEA	AW2	SD	AE3	MIA	AE2	IND	AC3	HOU
NE1	DAL	NE2	PHI	NW1	SF	NW2	ATL	NC1	GB	NC2	DET
NE3	WAS	NE4	NYG	NW3	STL	NW4	CAR	NC3	CHI	NC4	MIN
2	IND			2	CIN			2	SD		
Home		*Away*		*Home*		*Away*		*Home*		*Away*	
AW2	SD	AC2	CIN	AE2	IND	AW2	SD	AC2	CIN	AE2	IND
AC4	BAL	AW1	KC	AW4	DEN	AE1	BUF	AE4	NE	AC1	PIT
NE2	PHI	NE1	DAL	NW2	ATL	NW1	SF	NC2	DET	NC1	GB
NE5	ARI	NE3	WAS	NW5	NO	NW3	STL	NC5	TB	NC3	CHI
3	MIA			3	HOU			3	SEA		
Home		*Away*		*Home*		*Away*		*Home*		*Away*	
AW3	SEA	AC3	HOU	AE3	MIA	AW3	SEA	AC3	HOU	AE3	MIA
AC1	PIT	AW5	OAK	AW1	KC	AE5	NYJ	AE1	BUF	AC5	JAC
NE1	DAL	NE2	PHI	NW1	SF	NW2	ATL	NC1	GB	NC2	DET
NE4	NYG	NE5	ARI	NW4	CAR	NW5	NO	NC4	MIN	NC5	TB

4	NE			4	BAL			4	DEN		
Home		*Away*		*Home*		*Away*		*Home*		*Away*	
AW4	DEN	AC4	BAL	AE4	NE	AW4	DEN	AC4	BAL	AE4	NE
AC5	JAC	AW2	SD	AW5	OAK	AE2	IND	AE5	NYJ	AC2	CIN
NE3	WAS	NE1	DAL	NW3	STL	NW1	SF	NC3	CHI	NC1	GB
NE5	ARI	NE4	NYG	NW5	NO	NW4	CAR	NC5	TB	NC4	MIN
5	NYJ			5	JAC			5	OAK		
Home		*Away*		*Home*		*Away*		*Home*		*Away*	
AW5	OAK	AC5	JAC	AE5	NYJ	AW5	OAK	AC5	JAC	AE5	NYJ
AC3	HOU	AW4	DEN	AW3	SEA	AE4	NE	AE3	MIA	AC4	BAL
NE2	PHI	NE3	WAS	NW2	ATL	NW3	STL	NC2	DET	NC3	CHI
NE4	NYG	NE5	ARI	NW4	CAR	NW5	NO	NC4	MIN	NC5	TB

1996 NON-DIVISIONAL OPPONENTS (NFC)

NFC East — NE NFC Central — NC NFC West — NW

1	DAL			1	GB			1	SF		
Home		*Away*		*Home*		*Away*		*Home*		*Away*	
NC1	GB	NW1	SF	NW1	SF	NE1	DAL	NE1	DAL	NC1	GB
NW2	ATL	NC3	CHI	NE2	PHI	NW3	STL	NC2	DET	NE3	WAS
AE2	IND	AE1	BUF	AW2	SD	AW1	KC	AC2	CIN	AC1	PIT
AE4	NE	AE3	MIA	AW4	DEN	AW3	SEA	AC4	BAL	AC3	HOU
2	PHI			2	DET			2	ATL		
Home		*Away*		*Home*		*Away*		*Home*		*Away*	
NC2	DET	NW2	ATL	NW2	ATL	NE2	PHI	NE2	PHI	NC2	DET
NW4	CAR	NC1	GB	NE4	NYG	NW1	SF	NC4	MIN	NE1	DAL
AE1	BUF	AE2	IND	AW1	KC	AW2	SD	AC1	PIT	AC2	CIN
AE3	MIA	AE5	NYJ	AW3	SEA	AW5	OAK	AC3	HOU	AC5	JAC
3	WAS			3	CHI			3	STL		
Home		*Away*		*Home*		*Away*		*Home*		*Away*	
NC3	CHI	NW3	STL	NW3	STL	NE3	WAS	NE3	WAS	NC3	CHI
NW1	SF	NC5	TB	NE1	DAL	NW5	NO	NC1	GB	NE5	ARI
AE2	IND	AE1	BUF	AW2	SD	AW1	KC	AC2	CIN	AC1	PIT
AE5	NYJ	AE4	NE	AW5	OAK	AW4	DEN	AC5	JAC	AC4	BAL
4	NYG			4	MIN			4	CAR		
Home		*Away*		*Home*		*Away*		*Home*		*Away*	
NC4	MIN	NW4	CAR	NW4	CAR	NE4	NYG	NE4	NYG	NC4	MIN
NW5	NO	NC2	DET	NE5	ARI	NW2	ATL	NC5	TB	NE2	PHI
AE1	BUF	AE3	MIA	AW1	KC	AW3	SEA	AC1	PIT	AC3	HOU
AE4	NE	AE5	NYJ	AW4	DEN	AW5	OAK	AC4	BAL	AC5	JAC
5	ARI			5	TB			5	NO		
Home		*Away*		*Home*		*Away*		*Home*		*Away*	
NC5	TB	NW5	NO	NW5	NO	NE5	ARI	NE5	ARI	NC5	TB
NW3	STL	NC4	MIN	NE3	WAS	NW4	CAR	NC3	CHI	NE4	NYG
AE3	MIA	AE2	IND	AW3	SEA	AW2	SD	AC3	HOU	AC2	CIN
AE5	NYJ	AE4	NE	AW5	OAK	AW4	DEN	AC5	JAC	AC4	BAL

1996 Final Standings
(To Determine 1997 Opponents)

AFC East AE	AFC Central AC	AFC West AW
1 NEW ENGLAND	1 PITTSBURGH	1 DENVER
2 BUFFALO	2 JACKSONVILLE	2 KANSAS CITY
3 INDIANAPOLIS	3 CINCINNATI	3 SAN DIEGO
4 MIAMI	4 HOUSTON[a]	4 OAKLAND
5 NY JETS	5 BALTIMORE	5 SEATTLE

NFC East NE	NFC Central NC	NFC West NW
1 DALLAS	1 GREEN BAY	1 CAROLINA
2 PHILADELPHIA	2 MINNESOTA	2 SAN FRANCISCO
3 WASHINGTON	3 CHICAGO	3 ST. LOUIS
4 ARIZONA	4 TAMPA BAY	4 ATLANTA
5 NY GIANTS	5 DETROIT	5 NEW ORLEANS

[a] In 1997, Houston moved to Tennessee and became the Tennessee Oilers.

1997 NON-DIVISIONAL OPPONENTS (AFC)

AFC East — AE

1 NE

Home		Away	
AC1	PIT	AW1	DEN
AW3	SD	AC2	JAC
NC1	GB	NC2	MIN
NC3	CHI	NC4	TB

2 BUF

Home		Away	
AC2	JAC	AW2	KC
AW1	DEN	AC4	TEN
NC2	MIN	NC1	GB
NC5	DET	NC3	CHI

3 IND

Home		Away	
AC3	CIN	AW3	SD
AW5	SEA	AC1	PIT
NC1	GB	NC2	MIN
NC4	TB	NC5	DET

4 MIA

Home		Away	
AC4	TEN	AW4	OAK
AW2	KC	AC5	BAL
NC3	CHI	NC1	GB
NC5	DET	NC4	TB

AFC Central — AC

1 PIT

Home		Away	
AW1	DEN	AE1	NE
AE3	IND	AW2	KC
NE1	DAL	NE2	PHI
NE3	WAS	NE4	ARI

2 JAC

Home		Away	
AW2	KC	AE2	BUF
AE1	NE	AW4	OAK
NE2	PHI	NE1	DAL
NE5	NYG	NE3	WAS

3 CIN

Home		Away	
AW3	SD	AE3	IND
AE5	NYJ	AW1	DEN
NE1	DAL	NE2	PHI
NE4	ARI	NE5	NYG

4 TEN

Home		Away	
AW4	OAK	AE4	MIA
AE2	BUF	AW5	SEA
NE3	WAS	NE1	DAL
NE5	NYG	NE4	ARI

AFC West — AW

1 DEN

Home		Away	
AE1	NE	AC1	PIT
AC3	CIN	AE2	BUF
NW1	CAR	NW2	SF
NW3	STL	NW4	ATL

2 KC

Home		Away	
AE2	BUF	AC2	JAC
AC1	PIT	AE4	MIA
NW2	SF	NW1	CAR
NW5	NO	NW3	STL

3 SD

Home		Away	
AE3	IND	AC3	CIN
AC5	BAL	AE1	NE
NW1	CAR	NW2	SF
NW4	ATL	NW5	NO

4 OAK

Home		Away	
AE4	MIA	AC4	TEN
AC2	JAC	AE5	NYJ
NW3	STL	NW1	CAR
NW5	NO	NW4	ATL

5	NYJ			5	BAL			5	SEA		
Home		*Away*		*Home*		*Away*		*Home*		*Away*	
AC5	BAL	AW5	SEA	AW5	SEA	AE5	NYJ	AE5	NYJ	AC5	BAL
AW4	OAK	AC3	CIN	AE4	MIA	AW3	SD	AC4	TEN	AE3	IND
NC2	MIN	NC3	CHI	NE2	PHI	NE3	WAS	NW2	SF	NW3	STL
NC4	TB	NC5	DET	NE4	ARI	NE5	NYG	NW4	ATL	NW5	NO

1997 NON-DIVISIONAL OPPONENTS (NFC)

NFC East
NE

NFC Central
NC

NFC West
NW

1	DAL			1	GB			1	CAR		
Home		*Away*		*Home*		*Away*		*Home*		*Away*	
NW1	CAR	NC1	GB	NE1	DAL	NW1	CAR	NC1	GB	NE1	DAL
NC3	CHI	NW2	SF	NW3	STL	NE2	PHI	NE3	WAS	NC2	MIN
AC2	JAC	AC1	PIT	AE2	BUF	AE1	NE	AW2	KC	AW1	DEN
AC4	TEN	AC3	CIN	AE4	MIA	AE3	IND	AW4	OAK	AW3	SD

2	PHI			2	MIN			2	SF		
Home		*Away*		*Home*		*Away*		*Home*		*Away*	
NW2	SF	NC2	MIN	NE2	PHI	NW2	SF	NC2	MIN	NE2	PHI
NC1	GB	NW4	ATL	NW1	CAR	NE4	ARI	NE1	DAL	NC4	TB
AC1	PIT	AC2	JAC	AE1	NE	AE2	BUF	AW1	DEN	AW2	KC
AC3	CIN	AC5	BAL	AE3	IND	AE5	NYJ	AW3	SD	AW5	SEA

3	WAS			3	CHI			3	STL		
Home		*Away*		*Home*		*Away*		*Home*		*Away*	
NW3	STL	NC3	CHI	NE3	WAS	NW3	STL	NC3	CHI	NE3	WAS
NC5	DET	NW1	CAR	NW5	NO	NE1	DAL	NE5	NYG	NC1	GB
AC2	JAC	AC1	PIT	AE2	BUF	AE1	NE	AW2	KC	AW1	DEN
AC5	BAL	AC4	TEN	AE5	NYJ	AE4	MIA	AW5	SEA	AW4	OAK

4	ARI			4	TB			4	ATL		
Home		*Away*		*Home*		*Away*		*Home*		*Away*	
NW4	ATL	NC4	TB	NE4	ARI	NW4	ATL	NC4	TB	NE4	ARI
NC2	MIN	NW5	NO	NW2	SF	NE5	NYG	NE2	PHI	NC5	DET
AC1	PIT	AC3	CIN	AE1	NE	AE3	IND	AW1	DEN	AW3	SD
AC4	TEN	AC5	BAL	AE4	MIA	AE5	NYJ	AW4	OAK	AW5	SEA

5	NYG			5	DET			5	NO		
Home		*Away*		*Home*		*Away*		*Home*		*Away*	
NW5	NO	NC5	DET	NE5	NYG	NW5	NO	NC5	DET	NE5	NYG
NC4	TB	NW3	STL	NW4	ATL	NE3	WAS	NE4	ARI	NC3	CHI
AC3	CIN	AC2	JAC	AE3	IND	AE2	BUF	AW3	SD	AW2	KC
AC5	BAL	AC4	TEN	AE5	NYJ	AE4	MIA	AW5	SEA	AW4	OAK

1997 Final Standings
(To Determine 1998 Opponents)

AFC East AE	AFC Central AC	AFC West AW
1 NEW ENGLAND	1 PITTSBURGH	1 KANSAS CITY
2 MIAMI	2 JACKSONVILLE	2 DENVER
3 NY JETS	3 TENNESSEE	3 SEATTLE
4 BUFFALO	4 CINCINNATI	4 OAKLAND
5 INDIANAPOLIS	5 BALTIMORE	5 SAN DIEGO

NFC East NE	NFC Central NC	NFC West NW
1 NY GIANTS	1 GREEN BAY	1 SAN FRANCISCO
2 WASHINGTON	2 TAMPA BAY	2 CAROLINA
3 PHILADELPHIA	3 DETROIT	3 ATLANTA
4 DALLAS	4 MINNESOTA	4 NEW ORLEANS
5 ARIZONA	5 CHICAGO	5 ST. LOUIS

1998 NON-DIVISIONAL OPPONENTS (AFC)

AFC East — AE

1 NE

Home		Away	
AW1	KC	AC1	PIT
AC3	TEN	AW2	DEN
NW	ATL	NW	NO
	SF		STL

2 MIA

Home		Away	
AW2	DEN	AC2	JAC
AC1	PIT	AW4	OAK
NW	NO	NW	ATL
	STL		CAR

3 NYJ

Home		Away	
AW3	SEA	AC3	TEN
AC5	BAL	AW1	KC
NW	ATL	NW	STL
	CAR		SF

4 BUF

Home		Away	
AW4	OAK	AC4	CIN
AC2	JAC	AW5	SD
NW	STL	NW	CAR
	SF		NO

AFC Central — AC

1 PIT

Home		Away	
AE1	NE	AW1	KC
AW3	SEA	AE2	MIA
NC	CHI	NC	DET
	GB		TB

2 JAC

Home		Away	
AE2	MIA	AW2	DEN
AW1	KC	AE4	BUF
NC	DET	NC	CHI
	TB		MIN

3 TEN

Home		Away	
AE3	NYJ	AW3	SEA
AW5	SD	AE1	NE
NC	CHI	NC	GB
	MIN		TB

4 CIN

Home		Away	
AE4	BUF	AW4	OAK
AW2	DEN	AE5	IND
NC	GB	NC	DET
	TB		MIN

AFC West — AW

1 KC

Home		Away	
AC1	PIT	AE1	NE
AE3	NYJ	AC2	JAC
NE	ARI	NE	NYG
	DAL		PHI

2 DEN

Home		Away	
AC2	JAC	AE2	MIA
AE1	NE	AC4	CIN
NE	DAL	NE	NYG
	PHI		WAS

3 SEA

Home		Away	
AC3	TEN	AE3	NYJ
AE5	IND	AC1	PIT
NE	ARI	NE	DAL
	WAS		PHI

4 OAK

Home		Away	
AC4	CIN	AE4	BUF
AE2	MIA	AC5	BAL
NE	NYG	NE	ARI
	WAS		DAL

5	IND			5	BAL			5	SD		
Home		Away		Home		Away		Home		Away	
AW5	SD	AC5	BAL	AE5	IND	AW5	SD	AC5	BAL	AE5	IND
AC4	CIN	AW3	SEA	AW4	OAK	AE3	NYJ	AE4	BUF	AC3	TEN
NW	CAR	NW	ATL	NC	DET	NC	CHI	NE	NYG	NE	ARI
	NO		SF		MIN		GB		PHI		WAS

1998 NON-DIVISIONAL OPPONENTS (NFC)

NFC East — NE   NFC Central — NC   NFC West — NW

1	NYG			1	GB			1	SF		
Home		Away		Home		Away		Home		Away	
NC1	GB	NW1	SF	NW1	SF	NE1	NYG	NE1	NYG	NC1	GB
NW3	ATL	NC2	TB	NE3	PHI	NW2	CAR	NC3	DET	NE2	WAS
AW	DEN	AW	OAK	AC	BAL	AC	CIN	AE	IND	AE	BUF
	KC		SD		TEN		PIT		NYJ		NE

2	WAS			2	TB			2	CAR		
Home		Away		Home		Away		Home		Away	
NC2	TB	NW2	CAR	NW2	CAR	NE2	WAS	NE2	WAS	NC2	TB
NW1	SF	NC4	MIN	NE1	NYG	NW4	NO	NC1	GB	NE4	DAL
AW	DEN	AW	OAK	AC	PIT	AC	CIN	AE	BUF	AE	IND
	SD		SEA		TEN		JAC		MIA		NYJ

3	PHI			3	DET			3	ATL		
Home		Away		Home		Away		Home		Away	
NC3	DET	NW3	ATL	NW3	ATL	NE3	PHI	NE3	PHI	NC3	DET
NW5	STL	NC1	GB	NE5	ARI	NW1	SF	NC5	CHI	NE1	NYG
AW	KC	AW	DEN	AC	CIN	AC	BAL	AE	IND	AE	NE
	SEA		SD		PIT		JAC		MIA		NYJ

4	DAL			4	MIN			4	NO		
Home		Away		Home		Away		Home		Away	
NC4	MIN	NW4	NO	NW4	NO	NE4	DAL	NE4	DAL	NC4	MIN
NW2	CAR	NC5	CHI	NE2	WAS	NW5	STL	NC2	TB	NE5	ARI
AW	OAK	AW	DEN	AC	CIN	AC	BAL	AE	BUF	AE	IND
	SEA		KC		JAC		TEN		NE		MIA

5	ARI			5	CHI			5	STL		
Home		Away		Home		Away		Home		Away	
NC5	CHI	NW5	STL	NW5	STL	NE5	ARI	NE5	ARI	NC5	CHI
NW4	NO	NC3	DET	NE4	DAL	NW3	ATL	NC4	MIN	NE3	PHI
AW	OAK	AW	KC	AC	BAL	AC	PIT	AE	NE	AE	BUF
	SD		SEA		JAC		TEN		NYJ		MIA

1999–2001

AMERICAN CONFERENCE	NATIONAL CONFERENCE
Eastern Division	**Eastern Division**
Buffalo Bills	Arizona Cardinals
Indianapolis Colts	Dallas Cowboys
Miami Dolphins	New York Giants
New England Patriots	Philadelphia Eagles
New York Jets	Washington Redskins
Central Division	**Central Division**
Baltimore Ravens	Chicago Bears
Cincinnati Bengals	Detroit Lions
Cleveland Browns	Green Bay Packers
Jacksonville Jaguars	Minnesota Vikings
Pittsburgh Steelers	Tampa Bay Buccaneers
Tennessee Titans	
Western Division	**Western Division**
Denver Broncos	Atlanta Falcons
Kansas City Chiefs	Carolina Panthers
Oakland Raiders	New Orleans Saints
San Diego Chargers	St. Louis Rams
Seattle Seahawks	San Francisco 49ers

1999–2001

Source: 1999 NFL Record & Fact Book, p. 14

The 16-game regular season schedule of any NFL team is determined by one of the following formulas. (The reference point for figuring is the team's final division standing):[1]

A. AFC East, AFC West and all NFC teams.

1. *Divisional Games*: Home and away against its four division opponents (8 games).
2. *Intraconference Games*: Four games against teams from the other two divisions within the conference (4 games). In the NFC, first-place teams will play the other two first-place teams, a second- and a third-place team. Second-place teams will play the other two second-place teams, a first- and a fourth-place team, etc. AFC East and AFC West teams will also be matched with four other teams within the conference based on the prior year's standings, as shown below:

1999

Prior Year's Finish in Division	NFC Teams	AFC East	AFC West
1	1–1–2–3	1–1–2–3	1–1–2–4
2	1–2–2–4	1–2–2–5	1–2–2–3
3	1–3–3–5	2–3–3–4	1–3–3–5
4	2–4–4–5	1–4–4–6	3–4–4–5
5	3–4–5–5	4–5–5–6	2–5–5–6

2000 AND 2001

Prior Year's Finish in Division	NFC Teams	AFC East	AFC West
1	1-1-2-3	1-1-2-4	1-1-2-3
2	1-2-2-4	1-2-2-3	1-2-2-5
3	1-3-3-5	1-3-3-5	2-3-3-4
4	2-4-4-5	3-4-4-5	1-4-4-6
5	3-4-5-5	2-5-5-6	4-5-5-6

3. *Interconference Games*: Four games against teams from a division of the other conference (4 games). The following divisional matchups will take place from 1999 to 2001 based on the divisional rotation that began in 1978:

	1999	2000	2001
AFC EAST	NFCE	NFCC	NFCW
AFC CENTRAL	NFCW	NFCE	NFCC
AFC WEST	NFCC	NFCW	NFCE
NFC EAST	AFCE	AFCC	AFCW
NFC CENTRAL	AFCW	AFCE	AFCC
NFC WEST	AFCC	AFCW	AFCE

This completes the 16-game schedule.

Note: From 1999 to 2001, the interconference rotation that initiated in 1995 would continue between all NFC teams and teams from the AFC East and AFC West. Interconference matchups between all NFC teams and teams from the AFC Central would be based on the prior year's standings (see chart below in B3). Originally, it was arranged that each team would face every team from the other conference four times, twice at home and twice away, from 1995 to 2009. This would be revised, however, when the NFL realigned in 2002 and instituted a new scheduling formula.

B. AFC Central first- and second-place teams.
1. *Divisional Games*: Home and away against its five division opponents (10 games).
2. *Intraconference Games*: Two games against teams from the other two divisions within the conference (2 games). The AFC Central first-place team will play the other two first-place teams in the conference, and the AFC Central second-place team will play the other two second-place teams in the conference based on the prior year's standings, as shown below:

1999–2001

Prior Year's Finish in Division	AFC Central
1	1-1
2	2-2
3	3-3-4
4	3-4-4
5	3-5-5
6	4-5-5

3. *Interconference Games*: Four games against teams from a division of the other conference (4 games). The AFC Central first-place team will play the first-, second-, third-, and fourth-place teams from the NFC division. The AFC Central second-place team

will play the first-, second-, third-, and fifth-place teams from the NFC division. NFC teams scheduled to play the AFC Central will also be matched with four teams based on the prior year's standings, as shown below:

Prior Year's Finish In Division	AFC Central Schedule vs. NFC Division	NFC Division Schedule vs. AFC Central
1	1-2-3-4	1-2-3-4
2	1-2-3-5	1-2-3-5
3	1-2-4	1-2-4-6
4	1-3-5	1-3-5-6
5	2-4-5	2-4-5-6
6	3-4-5	

This completes the 16-game schedule.

C. AFC Central third-, fourth-, fifth-, and sixth-place teams.
  1. *Divisional Games*: Home and away against its five division opponents (10 games).
  2. *Intraconference Games*: Three games against teams from the other two divisions within the conference (3 games). The AFC Central third-place team will play the other two third-place teams and a fourth-place team in the conference. The AFC Central fourth-place team will play the other two fourth-place teams and a third-place team in the conference based on the prior year's standings, etc. See AFC Central intraconference opponent chart above in B2.
  3. *Interconference Games*: Three games against teams from a division of the other conference (3 games). The AFC Central third-place team will play the first-, second-, and fourth-place teams from the NFC division. The AFC Central fourth-place team will play the first-, third-, and fifth-place teams from the NFC division, etc. See AFC Central vs. NFC division chart above in B3.

This completes the 16-game schedule.

1998 Final Standings
(To Determine 1999 Opponents)

AFC EAST AE	AFC CENTRAL AC	AFC WEST AW
1 NY JETS	1 JACKSONVILLE	1 DENVER
2 MIAMI	2 TENNESSEE	2 OAKLAND
3 BUFFALO	3 PITTSBURGH	3 SEATTLE
4 NEW ENGLAND	4 BALTIMORE	4 KANSAS CITY
5 INDIANAPOLIS	5 CINCINNATI	5 SAN DIEGO

NFC EAST NE	NFC CENTRAL NC	NFC WEST NW
1 DALLAS	1 MINNESOTA	1 ATLANTA
2 ARIZONA	2 GREEN BAY	2 SAN FRANCISCO
3 NY GIANTS	3 TAMPA BAY	3 NEW ORLEANS
4 WASHINGTON	4 DETROIT	4 CAROLINA
5 PHILADELPHIA	5 CHICAGO	5 ST. LOUIS

Note: In 1999, the Cleveland Browns assigned sixth-place schedule in AFC Central.

1999 NON-DIVISIONAL OPPONENTS (AFC)

AFC East
AE

1	NYJ		
Home		*Away*	
AC1	JAC	AW1	DEN
AW3	SEA	AW2	OAK
NE	ARI	NE	DAL
	WAS		NYG

2	MIA		
Home		*Away*	
AC2	TEN	AW2	OAK
AW5	SD	AW1	DEN
NE	ARI	NE	DAL
	PHI		WAS

3	BUF		
Home		*Away*	
AC3	PIT	AW3	SEA
AW2	OAK	AC4	BAL
NE	NYG	NE	ARI
	PHI		WAS

4	NE		
Home		*Away*	
AC4	BAL	AW4	KC
AW1	DEN	AC6	CLE
NE	DAL	NE	ARI
	NYG		PHI

5	IND		
Home		*Away*	
AC5	CIN	AW5	SD
AW4	KC	AC6	CLE
NE	DAL	NE	NYG
	WAS		PHI

AFC Central
AC

1	JAC		
Home		*Away*	
AW1	DEN	AE1	NYJ
NW2	SF	NW1	ATL
NW3	NO	NW4	CAR

2	TEN		
Home		*Away*	
AW2	OAK	AE2	MIA
NW1	ATL	NW2	SF
NW5	STL	NW3	NO

3	PIT		
Home		*Away*	
AW3	SEA	AE3	BUF
		AW4	KC
NW1	ATL	NW2	SF
NW4	CAR		

4	BAL		
Home		*Away*	
AW4	KC	AE4	NE
AE3	BUF		
NW3	NO	NW1	ATL
		NW5	STL

5	CIN		
Home		*Away*	
AW5	SD	AE5	IND
		AW3	SEA
NW2	SF	NW4	CAR
NW5	STL		

6	CLE		
Home		*Away*	
AE5	IND	AW5	SD
AE4	NE		
NW4	CAR	NW3	NO
		NW5	STL

AFC West
AW

1	DEN		
Home		*Away*	
AE1	NYJ	AC1	JAC
AE2	MIA	AE4	NE
NC	GB	NC	DET
	MIN		TB

2	OAK		
Home		*Away*	
AE2	MIA	AC2	TEN
AE1	NYJ	AE3	BUF
NC	CHI	NC	GB
	TB		MIN

3	SEA		
Home		*Away*	
AE3	BUF	AC3	PIT
AC5	CIN	AE1	NYJ
NC	DET	NC	CHI
	TB		GB

4	KC		
Home		*Away*	
AE4	NE	AC4	BAL
AC3	PIT	AE5	IND
NC	DET	NC	CHI
	MIN		TB

5	SD		
Home		*Away*	
AE5	IND	AC5	CIN
AC6	CLE	AE2	MIA
NC	CHI	NC	DET
	GB		MIN

1999 NON-DIVISIONAL OPPONENTS (NFC)

NFC East NE		NFC Central NC		NFC West NW	
1 DAL		**1 MIN**		**1 ATL**	
Home	*Away*	*Home*	*Away*	*Home*	*Away*
NW1 ATL	NC1 MIN	NE1 DAL	NW1 ATL	NC1 MIN	NE1 DAL
NC2 GB	NW3 NO	NW2 SF	NE3 NYG	NE2 ARI	NC3 TB
AE MIA	AE IND	AW OAK	AW DEN	AC1 JAC	AC2 TEN
NYJ	NE	SD	KC	AC4 BAL	AC3 PIT
2 ARI		**2 GB**		**2 SF**	
Home	*Away*	*Home*	*Away*	*Home*	*Away*
NW2 SF	NC2 GB	NE2 ARI	NW2 SF	NC2 GB	NE2 ARI
NC4 DET	NW1 ATL	NW4 CAR	NE1 DAL	NE4 WAS	NC1 MIN
AE BUF	AE MIA	AW OAK	AW DEN	AC2 TEN	AC1 JAC
NE	NYJ	SEA	SD	AC3 PIT	AC5 CIN
3 NYG		**3 TB**		**3 NO**	
Home	*Away*	*Home*	*Away*	*Home*	*Away*
NW3 NO	NC3 TB	NE3 NYG	NW3 NO	NC3 TB	NE3 NYG
NC1 MIN	NW5 STL	NW1 ATL	NE5 PHI	NE1 DAL	NC5 CHI
AE IND	AE BUF	AW DEN	AW OAK	AC2 TEN	AC1 JAC
NYJ	NE	KC	SEA	AC6 CLE	AC4 BAL
4 WAS		**4 DET**		**4 CAR**	
Home	*Away*	*Home*	*Away*	*Home*	*Away*
NW4 CAR	NC4 DET	NE4 WAS	NW4 CAR	NC4 DET	NE4 WAS
NC5 CHI	NW2 SF	NW5 STL	NE2 ARI	NE5 PHI	NC2 GB
AE BUF	AE IND	AW DEN	AW KC	AC1 JAC	AC3 PIT
MIA	NYJ	SD	SEA	AC5 CIN	AC6 CLE
5 PHI		**5 CHI**		**5 STL**	
Home	*Away*	*Home*	*Away*	*Home*	*Away*
NW5 STL	NC5 CHI	NE5 PHI	NW5 STL	NC5 CHI	NE5 PHI
NC3 TB	NW4 CAR	NW3 NO	NE4 WAS	NE3 NYG	NC4 DET
AE IND	AE BUF	AW KC	AW OAK	AC4 BAL	AC2 TEN
NE	MIA	SEA	SD	AC6 CLE	AC5 CIN

1999 Final Standings
(To Determine 2000 Opponents)

AFC East AE	AFC Central AC	AFC West AW
1 INDIANAPOLIS	1 JACKSONVILLE	1 SEATTLE
2 BUFFALO	2 TENNESSEE	2 KANSAS CITY
3 MIAMI	3 BALTIMORE	3 SAN DIEGO
4 NY JETS	4 PITTSBURGH	4 OAKLAND
5 NEW ENGLAND	5 CINCINNATI	5 DENVER
	6 CLEVELAND	

| NFC East | NFC Central | NFC West |
NE	NC	NW
1 WASHINGTON	1 TAMPA BAY	1 ST. LOUIS
2 DALLAS	2 MINNESOTA	2 CAROLINA
3 NY GIANTS	3 DETROIT	3 ATLANTA
4 ARIZONA	4 GREEN BAY	4 SAN FRANCISCO
5 PHILADELPHIA	5 CHICAGO	5 NEW ORLEANS

2000 NON-DIVISIONAL OPPONENTS (AFC)

AFC East — AE

1 IND

Home		Away	
AC1	JAC	AW1	SEA
AW4	OAK	AW2	KC
NC	DET	NC	CHI
	MIN		GB

2 BUF

Home		Away	
AC2	TEN	AW2	KC
AW3	SD	AW1	SEA
NC	CHI	NC	MIN
	GB		TB

3 MIA

Home		Away	
AC3	BAL	AW3	SD
AW1	SEA	AC5	CIN
NC	GB	NC	DET
	TB		MIN

4 NYJ

Home		Away	
AC4	PIT	AW4	OAK
AW5	DEN	AC3	BAL
NC	CHI	NC	GB
	DET		TB

5 NE

Home		Away	
AC5	CIN	AW5	DEN
AW2	KC	AC6	CLE
NC	MIN	NC	CHI
	TB		DET

AFC Central — AC

1 JAC

Home		Away	
AW1	SEA	AE1	IND
NE1	WAS	NE2	DAL
NE4	ARI	NE3	NYG

2 TEN

Home		Away	
AW2	KC	AE2	BUF
NE2	DAL	NE1	WAS
NE3	NYG	NE5	PHI

3 BAL

Home		Away	
AW3	SD	AE3	MIA
AE4	NYJ		
NE2	DAL	NE1	WAS
		NE4	ARI

4 PIT

Home		Away	
AW4	OAK	AE4	NYJ
		AW3	SD
NE1	WAS	NE3	NYG
NE5	PHI		

5 CIN

Home		Away	
AW5	DEN	AE5	NE
AE3	MIA		
NE4	ARI	NE2	DAL
		NE5	PHI

6 CLE

Home		Away	
AE5	NE	AW5	DEN
		AW4	OAK
NE3	NYG	NE4	ARI
NE5	PHI		

AFC West — AW

1 SEA

Home		Away	
AE1	IND	AC1	JAC
AE2	BUF	AE3	MIA
NW	NO	NW	ATL
	STL		CAR

2 KC

Home		Away	
AE2	BUF	AC2	TEN
AE1	IND	AE5	NE
NW	CAR	NW	ATL
	STL		SF

3 SD

Home		Away	
AE3	MIA	AC3	BAL
AC4	PIT	AE2	BUF
NW	NO	NW	CAR
	SF		STL

4 OAK

Home		Away	
AE4	NYJ	AC4	PIT
AC6	CLE	AE1	IND
NW	ATL	NW	NO
	CAR		SF

5 DEN

Home		Away	
AE5	NE	AC5	CIN
AC6	CLE	AE4	NYJ
NW	ATL	NW	NO
	SF		STL

2000 NON-DIVISIONAL OPPONENTS (NFC)

NFC East — NE

1 WAS
Home		Away	
NC1	TB	NW1	STL
NW2	CAR	NC3	DET
AC2	TEN	AC1	JAC
AC3	BAL	AC4	PIT

2 DAL
Home		Away	
NC2	MIN	NW2	CAR
NW4	SF	NC1	TB
AC1	JAC	AC2	TEN
AC5	CIN	AC3	BAL

3 NYG
Home		Away	
NC3	DET	NW3	ATL
NW1	STL	NC5	CHI
AC1	JAC	AC2	TEN
AC4	PIT	AC6	CLE

4 ARI
Home		Away	
NC4	GB	NW4	SF
NW5	NO	NC2	MIN
AC3	BAL	AC1	JAC
AC6	CLE	AC5	CIN

5 PHI
Home		Away	
NC5	CHI	NW5	NO
NW3	ATL	NC4	GB
AC2	TEN	AC4	PIT
AC5	CIN	AC6	CLE

NFC Central — NC

1 TB
Home		Away	
NW1	STL	NE1	WAS
NE2	DAL	NW3	ATL
AE	BUF	AE	MIA
	NYJ		NE

2 MIN
Home		Away	
NW2	CAR	NE2	DAL
NE4	ARI	NW1	STL
AE	BUF	AE	IND
	MIA		NE

3 DET
Home		Away	
NW3	ATL	NE3	NYG
NE1	WAS	NW5	NO
AE	MIA	AE	IND
	NE		NYJ

4 GB
Home		Away	
NW4	SF	NE4	ARI
NE5	PHI	NW2	CAR
AE	IND	AE	BUF
	NYJ		MIA

5 CHI
Home		Away	
NW5	NO	NE5	PHI
NE3	NYG	NW4	SF
AE	IND	AE	BUF
	NE		NYJ

NFC West — NW

1 STL
Home		Away	
NE1	WAS	NC1	TB
NC2	MIN	NE3	NYG
AW	DEN	AW	KC
	SD		SEA

2 CAR
Home		Away	
NE2	DAL	NC2	MIN
NC4	GB	NE1	WAS
AW	SD	AW	KC
	SEA		OAK

3 ATL
Home		Away	
NE3	NYG	NC3	DET
NC1	TB	NE5	PHI
AW	KC	AW	DEN
	SEA		OAK

4 SF
Home		Away	
NE4	ARI	NC4	GB
NC5	CHI	NE2	DAL
AW	KC	AW	DEN
	OAK		SD

5 NO
Home		Away	
NE5	PHI	NC5	CHI
NC3	DET	NE4	ARI
AW	DEN	AW	SD
	OAK		SEA

2000 Final Standings
(To Determine 2001 Opponents)

AFC East — AE
1. MIAMI
2. INDIANAPOLIS
3. NY JETS
4. BUFFALO
5. NEW ENGLAND

AFC Central — AC
1. TENNESSEE
2. BALTIMORE
3. PITTSBURGH
4. JACKSONVILLE
5. CINCINNATI
6. CLEVELAND

AFC West — AW
1. OAKLAND
2. DENVER
3. KANSAS CITY
4. SEATTLE
5. SAN DIEGO

NFC East
NE
1. NY GIANTS
2. PHILADELPHIA
3. WASHINGTON
4. DALLAS
5. ARIZONA

NFC Central
NC
1. MINNESOTA
2. TAMPA BAY
3. GREEN BAY
4. DETROIT
5. CHICAGO

NFC West
NW
1. NEW ORLEANS
2. ST. LOUIS
3. CAROLINA
4. SAN FRANCISCO
5. ATLANTA

2001 NON-DIVISIONAL OPPONENTS (AFC)

AFC East
AE

1 MIA

Home		Away	
AW1	OAK	AC1	TEN
AW2	DEN	AW4	SEA
NW	ATL	NW	STL
	CAR		SF

2 IND

Home		Away	
AW2	DEN	AC2	BAL
AW1	OAK	AW3	KC
NW	ATL	NW	NO
	SF		STL

3 NYJ

Home		Away	
AW3	KC	AC3	PIT
AC5	CIN	AW1	OAK
NW	STL	NW	CAR
	SF		NO

4 BUF

Home		Away	
AW4	SEA	AC4	JAC
AC3	PIT	AW5	SD
NW	CAR	NW	ATL
	NO		SF

5 NE

Home		Away	
AW5	SD	AC5	CIN
AC6	CLE	AW2	DEN
NW	NO	NW	ATL
	STL		CAR

AFC Central
AC

1 TEN

Home		Away	
AE1	MIA	AW1	OAK
NC2	TB	NC1	MIN
NC3	GB	NC4	DET

2 BAL

Home		Away	
AE2	IND	AW2	DEN
NC1	MIN	NC2	TB
NC5	CHI	NC3	GB

3 PIT

Home		Away	
AE3	NYJ	AW3	KC
		AE4	BUF
NC1	MIN	NC2	TB
NC4	DET		

4 JAC

Home		Away	
AE4	BUF	AW4	SEA
AW3	KC		
NC3	GB	NC1	MIN
		NC5	CHI

5 CIN

Home		Away	
AE5	NE	AW5	SD
		AE3	NYJ
NC2	TB	NC4	DET
NC5	CHI		

6 CLE

Home		Away	
AW5	SD	AE5	NE
AW4	SEA		
NC4	DET	NC3	GB
		NC5	CHI

AFC West
AW

1 OAK

Home		Away	
AC1	TEN	AE1	MIA
AE3	NYJ	AE2	IND
NE	ARI	NE	NYG
	DAL		PHI

2 DEN

Home		Away	
AC2	BAL	AE2	IND
AE5	NE	AE1	MIA
NE	NYG	NE	ARI
	WAS		DAL

3 KC

Home		Away	
AC3	PIT	AE3	NYJ
AE2	IND	AC4	JAC
NE	NYG	NE	ARI
	PHI		WAS

4 SEA

Home		Away	
AC4	JAC	AE4	BUF
AE1	MIA	AC6	CLE
NE	DAL	NE	NYG
	PHI		WAS

5 SD

Home		Away	
AC5	CIN	AE5	NE
AE4	BUF	AC6	CLE
NE	ARI	NE	DAL
	WAS		PHI

2001 NON-DIVISIONAL OPPONENTS (NFC)

NFC East
NE

1 NYG

Home		Away	
NW1	NO	NC1	MIN
NC3	GB	NW2	STL
AW	OAK	AW	DEN
	SEA		KC

2 PHI

Home		Away	
NW2	STL	NC2	TB
NC1	MIN	NW4	SF
AW	OAK	AW	KC
	SD		SEA

3 WAS

Home		Away	
NW3	CAR	NC3	GB
NC5	CHI	NW1	NO
AW	KC	AW	DEN
	SEA		SD

4 DAL

Home		Away	
NW4	SF	NC4	DET
NC2	TB	NW5	ATL
AW	DEN	AW	OAK
	SD		SEA

5 ARI

Home		Away	
NW5	ATL	NC5	CHI
NC4	DET	NW3	CAR
AW	DEN	AW	OAK
	KC		SD

NFC Central
NC

1 MIN

Home		Away	
NE1	NYG	NW1	NO
NW3	CAR	NE2	PHI
AC1	TEN	AC2	BAL
AC4	JAC	AC3	PIT

2 TB

Home		Away	
NE2	PHI	NW2	STL
NW1	NO	NE4	DAL
AC2	BAL	AC1	TEN
AC3	PIT	AC5	CIN

3 GB

Home		Away	
NE3	WAS	NW3	CAR
NW5	ATL	NE1	NYG
AC2	BAL	AC1	TEN
AC6	CLE	AC4	JAC

4 DET

Home		Away	
NE4	DAL	NW4	SF
NW2	STL	NE5	ARI
AC1	TEN	AC3	PIT
AC5	CIN	AC6	CLE

5 CHI

Home		Away	
NE5	ARI	NW5	ATL
NW4	SF	NE3	WAS
AC4	JAC	AC2	BAL
AC6	CLE	AC5	CIN

NFC West
NW

1 NO

Home		Away	
NC1	MIN	NE1	NYG
NE3	WAS	NC2	TB
AE	IND	AE	BUF
	NYJ		NE

2 STL

Home		Away	
NC2	TB	NE2	PHI
NE1	NYG	NC4	DET
AE	IND	AE	NE
	MIA		NYJ

3 CAR

Home		Away	
NC3	GB	NE3	WAS
NE5	ARI	NC1	MIN
AE	NE	AE	BUF
	NYJ		MIA

4 SF

Home		Away	
NC4	DET	NE4	DAL
NE2	PHI	NC5	CHI
AE	BUF	AE	IND
	MIA		NYJ

5 ATL

Home		Away	
NC5	CHI	NE5	ARI
NE4	DAL	NC3	GB
AE	BUF	AE	IND
	NE		MIA

2002–2017

American Conference	National Conference
East Division	**East Division**
Buffalo Bills	Dallas Cowboys
Miami Dolphins	New York Giants
New England Patriots	Philadelphia Eagles
New York Jets	Washington Redskins
North Division	**North Division**
Baltimore Ravens	Chicago Bears
Cincinnati Bengals	Detroit Lions
Cleveland Browns	Green Bay Packers
Pittsburgh Steelers	Minnesota Vikings
South Division	**South Division**
Houston Texans	Atlanta Falcons
Indianapolis Colts	Carolina Panthers
Jacksonville Jaguars	New Orleans Saints
Tennessee Titans	Tampa Bay Buccaneers
West Division	**West Division**
Denver Broncos	Arizona Cardinals
Kansas City Chiefs	St. Louis Rams
Oakland Raiders	San Francisco 49ers
San Diego Chargers	Seattle Seahawks

2002–2017

Source: 2002 NFL Record & Fact Book, p. 16.

The 16-game regular season schedule of all NFL teams is determined by the following formula:[1]

- *Divisional Games*: Six games (one each home and away) vs. its three divisional opponents.
- *Intraconference Rotation*: Four games (two home, two away) vs. teams from another division, by rotation, within the conference.
- *Interconference Rotation*: Four games (two home, two away) vs. teams from another division, by rotation, from the opposite conference.
- *Standings-based Matchups*: Two games (one home, one away) vs. teams that finished in the same position in the prior year's standing from the two remaining divisions within the conference.

This completes the 16-game schedule.

Each team will face every conference opponent at least once every three years, and home and away every six years. AFC teams will play every NFC team once every four years, and home and away every eight years.

In March 2009, NFL owners voted to modify the West Coast rotation so that no team would play four games on the West Coast in one season, as did New England and the N.Y. Jets in 2008. Rather than having the alphabetical pairings used from 2002–2009, beginning with the 2010 season the pairings will be Denver/Oakland and Kansas City/San Diego in the AFC West. In the NFC West the new pairings will be Arizona/San Francisco and St. Louis/Seattle.

Note: In this section, matchups for 2014 and beyond are based on the NFL continuing its current scheduling format.

2002–2009 Scheduling Rotation

		2002	2003	2004	2005	2006	2007	2008	2009
AFC EAST	Intraconference	AFCW	AFCS	AFCN	AFCW	AFCS	AFCN	AFCW	AFCS
	Interconference	NFCN	NFCE	NFCW	NFCS	NFCN	NFCE	NFCW	NFCS
AFC NORTH	Intraconference	AFCS	AFCW	AFCE	AFCS	AFCW	AFCE	AFCS	AFCW
	Interconference	NFCS	NFCW	NFCE	NFCN	NFCS	NFCW	NFCE	NFCN
AFC SOUTH	Intraconference	AFCN	AFCE	AFCW	AFCN	AFCE	AFCW	AFCN	AFCE
	Interconference	NFCE	NFCS	NFCN	NFCW	NFCE	NFCS	NFCN	NFCW
AFC WEST	Intraconference	AFCE	AFCN	AFCS	AFCE	AFCN	AFCS	AFCE	AFCN
	Interconference	NFCW	NFCN	NFCS	NFCE	NFCW	NFCN	NFCS	NFCE
NFC EAST	Intraconference	NFCW	NFCS	NFCN	NFCW	NFCS	NFCN	NFCW	NFCS
	Interconference	AFCS	AFCE	AFCN	AFCW	AFCS	AFCE	AFCN	AFCW
NFC NORTH	Intraconference	NFCS	NFCW	NFCE	NFCS	NFCW	NFCE	NFCS	NFCW
	Interconference	AFCE	AFCW	AFCS	AFCN	AFCE	AFCW	AFCS	AFCN
NFC SOUTH	Intraconference	NFCN	NFCE	NFCW	NFCN	NFCE	NFCW	NFCN	NFCE
	Interconference	AFCN	AFCS	AFCW	AFCE	AFCN	AFCS	AFCW	AFCE
NFC WEST	Intraconference	NFCE	NFCN	NFCS	NFCE	NFCN	NFCS	NFCE	NFCN
	Interconference	AFCW	AFCN	AFCE	AFCS	AFCW	AFCN	AFCE	AFCS

2010–2017 Scheduling Rotation

		2010	2011	2012	2013	2014	2015	2016	2017
AFC EAST	Intraconference	AFCN	AFCW	AFCS	AFCN	AFCW	AFCS	AFCN	AFCW
	Interconference	NFCN	NFCE	NFCW	NFCS	NFCN	NFCE	NFCW	NFCS
AFC NORTH	Intraconference	AFCE	AFCS	AFCW	AFCE	AFCS	AFCW	AFCE	AFCS
	Interconference	NFCS	NFCW	NFCE	NFCN	NFCS	NFCW	NFCE	NFCN
AFC SOUTH	Intraconference	AFCW	AFCN	AFCE	AFCW	AFCN	AFCE	AFCW	AFCN
	Interconference	NFCE	NFCS	NFCN	NFCW	NFCE	NFCS	NFCN	NFCW
AFC WEST	Intraconference	AFCS	AFCE	AFCN	AFCS	AFCE	AFCN	AFCS	AFCE
	Interconference	NFCW	NFCN	NFCS	NFCE	NFCW	NFCN	NFCS	NFCE
NFC EAST	Intraconference	NFCN	NFCW	NFCS	NFCN	NFCW	NFCS	NFCN	NFCW
	Interconference	AFCS	AFCE	AFCN	AFCW	AFCS	AFCE	AFCN	AFCW
NFC NORTH	Intraconference	NFCE	NFCS	NFCW	NFCE	NFCS	NFCW	NFCE	NFCS
	Interconference	AFCE	AFCW	AFCS	AFCN	AFCE	AFCW	AFCS	AFCN
NFC SOUTH	Intraconference	NFCW	NFCN	NFCE	NFCW	NFCN	NFCE	NFCW	NFCN
	Interconference	AFCN	AFCS	AFCW	AFCE	AFCN	AFCS	AFCW	AFCE
NFC WEST	Intraconference	NFCS	NFCE	NFCN	NFCS	NFCE	NFCN	NFCS	NFCE
	Interconference	AFCW	AFCN	AFCE	AFCS	AFCW	AFCN	AFCE	AFCS

STANDINGS-BASED MATCHUPS

Below are the home and away pairings for each team's two intraconference games against teams that finished in the same position in the prior year's standings. The two games will be against teams from the two divisions that the team is not scheduled to play that season. For example, as noted in the scheduling rotation chart above, in 2013 the AFC East plays the AFC North. For the two "position games," AFC East teams will host the AFC West team and will play at the AFC South team that finished in the same position in the standings the year before. AFC North teams will host an AFC South team and will play at an AFC West team, etc. Every six years, each division would be matched with the other three divisions in its conference a total of four times, twice home and twice away.

	2002 2008 2014[a] Home Away	2003 2009 2015[a] Home Away	2004 2010 2016[a] Home Away	2005 2011 2017[a] Home Away	2006 2012 2018[a] Home Away	2007 2013 2019[a] Home Away
AFC EAST	AFCN AFCS	AFCN AFCW	AFCS AFCW	AFCS AFCN	AFCW AFCN	AFCW AFCS
AFC NORTH	AFCW AFCE	AFCS AFCE	AFCW AFCS	AFCE AFCW	AFCE AFCS	AFCS AFCW
AFC SOUTH	AFCE AFCW	AFCW AFCN	AFCN AFCE	AFCW AFCE	AFCN AFCW	AFCE AFCN
AFC WEST	AFCS AFCN	AFCE AFCS	AFCE AFCN	AFCN AFCS	AFCS AFCE	AFCN AFCE
NFC EAST	NFCS NFCN	NFCW NFCN	NFCS NFCW	NFCN NFCS	NFCN NFCW	NFCW NFCS
NFC NORTH	NFCE NFCW	NFCE NFCS	NFCW NFCS	NFCW NFCE	NFCS NFCE	NFCS NFCW
NFC SOUTH	NFCW NFCE	NFCN NFCW	NFCN NFCE	NFCE NFCW	NFCW NFCN	NFCE NFCN
NFC WEST	NFCN NFCS	NFCS NFCE	NFCE NFCN	NFCS NFCN	NFCE NFCS	NFCN NFCE

[a]Matchups for 2014 and beyond are based on the NFL continuing its current scheduling format.

2002 NON-DIVISIONAL OPPONENTS (AFC)

2001 FINAL STANDINGS

	East	Central	West
1	NE	PIT	OAK
2	MIA	BAL	SEA[b]
3	NYJ	CLE	DEN
4	IND[a]	TEN[a]	KC
5	BUF	JAC[a]	SD
6		CIN	

		East NEW ENGLAND		West OAKLAND		North PITTSBURGH		South TENNESSEE	
1		Home	Away	Home	Away	Home	Away	Home	Away
Intraconference		DEN	OAK	NE	BUF	HOU	JAC	CLE	BAL
		KC	SD	NYJ	MIA	IND	TEN	PIT	CIN
Interconference		GB	CHI	SF	ARI	ATL	NO	PHI	DAL
		MIN	DET	SEA	STL	CAR	TB	WAS	NYG
By Position		PIT	TEN	TEN	PIT	OAK	NE	NE	OAK
2		MIAMI		DENVER		BALTIMORE		INDIANAPOLIS	
		Home	Away	Home	Away	Home	Away	Home	Away
Intraconference		OAK	DEN	BUF	NE	JAC	HOU	BAL	CLE
		SD	KC	MIA	NYJ	TEN	IND	CIN	PIT
Interconference		CHI	GB	ARI	SF	NO	ATL	DAL	PHI
		DET	MIN	STL	SEA	TB	CAR	NYG	WAS
By Position		BAL	IND	IND	BAL	DEN	MIA	MIA	DEN

		NY JETS		KANSAS CITY		CLEVELAND		JACKSONVILLE	
3		Home	Away	Home	Away	Home	Away	Home	Away
Intraconference		DEN	OAK	BUF	NE	HOU	JAC	CLE	BAL
		KC	SD	MIA	NYJ	IND	TEN	PIT	CIN
Interconference		GB	CHI	ARI	SF	ATL	NO	PHI	DAL
		MIN	DET	STL	SEA	CAR	TB	WAS	NYG
By Position		CLE	JAC	JAC	CLE	KC	NYJ	NYJ	KC
4		BUFFALO		SAN DIEGO		CINCINNATI		HOUSTON[a]	
		Home	Away	Home	Away	Home	Away	Home	Away
Intraconference		OAK	DEN	NE	BUF	JAC	HOU	BAL	CLE
		SD	KC	NYJ	MIA	TEN	IND	CIN	PIT
Interconference		CHI	GB	SF	ARI	NO	ATL	DAL	PHI
		DET	MIN	SEA	STL	TB	CAR	NYG	WAS
By Position		CIN	HOU	HOU	CIN	SD	BUF	BUF	SD

[a]Tennessee, Indianapolis and Jacksonville assigned 1st, 2nd and 3rd place, respectively, based on 2001 records. Expansion Houston Texans assigned 4th place in AFC South.
[b]Based on 2001 record, Seattle assigned 3rd place in NFC West.

2002 NON-DIVISIONAL OPPONENTS (NFC)

2001 FINAL STANDINGS

	East	Central	West
1	PHI	CHI	STL
2	WAS	GB	SF
3	NYG	TB[a]	NO[a]
4	ARI[b]	MIN	ATL[a]
5	DAL	DET	CAR[a]

		East		West		North		South	
1		PHILADELPHIA		ST. LOUIS		CHICAGO		TAMPA BAY	
		Home	Away	Home	Away	Home	Away	Home	Away
Intraconference		ARI	SF	DAL	PHI	NO	ATL	GB	CHI
		STL	SEA	NYG	WAS	TB	CAR	MIN	DET
Interconference		HOU	JAC	OAK	DEN	NE	BUF	CLE	BAL
		IND	TEN	SD	KC	NYJ	MIA	PIT	CIN
By Position		TB	CHI	CHI	TB	PHI	STL	STL	PHI
2		WASHINGTON		SAN FRANCISCO		GREEN BAY		NEW ORLEANS	
		Home	Away	Home	Away	Home	Away	Home	Away
Intraconference		ARI	SF	PHI	DAL	ATL	NO	GB	CHI
		STL	SEA	WAS	NYG	CAR	TB	MIN	DET
Interconference		HOU	JAC	DEN	OAK	BUF	NE	CLE	BAL
		IND	TEN	KC	SD	MIA	NYJ	PIT	CIN
By Position		NO	GB	GB	NO	WAS	SF	SF	WAS
3		NY GIANTS		SEATTLE		MINNESOTA		ATLANTA	
		Home	Away	Home	Away	Home	Away	Home	Away
Intraconference		SF	ARI	PHI	DAL	ATL	NO	CHI	GB
		SEA	STL	WAS	NYG	CAR	TB	DET	MIN
Interconference		JAC	HOU	DEN	OAK	BUF	NE	BAL	CLE
		TEN	IND	KC	SD	MIA	NYJ	CIN	PIT
By Position		ATL	MIN	MIN	ATL	NYG	SEA	SEA	NYG

		DALLAS		ARIZONA		DETROIT		CAROLINA	
4		Home	Away	Home	Away	Home	Away	Home	Away
Intraconference		SF	ARI	DAL	PHI	NO	ATL	CHI	GB
		SEA	STL	NYG	WAS	TB	CAR	DET	MIN
Interconference		JAC	HOU	OAK	DEN	NE	BUF	BAL	CLE
		TEN	IND	SD	KC	NYJ	MIA	CIN	PIT
By Position		CAR	DET	DET	CAR	DAL	ARI	ARI	DAL

[a]TB, NO, ATL and CAR assigned 1st, 2nd, 3rd and 4th place, respectively, based on 2001 records.
[b]ARI assigned 4th place in NFC West based on final 2001 records.

2003 NON-DIVISIONAL OPPONENTS (AFC)

2002 FINAL STANDINGS

	East	South	North	West
1	NYJ	TEN	PIT	OAK
2	NE	IND	CLE	DEN
3	MIA	JAC	BAL	SD
4	BUF	HOU	CIN	KC

	East		South		North		West	
1	NY JETS		TENNESSEE		PITTSBURGH		OAKLAND	
	Home	Away	Home	Away	Home	Away	Home	Away
Intraconference	JAC	HOU	BUF	NE	OAK	DEN	BAL	CLE
	TEN	IND	MIA	NYJ	SD	KC	CIN	PIT
Interconference	DAL	PHI	NO	ATL	ARI	SF	GB	CHI
	NYG	WAS	TB	CAR	STL	SEA	MIN	DET
By Position	PIT	OAK	OAK	PIT	TEN	NYJ	NYJ	TEN
2	NEW ENGLAND		INDIANAPOLIS		CLEVELAND		DENVER	
	Home	Away	Home	Away	Home	Away	Home	Away
Intraconference	JAC	HOU	NE	BUF	OAK	DEN	CLE	BAL
	TEN	IND	NYJ	MIA	SD	KC	PIT	CIN
Interconference	DAL	PHI	ATL	NO	ARI	SF	CHI	GB
	NYG	WAS	CAR	TB	STL	SEA	DET	MIN
By Position	CLE	DEN	DEN	CLE	IND	NE	NE	IND
3	MIAMI		JACKSONVILLE		BALTIMORE		SAN DIEGO	
	Home	Away	Home	Away	Home	Away	Home	Away
Intraconference	HOU	JAC	BUF	NE	DEN	OAK	BAL	CLE
	IND	TEN	MIA	NYJ	KC	SD	CIN	PIT
Interconference	PHI	DAL	NO	ATL	SF	ARI	GB	CHI
	WAS	NYG	TB	CAR	SEA	STL	MIN	DET
By Position	BAL	SD	SD	BAL	JAC	MIA	MIA	JAC
4	BUFFALO		HOUSTON		CINCINNATI		KANSAS CITY	
	Home	Away	Home	Away	Home	Away	Home	Away
Intraconference	HOU	JAC	NE	BUF	DEN	OAK	CLE	BAL
	IND	TEN	NYJ	MIA	KC	SD	PIT	CIN
Interconference	PHI	DAL	ATL	NO	SF	ARI	CHI	GB
	WAS	NYG	CAR	TB	SEA	STL	DET	MIN
By Position	CIN	KC	KC	CIN	HOU	BUF	BUF	HOU

2003 NON-DIVISIONAL OPPONENTS (NFC)

2002 FINAL STANDINGS

	East	South	North	West
1	PHI	TB	GB	SF
2	NYG	ATL	MIN	STL
3	WAS	NO	CHI	SEA
4	DAL	CAR	DET	ARI

		East **PHILADELPHIA**		*South* **TAMPA BAY**		*North* **GREEN BAY**		*West* **SAN FRANCISCO**	
1		Home	Away	Home	Away	Home	Away	Home	Away
Intraconference		NO	ATL	DAL	PHI	SF	ARI	CHI	GB
		TB	CAR	NYG	WAS	SEA	STL	DET	MIN
Interconference		NE	BUF	HOU	JAC	DEN	OAK	CLE	BAL
		NYJ	MIA	IND	TEN	KC	SD	PIT	CIN
By Position		SF	GB	GB	SF	PHI	TB	TB	PHI
2		**NY GIANTS**		**ATLANTA**		**MINNESOTA**		**ST. LOUIS**	
		Home	Away	Home	Away	Home	Away	Home	Away
Intraconference		ATL	NO	PHI	DAL	SF	ARI	GB	CHI
		CAR	TB	WAS	NYG	SEA	STL	MIN	DET
Interconference		BUF	NE	JAC	HOU	DEN	OAK	BAL	CLE
		MIA	NYJ	TEN	IND	KC	SD	CIN	PIT
By Position		STL	MIN	MIN	STL	NYG	ATL	ATL	NYG
3		**WASHINGTON**		**NEW ORLEANS**		**CHICAGO**		**SEATTLE**	
		Home	Away	Home	Away	Home	Away	Home	Away
Intraconference		NO	ATL	DAL	PHI	ARI	SF	CHI	GB
		TB	CAR	NYG	WAS	STL	SEA	DET	MIN
Interconference		NE	BUF	HOU	JAC	OAK	DEN	CLE	BAL
		NYJ	MIA	IND	TEN	SD	KC	PIT	CIN
By Position		SEA	CHI	CHI	SEA	WAS	NO	NO	WAS
4		**DALLAS**		**CAROLINA**		**DETROIT**		**ARIZONA**	
		Home	Away	Home	Away	Home	Away	Home	Away
Intraconference		ATL	NO	PHI	DAL	ARI	SF	GB	CHI
		CAR	TB	WAS	NYG	STL	SEA	MIN	DET
Interconference		BUF	NE	JAC	HOU	OAK	DEN	BAL	CLE
		MIA	NYJ	TEN	IND	SD	KC	CIN	PIT
By Position		ARI	DET	DET	ARI	DAL	CAR	CAR	DAL

2004 NON-DIVISIONAL OPPONENTS (AFC)

2003 FINAL STANDINGS

	East	North	South	West
1	NE	BAL	IND	KC
2	MIA	CIN	TEN	DEN
3	BUF	PIT	JAC	OAK
4	NYJ	CLE	HOU	SD

	East		North		South		West	
1	**NEW ENGLAND**		**BALTIMORE**		**INDIANAPOLIS**		**KANSAS CITY**	
	Home	Away	Home	Away	Home	Away	Home	Away
Intraconference	BAL	CLE	BUF	NE	OAK	DEN	HOU	JAC
	CIN	PIT	MIA	NYJ	SD	KC	IND	TEN
Interconference	SF	ARI	DAL	PHI	GB	CHI	ATL	NO
	SEA	STL	NYG	WAS	MIN	DET	CAR	TB
By Position	IND	KC	KC	IND	BAL	NE	NE	BAL
2	**MIAMI**		**CINCINNATI**		**TENNESSEE**		**DENVER**	
	Home	Away	Home	Away	Home	Away	Home	Away
Intraconference	CLE	BAL	BUF	NE	DEN	OAK	HOU	JAC
	PIT	CIN	MIA	NYJ	KC	SD	IND	TEN
Interconference	ARI	SF	DAL	PHI	CHI	GB	ATL	NO
	STL	SEA	NYG	WAS	DET	MIN	CAR	TB
By Position	TEN	DEN	DEN	TEN	CIN	MIA	MIA	CIN
3	**BUFFALO**		**PITTSBURGH**		**JACKSONVILLE**		**OAKLAND**	
	Home	Away	Home	Away	Home	Away	Home	Away
Intraconference	CLE	BAL	NE	BUF	DEN	OAK	JAC	HOU
	PIT	CIN	NYJ	MIA	KC	SD	TEN	IND
Interconference	ARI	SF	PHI	DAL	CHI	GB	NO	ATL
	STL	SEA	WAS	NYG	DET	MIN	TB	CAR
By Position	JAC	OAK	OAK	JAC	PIT	BUF	BUF	PIT
4	**NY JETS**		**CLEVELAND**		**HOUSTON**		**SAN DIEGO**	
	Home	Away	Home	Away	Home	Away	Home	Away
Intraconference	BAL	CLE	NE	BUF	OAK	DEN	JAC	HOU
	CIN	PIT	NYJ	MIA	SD	KC	TEN	IND
Interconference	SF	ARI	PHI	DAL	GB	CHI	NO	ATL
	SEA	STL	WAS	NYG	MIN	DET	TB	CAR
By Position	HOU	SD	SD	HOU	CLE	NYJ	NYJ	CLE

2004 NON-DIVISIONAL OPPONENTS (NFC)

2003 FINAL STANDINGS

	East	North	South	West
1	PHI	GB	CAR	STL
2	DAL	MIN	NO	SEA
3	WAS	CHI	TB	SF
4	NYG	DET	ATL	ARI

	East		North		South		West	
1	**PHILADELPHIA**		**GREEN BAY**		**CAROLINA**		**ST. LOUIS**	
	Home	Away	Home	Away	Home	Away	Home	Away
Intraconference	GB	CHI	DAL	PHI	ARI	SF	NO	ATL
	MIN	DET	NYG	WAS	STL	SEA	TB	CAR
Interconference	BAL	CLE	JAC	HOU	OAK	DEN	NE	BUF
	CIN	PIT	TEN	IND	SD	KC	NYJ	MIA
By Position	CAR	STL	STL	CAR	GB	PHI	PHI	GB

2		DALLAS		MINNESOTA		NEW ORLEANS		SEATTLE	
		Home	*Away*	*Home*	*Away*	*Home*	*Away*	*Home*	*Away*
Intraconference		CHI	GB	DAL	PHI	SF	ARI	ATL	NO
		DET	MIN	NYG	WAS	SEA	STL	CAR	TB
Interconference		CLE	BAL	JAC	HOU	DEN	OAK	BUF	NE
		PIT	CIN	TEN	IND	KC	SD	MIA	NYJ
By Position		NO	SEA	SEA	NO	MIN	DAL	DAL	MIN
3		WASHINGTON		CHICAGO		TAMPA BAY		SAN FRANCISCO	
		Home	*Away*	*Home*	*Away*	*Home*	*Away*	*Home*	*Away*
Intraconference		GB	CHI	PHI	DAL	SF	ARI	ATL	NO
		MIN	DET	WAS	NYG	SEA	STL	CAR	TB
Interconference		BAL	CLE	HOU	JAC	DEN	OAK	BUF	NE
		CIN	PIT	IND	TEN	KC	SD	MIA	NYJ
By Position		TB	SF	SF	TB	CHI	WAS	WAS	CHI
4		NY GIANTS		DETROIT		ATLANTA		ARIZONA	
		Home	*Away*	*Home*	*Away*	*Home*	*Away*	*Home*	*Away*
Intraconference		CHI	GB	PHI	DAL	ARI	SF	NO	ATL
		DET	MIN	WAS	NYG	STL	SEA	TB	CAR
Interconference		CLE	BAL	HOU	JAC	OAK	DEN	NE	BUF
		PIT	CIN	IND	TEN	SD	KC	NYJ	MIA
By Position		ATL	ARI	ARI	ATL	DET	NYG	NYG	DET

2005 NON-DIVISIONAL OPPONENTS (AFC)

2004 FINAL STANDINGS

	East	West	North	South
1	NE	SD	PIT	IND
2	NYJ	DEN	BAL	JAC
3	BUF	KC	CIN	HOU
4	MIA	OAK	CLE	TEN

		East		West		North		South	
1		NEW ENGLAND		SAN DIEGO		PITTSBURGH		INDIANAPOLIS	
		Home	*Away*	*Home*	*Away*	*Home*	*Away*	*Home*	*Away*
Intraconference		OAK	DEN	BUF	NE	JAC	HOU	CLE	BAL
		SD	KC	MIA	NYJ	TEN	IND	PIT	CIN
Interconference		NO	ATL	DAL	PHI	CHI	GB	ARI	SF
		TB	CAR	NYG	WAS	DET	MIN	STL	SEA
By Position		IND	PIT	PIT	IND	NE	SD	SD	NE
2		NY JETS		DENVER		BALTIMORE		JACKSONVILLE	
		Home	*Away*	*Home*	*Away*	*Home*	*Away*	*Home*	*Away*
Intraconference		OAK	DEN	NE	BUF	HOU	JAC	BAL	CLE
		SD	KC	NYJ	MIA	IND	TEN	CIN	PIT
Interconference		NO	ATL	PHI	DAL	GB	CHI	SF	ARI
		TB	CAR	WAS	NYG	MIN	DET	SEA	STL
By Position		JAC	BAL	BAL	JAC	NYJ	DEN	DEN	NYJ
3		BUFFALO		KANSAS CITY		CINCINNATI		HOUSTON	
		Home	*Away*	*Home*	*Away*	*Home*	*Away*	*Home*	*Away*
Intraconference		DEN	OAK	NE	BUF	HOU	JAC	CLE	BAL
		KC	SD	NYJ	MIA	IND	TEN	PIT	CIN
Interconference		ATL	NO	PHI	DAL	GB	CHI	ARI	SF
		CAR	TB	WAS	NYG	MIN	DET	STL	SEA
By Position		HOU	CIN	CIN	HOU	BUF	KC	KC	BUF

	MIAMI		**OAKLAND**		**CLEVELAND**		**TENNESSEE**	
4	Home	Away	Home	Away	Home	Away	Home	Away
Intraconference	DEN	OAK	BUF	NE	JAC	HOU	BAL	CLE
	KC	SD	MIA	NYJ	TEN	IND	CIN	PIT
Interconference	ATL	NO	DAL	PHI	CHI	GB	SF	ARI
	CAR	TB	NYG	WAS	DET	MIN	SEA	STL
By Position	TEN	CLE	CLE	TEN	MIA	OAK	OAK	MIA

2005 NON-DIVISIONAL OPPONENTS (NFC)

2004 FINAL STANDINGS

	East	West	North	South
1	PHI	SEA	GB	ATL
2	NYG	STL	MIN	NO
3	DAL	ARI	DET	CAR
4	WAS	SF	CHI	TB

	East		West		North		South	
1	**PHILADELPHIA**		**SEATTLE**		**GREEN BAY**		**ATLANTA**	
	Home	Away	Home	Away	Home	Away	Home	Away
Intraconference	SF	ARI	DAL	PHI	NO	ATL	GB	CHI
	SEA	STL	NYG	WAS	TB	CAR	MIN	DET
Interconference	OAK	DEN	HOU	JAC	CLE	BAL	NE	BUF
	SD	KC	IND	TEN	PIT	CIN	NYJ	MIA
By Position	GB	ATL	ATL	GB	SEA	PHI	PHI	SEA
2	**NY GIANTS**		**ST. LOUIS**		**MINNESOTA**		**NEW ORLEANS**	
	Home	Away	Home	Away	Home	Away	Home	Away
Intraconference	ARI	SF	PHI	DAL	NO	ATL	CHI	GB
	STL	SEA	WAS	NYG	TB	CAR	DET	MIN
Interconference	DEN	OAK	JAC	HOU	CLE	BAL	BUF	NE
	KC	SD	TEN	IND	PIT	CIN	MIA	NYJ
By Position	MIN	NO	NO	MIN	STL	NYG	NYG	STL
3	**DALLAS**		**ARIZONA**		**DETROIT**		**CAROLINA**	
	Home	Away	Home	Away	Home	Away	Home	Away
Intraconference	ARI	SF	PHI	DAL	ATL	NO	GB	CHI
	STL	SEA	WAS	NYG	CAR	TB	MIN	DET
Interconference	DEN	OAK	JAC	HOU	BAL	CLE	NE	BUF
	KC	SD	TEN	IND	CIN	PIT	NYJ	MIA
By Position	DET	CAR	CAR	DET	ARI	DAL	DAL	ARI
4	**WASHINGTON**		**SAN FRANCISCO**		**CHICAGO**		**TAMPA BAY**	
	Home	Away	Home	Away	Home	Away	Home	Away
Intraconference	SF	ARI	DAL	PHI	ATL	NO	CHI	GB
	SEA	STL	NYG	WAS	CAR	TB	DET	MIN
Interconference	OAK	DEN	HOU	JAC	BAL	CLE	BUF	NE
	SD	KC	IND	TEN	CIN	PIT	MIA	NYJ
By Position	CHI	TB	TB	CHI	SF	WAS	WAS	SF

2006 NON-DIVISIONAL OPPONENTS (AFC)

2005 FINAL STANDINGS

	East	South	North	West
1	NE	IND	CIN	DEN
2	MIA	JAC	PIT	KC
3	BUF	TEN	BAL	SD
4	NYJ	HOU	CLE	OAK

		East NEW ENGLAND		South INDIANAPOLIS		North CINCINNATI		West DENVER	
1		Home	Away	Home	Away	Home	Away	Home	Away
Intraconference		HOU	JAC	BUF	NE	OAK	DEN	BAL	CLE
		IND	TEN	MIA	NYJ	SD	KC	CIN	PIT
Interconference		CHI	GB	PHI	DAL	ATL	NO	SF	ARI
		DET	MIN	WAS	NYG	CAR	TB	SEA	STL
By Position		DEN	CIN	CIN	DEN	NE	IND	IND	NE
2		MIAMI		JACKSONVILLE		PITTSBURGH		KANSAS CITY	
		Home	Away	Home	Away	Home	Away	Home	Away
Intraconference		JAC	HOU	NE	BUF	DEN	OAK	BAL	CLE
		TEN	IND	NYJ	MIA	KC	SD	CIN	PIT
Interconference		GB	CHI	DAL	PHI	NO	ATL	SF	ARI
		MIN	DET	NYG	WAS	TB	CAR	SEA	STL
By Position		KC	PIT	PIT	KC	MIA	JAC	JAC	MIA
3		BUFFALO		TENNESSEE		BALTIMORE		SAN DIEGO	
		Home	Away	Home	Away	Home	Away	Home	Away
Intraconference		JAC	HOU	NE	BUF	OAK	DEN	CLE	BAL
		TEN	IND	NYJ	MIA	SD	KC	PIT	CIN
Interconference		GB	CHI	DAL	PHI	ATL	NO	ARI	SF
		MIN	DET	NYG	WAS	CAR	TB	STL	SEA
By Position		SD	BAL	BAL	SD	BUF	TEN	TEN	BUF
4		NY JETS		HOUSTON		CLEVELAND		OAKLAND	
		Home	Away	Home	Away	Home	Away	Home	Away
Intraconference		HOU	JAC	BUF	NE	DEN	OAK	CLE	BAL
		IND	TEN	MIA	NYJ	KC	SD	PIT	CIN
Interconference		CHI	GB	PHI	DAL	NO	ATL	ARI	SF
		DET	MIN	WAS	NYG	TB	CAR	STL	SEA
By Position		OAK	CLE	CLE	OAK	NYJ	HOU	HOU	NYJ

2006 NON-DIVISIONAL OPPONENTS (NFC)

2005 FINAL STANDINGS

	East	South	North	West
1	NYG	TB	CHI	SEA
2	WAS	CAR	MIN	STL
3	DAL	ATL	DET	ARI
4	PHI	NO	GB	SF

		East NY GIANTS		South TAMPA BAY		North CHICAGO		West SEATTLE	
1		Home	Away	Home	Away	Home	Away	Home	Away
Intraconference		NO	ATL	PHI	DAL	SF	ARI	GB	CHI
		TB	CAR	WAS	NYG	SEA	STL	MIN	DET
Interconference		HOU	JAC	BAL	CLE	BUF	NE	OAK	DEN
		IND	TEN	CIN	PIT	MIA	NYJ	SD	KC
By Position		CHI	SEA	SEA	CHI	TB	NYG	NYG	TB

2	WASHINGTON		CAROLINA		MINNESOTA		ST. LOUIS	
	Home	Away	Home	Away	Home	Away	Home	Away
Intraconference	ATL	NO	DAL	PHI	ARI	SF	CHI	GB
	CAR	TB	NYG	WAS	STL	SEA	DET	MIN
Interconference	JAC	HOU	CLE	BAL	NE	BUF	DEN	OAK
	TEN	IND	PIT	CIN	NYJ	MIA	KC	SD
By Position	MIN	STL	STL	MIN	CAR	WAS	WAS	CAR
3	DALLAS		ATLANTA		DETROIT		ARIZONA	
	Home	Away	Home	Away	Home	Away	Home	Away
Intraconference	NO	ATL	DAL	PHI	SF	ARI	CHI	GB
	TB	CAR	NYG	WAS	SEA	STL	DET	MIN
Interconference	HOU	JAC	CLE	BAL	BUF	NE	DEN	OAK
	IND	TEN	PIT	CIN	MIA	NYJ	KC	SD
By Position	DET	ARI	ARI	DET	ATL	DAL	DAL	ATL
4	PHILADELPHIA		NEW ORLEANS		GREEN BAY		SAN FRANCISCO	
	Home	Away	Home	Away	Home	Away	Home	Away
Intraconference	ATL	NO	PHI	DAL	ARI	SF	GB	CHI
	CAR	TB	WAS	NYG	STL	SEA	MIN	DET
Interconference	JAC	HOU	BAL	CLE	NE	BUF	OAK	DEN
	TEN	IND	CIN	PIT	NYJ	MIA	SD	KC
By Position	GB	SF	SF	GB	NO	PHI	PHI	NO

2007 NON-DIVISIONAL OPPONENTS (AFC)

2006 FINAL STANDINGS

	East	North	South	West
1	NE	BAL	IND	SD
2	NYJ	CIN	TEN	KC
3	BUF	PIT	JAC	DEN
4	MIA	CLE	HOU	OAK

	East		North		South		West	
1	NEW ENGLAND		BALTIMORE		INDIANAPOLIS		SAN DIEGO	
	Home	Away	Home	Away	Home	Away	Home	Away
Intraconference	CLE	BAL	NE	BUF	DEN	OAK	HOU	JAC
	PIT	CIN	NYJ	MIA	KC	SD	IND	TEN
Interconference	PHI	DAL	ARI	SF	NO	ATL	CHI	GB
	WAS	NYG	STL	SEA	TB	CAR	DET	MIN
By Position	SD	IND	IND	SD	NE	BAL	BAL	NE
2	NY JETS		CINCINNATI		TENNESSEE		KANSAS CITY	
	Home	Away	Home	Away	Home	Away	Home	Away
Intraconference	CLE	BAL	NE	BUF	OAK	DEN	JAC	HOU
	PIT	CIN	NYJ	MIA	SD	KC	TEN	IND
Interconference	PHI	DAL	ARI	SF	ATL	NO	GB	CHI
	WAS	NYG	STL	SEA	CAR	TB	MIN	DET
By Position	KC	TEN	TEN	KC	NYJ	CIN	CIN	NYJ
3	BUFFALO		PITTSBURGH		JACKSONVILLE		DENVER	
	Home	Away	Home	Away	Home	Away	Home	Away
Intraconference	BAL	CLE	BUF	NE	OAK	DEN	JAC	HOU
	CIN	PIT	MIA	NYJ	SD	KC	TEN	IND
Interconference	DAL	PHI	SF	ARI	ATL	NO	GB	CHI
	NYG	WAS	SEA	STL	CAR	TB	MIN	DET
By Position	DEN	JAC	JAC	DEN	BUF	PIT	PIT	BUF

4	MIAMI		CLEVELAND		HOUSTON		OAKLAND	
	Home	Away	Home	Away	Home	Away	Home	Away
Intraconference	BAL	CLE	BUF	NE	DEN	OAK	HOU	JAC
	CIN	PIT	MIA	NYJ	KC	SD	IND	TEN
Interconference	DAL	PHI	SF	ARI	NO	ATL	CHI	GB
	NYG	WAS	SEA	STL	TB	CAR	DET	MIN
By Position	OAK	HOU	HOU	OAK	MIA	CLE	CLE	MIA

2007 NON-DIVISIONAL OPPONENTS (NFC)

2006 FINAL STANDINGS

	East	North	South	West
1	PHI	CHI	NO	SEA
2	DAL	GB	CAR	STL
3	NYG	MIN	ATL	SF
4	WAS	DET	TB	ARI

	East		North		South		West	
1	PHILADELPHIA		CHICAGO		NEW ORLEANS		SEATTLE	
	Home	Away	Home	Away	Home	Away	Home	Away
Intraconference	CHI	GB	DAL	PHI	ARI	SF	NO	ATL
	DET	MIN	NYG	WAS	STL	SEA	TB	CAR
Interconference	BUF	NE	DEN	OAK	JAC	HOU	BAL	CLE
	MIA	NYJ	KC	SD	TEN	IND	CIN	PIT
By Position	SEA	NO	NO	SEA	PHI	CHI	CHI	PHI
2	DALLAS		GREEN BAY		CAROLINA		ST. LOUIS	
	Home	Away	Home	Away	Home	Away	Home	Away
Intraconference	GB	CHI	PHI	DAL	SF	ARI	ATL	NO
	MIN	DET	WAS	NYG	SEA	STL	CAR	TB
Interconference	NE	BUF	OAK	DEN	HOU	JAC	CLE	BAL
	NYJ	MIA	SD	KC	IND	TEN	PIT	CIN
By Position	STL	CAR	CAR	STL	DAL	GB	GB	DAL
3	NY GIANTS		MINNESOTA		ATLANTA		SAN FRANCISCO	
	Home	Away	Home	Away	Home	Away	Home	Away
Intraconference	GB	CHI	PHI	DAL	SF	ARI	NO	ATL
	MIN	DET	WAS	NYG	SEA	STL	TB	CAR
Interconference	NE	BUF	OAK	DEN	HOU	JAC	BAL	CLE
	NYJ	MIA	SD	KC	IND	TEN	CIN	PIT
By Position	SF	ATL	ATL	SF	NYG	MIN	MIN	NYG
4	WASHINGTON		DETROIT		TAMPA BAY		ARIZONA	
	Home	Away	Home	Away	Home	Away	Home	Away
Intraconference	CHI	GB	DAL	PHI	ARI	SF	ATL	NO
	DET	MIN	NYG	WAS	STL	SEA	CAR	TB
Interconference	BUF	NE	DEN	OAK	JAC	HOU	CLE	BAL
	MIA	NYJ	KC	SD	TEN	IND	PIT	CIN
By Position	ARI	TB	TB	ARI	WAS	DET	DET	WAS

2008 NON-DIVISIONAL OPPONENTS (AFC)

2007 FINAL STANDINGS

	East	West	North	South
1	NE	SD	PIT	IND
2	BUF	DEN	CLE	JAC
3	NYJ	KC	CIN	TEN
4	MIA	OAK	BAL	HOU

		East NEW ENGLAND		West SAN DIEGO		North PITTSBURGH		South INDIANAPOLIS	
1		Home	Away	Home	Away	Home	Away	Home	Away
Intraconference		DEN	OAK	NE	BUF	HOU	JAC	BAL	CLE
		KC	SD	NYJ	MIA	IND	TEN	CIN	PIT
Interconference		ARI	SF	ATL	NO	DAL	PHI	CHI	GB
		STL	SEA	CAR	TB	NYG	WAS	DET	MIN
By Position		PIT	IND	IND	PIT	SD	NE	NE	SD
2		BUFFALO		DENVER		CLEVELAND		JACKSONVILLE	
		Home	Away	Home	Away	Home	Away	Home	Away
Intraconference		OAK	DEN	BUF	NE	HOU	JAC	CLE	BAL
		SD	KC	MIA	NYJ	IND	TEN	PIT	CIN
Interconference		SF	ARI	NO	ATL	DAL	PHI	GB	CHI
		SEA	STL	TB	CAR	NYG	WAS	MIN	DET
By Position		CLE	JAC	JAC	CLE	DEN	BUF	BUF	DEN
3		NY JETS		KANSAS CITY		CINCINNATI		TENNESSEE	
		Home	Away	Home	Away	Home	Away	Home	Away
Intraconference		DEN	OAK	BUF	NE	JAC	HOU	CLE	BAL
		KC	SD	MIA	NYJ	TEN	IND	PIT	CIN
Interconference		ARI	SF	NO	ATL	PHI	DAL	GB	CHI
		STL	SEA	TB	CAR	WAS	NYG	MIN	DET
By Position		CIN	TEN	TEN	CIN	KC	NYJ	NYJ	KC
4		MIAMI		OAKLAND		BALTIMORE		HOUSTON	
		Home	Away	Home	Away	Home	Away	Home	Away
Intraconference		OAK	DEN	NE	BUF	JAC	HOU	BAL	CLE
		SD	KC	NYJ	MIA	TEN	IND	CIN	PIT
Interconference		SF	ARI	ATL	NO	PHI	DAL	CHI	GB
		SEA	STL	CAR	TB	WAS	NYG	DET	MIN
By Position		BAL	HOU	HOU	BAL	OAK	MIA	MIA	OAK

2008 NON-DIVISIONAL OPPONENTS (NFC)

2007 FINAL STANDINGS

	East	West	North	South
1	DAL	SEA	GB	TB
2	NYG	ARI	MIN	CAR
3	WAS	SF	DET	NO
4	PHI	STL	CHI	ATL

		East DALLAS		West SEATTLE		North GREEN BAY		South TAMPA BAY	
1		Home	Away	Home	Away	Home	Away	Home	Away
Intraconference		SF	ARI	PHI	DAL	ATL	NO	GB	CHI
		SEA	STL	WAS	NYG	CAR	TB	MIN	DET
Interconference		BAL	CLE	NE	BUF	HOU	JAC	OAK	DEN
		CIN	PIT	NYJ	MIA	IND	TEN	SD	KC
By Position		TB	GB	GB	TB	DAL	SEA	SEA	DAL

		NY GIANTS		ARIZONA		MINNESOTA		CAROLINA	
		Home	*Away*	*Home*	*Away*	*Home*	*Away*	*Home*	*Away*
2	Intraconference	SF	ARI	DAL	PHI	ATL	NO	CHI	GB
		SEA	STL	NYG	WAS	CAR	TB	DET	MIN
	Interconference	BAL	CLE	BUF	NE	HOU	JAC	DEN	OAK
		CIN	PIT	MIA	NYJ	IND	TEN	KC	SD
	By Position	CAR	MIN	MIN	CAR	NYG	ARI	ARI	NYG
		WASHINGTON		SAN FRANCISCO		DETROIT		NEW ORLEANS	
		Home	*Away*	*Home*	*Away*	*Home*	*Away*	*Home*	*Away*
3	Intraconference	ARI	SF	PHI	DAL	NO	ATL	GB	CHI
		STL	SEA	WAS	NYG	TB	CAR	MIN	DET
	Interconference	CLE	BAL	NE	BUF	JAC	HOU	OAK	DEN
		PIT	CIN	NYJ	MIA	TEN	IND	SD	KC
	By Position	NO	DET	DET	NO	WAS	SF	SF	WAS
		PHILADELPHIA		ST. LOUIS		CHICAGO		ATLANTA	
		Home	*Away*	*Home*	*Away*	*Home*	*Away*	*Home*	*Away*
4	Intraconference	ARI	SF	DAL	PHI	NO	ATL	CHI	GB
		STL	SEA	NYG	WAS	TB	CAR	DET	MIN
	Interconference	CLE	BAL	BUF	NE	JAC	HOU	DEN	OAK
		PIT	CIN	MIA	NYJ	TEN	IND	KC	SD
	By Position	ATL	CHI	CHI	ATL	PHI	STL	STL	PHI

2009 NON-DIVISIONAL OPPONENTS (AFC)

2008 FINAL STANDINGS

	East	South	North	West
1	MIA	TEN	PIT	SD
2	NE	IND	BAL	DEN
3	NYJ	HOU	CIN	OAK
4	BUF	JAC	CLE	KC

		East		South		North		West	
		MIAMI		TENNESSEE		PITTSBURGH		SAN DIEGO	
		Home	*Away*	*Home*	*Away*	*Home*	*Away*	*Home*	*Away*
1	Intraconference	HOU	JAC	BUF	NE	OAK	DEN	BAL	CLE
		IND	TEN	MIA	NYJ	SD	KC	CIN	PIT
	Interconference	NO	ATL	ARI	SF	GB	CHI	PHI	DAL
		TB	CAR	STL	SEA	MIN	DET	WAS	NYG
	By Position	PIT	SD	SD	PIT	TEN	MIA	MIA	TEN
		NEW ENGLAND		INDIANAPOLIS		BALTIMORE		DENVER	
		Home	*Away*	*Home*	*Away*	*Home*	*Away*	*Home*	*Away*
2	Intraconference	JAC	HOU	NE	BUF	DEN	OAK	CLE	BAL
		TEN	IND	NYJ	MIA	KC	SD	PIT	CIN
	Interconference	ATL	NO	SF	ARI	CHI	GB	DAL	PHI
		CAR	TB	SEA	STL	DET	MIN	NYG	WAS
	By Position	BAL	DEN	DEN	BAL	IND	NE	NE	IND
		NY JETS		HOUSTON		CINCINNATI		OAKLAND	
		Home	*Away*	*Home*	*Away*	*Home*	*Away*	*Home*	*Away*
3	Intraconference	JAC	HOU	NE	BUF	DEN	OAK	BAL	CLE
		TEN	IND	NYJ	MIA	KC	SD	CIN	PIT
	Interconference	ATL	NO	SF	ARI	CHI	GB	PHI	DAL
		CAR	TB	SEA	STL	DET	MIN	WAS	NYG
	By Position	CIN	OAK	OAK	CIN	HOU	NYJ	NYJ	HOU

	4	BUFFALO		JACKSONVILLE		CLEVELAND		KANSAS CITY	
		Home	Away	Home	Away	Home	Away	Home	Away
Intraconference		HOU	JAC	BUF	NE	OAK	DEN	CLE	BAL
		IND	TEN	MIA	NYJ	SD	KC	PIT	CIN
Interconference		NO	ATL	ARI	SF	GB	CHI	DAL	PHI
		TB	CAR	STL	SEA	MIN	DET	NYG	WAS
By Position		CLE	KC	KC	CLE	JAC	BUF	BUF	JAC

2009 NON-DIVISIONAL OPPONENTS (NFC)

2008 FINAL STANDINGS

	East	South	North	West
1	NYG	CAR	MIN	ARI
2	PHI	ATL	CHI	SF
3	DAL	TB	GB	SEA
4	WAS	NO	DET	STL

		East		South		North		West	
1		NY GIANTS		CAROLINA		MINNESOTA		ARIZONA	
		Home	Away	Home	Away	Home	Away	Home	Away
Intraconference		ATL	NO	PHI	DAL	SF	ARI	GB	CHI
		CAR	TB	WAS	NYG	SEA	STL	MIN	DET
Interconference		OAK	DEN	BUF	NE	BAL	CLE	HOU	JAC
		SD	KC	MIA	NYJ	CIN	PIT	IND	TEN
By Position		ARI	MIN	MIN	ARI	NYG	CAR	CAR	NYG
2		PHILADELPHIA		ATLANTA		CHICAGO		SAN FRANCISCO	
		Home	Away	Home	Away	Home	Away	Home	Away
Intraconference		NO	ATL	PHI	DAL	ARI	SF	CHI	GB
		TB	CAR	WAS	NYG	STL	SEA	DET	MIN
Interconference		DEN	OAK	BUF	NE	CLE	BAL	JAC	HOU
		KC	SD	MIA	NYJ	PIT	CIN	TEN	IND
By Position		SF	CHI	CHI	SF	PHI	ATL	ATL	PHI
3		DALLAS		TAMPA BAY		GREEN BAY		SEATTLE	
		Home	Away	Home	Away	Home	Away	Home	Away
Intraconference		ATL	NO	DAL	PHI	SF	ARI	CHI	GB
		CAR	TB	NYG	WAS	SEA	STL	DET	MIN
Interconference		OAK	DEN	NE	BUF	BAL	CLE	JAC	HOU
		SD	KC	NYJ	MIA	CIN	PIT	TEN	IND
By Position		SEA	GB	GB	SEA	DAL	TB	TB	DAL
4		WASHINGTON		NEW ORLEANS		DETROIT		ST. LOUIS	
		Home	Away	Home	Away	Home	Away	Home	Away
Intraconference		NO	ATL	DAL	PHI	ARI	SF	GB	CHI
		TB	CAR	NYG	WAS	STL	SEA	MIN	DET
Interconference		DEN	OAK	NE	BUF	CLE	BAL	HOU	JAC
		KC	SD	NYJ	MIA	PIT	CIN	IND	TEN
By Position		STL	DET	DET	STL	WAS	NO	NO	WAS

2010 NON-DIVISIONAL OPPONENTS (AFC)

2009 FINAL STANDINGS

	East	North	South	West
1	NE	CIN	IND	SD
2	NYJ	BAL	HOU	DEN
3	MIA	PIT	TEN	OAK
4	BUF	CLE	JAC	KC

	East NEW ENGLAND		North CINCINNATI		South INDIANAPOLIS		West SAN DIEGO	
1	Home	Away	Home	Away	Home	Away	Home	Away
Intraconference	BAL	CLE	BUF	NE	KC	DEN	JAC	HOU
	CIN	PIT	MIA	NYJ	SD	OAK	TEN	IND
Interconference	GB	CHI	NO	ATL	DAL	PHI	ARI	STL
	MIN	DET	TB	CAR	NYG	WAS	SF	SEA
By Position	IND	SD	SD	IND	CIN	NE	NE	CIN
2	NY JETS		BALTIMORE		HOUSTON		DENVER	
	Home	Away	Home	Away	Home	Away	Home	Away
Intraconference	BAL	CLE	BUF	NE	KC	DEN	HOU	JAC
	CIN	PIT	MIA	NYJ	SD	OAK	IND	TEN
Interconference	GB	CHI	NO	ATL	DAL	PHI	STL	ARI
	MIN	DET	TB	CAR	NYG	WAS	SEA	SF
By Position	HOU	DEN	DEN	HOU	BAL	NYJ	NYJ	BAL
3	MIAMI		PITTSBURGH		TENNESSEE		OAKLAND	
	Home	Away	Home	Away	Home	Away	Home	Away
Intraconference	CLE	BAL	NE	BUF	DEN	KC	HOU	JAC
	PIT	CIN	NYJ	MIA	OAK	SD	IND	TEN
Interconference	CHI	GB	ATL	NO	PHI	DAL	STL	ARI
	DET	MIN	CAR	TB	WAS	NYG	SEA	SF
By Position	TEN	OAK	OAK	TEN	PIT	MIA	MIA	PIT
4	BUFFALO		CLEVELAND		JACKSONVILLE		KANSAS CITY	
	Home	Away	Home	Away	Home	Away	Home	Away
Intraconference	CLE	BAL	NE	BUF	DEN	KC	JAC	HOU
	PIT	CIN	NYJ	MIA	OAK	SD	TEN	IND
Interconference	CHI	GB	ATL	NO	PHI	DAL	ARI	STL
	DET	MIN	CAR	TB	WAS	NYG	SF	SEA
By Position	JAC	KC	KC	JAC	CLE	BUF	BUF	CLE

2010 NON-DIVISIONAL OPPONENTS (NFC)

2009 FINAL STANDINGS

	East	North	South	West
1	DAL	MIN	NO	ARI
2	PHI	GB	ATL	SF
3	NYG	CHI	CAR	SEA
4	WAS	DET	TB	STL

	East DALLAS		North MINNESOTA		South NEW ORLEANS		West ARIZONA	
1	Home	Away	Home	Away	Home	Away	Home	Away
Intraconference	CHI	GB	DAL	PHI	STL	ARI	NO	ATL
	DET	MIN	NYG	WAS	SEA	SF	TB	CAR
Interconference	JAC	HOU	BUF	NE	CLE	BAL	DEN	KC
	TEN	IND	MIA	NYJ	PIT	CIN	OAK	SD
By Position	NO	ARI	ARI	NO	MIN	DAL	DAL	MIN
2	PHILADELPHIA		GREEN BAY		ATLANTA		SAN FRANCISCO	
	Home	Away	Home	Away	Home	Away	Home	Away
Intraconference	GB	CHI	DAL	PHI	ARI	STL	NO	ATL
	MIN	DET	NYG	WAS	SF	SEA	TB	CAR
Interconference	HOU	JAC	BUF	NE	BAL	CLE	DEN	KC
	IND	TEN	MIA	NYJ	CIN	PIT	OAK	SD
By Position	ATL	SF	SF	ATL	GB	PHI	PHI	GB

	NY GIANTS		CHICAGO		CAROLINA		SEATTLE	
3	Home	Away	Home	Away	Home	Away	Home	Away
Intraconference	CHI	GB	PHI	DAL	ARI	STL	ATL	NO
	DET	MIN	WAS	NYG	SF	SEA	CAR	TB
Interconference	JAC	HOU	NE	BUF	BAL	CLE	KC	DEN
	TEN	IND	NYJ	MIA	CIN	PIT	SD	OAK
By Position	CAR	SEA	SEA	CAR	CHI	NYG	NYG	CHI
	WASHINGTON		DETROIT		TAMPA BAY		ST. LOUIS	
4	Home	Away	Home	Away	Home	Away	Home	Away
Intraconference	GB	CHI	PHI	DAL	STL	ARI	ATL	NO
	MIN	DET	WAS	NYG	SEA	SF	CAR	TB
Interconference	HOU	JAC	NE	BUF	CLE	BAL	KC	DEN
	IND	TEN	NYJ	MIA	PIT	CIN	SD	OAK
By Position	TB	STL	STL	TB	DET	WAS	WAS	DET

2011 NON-DIVISIONAL OPPONENTS (AFC)

2010 FINAL STANDINGS

	East	West	North	South
1	NE	KC	PIT	IND
2	NYJ	SD	BAL	JAC
3	MIA	OAK	CLE	HOU
4	BUF	DEN	CIN	TEN

	East		West		North		South	
	NEW ENGLAND		KANSAS CITY		PITTSBURGH		INDIANAPOLIS	
1	Home	Away	Home	Away	Home	Away	Home	Away
Intraconference	KC	DEN	BUF	NE	JAC	HOU	CLE	BAL
	SD	OAK	MIA	NYJ	TEN	IND	PIT	CIN
Interconference	DAL	PHI	GB	CHI	STL	ARI	ATL	NO
	NYG	WAS	MIN	DET	SEA	SF	CAR	TB
By Position	IND	PIT	PIT	IND	NE	KC	KC	NE
	NY JETS		SAN DIEGO		BALTIMORE		JACKSONVILLE	
2	Home	Away	Home	Away	Home	Away	Home	Away
Intraconference	KC	DEN	BUF	NE	HOU	JAC	BAL	CLE
	SD	OAK	MIA	NYJ	IND	TEN	CIN	PIT
Interconference	DAL	PHI	GB	CHI	ARI	STL	NO	ATL
	NYG	WAS	MIN	DET	SF	SEA	TB	CAR
By Position	JAC	BAL	BAL	JAC	NYJ	SD	SD	NYJ
	MIAMI		OAKLAND		CLEVELAND		HOUSTON	
3	Home	Away	Home	Away	Home	Away	Home	Away
Intraconference	DEN	KC	NE	BUF	JAC	HOU	CLE	BAL
	OAK	SD	NYJ	MIA	TEN	IND	PIT	CIN
Interconference	PHI	DAL	CHI	GB	STL	ARI	ATL	NO
	WAS	NYG	DET	MIN	SEA	SF	CAR	TB
By Position	HOU	CLE	CLE	HOU	MIA	OAK	OAK	MIA
	BUFFALO		DENVER		CINCINNATI		TENNESSEE	
4	Home	Away	Home	Away	Home	Away	Home	Away
Intraconference	DEN	KC	NE	BUF	HOU	JAC	BAL	CLE
	OAK	SD	NYJ	MIA	IND	TEN	CIN	PIT
Interconference	PHI	DAL	CHI	GB	ARI	STL	NO	ATL
	WAS	NYG	DET	MIN	SF	SEA	TB	CAR
By Position	TEN	CIN	CIN	TEN	BUF	DEN	DEN	BUF

2011 NON-DIVISIONAL OPPONENTS (NFC)

2010 FINAL STANDINGS

	East	West	North	South
1	PHI	SEA	CHI	ATL
2	NYG	STL	GB	NO
3	DAL	SF	DET	TB
4	WAS	ARI	MIN	CAR

	East		West		North		South	
1	**PHILADELPHIA**		**SEATTLE**		**CHICAGO**		**ATLANTA**	
	Home	Away	Home	Away	Home	Away	Home	Away
Intraconference	ARI	STL	PHI	DAL	ATL	NO	GB	CHI
	SF	SEA	WAS	NYG	CAR	TB	MIN	DET
Interconference	NE	BUF	BAL	CLE	KC	DEN	JAC	HOU
	NYJ	MIA	CIN	PIT	SD	OAK	TEN	IND
By Position	CHI	ATL	ATL	CHI	SEA	PHI	PHI	SEA
2	**NY GIANTS**		**ST. LOUIS**		**GREEN BAY**		**NEW ORLEANS**	
	Home	Away	Home	Away	Home	Away	Home	Away
Intraconference	STL	ARI	PHI	DAL	NO	ATL	CHI	GB
	SEA	SF	WAS	NYG	TB	CAR	DET	MIN
Interconference	BUF	NE	BAL	CLE	DEN	KC	HOU	JAC
	MIA	NYJ	CIN	PIT	OAK	SD	IND	TEN
By Position	GB	NO	NO	GB	STL	NYG	NYG	STL
3	**DALLAS**		**SAN FRANCISCO**		**DETROIT**		**TAMPA BAY**	
	Home	Away	Home	Away	Home	Away	Home	Away
Intraconference	STL	ARI	DAL	PHI	ATL	NO	CHI	GB
	SEA	SF	NYG	WAS	CAR	TB	DET	MIN
Interconference	BUF	NE	CLE	BAL	KC	DEN	HOU	JAC
	MIA	NYJ	PIT	CIN	SD	OAK	IND	TEN
By Position	DET	TB	TB	DET	SF	DAL	DAL	SF
4	**WASHINGTON**		**ARIZONA**		**MINNESOTA**		**CAROLINA**	
	Home	Away	Home	Away	Home	Away	Home	Away
Intraconference	ARI	STL	DAL	PHI	NO	ATL	GB	CHI
	SF	SEA	NYG	WAS	TB	CAR	MIN	DET
Interconference	NE	BUF	CLE	BAL	DEN	KC	JAC	HOU
	NYJ	MIA	PIT	CIN	OAK	SD	TEN	IND
By Position	MIN	CAR	CAR	MIN	ARI	WAS	WAS	ARI

2012 NON-DIVISIONAL OPPONENTS (AFC)

2011 FINAL STANDINGS

	East	South	North	West
1	NE	HOU	BAL	DEN
2	NYJ	TEN	PIT	SD
3	MIA	JAC	CIN	OAK
4	BUF	IND	CLE	KC

	East		South		North		West	
1	**NEW ENGLAND**		**HOUSTON**		**BALTIMORE**		**DENVER**	
	Home	Away	Home	Away	Home	Away	Home	Away
Intraconference	HOU	JAC	BUF	NE	DEN	KC	CLE	BAL
	IND	TEN	MIA	NYJ	OAK	SD	PIT	CIN
Interconference	ARI	STL	GB	CHI	DAL	PHI	NO	ATL
	SF	SEA	MIN	DET	NYG	WAS	TB	CAR
By Position	DEN	BAL	BAL	DEN	NE	HOU	HOU	NE

2		NY JETS		TENNESSEE		PITTSBURGH		SAN DIEGO	
		Home	*Away*	*Home*	*Away*	*Home*	*Away*	*Home*	*Away*
Intraconference		HOU	JAC	NE	BUF	KC	DEN	BAL	CLE
		IND	TEN	NYJ	MIA	SD	OAK	CIN	PIT
Interconference		ARI	STL	CHI	GB	PHI	DAL	ATL	NO
		SF	SEA	DET	MIN	WAS	NYG	CAR	TB
By Position		SD	PIT	PIT	SD	NYJ	TEN	TEN	NYJ
3		MIAMI		JACKSONVILLE		CINCINNATI		OAKLAND	
		Home	*Away*	*Home*	*Away*	*Home*	*Away*	*Home*	*Away*
Intraconference		JAC	HOU	NE	BUF	DEN	KC	CLE	BAL
		TEN	IND	NYJ	MIA	OAK	SD	PIT	CIN
Interconference		STL	ARI	CHI	GB	DAL	PHI	NO	ATL
		SEA	SF	DET	MIN	NYG	WAS	TB	CAR
By Position		OAK	CIN	CIN	OAK	MIA	JAC	JAC	MIA
4		BUFFALO		INDIANAPOLIS		CLEVELAND		KANSAS CITY	
		Home	*Away*	*Home*	*Away*	*Home*	*Away*	*Home*	*Away*
Intraconference		JAC	HOU	BUF	NE	KC	DEN	BAL	CLE
		TEN	IND	MIA	NYJ	SD	OAK	CIN	PIT
Interconference		STL	ARI	GB	CHI	PHI	DAL	ATL	NO
		SEA	SF	MIN	DET	WAS	NYG	CAR	TB
By Position		KC	CLE	CLE	KC	BUF	IND	IND	BUF

2012 NON-DIVISIONAL OPPONENTS (NFC)

2011 FINAL STANDINGS

	East	South	North	West
1	NYG	NO	GB	SF
2	PHI	ATL	DET	ARI
3	DAL	CAR	CHI	SEA
4	WAS	TB	MIN	STL

		East		South		North		West	
1		NY GIANTS		NEW ORLEANS		GREEN BAY		SAN FRANCISCO	
		Home	*Away*	*Home*	*Away*	*Home*	*Away*	*Home*	*Away*
Intraconference		NO	ATL	PHI	DAL	ARI	STL	CHI	GB
		TB	CAR	WAS	NYG	SF	SEA	DET	MIN
Interconference		CLE	BAL	KC	DEN	JAC	HOU	BUF	NE
		PIT	CIN	SD	OAK	TEN	IND	MIA	NYJ
By Position		GB	SF	SF	GB	NO	NYG	NYG	NO
2		PHILADELPHIA		ATLANTA		DETROIT		ARIZONA	
		Home	*Away*	*Home*	*Away*	*Home*	*Away*	*Home*	*Away*
Intraconference		ATL	NO	DAL	PHI	STL	ARI	CHI	GB
		CAR	TB	NYG	WAS	SEA	SF	DET	MIN
Interconference		BAL	CLE	DEN	KC	HOU	JAC	BUF	NE
		CIN	PIT	OAK	SD	IND	TEN	MIA	NYJ
By Position		DET	ARI	ARI	DET	ATL	PHI	PHI	ATL
3		DALLAS		CAROLINA		CHICAGO		SEATTLE	
		Home	*Away*	*Home*	*Away*	*Home*	*Away*	*Home*	*Away*
Intraconference		NO	ATL	DAL	PHI	STL	ARI	GB	CHI
		TB	CAR	NYG	WAS	SEA	SF	MIN	DET
Interconference		CLE	BAL	DEN	KC	HOU	JAC	NE	BUF
		PIT	CIN	OAK	SD	IND	TEN	NYJ	MIA
By Position		CHI	SEA	SEA	CHI	CAR	DAL	DAL	CAR

	WASHINGTON		TAMPA BAY		MINNESOTA		ST. LOUIS	
4	Home	Away	Home	Away	Home	Away	Home	Away
Intraconference	ATL	NO	PHI	DAL	ARI	STL	GB	CHI
	CAR	TB	WAS	NYG	SF	SEA	MIN	DET
Interconference	BAL	CLE	KC	DEN	JAC	HOU	NE	BUF
	CIN	PIT	SD	OAK	TEN	IND	NYJ	MIA
By Position	MIN	STL	STL	MIN	TB	WAS	WAS	TB

2013 NON-DIVISIONAL OPPONENTS (AFC)

2012 FINAL STANDINGS

	East	North	South	West
1	NE	BAL	HOU	DEN
2	MIA	CIN	IND	SD
3	NYJ	PIT	TEN	OAK
4	BUF	CLE	JAC	KC

	East		North		South		West	
1	NEW ENGLAND		BALTIMORE		HOUSTON		DENVER	
	Home	Away	Home	Away	Home	Away	Home	Away
Intraconference	CLE	BAL	NE	BUF	DEN	KC	JAC	HOU
	PIT	CIN	NYJ	MIA	OAK	SD	TEN	IND
Interconference	NO	ATL	GB	CHI	STL	ARI	PHI	DAL
	TB	CAR	MIN	DET	SEA	SF	WAS	NYG
By Position	DEN	HOU	HOU	DEN	NE	BAL	BAL	NE

2	MIAMI		CINCINNATI		INDIANAPOLIS		SAN DIEGO	
	Home	Away	Home	Away	Home	Away	Home	Away
Intraconference	BAL	CLE	NE	BUF	DEN	KC	HOU	JAC
	CIN	PIT	NYJ	MIA	OAK	SD	IND	TEN
Interconference	ATL	NO	GB	CHI	STL	ARI	DAL	PHI
	CAR	TB	MIN	DET	SEA	SF	NYG	WAS
By Position	SD	IND	IND	SD	MIA	CIN	CIN	MIA

3	NY JETS		PITTSBURGH		TENNESSEE		OAKLAND	
	Home	Away	Home	Away	Home	Away	Home	Away
Intraconference	CLE	BAL	BUF	NE	KC	DEN	JAC	HOU
	PIT	CIN	MIA	NYJ	SD	OAK	TEN	IND
Interconference	NO	ATL	CHI	GB	ARI	STL	PHI	DAL
	TB	CAR	DET	MIN	SF	SEA	WAS	NYG
By Position	OAK	TEN	TEN	OAK	NYJ	PIT	PIT	NYJ

4	BUFFALO		CLEVELAND		JACKSONVILLE		KANSAS CITY	
	Home	Away	Home	Away	Home	Away	Home	Away
Intraconference	BAL	CLE	BUF	NE	KC	DEN	HOU	JAC
	CIN	PIT	MIA	NYJ	SD	OAK	IND	TEN
Interconference	ATL	NO	CHI	GB	ARI	STL	DAL	PHI
	CAR	TB	DET	MIN	SF	SEA	NYG	WAS
By Position	KC	JAC	JAC	KC	BUF	CLE	CLE	BUF

2013 NON-DIVISIONAL OPPONENTS (NFC)

2012 FINAL STANDINGS

	East	North	South	West
1	WAS	GB	ATL	SF
2	NYG	MIN	CAR	SEA
3	DAL	CHI	NO	STL
4	PHI	DET	TB	ARI

		East WASHINGTON		North GREEN BAY		South ATLANTA		West SAN FRANCISCO	
		Home	Away	Home	Away	Home	Away	Home	Away
1	Intraconference	CHI	GB	PHI	DAL	STL	ARI	ATL	NO
		DET	MIN	WAS	NYG	SEA	SF	CAR	TB
	Interconference	KC	DEN	CLE	BAL	NE	BUF	HOU	JAC
		SD	OAK	PIT	CIN	NYJ	MIA	IND	TEN
	By Position	SF	ATL	ATL	SF	WAS	GB	GB	WAS
2		NY GIANTS		MINNESOTA		CAROLINA		SEATTLE	
		Home	Away	Home	Away	Home	Away	Home	Away
	Intraconference	GB	CHI	PHI	DAL	STL	ARI	NO	ATL
		MIN	DET	WAS	NYG	SEA	SF	TB	CAR
	Interconference	DEN	KC	CLE	BAL	NE	BUF	JAC	HOU
		OAK	SD	PIT	CIN	NYJ	MIA	TEN	IND
	By Position	SEA	CAR	CAR	SEA	NYG	MIN	MIN	NYG
3		DALLAS		CHICAGO		NEW ORLEANS		ST. LOUIS	
		Home	Away	Home	Away	Home	Away	Home	Away
	Intraconference	GB	CHI	DAL	PHI	ARI	STL	NO	ATL
		MIN	DET	NYG	WAS	SF	SEA	TB	CAR
	Interconference	DEN	KC	BAL	CLE	BUF	NE	JAC	HOU
		OAK	SD	CIN	PIT	MIA	NYJ	TEN	IND
	By Position	STL	NO	NO	STL	DAL	CHI	CHI	DAL
4		PHILADELPHIA		DETROIT		TAMPA BAY		ARIZONA	
		Home	Away	Home	Away	Home	Away	Home	Away
	Intraconference	CHI	GB	DAL	PHI	ARI	STL	ATL	NO
		DET	MIN	NYG	WAS	SF	SEA	CAR	TB
	Interconference	KC	DEN	BAL	CLE	BUF	NE	HOU	JAC
		SD	OAK	CIN	PIT	MIA	NYJ	IND	TEN
	By Position	ARI	TB	TB	ARI	PHI	DET	DET	PHI

2002–2017 NON-DIVISIONAL OPPONENTS (By Team)

AFC East

BUFFALO BILLS

	2002				2003			
	Home		Away		Home		Away	
Intraconference by Division	AFCW	OAK	AFCW	DEN	AFCS	HOU	AFCS	JAC
		SD		KC		IND		TEN
Interconference by Division	NFCN	CHI	NFCN	GB	NFCE	PHI	NFCE	DAL
		DET		MIN		WAS		NYG
Intraconference by Position	AFCN	CIN	AFCS	HOU	AFCN	CIN	AFCW	KC

	2004		2005	
	Home	*Away*	*Home*	*Away*
Intraconference by Division	AFCN CLE PIT	AFCN BAL CIN	AFCW DEN KC	AFCW OAK SD
Interconference by Division	NFCW ARI STL	NFCW SF SEA	NFCS ATL CAR	NFCS NO[1] TB
Intraconference by Position	AFCS JAC	AFCW OAK	AFCS HOU	AFCN CIN

	2006		2007	
	Home	*Away*	*Home*	*Away*
Intraconference by Division	AFCS JAC TEN	AFCS HOU IND	AFCN BAL CIN	AFCN CLE PIT
Interconference by Division	NFCN GB MIN	NFCN CHI DET	NFCE DAL NYG	NFCE PHI WAS
Intraconference by Position	AFCW SD	AFCN BAL	AFCW DEN	AFCS JAC

	2008		2009	
	Home	*Away*	*Home*	*Away*
Intraconference by Division	AFCW OAK SD	AFCW DEN KC	AFCS HOU IND	AFCS JAC TEN
Interconference by Division	NFCW SF SEA	NFCW ARI STL	NFCS NO TB	NFCS ATL CAR
Intraconference by Position	AFCN CLE	AFCS JAC	AFCN CLE	AFCW KC

	2010		2011	
	Home	*Away*	*Home*	*Away*
Intraconference by Division	AFCN CLE PIT	AFCN BAL CIN	AFCW DEN OAK	AFCW KC SD
Interconference by Division	NFCN CHI[2] DET	NFCN GB MIN	NFCE PHI WAS[2]	NFCE DAL NYG
Intraconference by Position	AFCS JAC	AFCW KC	AFCS TEN	AFCN CIN

	2012		2013	
	Home	*Away*	*Home*	*Away*
Intraconference by Division	AFCS JAC TEN	AFCS HOU IND	AFCN BAL CIN	AFCN CLE PIT
Interconference by Division	NFCW STL SEA[2]	NFCW ARI SF	NFCS ATL[2] CAR	NFCS NO TB
Intraconference by Position	AFCW KC	AFCN CLE	AFCW KC	AFCS JAC

	2014		2015	
	Home	*Away*	*Home*	*Away*
Intraconference by Division	AFCW KC SD	AFCW DEN OAK	AFCS HOU IND	AFCS JAC TEN
Interconference by Division	NFCN GB MIN	NFCN CHI DET	NFCE DAL NYG	NFCE PHI WAS
Intraconference by Position	AFCN	AFCS	AFCN	AFCW

	2016		2017	
	Home	*Away*	*Home*	*Away*
Intraconference by Division	AFCN CLE PIT	AFCN BAL CIN	AFCW DEN OAK	AFCW KC SD
Interconference by Division	NFCW ARI SF	NFCW STL SEA	NFCS NO TB	NFCS ATL CAR
Intraconference by Position	AFCS	AFCW	AFCS	AFCN

[1] Due to Hurricane Katrina, game moved to San Antonio, TX.
[2] Game played at Toronto.

MIAMI DOLPHINS

2002
	Home		Away	
Intraconference by Division	AFCW	OAK SD	AFCW	DEN KC
Interconference by Division	NFCN	CHI DET	NFCN	GB MIN
Intraconference by Position	AFCN	BAL	AFCS	IND

2003
	Home		Away	
Intraconference by Division	AFCS	HOU IND	AFCS	JAC TEN
Interconference by Division	NFCE	PHI WAS	NFCE	DAL NYG
Intraconference by Position	AFCN	BAL	AFCW	SD[1]

2004
	Home		Away	
Intraconference by Division	AFCN	CLE PIT	AFCN	BAL CIN
Interconference by Division	NFCW	ARI STL	NFCW	SF SEA
Intraconference by Position	AFCS	TEN	AFCW	DEN

2005
	Home		Away	
Intraconference by Division	AFCW	DEN KC	AFCW	OAK SD
Interconference by Division	NFCS	ATL CAR	NFCS	NO[2] TB
Intraconference by Position	AFCS	TEN	AFCN	CLE

2006
	Home		Away	
Intraconference by Division	AFCS	JAC TEN	AFCS	HOU IND
Interconference by Division	NFCN	GB MIN	NFCN	CHI DET
Intraconference by Position	AFCW	KC	AFCN	PIT

2007
	Home		Away	
Intraconference by Division	AFCN	BAL CIN	AFCN	CLE PIT
Interconference by Division	NFCE	DAL NYG[3]	NFCE	PHI WAS
Intraconference by Position	AFCW	OAK	AFCS	HOU

2008
	Home		Away	
Intraconference by Division	AFCW	OAK SD	AFCW	DEN KC
Interconference by Division	NFCW	SF SEA	NFCW	ARI STL
Intraconference by Position	AFCN	BAL	AFCS	HOU

2009
	Home		Away	
Intraconference by Division	AFCS	HOU IND	AFCS	JAC TEN
Interconference by Division	NFCS	NO TB	NFCS	ATL CAR
Intraconference by Position	AFCN	PIT	AFCW	SD

2010
	Home		Away	
Intraconference by Division	AFCN	CLE PIT	AFCN	BAL CIN
Interconference by Division	NFCN	CHI DET	NFCN	GB MIN
Intraconference by Position	AFCS	TEN	AFCW	OAK

2011
	Home		Away	
Intraconference by Division	AFCW	DEN OAK	AFCW	KC SD
Interconference by Division	NFCE	PHI WAS	NFCE	DAL NYG
Intraconference by Position	AFCS	HOU	AFCN	CLE

2012
	Home		Away	
Intraconference by Division	AFCS	JAC TEN	AFCS	HOU IND
Interconference by Division	NFCW	STL SEA	NFCW	ARI SF
Intraconference by Position	AFCW	OAK	AFCN	CIN

2013
	Home		Away	
Intraconference by Division	AFCN	BAL CIN	AFCN	CLE PIT
Interconference by Division	NFCS	ATL CAR	NFCS	NO TB
Intraconference by Position	AFCW	SD	AFCS	IND

2014
	Home		Away	
Intraconference by Division	AFCW	KC SD	AFCW	DEN OAK
Interconference by Division	NFCN	GB MIN	NFCN	CHI DET
Intraconference by Position	AFCN		AFCS	

2015
	Home		Away	
Intraconference by Division	AFCS	HOU IND	AFCS	JAC TEN
Interconference by Division	NFCE	DAL NYG	NFCE	PHI WAS
Intraconference by Position	AFCN		AFCW	

	2016		2017	
	Home	**Away**	**Home**	**Away**
Intraconference by Division	AFCN CLE / PIT	AFCN BAL / CIN	AFCW DEN / OAK	AFCW KC / SD
Interconference by Division	NFCW ARI / SF	NFCW STL / SEA	NFCS NO / TB	NFCS ATL / CAR
Intraconference by Position	AFCS	AFCW	AFCS	AFCN

[1] Game moved to Tempe, AZ due to wildfires in the San Diego area.
[2] Due to Hurricane Katrina, game moved to Baton Rouge, LA.
[3] Game played at London, England.

NEW ENGLAND PATRIOTS

	2002		2003	
	Home	**Away**	**Home**	**Away**
Intraconference by Division	AFCW DEN / KC	AFCW OAK / SD	AFCS JAC / TEN	AFCS HOU / IND
Interconference by Division	NFCN GB / MIN	NFCN CHI[1] / DET	NFCE DAL / NYG	NFCE PHI / WAS
Intraconference by Position	AFCN PIT	AFCS TEN	AFCN CLE	AFCW DEN

	2004		2005	
	Home	**Away**	**Home**	**Away**
Intraconference by Division	AFCN BAL / CIN	AFCN CLE / PIT	AFCW OAK / SD	AFCW DEN / KC
Interconference by Division	NFCW SF / SEA	NFCW ARI / STL	NFCS NO / TB	NFCS ATL / CAR
Intraconference by Position	AFCS IND	AFCW KC	AFCS IND	AFCN PIT

	2006		2007	
	Home	**Away**	**Home**	**Away**
Intraconference by Division	AFCS HOU / IND	AFCS JAC / TEN	AFCN CLE / PIT	AFCN BAL / CIN
Interconference by Division	NFCN CHI / DET	NFCN GB / MIN	NFCE PHI / WAS	NFCE DAL / NYG
Intraconference by Position	AFCW DEN	AFCN CIN	AFCW SD	AFCS IND

	2008		2009	
	Home	**Away**	**Home**	**Away**
Intraconference by Division	AFCW DEN / KC	AFCW OAK / SD	AFCS JAC / TEN	AFCS HOU / IND
Interconference by Division	NFCW ARI / STL	NFCW SF / SEA	NFCS ATL / CAR	NFCS NO / TB[2]
Intraconference by Position	AFCN PIT	AFCS IND	AFCN BAL	AFCW DEN

	2010		2011	
	Home	**Away**	**Home**	**Away**
Intraconference by Division	AFCN BAL / CIN	AFCN CLE / PIT	AFCW KC / SD	AFCW DEN / OAK
Interconference by Division	NFCN GB / MIN	NFCN CHI / DET	NFCE DAL / NYG	NFCE PHI / WAS
Intraconference by Position	AFCS IND	AFCW SD	AFCS IND	AFCN PIT

	2012		2013	
	Home	**Away**	**Home**	**Away**
Intraconference by Division	AFCS HOU / IND	AFCS JAC / TEN	AFCN CLE / PIT	AFCN BAL / CIN
Interconference by Division	NFCW ARI / SF	NFCW STL[2] / SEA	NFCS NO / TB	NFCS ATL / CAR
Intraconference by Position	AFCW DEN	AFCN BAL	AFCW DEN	AFCS HOU

2014

	Home		Away	
Intraconference by Division	AFCW	DEN	AFCW	KC
		OAK		SD
Interconference by Division	NFCN	CHI	NFCN	GB
		DET		MIN
Intraconference by Position	AFCN		AFCS	

2015

	Home		Away	
Intraconference by Division	AFCS	JAC	AFCS	HOU
		TEN		IND
Interconference by Division	NFCE	PHI	NFCE	DAL
		WAS		NYG
Intraconference by Position	AFCN		AFCW	

2016

	Home		Away	
Intraconference by Division	AFCN	BAL	AFCN	CLE
		CIN		PIT
Interconference by Division	NFCW	STL	NFCW	ARI
		SEA		SF
Intraconference by Position	AFCS		AFCW	

2017

	Home		Away	
Intraconference by Division	AFCW	KC	AFCW	DEN
		SD		OAK
Interconference by Division	NFCS	ATL	NFCS	NO
		CAR		TB
Intraconference by Position	AFCS		AFCN	

¹Game played at Champaign, IL.
²Game played at London, England.

NEW YORK JETS

2002

	Home		Away	
Intraconference by Division	AFCW	DEN	AFCW	OAK
		KC		SD
Interconference by Division	NFCN	GB	NFCN	CHI¹
		MIN		DET
Intraconference by Position	AFCN	CLE	AFCS	JAC

2003

	Home		Away	
Intraconference by Division	AFCS	JAC	AFCS	HOU
		TEN		IND
Interconference by Division	NFCE	DAL	NFCE	PHI
		NYG		WAS
Intraconference by Position	AFCN	PIT	AFCW	OAK

2004

	Home		Away	
Intraconference by Division	AFCN	BAL	AFCN	CLE
		CIN		PIT
Interconference by Division	NFCW	SF	NFCW	ARI
		SEA		STL
Intraconference by Position	AFCS	HOU	AFCW	SD

2005

	Home		Away	
Intraconference by Division	AFCW	OAK	AFCW	DEN
		SD		KC
Interconference by Division	NFCS	NO	NFCS	ATL
		TB		CAR
Intraconference by Position	AFCS	JAC	AFCN	BAL

2006

	Home		Away	
Intraconference by Division	AFCS	HOU	AFCS	JAC
		IND		TEN
Interconference by Division	NFCN	CHI	NFCN	GB
		DET		MIN
Intraconference by Position	AFCW	OAK	AFCN	CLE

2007

	Home		Away	
Intraconference by Division	AFCN	CLE	AFCN	BAL
		PIT		CIN
Interconference by Division	NFCE	PHI	NFCE	DAL
		WAS		NYG
Intraconference by Position	AFCW	KC	AFCS	TEN

2008

	Home		Away	
Intraconference by Division	AFCW	DEN	AFCW	OAK
		KC		SD
Interconference by Division	NFCW	ARI	NFCW	SF
		STL		SEA
Intraconference by Position	AFCN	CIN	AFCS	TEN

2009

	Home		Away	
Intraconference by Division	AFCS	JAC	AFCS	HOU
		TEN		IND
Interconference by Division	NFCS	ATL	NFCS	NO
		CAR		TB
Intraconference by Position	AFCN	CIN	AFCW	OAK

2010

	Home		Away	
Intraconference by Division	AFCN	BAL	AFCN	CLE
		CIN		PIT
Interconference by Division	NFCN	GB	NFCN	CHI
		MIN		DET
Intraconference by Position	AFCS	HOU	AFCW	DEN

2011

	Home		Away	
Intraconference by Division	AFCW	KC	AFCW	DEN
		SD		OAK
Interconference by Division	NFCE	DAL	NFCE	PHI
		NYG		WAS
Intraconference by Position	AFCS	JAC	AFCN	BAL

	2012		2013	
	Home	Away	Home	Away
Intraconference by Division	AFCS HOU IND	AFCS JAC TEN	AFCN CLE PIT	AFCN BAL CIN
Interconference by Division	NFCW ARI SF	NFCW STL SEA	NFCS NO TB	NFCS ATL CAR
Intraconference by Position	AFCW SD	AFCN PIT	AFCW OAK	AFCS TEN

	2014		2015	
	Home	Away	Home	Away
Intraconference by Division	AFCW DEN OAK	AFCW KC SD	AFCS JAC TEN	AFCS HOU IND
Interconference by Division	NFCN CHI DET	NFCN GB MIN	NFCE PHI WAS	NFCE DAL NYG
Intraconference by Position	AFCN	AFCS	AFCN	AFCW

	2016		2017	
	Home	Away	Home	Away
Intraconference by Division	AFCN BAL CIN	AFCN CLE PIT	AFCW KC SD	AFCW DEN OAK
Interconference by Division	NFCW STL SEA	NFCW ARI SF	NFCS ATL CAR	NFCS NO TB
Intraconference by Position	AFCS	AFCW	AFCS	AFCN

¹Game played at Champaign, IL.

2002–2017 NON-DIVISIONAL OPPONENTS (By Team)

AFC North

BALTIMORE RAVENS

	2002		2003	
	Home	Away	Home	Away
Intraconference by Division	AFCS JAC TEN	AFCS HOU IND	AFCW DEN KC	AFCW OAK SD
Interconference by Division	NFCS NO TB	NFCS ATL CAR	NFCW SF SEA	NFCW ARI STL
Intraconference by Position	AFCW DEN	AFCE MIA	AFCS JAC	AFCE MIA

	2004		2005	
	Home	Away	Home	Away
Intraconference by Division	AFCE BUF MIA	AFCE NE NYJ	AFCS HOU IND	AFCS JAC TEN
Interconference by Division	NFCE DAL NYG	NFCE PHI WAS	NFCN GB MIN	NFCN CHI DET
Intraconference by Position	AFCW KC	AFCS IND	AFCE NYJ	AFCW DEN

	2006		2007	
	Home	Away	Home	Away
Intraconference by Division	AFCW OAK SD	AFCW DEN KC	AFCE NE NYJ	AFCE BUF MIA
Interconference by Division	NFCS ATL CAR	NFCS NO TB	NFCW ARI STL	NFCW SF SEA
Intraconference by Position	AFCE BUF	AFCS TEN	AFCS IND	AFCW SD

	2008				2009			
	Home		*Away*		*Home*		*Away*	
Intraconference by Division	AFCS	JAC	AFCS	HOU	AFCW	DEN	AFCW	OAK
		TEN		IND		KC		SD
Interconference by Division	NFCE	PHI	NFCE	DAL	NFCN	CHI	NFCN	GB
		WAS		NYG		DET		MIN
Intraconference by Position	AFCW	OAK	AFCE	MIA	AFCS	IND	AFCE	NE

	2010				2011			
	Home		*Away*		*Home*		*Away*	
Intraconference by Division	AFCE	BUF	AFCE	NE	AFCS	HOU	AFCS	JAC
		MIA		NYJ		IND		TEN
Interconference by Division	NFCS	NO	NFCS	ATL	NFCW	ARI	NFCW	STL
		TB		CAR		SF		SEA
Intraconference by Position	AFCW	DEN	AFCS	HOU	AFCE	NYJ	AFCW	SD

	2012				2013			
	Home		*Away*		*Home*		*Away*	
Intraconference by Division	AFCW	DEN	AFCW	KC	AFCE	NE	AFCE	BUF
		OAK		SD		NYJ		MIA
Interconference by Division	NFCE	DAL	NFCE	PHI	NFCN	GB	NFCN	CHI
		NYG		WAS		MIN		DET
Intraconference by Position	AFCE	NE	AFCS	HOU	AFCS	HOU	AFCW	DEN

	2014				2015			
	Home		*Away*		*Home*		*Away*	
Intraconference by Division	AFCS	JAC	AFCS	HOU	AFCW	KC	AFCW	DEN
		TEN		IND		SD		OAK
Interconference by Division	NFCS	ATL	NFCS	NO	NFCW	STL	NFCW	ARI
		CAR		TB		SEA		SF
Intraconference by Position	AFCW		AFCE		AFCS		AFCE	

	2016				2017			
	Home		*Away*		*Home*		*Away*	
Intraconference by Division	AFCE	BUF	AFCE	NE	AFCS	HOU	AFCS	JAC
		MIA		NYJ		IND		TEN
Interconference by Division	NFCE	PHI	NFCE	DAL	NFCN	CHI	NFCN	GB
		WAS		NYG		DET		MIN
Intraconference by Position	AFCW		AFCS		AFCE		AFCW	

CINCINNATI BENGALS

	2002				2003			
	Home		*Away*		*Home*		*Away*	
Intraconference by Division	AFCS	JAC	AFCS	HOU	AFCW	DEN	AFCW	OAK
		TEN		IND		KC		SD
Interconference by Division	NFCS	NO	NFCS	ATL	NFCW	SF	NFCW	ARI
		TB		CAR		SEA		STL
Intraconference by Position	AFCW	SD	AFCE	BUF	AFCS	HOU	AFCE	BUF

	2004				2005			
	Home		*Away*		*Home*		*Away*	
Intraconference by Division	AFCE	BUF	AFCE	NE	AFCS	HOU	AFCS	JAC
		MIA		NYJ		IND		TEN
Interconference by Division	NFCE	DAL	NFCE	PHI	NFCN	GB	NFCN	CHI
		NYG		WAS		MIN		DET
Intraconference by Position	AFCW	DEN	AFCS	TEN	AFCE	BUF	AFCW	KC

	2006		2007	
	Home	Away	Home	Away
Intraconference by Division	AFCW OAK SD	AFCW DEN KC	AFCE NE NYJ	AFCE BUF MIA
Interconference by Division	NFCS ATL CAR	NFCS NO TB	NFCW ARI STL	NFCW SF SEA
Intraconference by Position	AFCE NE	AFCS IND	AFCS TEN	AFCW KC

	2008		2009	
	Home	Away	Home	Away
Intraconference by Division	AFCS JAC TEN	AFCS HOU IND	AFCW DEN KC	AFCW OAK SD
Interconference by Division	NFCE PHI WAS	NFCE DAL NYG	NFCN CHI DET	NFCN GB MIN
Intraconference by Position	AFCW KC	AFCE NYJ	AFCS HOU	AFCE NYJ

	2010		2011	
	Home	Away	Home	Away
Intraconference by Division	AFCE BUF MIA	AFCE NE NYJ	AFCS HOU IND	AFCS JAC TEN
Interconference by Division	NFCS NO TB	NFCS ATL CAR	NFCW ARI SF	NFCW STL SEA
Intraconference by Position	AFCW SD	AFCS IND	AFCE BUF	AFCW DEN

	2012		2013	
	Home	Away	Home	Away
Intraconference by Division	AFCW DEN OAK	AFCW KC SD	AFCE NE NYJ	AFCE BUF MIA
Interconference by Division	NFCE DAL NYG	NFCE PHI WAS	NFCN GB MIN	NFCN CHI DET
Intraconference by Position	AFCE MIA	AFCS JAC	AFCS IND	AFCW SD

	2014		2015	
	Home	Away	Home	Away
Intraconference by Division	AFCS JAC TEN	AFCS HOU IND	AFCW KC SD	AFCW DEN OAK
Interconference by Division	NFCS ATL CAR	NFCS NO TB	NFCW STL SEA	NFCW ARI SF
Intraconference by Position	AFCW	AFCE	AFCS	AFCE

	2016		2017	
	Home	Away	Home	Away
Intraconference by Division	AFCE BUF MIA	AFCE NE NYJ	AFCS HOU IND	AFCS JAC TEN
Interconference by Division	NFCE PHI WAS	NFCE DAL NYG	NFCN CHI DET	NFCN GB MIN
Intraconference by Position	AFCW	AFCS	AFCE	AFCW

CLEVELAND BROWNS

	2002		2003	
	Home	Away	Home	Away
Intraconference by Division	AFCS HOU IND	AFCS JAC TEN	AFCW OAK SD	AFCW DEN KC
Interconference by Division	NFCS ATL CAR	NFCS NO TB	NFCW ARI STL	NFCW SF SEA
Intraconference by Position	AFCW KC	AFCE NYJ	AFCS IND	AFCE NE

	2004				2005			
	Home		*Away*		*Home*		*Away*	
Intraconference by Division	AFCE	NE	AFCE	BUF	AFCS	JAC	AFCS	HOU
		NYJ		MIA		TEN		IND
Interconference by Division	NFCE	PHI	NFCE	DAL	NFCN	CHI	NFCN	GB
		WAS		NYG		DET		MIN
Intraconference by Position	AFCW	SD	AFCS	HOU	AFCE	MIA	AFCW	OAK

	2006				2007			
	Home		*Away*		*Home*		*Away*	
Intraconference by Division	AFCW	DEN	AFCW	OAK	AFCE	BUF	AFCE	NE
		KC		SD		MIA		NYJ
Interconference by Division	NFCS	NO	NFCS	ATL	NFCW	SF	NFCW	ARI
		TB		CAR		SEA		STL
Intraconference by Position	AFCE	NYJ	AFCS	HOU	AFCS	HOU	AFCW	OAK

	2008				2009			
	Home		*Away*		*Home*		*Away*	
Intraconference by Division	AFCS	HOU	AFCS	JAC	AFCW	OAK	AFCW	DEN
		IND		TEN		SD		KC
Interconference by Division	NFCE	DAL	NFCE	PHI	NFCN	GB	NFCN	CHI
		NYG		WAS		MIN		DET
Intraconference by Position	AFCW	DEN	AFCE	BUF	AFCS	JAC	AFCE	BUF

	2010				2011			
	Home		*Away*		*Home*		*Away*	
Intraconference by Division	AFCE	NE	AFCE	BUF	AFCS	JAC	AFCS	HOU
		NYJ		MIA		TEN		IND
Interconference by Division	NFCS	ATL	NFCS	NO	NFCW	STL	NFCW	ARI
		CAR		TB		SEA		SF
Intraconference by Position	AFCW	KC	AFCS	JAC	AFCE	MIA	AFCW	OAK

	2012				2013			
	Home		*Away*		*Home*		*Away*	
Intraconference by Division	AFCW	KC	AFCW	DEN	AFCE	BUF	AFCE	NE
		SD		OAK		MIA		NYJ
Interconference by Division	NFCE	PHI	NFCE	DAL	NFCN	CHI	NFCN	GB
		WAS		NYG		DET		MIN
Intraconference by Position	AFCE	BUF	AFCS	IND	AFCS	JAC	AFCW	KC

	2014				2015			
	Home		*Away*		*Home*		*Away*	
Intraconference by Division	AFCS	HOU	AFCS	JAC	AFCW	DEN	AFCW	KC
		IND		TEN		OAK		SD
Interconference by Division	NFCS	NO	NFCS	ATL	NFCW	ARI	NFCW	STL
		TB		CAR		SF		SEA
Intraconference by Position	AFCW		AFCE		AFCS		AFCE	

	2016				2017			
	Home		*Away*		*Home*		*Away*	
Intraconference by Division	AFCE	NE	AFCE	BUF	AFCS	JAC	AFCS	HOU
		NYJ		MIA		TEN		IND
Interconference by Division	NFCE	DAL	NFCE	PHI	NFCN	GB	NFCN	CHI
		NYG		WAS		MIN		DET
Intraconference by Position	AFCW		AFCS		AFCE		AFCW	

PITTSBURGH STEELERS

2002

	Home		Away	
Intraconference by Division	AFCS	HOU	AFCS	JAC
		IND		TEN
Interconference by Division	NFCS	ATL	NFCS	NO
		CAR		TB
Intraconference by Position	AFCW	OAK	AFCE	NE

2003

	Home		Away	
Intraconference by Division	AFCW	OAK	AFCW	DEN
		SD		KC
Interconference by Division	NFCW	ARI	NFCW	SF
		STL		SEA
Intraconference by Position	AFCS	TEN	AFCE	NYJ

2004

	Home		Away	
Intraconference by Division	AFCE	NE	AFCE	BUF
		NYJ		MIA
Interconference by Division	NFCE	PHI	NFCE	DAL
		WAS		NYG
Intraconference by Position	AFCW	OAK	AFCS	JAC

2005

	Home		Away	
Intraconference by Division	AFCS	JAC	AFCS	HOU
		TEN		IND
Interconference by Division	NFCN	CHI	NFCN	GB
		DET		MIN
Intraconference by Position	AFCE	NE	AFCW	SD

2006

	Home		Away	
Intraconference by Division	AFCW	DEN	AFCW	OAK
		KC		SD
Interconference by Division	NFCS	NO	NFCS	ATL
		TB		CAR
Intraconference by Position	AFCE	MIA	AFCS	JAC

2007

	Home		Away	
Intraconference by Division	AFCE	BUF	AFCE	NE
		MIA		NYJ
Interconference by Division	NFCW	SF	NFCW	ARI
		SEA		STL
Intraconference by Position	AFCS	JAC	AFCW	DEN

2008

	Home		Away	
Intraconference by Division	AFCS	HOU	AFCS	JAC
		IND		TEN
Interconference by Division	NFCE	DAL	NFCE	PHI
		NYG		WAS
Intraconference by Position	AFCW	SD	AFCE	NE

2009

	Home		Away	
Intraconference by Division	AFCW	OAK	AFCW	DEN
		SD		KC
Interconference by Division	NFCN	GB	NFCN	CHI
		MIN		DET
Intraconference by Position	AFCS	TEN	AFCE	MIA

2010

	Home		Away	
Intraconference by Division	AFCE	NE	AFCE	BUF
		NYJ		MIA
Interconference by Division	NFCS	ATL	NFCS	NO
		CAR		TB
Intraconference by Position	AFCW	OAK	AFCS	TEN

2011

	Home		Away	
Intraconference by Division	AFCS	JAC	AFCS	HOU
		TEN		IND
Interconference by Division	NFCW	STL	NFCW	ARI
		SEA		SF
Intraconference by Position	AFCE	NE	AFCW	KC

2012

	Home		Away	
Intraconference by Division	AFCW	KC	AFCW	DEN
		SD		OAK
Interconference by Division	NFCE	PHI	NFCE	DAL
		WAS		NYG
Intraconference by Position	AFCE	NYJ	AFCS	TEN

2013

	Home		Away	
Intraconference by Division	AFCE	BUF	AFCE	NE
		MIA		NYJ
Interconference by Division	NFCN	CHI	NFCN	GB
		DET		MIN[1]
Intraconference by Position	AFCS	TEN	AFCW	OAK

2014

	Home		Away	
Intraconference by Division	AFCS	HOU	AFCS	JAC
		IND		TEN
Interconference by Division	NFCS	NO	NFCS	ATL
		TB		CAR
Intraconference by Position	AFCW		AFCE	

2015

	Home		Away	
Intraconference by Division	AFCW	DEN	AFCW	KC
		OAK		SD
Interconference by Division	NFCW	ARI	NFCW	STL
		SF		SEA
Intraconference by Position	AFCS		AFCE	

	2016				2017			
	Home		*Away*		*Home*		*Away*	
Intraconference by Division	AFCE	NE	AFCE	BUF	AFCS	JAC	AFCS	HOU
		NYJ		MIA		TEN		IND
Interconference by Division	NFCE	DAL	NFCE	PHI	NFCN	GB	NFCN	CHI
		NYG		WAS		MIN		DET
Intraconference by Position	AFCW		AFCS		AFCE		AFCW	

[1]Game played at London, England.

2002–2017 NON-DIVISIONAL OPPONENTS (By Team)
AFC South
HOUSTON TEXANS

	2002				2003			
	Home		*Away*		*Home*		*Away*	
Intraconference by Division	AFCN	BAL	AFCN	CLE	AFCE	NE	AFCE	BUF
		CIN		PIT		NYJ		MIA
Interconference by Division	NFCE	DAL	NFCE	PHI	NFCS	ATL	NFCS	NO
		NYG		WAS		CAR		TB
Intraconference by Position	AFCE	BUF	AFCW	SD	AFCW	KC	AFCN	CIN

	2004				2005			
	Home		*Away*		*Home*		*Away*	
Intraconference by Division	AFCW	OAK	AFCW	DEN	AFCN	CLE	AFCN	BAL
		SD		KC		PIT		CIN
Interconference by Division	NFCN	GB	NFCN	CHI	NFCW	ARI	NFCW	SF
		MIN		DET		STL		SEA
Intraconference by Position	AFCN	CLE	AFCE	NYJ	AFCW	KC	AFCE	BUF

	2006				2007			
	Home		*Away*		*Home*		*Away*	
Intraconference by Division	AFCE	BUF	AFCE	NE	AFCW	DEN	AFCW	OAK
		MIA		NYJ		KC		SD
Interconference by Division	NFCE	PHI	NFCE	DAL	NFCS	NO	NFCS	ATL
		WAS		NYG		TB		CAR
Intraconference by Position	AFCN	CLE	AFCW	OAK	AFCE	MIA	AFCN	CLE

	2008				2009			
	Home		*Away*		*Home*		*Away*	
Intraconference by Division	AFCN	BAL	AFCN	CLE	AFCE	NE	AFCE	BUF
		CIN		PIT		NYJ		MIA
Interconference by Division	NFCN	CHI	NFCN	GB	NFCW	SF	NFCW	ARI
		DET		MIN		SEA		STL
Intraconference by Position	AFCE	MIA	AFCW	OAK	AFCW	OAK	AFCN	CIN

	2010				2011			
	Home		*Away*		*Home*		*Away*	
Intraconference by Division	AFCW	KC	AFCW	DEN	AFCN	CLE	AFCN	BAL
		SD		OAK		PIT		CIN
Interconference by Division	NFCE	DAL	NFCE	PHI	NFCS	ATL	NFCS	NO
		NYG		WAS		CAR		TB
Intraconference by Position	AFCN	BAL	AFCE	NYJ	AFCW	OAK	AFCE	MIA

	2012				2013			
	Home		*Away*		*Home*		*Away*	
Intraconference by Division	AFCE	BUF	AFCE	NE	AFCW	DEN	AFCW	KC
		MIA		NYJ		OAK		SD

Interconference by Division	NFCN	GB	NFCN	CHI	NFCW	STL	NFCW	ARI
		MIN		DET		SEA		SF
Intraconference by Position	AFCN	BAL	AFCW	DEN	AFCE	NE	AFCN	BAL

	2014				2015			
	Home		*Away*		*Home*		*Away*	
Intraconference by Division	AFCN	BAL	AFCN	CLE	AFCE	NE	AFCE	BUF
		CIN		PIT		NYJ		MIA
Interconference by Division	NFCE	PHI	NFCE	DAL	NFCS	NO	NFCS	ATL
		WAS		NYG		TB		CAR
Intraconference by Position	AFCE		AFCW		AFCW		AFCN	

	2016				2017			
	Home		*Away*		*Home*		*Away*	
Intraconference by Division	AFCW	KC	AFCW	DEN	AFCN	CLE	AFCN	BAL
		SD		OAK		PIT		CIN
Interconference by Division	NFCN	CHI	NFCN	GB	NFCW	ARI	NFCW	STL
		DET		MIN		SF		SEA
Intraconference by Position	AFCN		AFCE		AFCW		AFCE	

INDIANAPOLIS COLTS

	2002				2003			
	Home		*Away*		*Home*		*Away*	
Intraconference by Division	AFCN	BAL	AFCN	CLE	AFCE	NE	AFCE	BUF
		CIN		PIT		NYJ		MIA
Interconference by Division	NFCE	DAL	NFCE	PHI	NFCS	ATL	NFCS	NO
		NYG		WAS		CAR		TB
Intraconference by Position	AFCE	MIA	AFCW	DEN	AFCW	DEN	AFCN	CLE

	2004				2005			
	Home		*Away*		*Home*		*Away*	
Intraconference by Division	AFCW	OAK	AFCW	DEN	AFCN	CLE	AFCN	BAL
		SD		KC		PIT		CIN
Interconference by Division	NFCN	GB	NFCN	CHI	NFCW	ARI	NFCW	SF
		MIN		DET		STL		SEA
Intraconference by Position	AFCN	BAL	AFCE	NE	AFCW	SD	AFCE	NE

	2006				2007			
	Home		*Away*		*Home*		*Away*	
Intraconference by Division	AFCE	BUF	AFCE	NE	AFCW	DEN	AFCW	OAK
		MIA		NYJ		KC		SD
Interconference by Division	NFCE	PHI	NFCE	DAL	NFCS	NO	NFCS	ATL
		WAS		NYG		TB		CAR
Intraconference by Position	AFCN	CIN	AFCW	DEN	AFCE	NE	AFCN	BAL

	2008				2009			
	Home		*Away*		*Home*		*Away*	
Intraconference by Division	AFCN	BAL	AFCN	CLE	AFCE	NE	AFCE	BUF
		CIN		PIT		NYJ		MIA
Interconference by Division	NFCN	CHI	NFCN	GB	NFCW	SF	NFCW	ARI
		DET		MIN		SEA		STL
Intraconference by Position	AFCE	NE	AFCW	SD	AFCW	DEN	AFCN	BAL

	2010				2011			
	Home		*Away*		*Home*		*Away*	
Intraconference by Division	AFCW	KC	AFCW	DEN	AFCN	CLE	AFCN	BAL
		SD		OAK		PIT		CIN
Interconference by Division	NFCE	DAL	NFCE	PHI	NFCS	ATL	NFCS	NO
		NYG		WAS		CAR		TB
Intraconference by Position	AFCN	CIN	AFCE	NE	AFCW	KC	AFCE	NE

	2012				2013			
	Home		*Away*		*Home*		*Away*	
Intraconference by Division	AFCE	BUF	AFCE	NE	AFCW	DEN	AFCW	KC
		MIA		NYJ		OAK		SD
Interconference by Division	NFCN	GB	NFCN	CHI	NFCW	STL	NFCW	ARI
		MIN		DET		SEA		SF
Intraconference by Position	AFCN	CLE	AFCW	KC	AFCE	MIA	AFCN	CIN

	2014				2015			
	Home		*Away*		*Home*		*Away*	
Intraconference by Division	AFCN	BAL	AFCN	CLE	AFCE	NE	AFCE	BUF
		CIN		PIT		NYJ		MIA
Interconference by Division	NFCE	PHI	NFCE	DAL	NFCS	NO	NFCS	ATL
		WAS		NYG		TB		CAR
Intraconference by Position	AFCE		AFCW		AFCW		AFCN	

	2016				2017			
	Home		*Away*		*Home*		*Away*	
Intraconference by Division	AFCW	KC	AFCW	DEN	AFCN	CLE	AFCN	BAL
		SD		OAK		PIT		CIN
Interconference by Division	NFCN	CHI	NFCN	GB	NFCW	ARI	NFCW	STL
		DET		MIN		SF		SEA
Intraconference by Position	AFCN		AFCE		AFCW		AFCE	

JACKSONVILLE JAGUARS

	2002				2003			
	Home		*Away*		*Home*		*Away*	
Intraconference by Division	AFCN	CLE	AFCN	BAL	AFCE	BUF	AFCE	NE
		PIT		CIN		MIA		NYJ
Interconference by Division	NFCE	PHI	NFCE	DAL	NFCS	NO	NFCS	ATL
		WAS		NYG		TB		CAR
Intraconference by Position	AFCE	NYJ	AFCW	KC	AFCW	SD	AFCN	BAL

	2004				2005			
	Home		*Away*		*Home*		*Away*	
Intraconference by Division	AFCW	DEN	AFCW	OAK	AFCN	BAL	AFCN	CLE
		KC		SD		CIN		PIT
Interconference by Division	NFCN	CHI	NFCN	GB	NFCW	SF	NFCW	ARI
		DET		MIN		SEA		STL
Intraconference by Position	AFCN	PIT	AFCE	BUF	AFCW	DEN	AFCE	NYJ

	2006				2007			
	Home		*Away*		*Home*		*Away*	
Intraconference by Division	AFCE	NE	AFCE	BUF	AFCW	OAK	AFCW	DEN
		NYJ		MIA		SD		KC
Interconference by Division	NFCE	DAL	NFCE	PHI	NFCS	ATL	NFCS	NO
		NYG		WAS		CAR		TB
Intraconference by Position	AFCN	PIT	AFCW	KC	AFCE	BUF	AFCN	PIT

	2008				2009			
	Home		*Away*		*Home*		*Away*	
Intraconference by Division	AFCN	CLE	AFCN	BAL	AFCE	BUF	AFCE	NE
		PIT		CIN		MIA		NYJ
Interconference by Division	NFCN	GB	NFCN	CHI	NFCW	ARI	NFCW	SF
		MIN		DET		STL		SEA
Intraconference by Position	AFCE	BUF	AFCW	DEN	AFCW	KC	AFCN	CLE

	2010		2011	
	Home	Away	Home	Away
Intraconference by Division	AFCW DEN OAK	AFCW KC SD	AFCN BAL CIN	AFCN CLE PIT
Interconference by Division	NFCE PHI WAS	NFCE DAL NYG	NFCS NO TB	NFCS ATL CAR
Intraconference by Position	AFCN CLE	AFCE BUF	AFCW SD	AFCE NYJ

	2012		2013	
	Home	Away	Home	Away
Intraconference by Division	AFCE NE NYJ	AFCE BUF MIA	AFCW KC SD	AFCW DEN OAK
Interconference by Division	NFCN CHI DET	NFCN GB MIN	NFCW ARI SF[1]	NFCW STL SEA
Intraconference by Position	AFCN CIN	AFCW OAK	AFCE BUF	AFCN CLE

	2014		2015	
	Home	Away	Home	Away
Intraconference by Division	AFCN CLE PIT	AFCN BAL CIN	AFCE BUF MIA	AFCE NE NYJ
Interconference by Division	NFCE DAL NYG	NFCE PHI WAS	NFCS ATL CAR	NFCS NO TB
Intraconference by Position	AFCE	AFCW	AFCW	AFCN

	2016		2017	
	Home	Away	Home	Away
Intraconference by Division	AFCW DEN OAK	AFCW KC SD	AFCN BAL CIN	AFCN CLE PIT
Interconference by Division	NFCN GB MIN	NFCN CHI DET	NFCW STL SEA	NFCW ARI SF
Intraconference by Position	AFCN	AFCE	AFCW	AFCE

[1] Game played at London, England. Jacksonville will play one regular-season home game in London each year from 2013–2016.

TENNESSEE TITANS

	2002		2003	
	Home	Away	Home	Away
Intraconference by Division	AFCN CLE PIT	AFCN BAL CIN	AFCE BUF MIA	AFCE NE NYJ
Interconference by Division	NFCE PHI WAS	NFCE DAL NYG	NFCS NO TB	NFCS ATL CAR
Intraconference by Position	AFCE NE	AFCW OAK	AFCW OAK	AFCN PIT

	2004		2005	
	Home	Away	Home	Away
Intraconference by Division	AFCW DEN KC	AFCW OAK SD	AFCN BAL CIN	AFCN CLE PIT
Interconference by Division	NFCN CHI DET	NFCN GB MIN	NFCW SF SEA	NFCW ARI STL
Intraconference by Position	AFCN CIN	AFCE MIA	AFCW OAK	AFCE MIA

2006

	Home	Away
Intraconference by Division	AFCE NE / NYJ	AFCE BUF / MIA
Interconference by Division	NFCE DAL / NYG	NFCE PHI / WAS
Intraconference by Position	AFCN BAL	AFCW SD

2007

	Home	Away
Intraconference by Division	AFCW OAK / SD	AFCW DEN / KC
Interconference by Division	NFCS ATL / CAR	NFCS NO / TB
Intraconference by Position	AFCE NYJ	AFCN CIN

2008

	Home	Away
Intraconference by Division	AFCN CLE / PIT	AFCN BAL / CIN
Interconference by Division	NFCN GB / MIN	NFCN CHI / DET
Intraconference by Position	AFCE NYJ	AFCW KC

2009

	Home	Away
Intraconference by Division	AFCE BUF / MIA	AFCE NE / NYJ
Interconference by Division	NFCW ARI / STL	NFCW SF / SEA
Intraconference by Position	AFCW SD	AFCN PIT

2010

	Home	Away
Intraconference by Division	AFCW DEN / OAK	AFCW KC / SD
Interconference by Division	NFCE PHI / WAS	NFCE DAL / NYG
Intraconference by Position	AFCN PIT	AFCE MIA

2011

	Home	Away
Intraconference by Division	AFCN BAL / CIN	AFCN CLE / PIT
Interconference by Division	NFCS NO / TB	NFCS ATL / CAR
Intraconference by Position	AFCW DEN	AFCE BUF

2012

	Home	Away
Intraconference by Division	AFCE NE / NYJ	AFCE BUF / MIA
Interconference by Division	NFCN CHI / DET	NFCN GB / MIN
Intraconference by Position	AFCN PIT	AFCW SD

2013

	Home	Away
Intraconference by Division	AFCW KC / SD	AFCW DEN / OAK
Interconference by Division	NFCW ARI / SF	NFCW STL / SEA
Intraconference by Position	AFCE NYJ	AFCN PIT

2014

	Home	Away
Intraconference by Division	AFCN CLE / PIT	AFCN BAL / CIN
Interconference by Division	NFCE DAL / NYG	NFCE PHI / WAS
Intraconference by Position	AFCE	AFCW

2015

	Home	Away
Intraconference by Division	AFCE BUF / MIA	AFCE NE / NYJ
Interconference by Division	NFCS ATL / CAR	NFCS NO / TB
Intraconference by Position	AFCW	AFCN

2016

	Home	Away
Intraconference by Division	AFCW DEN / OAK	AFCW KC / SD
Interconference by Division	NFCN GB / MIN	NFCN CHI / DET
Intraconference by Position	AFCN	AFCE

2017

	Home	Away
Intraconference by Division	AFCN BAL / CIN	AFCN CLE / PIT
Interconference by Division	NFCW STL / SEA	NFCW ARI / SF
Intraconference by Position	AFCW	AFCE

2002–2017 NON-DIVISIONAL OPPONENTS (By Team)
AFC WEST
DENVER BRONCOS

	2002 Home	2002 Away	2003 Home	2003 Away
Intraconference by Division	AFCE BUF MIA	AFCE NE NYJ	AFCN CLE PIT	AFCN BAL CIN
Interconference by Division	NFCW ARI STL	NFCW SF SEA	NFCN CHI DET	NFCN GB MIN
Intraconference by Position	AFCS IND	AFCN BAL	AFCE NE	AFCS IND

	2004 Home	2004 Away	2005 Home	2005 Away
Intraconference by Division	AFCS HOU IND	AFCS JAC TEN	AFCE NE NYJ	AFCE BUF MIA
Interconference by Division	NFCS ATL CAR	NFCS NO TB	NFCE PHI WAS	NFCE DAL NYG
Intraconference by Position	AFCE MIA	AFCN CIN	AFCN BAL	AFCS JAC

	2006 Home	2006 Away	2007 Home	2007 Away
Intraconference by Division	AFCN BAL CIN	AFCN CLE PIT	AFCS JAC TEN	AFCS HOU IND
Interconference by Division	NFCW SF SEA	NFCW ARI STL	NFCN GB MIN	NFCN CHI DET
Intraconference by Position	AFCS IND	AFCE NE	AFCN PIT	AFCE BUF

	2008 Home	2008 Away	2009 Home	2009 Away
Intraconference by Division	AFCE BUF MIA	AFCE NE NYJ	AFCN CLE PIT	AFCN BAL CIN
Interconference by Division	NFCS NO TB	NFCS ATL CAR	NFCE DAL NYG	NFCE PHI WAS
Intraconference by Position	AFCS JAC	AFCN CLE	AFCE NE	AFCS IND

	2010 Home	2010 Away	2011 Home	2011 Away
Intraconference by Division	AFCS HOU IND	AFCS JAC TEN	AFCE NE NYJ	AFCE BUF MIA
Interconference by Division	NFCW STL SEA	NFCW ARI SF[1]	NFCN CHI DET	NFCN GB MIN
Intraconference by Position	AFCE NYJ	AFCN BAL	AFCN CIN	AFCS TEN

	2012 Home	2012 Away	2013 Home	2013 Away
Intraconference by Division	AFCN CLE PIT	AFCN BAL CIN	AFCS JAC TEN	AFCS HOU IND
Interconference by Division	NFCS NO TB	NFCS ATL CAR	NFCE PHI WAS	NFCE DAL NYG
Intraconference by Position	AFCS HOU	AFCE NE	AFCN BAL	AFCE NE

	2014 Home	2014 Away	2015 Home	2015 Away
Intraconference by Division	AFCE BUF MIA	AFCE NE NYJ	AFCN BAL CIN	AFCN CLE PIT
Interconference by Division	NFCW ARI SF	NFCW STL SEA	NFCN GB MIN	NFCN CHI DET
Intraconference by Position	AFCS	AFCN	AFCE	AFCS

	2016				2017		
	Home		*Away*		*Home*		*Away*
Intraconference by Division	AFCS	HOU	AFCS	JAC	AFCE	NE	AFCE	BUF
		IND		TEN		NYJ		MIA
Interconference by Division	NFCS	ATL	NFCS	NO	NFCE	DAL	NFCE	PHI
		CAR		TB		NYG		WAS
Intraconference by Position	AFCE		AFCN		AFCN		AFCS	

[1]Game played at London, England.

KANSAS CITY CHIEFS

	2002				2003		
	Home		*Away*		*Home*		*Away*
Intraconference by Division	AFCE	BUF	AFCE	NE	AFCN	CLE	AFCN	BAL
		MIA		NYJ		PIT		CIN
Interconference by Division	NFCW	ARI	NFCW	SF	NFCN	CHI	NFCN	GB
		STL		SEA		DET		MIN
Intraconference by Position	AFCS	JAC	AFCN	CLE	AFCE	BUF	AFCS	HOU

	2004				2005		
	Home		*Away*		*Home*		*Away*
Intraconference by Division	AFCS	HOU	AFCS	JAC	AFCE	NE	AFCE	BUF
		IND		TEN		NYJ		MIA
Interconference by Division	NFCS	ATL	NFCS	NO	NFCE	PHI	NFCE	DAL
		CAR		TB		WAS		NYG
Intraconference by Position	AFCE	NE	AFCN	BAL	AFCN	CIN	AFCS	HOU

	2006				2007		
	Home		*Away*		*Home*		*Away*
Intraconference by Division	AFCN	BAL	AFCN	CLE	AFCS	JAC	AFCS	HOU
		CIN		PIT		TEN		IND
Interconference by Division	NFCW	SF	NFCW	ARI	NFCN	GB	NFCN	CHI
		SEA		STL		MIN		DET
Intraconference by Position	AFCS	JAC	AFCE	MIA	AFCN	CIN	AFCE	NYJ

	2008				2009		
	Home		*Away*		*Home*		*Away*
Intraconference by Division	AFCE	BUF	AFCE	NE	AFCN	CLE	AFCN	BAL
		MIA		NYJ		PIT		CIN
Interconference by Division	NFCS	NO	NFCS	ATL	NFCE	DAL	NFCE	PHI
		TB		CAR		NYG		WAS
Intraconference by Position	AFCS	TEN	AFCN	CIN	AFCE	BUF	AFCS	JAC

	2010				2011		
	Home		*Away*		*Home*		*Away*
Intraconference by Division	AFCS	JAC	AFCS	HOU	AFCE	BUF	AFCE	NE
		TEN		IND		MIA		NYJ
Interconference by Division	NFCW	ARI	NFCW	STL	NFCN	GB	NFCN	CHI
		SF		SEA		MIN		DET
Intraconference by Position	AFCE	BUF	AFCN	CLE	AFCN	PIT	AFCS	IND

	2012				2013		
	Home		*Away*		*Home*		*Away*
Intraconference by Division	AFCN	BAL	AFCN	CLE	AFCS	HOU	AFCS	JAC
		CIN		PIT		IND		TEN
Interconference by Division	NFCS	ATL	NFCS	NO	NFCE	DAL	NFCE	PHI
		CAR		TB		NYG		WAS
Intraconference by Position	AFCS	IND	AFCE	BUF	AFCN	CLE	AFCE	BUF

	2014			2015		
	Home		*Away*	*Home*		*Away*
Intraconference by Division	AFCE	NE	AFCE BUF	AFCN	CLE	AFCN BAL
		NYJ	MIA		PIT	CIN
Interconference by Division	NFCW	STL	NFCW ARI	NFCN	CHI	NFCN GB
		SEA	SF		DET	MIN
Intraconference by Position	AFCS		AFCN	AFCE		AFCS

	2016			2017		
	Home		*Away*	*Home*		*Away*
Intraconference by Division	AFCS	JAC	AFCS HOU	AFCE	BUF	AFCE NE
		TEN	IND		MIA	NYJ
Interconference by Division	NFCS	NO	NFCS ATL	NFCE	PHI	NFCE DAL
		TB	CAR		WAS	NYG
Intraconference by Position	AFCE		AFCN	AFCN		AFCS

OAKLAND RAIDERS

	2002			2003		
	Home		*Away*	*Home*		*Away*
Intraconference by Division	AFCE	NE	AFCE BUF	AFCN	BAL	AFCN CLE
		NYJ	MIA		CIN	PIT
Interconference by Division	NFCW	SF	NFCW ARI	NFCN	GB	NFCN CHI
		SEA	STL		MIN	DET
Intraconference by Position	AFCS	TEN	AFCN PIT	AFCE	NYJ	AFCS TEN

	2004			2005		
	Home		*Away*	*Home*		*Away*
Intraconference by Division	AFCS	JAC	AFCS HOU	AFCE	BUF	AFCE NE
		TEN	IND		MIA	NYJ
Interconference by Division	NFCS	NO	NFCS ATL	NFCE	DAL	NFCE PHI
		TB	CAR		NYG	WAS
Intraconference by Position	AFCE	BUF	AFCN PIT	AFCN	CLE	AFCS TEN

	2006			2007		
	Home		*Away*	*Home*		*Away*
Intraconference by Division	AFCN	CLE	AFCN BAL	AFCS	HOU	AFCS JAC
		PIT	CIN		IND	TEN
Interconference by Division	NFCW	ARI	NFCW SF	NFCN	CHI	NFCN GB
		STL	SEA		DET	MIN
Intraconference by Position	AFCS	HOU	AFCE NYJ	AFCN	CLE	AFCE MIA

	2008			2009		
	Home		*Away*	*Home*		*Away*
Intraconference by Division	AFCE	NE	AFCE BUF	AFCN	BAL	AFCN CLE
		NYJ	MIA		CIN	PIT
Interconference by Division	NFCS	ATL	NFCS NO	NFCE	PHI	NFCE DAL
		CAR	TB		WAS	NYG
Intraconference by Position	AFCS	HOU	AFCN BAL	AFCE	NYJ	AFCS HOU

	2010			2011		
	Home		*Away*	*Home*		*Away*
Intraconference by Division	AFCS	HOU	AFCS JAC	AFCE	NE	AFCE BUF
		IND	TEN		NYJ	MIA
Interconference by Division	NFCW	STL	NFCW ARI	NFCN	CHI	NFCN GB
		SEA	SF		DET	MIN
Intraconference by Position	AFCE	MIA	AFCN PIT	AFCN	CLE	AFCS HOU

	2012				2013			
	Home		*Away*		*Home*		*Away*	
Intraconference by Division	AFCN	CLE PIT	AFCN	BAL CIN	AFCS	JAC TEN	AFCS	HOU IND
Interconference by Division	NFCS	NO TB	NFCS	ATL CAR	NFCE	PHI WAS	NFCE	DAL NYG
Intraconference by Position	AFCS	JAC	AFCE	MIA	AFCN	PIT	AFCE	NYJ

	2014				2015			
	Home		*Away*		*Home*		*Away*	
Intraconference by Division	AFCE	BUF MIA	AFCE	NE NYJ	AFCN	BAL CIN	AFCN	CLE PIT
Interconference by Division	NFCW	ARI SF	NFCW	STL SEA	NFCN	GB MIN	NFCN	CHI DET
Intraconference by Position	AFCS		AFCN		AFCE		AFCS	

	2016				2017			
	Home		*Away*		*Home*		*Away*	
Intraconference by Division	AFCS	HOU IND	AFCS	JAC TEN	AFCE	NE NYJ	AFCE	BUF MIA
Interconference by Division	NFCS	ATL CAR	NFCS	NO TB	NFCE	DAL NYG	NFCE	PHI WAS
Intraconference by Position	AFCE		AFCN		AFCN		AFCS	

SAN DIEGO CHARGERS

	2002				2003			
	Home		*Away*		*Home*		*Away*	
Intraconference by Division	AFCE	NE NYJ	AFCE	BUF MIA	AFCN	BAL CIN	AFCN	CLE PIT
Interconference by Division	NFCW	SF SEA	NFCW	ARI STL	NFCN	GB MIN	NFCN	CHI DET
Intraconference by Position	AFCS	HOU	AFCN	CIN	AFCE	MIA[1]	AFCS	JAC

	2004				2005			
	Home		*Away*		*Home*		*Away*	
Intraconference by Division	AFCS	JAC TEN	AFCS	HOU IND	AFCE	BUF MIA	AFCE	NE NYJ
Interconference by Division	NFCS	NO TB	NFCS	ATL CAR	NFCE	DAL NYG	NFCE	PHI WAS
Intraconference by Position	AFCE	NYJ	AFCN	CLE	AFCN	PIT	AFCS	IND

	2006				2007			
	Home		*Away*		*Home*		*Away*	
Intraconference by Division	AFCN	CLE PIT	AFCN	BAL CIN	AFCS	HOU IND	AFCS	JAC TEN
Interconference by Division	NFCW	ARI STL	NFCW	SF SEA	NFCN	CHI DET	NFCN	GB MIN
Intraconference by Position	AFCS	TEN	AFCE	BUF	AFCN	BAL	AFCE	NE

	2008				2009			
	Home		*Away*		*Home*		*Away*	
Intraconference by Division	AFCE	NE NYJ	AFCE	BUF MIA	AFCN	BAL CIN	AFCN	CLE PIT
Interconference by Division	NFCS	ATL CAR	NFCS	NO[2] TB	NFCE	PHI WAS	NFCE	DAL NYG
Intraconference by Position	AFCS	IND	AFCN	PIT	AFCE	MIA	AFCS	TEN

	2010				2011			
	Home		*Away*		*Home*		*Away*	
Intraconference by Division	AFCS	JAC	AFCS	HOU	AFCE	BUF	AFCE	NE

		TEN		IND		MIA		NYJ
Interconference by Division	NFCW	ARI	NFCW	STL	NFCN	GB	NFCN	CHI
		SF		SEA		MIN		DET
Intraconference by Position	AFCE	NE	AFCN	CIN	AFCN	BAL	AFCS	JAC

	2012				2013			
	Home		Away		Home		Away	
Intraconference by Division	AFCN	BAL	AFCN	CLE	AFCS	HOU	AFCS	JAC
		CIN		PIT		IND		TEN
Interconference by Division	NFCS	ATL	NFCS	NO	NFCE	DAL	NFCE	PHI
		CAR		TB		NYG		WAS
Intraconference by Position	AFCS	TEN	AFCE	NYJ	AFCN	CIN	AFCE	MIA

	2014				2015			
	Home		Away		Home		Away	
Intraconference by Division	AFCE	NE	AFCE	BUF	AFCN	CLE	AFCN	BAL
		NYJ		MIA		PIT		CIN
Interconference by Division	NFCW	STL	NFCW	ARI	NFCN	CHI	NFCN	GB
		SEA		SF		DET		MIN
Intraconference by Position	AFCS		AFCN		AFCE		AFCS	

	2016				2017			
	Home		Away		Home		Away	
Intraconference by Division	AFCS	JAC	AFCS	HOU	AFCE	BUF	AFCE	NE
		TEN		IND		MIA		NYJ
Interconference by Division	NFCS	NO	NFCS	ATL	NFCE	PHI	NFCE	DAL
		TB		CAR		WAS		NYG
Intraconference by Position	AFCE		AFCN		AFCN		AFCS	

[1]Game moved to Tempe, AZ due to wildfires in the San Diego area.
[2]Game played at London, England.

2002–2017 NON-DIVISIONAL OPPONENTS (By Team)

NFC East

DALLAS COWBOYS

	2002				2003			
	Home		Away		Home		Away	
Intraconference by Division	NFCW	SF	NFCW	ARI	NFCS	ATL	NFCS	NO
		SEA		STL		CAR		TB
Interconference by Division	AFCS	JAC	AFCS	HOU	AFCE	BUF	AFCE	NE
		TEN		IND		MIA		NYJ
Intraconference by Position	NFCS	CAR	NFCN	DET	NFCW	ARI	NFCN	DET

	2004				2005			
	Home		Away		Home		Away	
Intraconference by Division	NFCN	CHI	NFCN	GB	NFCW	ARI	NFCW	SF
		DET		MIN		STL		SEA
Interconference by Division	AFCN	CLE	AFCN	BAL	AFCW	DEN	AFCW	OAK
		PIT		CIN		KC		SD
Intraconference by Position	NFCS	NO	NFCW	SEA	NFCN	DET	NFCS	CAR

	2006				2007			
	Home		Away		Home		Away	
Intraconference by Division	NFCS	NO	NFCS	ATL	NFCN	GB	NFCN	CHI
		TB		CAR		MIN		DET
Interconference by Division	AFCS	HOU	AFCS	JAC	AFCE	NE	AFCE	BUF
		IND		TEN		NYJ		MIA
Intraconference by Position	NFCN	DET	NFCW	ARI	NFCW	STL	NFCS	CAR

	2008				2009		
	Home		*Away*		*Home*		*Away*
Intraconference by Division	NFCW	SF	NFCW	ARI	NFCS	ATL	NFCS	NO
		SEA		STL		CAR		TB
Interconference by Division	AFCN	BAL	AFCN	CLE	AFCW	OAK	AFCW	DEN
		CIN		PIT		SD		KC
Intraconference by Position	NFCS	TB	NFCN	GB	NFCW	SEA	NFCN	GB

	2010				2011			
	Home		*Away*		*Home*		*Away*	
Intraconference by Division	NFCN	CHI	NFCN	GB	NFCW	STL	NFCW	ARI
		DET		MIN		SEA		SF
Interconference by Division	AFCS	JAC	AFCS	HOU	AFCE	BUF	AFCE	NE
		TEN		IND		MIA		NYJ
Intraconference by Position	NFCS	NO	NFCW	ARI	NFCN	DET	NFCS	TB

	2012				2013			
	Home		*Away*		*Home*		*Away*	
Intraconference by Division	NFCS	NO	NFCS	ATL	NFCN	GB	NFCN	CHI
		TB		CAR		MIN		DET
Interconference by Division	AFCN	CLE	AFCN	BAL	AFCW	DEN	AFCW	KC
		PIT		CIN		OAK		SD
Intraconference by Position	NFCN	CHI	NFCW	SEA	NFCW	STL	NFCS	NO

	2014				2015			
	Home		*Away*		*Home*		*Away*	
Intraconference by Division	NFCW	ARI	NFCW	STL	NFCS	ATL	NFCS	NO
		SF		SEA		CAR		TB
Interconference by Division	AFCS	HOU	AFCS	JAC	AFCE	NE	AFCE	BUF
		IND		TEN		NYJ		MIA
Intraconference by Position	NFCS		NFCN		NFCW		NFCN	

	2016				2017			
	Home		*Away*		*Home*		*Away*	
Intraconference by Division	NFCN	CHI	NFCN	GB	NFCW	STL	NFCW	ARI
		DET		MIN		SEA		SF
Interconference by Division	AFCN	BAL	AFCN	CLE	AFCW	KC	AFCW	DEN
		CIN		PIT		SD		OAK
Intraconference by Position	NFCS		NFCW		NFCN		NFCS	

NEW YORK GIANTS

	2002				2003			
	Home		*Away*		*Home*		*Away*	
Intraconference by Division	NFCW	SF	NFCW	ARI	NFCS	ATL	NFCS	NO
		SEA		STL		CAR		TB
Interconference by Division	AFCS	JAC	AFCS	HOU	AFCE	BUF	AFCE	NE
		TEN		IND		MIA		NYJ
Intraconference by Position	NFCS	ATL	NFCN	MIN	NFCW	STL	NFCN	MIN

	2004				2005			
	Home		*Away*		*Home*		*Away*	
Intraconference by Division	NFCN	CHI	NFCN	GB	NFCW	ARI	NFCW	SF
		DET		MIN		STL		SEA
Interconference by Division	AFCN	CLE	AFCN	BAL	AFCW	DEN	AFCW	OAK
		PIT		CIN		KC		SD
Intraconference by Position	NFCS	ATL	NFCW	ARI	NFCN	MIN	NFCS	NO[1]

2006

	Home		Away	
Intraconference by Division	NFCS	NO TB	NFCS	ATL CAR
Interconference by Division	AFCS	HOU IND	AFCS	JAC TEN
Intraconference by Position	NFCN	CHI	NFCW	SEA

2007

	Home		Away	
Intraconference by Division	NFCN	GB MIN	NFCN	CHI DET
Interconference by Division	AFCE	NE NYJ	AFCE	BUF MIA[2]
Intraconference by Position	NFCW	SF	NFCS	ATL

2008

	Home		Away	
Intraconference by Division	NFCW	SF SEA	NFCW	ARI STL
Interconference by Division	AFCN	BAL CIN	AFCN	CLE PIT
Intraconference by Position	NFCS	CAR	NFCN	MIN

2009

	Home		Away	
Intraconference by Division	NFCS	ATL CAR	NFCS	NO TB
Interconference by Division	AFCW	OAK SD	AFCW	DEN KC
Intraconference by Position	NFCW	ARI	NFCN	MIN

2010

	Home		Away	
Intraconference by Division	NFCN	CHI DET	NFCN	GB MIN[3]
Interconference by Division	AFCS	JAC TEN	AFCS	HOU IND
Intraconference by Position	NFCS	CAR	NFCW	SEA

2011

	Home		Away	
Intraconference by Division	NFCW	STL SEA	NFCW	ARI SF
Interconference by Division	AFCE	BUF MIA	AFCE	NE NYJ
Intraconference by Position	NFCN	GB	NFCS	NO

2012

	Home		Away	
Intraconference by Division	NFCS	NO TB	NFCS	ATL CAR
Interconference by Division	AFCN	CLE PIT	AFCN	BAL CIN
Intraconference by Position	NFCN	GB	NFCW	SF

2013

	Home		Away	
Intraconference by Division	NFCN	GB MIN	NFCN	CHI DET
Interconference by Division	AFCW	DEN OAK	AFCW	KC SD
Intraconference by Position	NFCW	SEA	NFCS	CAR

2014

	Home		Away	
Intraconference by Division	NFCW	ARI SF	NFCW	STL SEA
Interconference by Division	AFCS	HOU IND	AFCS	JAC TEN
Intraconference by Position	NFCS		NFCN	

2015

	Home		Away	
Intraconference by Division	NFCS	ATL CAR	NFCS	NO TB
Interconference by Division	AFCE	NE NYJ	AFCE	BUF MIA
Intraconference by Position	NFCW		NFCN	

2016

	Home		Away	
Intraconference by Division	NFCN	CHI DET	NFCN	GB MIN
Interconference by Division	AFCN	BAL CIN	AFCN	CLE PIT
Intraconference by Position	NFCS		NFCW	

2017

	Home		Away	
Intraconference by Division	NFCW	STL SEA	NFCW	ARI SF
Interconference by Division	AFCW	KC SD	AFCW	DEN OAK
Intraconference by Position	NFCN		NFCS	

[1] Due to Hurricane Katrina, game moved to Giants Stadium, East Rutherford, NJ.
[2] Game played at London, England.
[3] Game moved to Detroit due to Minneapolis blizzard.

PHILADELPHIA EAGLES

2002

	Home		Away	
Intraconference by Division	NFCW	ARI STL	NFCW	SF SEA
Interconference by Division	AFCS	HOU IND	AFCS	JAC TEN
Intraconference by Position	NFCS	TB	NFCN	CHI[1]

2003

	Home		Away	
Intraconference by Division	NFCS	NO TB	NFCS	ATL CAR
Interconference by Division	AFCE	NE NYJ	AFCE	BUF MIA
Intraconference by Position	NFCW	SF	NFCN	GB

	2004			2005		
	Home		*Away*	*Home*		*Away*
Intraconference by Division	NFCN	GB	NFCN CHI	NFCW	SF	NFCW ARI
		MIN	DET		SEA	STL
Interconference by Division	AFCN	BAL	AFCN CLE	AFCW	OAK	AFCW DEN
		CIN	PIT		SD	KC
Intraconference by Position	NFCS	CAR	NFCW STL	NFCN	GB	NFCS ATL

	2006			2007		
	Home		*Away*	*Home*		*Away*
Intraconference by Division	NFCS	ATL	NFCS NO	NFCN	CHI	NFCN GB
		CAR	TB		DET	MIN
Interconference by Division	AFCS	JAC	AFCS HOU	AFCE	BUF	AFCE NE
		TEN	IND		MIA	NYJ
Intraconference by Position	NFCN	GB	NFCW SF	NFCW	SEA	NFCS NO

	2008			2009		
	Home		*Away*	*Home*		*Away*
Intraconference by Division	NFCW	ARI	NFCW SF	NFCS	NO	NFCS ATL
		STL	SEA		TB	CAR
Interconference by Division	AFCN	CLE	AFCN BAL	AFCW	DEN	AFCW OAK
		PIT	CIN		KC	SD
Intraconference by Position	NFCS	ATL	NFCN CHI	NFCW	SF	NFCN CHI

	2010			2011		
	Home		*Away*	*Home*		*Away*
Intraconference by Division	NFCN	GB	NFCN CHI	NFCW	ARI	NFCW STL
		MIN	DET		SF	SEA
Interconference by Division	AFCS	HOU	AFCS JAC	AFCE	NE	AFCE BUF
		IND	TEN		NYJ	MIA
Intraconference by Position	NFCS	ATL	NFCW SF	NFCN	CHI	NFCS ATL

	2012			2013		
	Home		*Away*	*Home*		*Away*
Intraconference by Division	NFCS	ATL	NFCS NO	NFCN	CHI	NFCN GB
		CAR	TB		DET	MIN
Interconference by Division	AFCN	BAL	AFCN CLE	AFCW	KC	AFCW DEN
		CIN	PIT		SD	OAK
Intraconference by Position	NFCN	DET	NFCW ARI	NFCW	ARI	NFCS TB

	2014			2015		
	Home		*Away*	*Home*		*Away*
Intraconference by Division	NFCW	STL	NFCW ARI	NFCS	NO	NFCS ATL
		SEA	SF		TB	CAR
Interconference by Division	AFCS	JAC	AFCS HOU	AFCE	BUF	AFCE NE
		TEN	IND		MIA	NYJ
Intraconference by Position	NFCS		NFCN	NFCW		NFCN

	2016			2017		
	Home		*Away*	*Home*		*Away*
Intraconference by Division	NFCN	GB	NFCN CHI	NFCW	ARI	NFCW STL
		MIN	DET		SF	SEA
Interconference by Division	AFCN	CLE	AFCN BAL	AFCW	DEN	AFCW KC
		PIT	CIN		OAK	SD
Intraconference by Position	NFCS		NFCW	NFCN		NFCS

[1]Game played at Champaign, IL.

WASHINGTON REDSKINS

2002

	Home		Away	
Intraconference by Division	NFCW	ARI STL	NFCW	SF SEA
Interconference by Division	AFCS	HOU IND	AFCS	JAC TEN
Intraconference by Position	NFCS	NO	NFCN	GB

2003

	Home		Away	
Intraconference by Division	NFCS	NO TB	NFCS	ATL CAR
Interconference by Division	AFCE	NE NYJ	AFCE	BUF MIA
Intraconference by Position	NFCW	SEA	NFCN	CHI

2004

	Home		Away	
Intraconference by Division	NFCN	GB MIN	NFCN	CHI DET
Interconference by Division	AFCN	BAL CIN	AFCN	CLE PIT
Intraconference by Position	NFCS	TB	NFCW	SF

2005

	Home		Away	
Intraconference by Division	NFCW	SF SEA	NFCW	ARI STL
Interconference by Division	AFCW	OAK SD	AFCW	DEN KC
Intraconference by Position	NFCN	CHI	NFCS	TB

2006

	Home		Away	
Intraconference by Division	NFCS	ATL CAR	NFCS	NO TB
Interconference by Division	AFCS	JAC TEN	AFCS	HOU IND
Intraconference by Position	NFCN	MIN	NFCW	STL

2007

	Home		Away	
Intraconference by Division	NFCN	CHI DET	NFCN	GB MIN
Interconference by Division	AFCE	BUF MIA	AFCE	NE NYJ
Intraconference by Position	NFCW	ARI	NFCS	TB

2008

	Home		Away	
Intraconference by Division	NFCW	ARI STL	NFCW	SF SEA
Interconference by Division	AFCN	CLE PIT	AFCN	BAL CIN
Intraconference by Position	NFCS	NO	NFCN	DET

2009

	Home		Away	
Intraconference by Division	NFCS	NO TB	NFCS	ATL CAR
Interconference by Division	AFCW	DEN KC	AFCW	OAK SD
Intraconference by Position	NFCW	STL	NFCN	DET

2010

	Home		Away	
Intraconference by Division	NFCN	GB MIN	NFCN	CHI DET
Interconference by Division	AFCS	HOU IND	AFCS	JAC TEN
Intraconference by Position	NFCS	TB	NFCW	STL

2011

	Home		Away	
Intraconference by Division	NFCW	ARI SF	NFCW	STL SEA
Interconference by Division	AFCE	NE NYJ	AFCE	BUF[1] MIA
Intraconference by Position	NFCN	MIN	NFCS	CAR

2012

	Home		Away	
Intraconference by Division	NFCS	ATL CAR	NFCS	NO TB
Interconference by Division	AFCN	BAL CIN	AFCN	CLE PIT
Intraconference by Position	NFCN	MIN	NFCW	STL

2013

	Home		Away	
Intraconference by Division	NFCN	CHI DET	NFCN	GB MIN
Interconference by Division	AFCW	KC SD	AFCW	DEN OAK
Intraconference by Position	NFCW	SF	NFCS	ATL

2014

	Home		Away	
Intraconference by Division	NFCW	STL SEA	NFCW	ARI SF
Interconference by Division	AFCS	JAC TEN	AFCS	HOU IND
Intraconference by Position	NFCS		NFCN	

2015

	Home		Away	
Intraconference by Division	NFCS	NO TB	NFCS	ATL CAR
Interconference by Division	AFCE	BUF MIA	AFCE	NE NYJ
Intraconference by Position	NFCW		NFCN	

	2016			2017		
	Home		**Away**	**Home**		**Away**
Intraconference by Division	NFCN	GB	NFCN CHI	NFCW	ARI	NFCW STL
		MIN	DET		SF	SEA
Interconference by Division	AFCN	CLE	AFCN BAL	AFCW	DEN	AFCW KC
		PIT	CIN		OAK	SD
Intraconference by Position	NFCS		NFCW	NFCN		NFCS

¹Game played at Toronto.

2002–2017 NON-DIVISIONAL OPPONENTS (By Team)

NFC NORTH

CHICAGO BEARS

	2002			2003		
	Home		**Away**	**Home**		**Away**
Intraconference by Division	NFCS	NO¹	NFCS ATL	NFCW	ARI	NFCW SF
		TB¹	CAR		STL	SEA
Interconference by Division	AFCE	NE¹	AFCE BUF	AFCW	OAK	AFCW DEN
		NYJ¹	MIA		SD	KC
Intraconference by Position	NFCE	PHI¹	NFCW STL	NFCE	WAS	NFCS NO

	2004			2005		
	Home		**Away**	**Home**		**Away**
Intraconference by Division	NFCE	PHI	NFCE DAL	NFCS	ATL	NFCS NO²
		WAS	NYG		CAR	TB
Interconference by Division	AFCS	HOU	AFCS JAC	AFCN	BAL	AFCN CLE
		IND	TEN		CIN	PIT
Intraconference by Position	NFCW	SF	NFCS TB	NFCW	SF	NFCE WAS

	2006			2007		
	Home		**Away**	**Home**		**Away**
Intraconference by Division	NFCW	SF	NFCW ARI	NFCE	DAL	NFCE PHI
		SEA	STL		NYG	WAS
Interconference by Division	AFCE	BUF	AFCE NE	AFCW	DEN	AFCW OAK
		MIA	NYJ		KC	SD
Intraconference by Position	NFCS	TB	NFCE NYG	NFCS	NO	NFCW SEA

	2008			2009		
	Home		**Away**	**Home**		**Away**
Intraconference by Division	NFCS	NO	NFCS ATL	NFCW	ARI	NFCW SF
		TB	CAR		STL	SEA
Interconference by Division	AFCS	JAC	AFCS HOU	AFCN	CLE	AFCN BAL
		TEN	IND		PIT	CIN
Intraconference by Position	NFCE	PHI	NFCW STL	NFCE	PHI	NFCS ATL

	2010			2011		
	Home		**Away**	**Home**		**Away**
Intraconference by Division	NFCE	PHI	NFCE DAL	NFCS	ATL	NFCS NO
		WAS	NYG		CAR	TB⁴
Interconference by Division	AFCE	NE	AFCE BUF³	AFCW	KC	AFCW DEN
		NYJ	MIA		SD	OAK
Intraconference by Position	NFCW	SEA	NFCS CAR	NFCW	SEA	NFCE PHI

	2012				2013			
	Home		*Away*		*Home*		*Away*	
Intraconference by Division	NFCW	STL	NFCW	ARI	NFCE	DAL	NFCE	PHI
		SEA		SF		NYG		WAS
Interconference by Division	AFCS	HOU	AFCS	JAC	AFCN	BAL	AFCN	CLE
		IND		TEN		CIN		PIT
Intraconference by Position	NFCS	CAR	NFCE	DAL	NFCS	NO	NFCW	STL

	2014				2015			
	Home		*Away*		*Home*		*Away*	
Intraconference by Division	NFCS	NO	NFCS	ATL	NFCW	ARI	NFCW	STL
		TB		CAR		SF		SEA
Interconference by Division	AFCE	BUF	AFCE	NE	AFCW	DEN	AFCW	KC
		MIA		NYJ		OAK		SD
Intraconference by Position	NFCE		NFCW		NFCE		NFCS	

	2016				2017			
	Home		*Away*		*Home*		*Away*	
Intraconference by Division	NFCE	PHI	NFCE	DAL	NFCS	ATL	NFCS	NO
		WAS		NYG		CAR		TB
Interconference by Division	AFCS	JAC	AFCS	HOU	AFCN	CLE	AFCN	BAL
		TEN		IND		PIT		CIN
Intraconference by Position	NFCW		NFCS		NFCW		NFCE	

[1] All 2002 home games played at Champaign, IL.
[2] Due to Hurricane Katrina, game moved to Baton Rouge, LA.
[3] Game played at Toronto.
[4] Game played at London, England.

DETROIT LIONS

	2002				2003			
	Home		*Away*		*Home*		*Away*	
Intraconference by Division	NFCS	NO	NFCS	ATL	NFCW	ARI	NFCW	SF
		TB		CAR		STL		SEA
Interconference by Division	AFCE	NE	AFCE	BUF	AFCW	OAK	AFCW	DEN
		NYJ		MIA		SD		KC
Intraconference by Position	NFCE	DAL	NFCW	ARI	NFCE	DAL	NFCS	CAR

	2004				2005			
	Home		*Away*		*Home*		*Away*	
Intraconference by Division	NFCE	PHI	NFCE	DAL	NFCS	ATL	NFCS	NO[1]
		WAS		NYG		CAR		TB
Interconference by Division	AFCS	HOU	AFCS	JAC	AFCN	BAL	AFCN	CLE
		IND		TEN		CIN		PIT
Intraconference by Position	NFCW	ARI	NFCS	ATL	NFCW	ARI	NFCE	DAL

	2006				2007			
	Home		*Away*		*Home*		*Away*	
Intraconference by Division	NFCW	SF	NFCW	ARI	NFCE	DAL	NFCE	PHI
		SEA		STL		NYG		WAS
Interconference by Division	AFCE	BUF	AFCE	NE	AFCW	DEN	AFCW	OAK
		MIA		NYJ		KC		SD
Intraconference by Position	NFCS	ATL	NFCE	DAL	NFCS	TB	NFCW	ARI

	2008			2009		
	Home		*Away*	*Home*		*Away*
Intraconference by Division	NFCS	NO TB	NFCS ATL CAR	NFCW	ARI STL	NFCW SF SEA
Interconference by Division	AFCS	JAC TEN	AFCS HOU IND	AFCN	CLE PIT	AFCN BAL CIN
Intraconference by Position	NFCE	WAS	NFCW SF	NFCE	WAS	NFCS NO

	2010			2011		
	Home		*Away*	*Home*		*Away*
Intraconference by Division	NFCE	PHI WAS	NFCE DAL NYG	NFCS	ATL CAR	NFCS NO TB
Interconference by Division	AFCE	NE NYJ	AFCE BUF MIA	AFCW	KC SD	AFCW DEN OAK
Intraconference by Position	NFCW	STL	NFCS TB	NFCW	SF	NFCE DAL

	2012			2013		
	Home		*Away*	*Home*		*Away*
Intraconference by Division	NFCW	STL SEA	NFCW ARI SF	NFCE	DAL NYG	NFCE PHI WAS
Interconference by Division	AFCS	HOU IND	AFCS JAC TEN	AFCN	BAL CIN	AFCN CLE PIT
Intraconference by Position	NFCS	ATL	NFCE PHI	NFCS	TB	NFCW ARI

	2014			2015		
	Home		*Away*	*Home*		*Away*
Intraconference by Division	NFCS	NO TB	NFCS ATL CAR	NFCW	ARI SF	NFCW STL SEA
Interconference by Division	AFCE	BUF MIA	AFCE NE NYJ	AFCW	DEN OAK	AFCW KC SD
Intraconference by Position	NFCE		NFCW	NFCE		NFCS

	2016			2017		
	Home		*Away*	*Home*		*Away*
Intraconference by Division	NFCE	PHI WAS	NFCE DAL NYG	NFCS	ATL CAR	NFCS NO TB
Interconference by Division	AFCS	JAC TEN	AFCS HOU IND	AFCN	CLE PIT	AFCN BAL CIN
Intraconference by Position	NFCW		NFCS	NFCW		NFCE

[1]Due to Hurricane Katrina, game moved to San Antonio, TX.

GREEN BAY PACKERS

	2002			2003		
	Home		*Away*	*Home*		*Away*
Intraconference by Division	NFCS	ATL CAR	NFCS NO TB	NFCW	SF SEA	NFCW ARI STL
Interconference by Division	AFCE	BUF MIA	AFCE NE NYJ	AFCW	DEN KC	AFCW OAK SD
Intraconference by Position	NFCE	WAS	NFCW SF	NFCE	PHI	NFCS TB

	2004			2005		
	Home		*Away*	*Home*		*Away*
Intraconference by Division	NFCE	DAL NYG	NFCE PHI WAS	NFCS	NO TB	NFCS ATL CAR
Interconference by Division	AFCS	JAC TEN	AFCS HOU IND	AFCN	CLE PIT	AFCN BAL CIN
Intraconference by Position	NFCW	STL	NFCS CAR	NFCW	SEA	NFCE PHI

	2006				2007			
	Home		*Away*		*Home*		*Away*	
Intraconference by Division	NFCW	ARI	NFCW	SF	NFCE	PHI	NFCE	DAL
		STL		SEA		WAS		NYG
Interconference by Division	AFCE	NE	AFCE	BUF	AFCW	OAK	AFCW	DEN
		NYJ		MIA		SD		KC
Intraconference by Position	NFCS	NO	NFCE	PHI	NFCS	CAR	NFCW	STL

	2008				2009			
	Home		*Away*		*Home*		*Away*	
Intraconference by Division	NFCS	ATL	NFCS	NO	NFCW	SF	NFCW	ARI
		CAR		TB		SEA		STL
Interconference by Division	AFCS	HOU	AFCS	JAC	AFCN	BAL	AFCN	CLE
		IND		TEN		CIN		PIT
Intraconference by Position	NFCE	DAL	NFCW	SEA	NFCE	DAL	NFCS	TB

	2010				2011			
	Home		*Away*		*Home*		*Away*	
Intraconference by Division	NFCE	DAL	NFCE	PHI	NFCS	NO	NFCS	ATL
		NYG		WAS		TB		CAR
Interconference by Division	AFCE	BUF	AFCE	NE	AFCW	DEN	AFCW	KC
		MIA		NYJ		OAK		SD
Intraconference by Position	NFCW	SF	NFCS	ATL	NFCW	STL	NFCE	NYG

	2012				2013			
	Home		*Away*		*Home*		*Away*	
Intraconference by Division	NFCW	ARI	NFCW	STL	NFCE	PHI	NFCE	DAL
		SF		SEA		WAS		NYG
Interconference by Division	AFCS	JAC	AFCS	HOU	AFCN	CLE	AFCN	BAL
		TEN		IND		PIT		CIN
Intraconference by Position	NFCS	NO	NFCE	NYG	NFCS	ATL	NFCW	SF

	2014				2015			
	Home		*Away*		*Home*		*Away*	
Intraconference by Division	NFCS	ATL	NFCS	NO	NFCW	STL	NFCW	ARI
		CAR		TB		SEA		SF
Interconference by Division	AFCE	NE	AFCE	BUF	AFCW	KC	AFCW	DEN
		NYJ		MIA		SD		OAK
Intraconference by Position	NFCE		NFCW		NFCE		NFCS	

	2016				2017			
	Home		*Away*		*Home*		*Away*	
Intraconference by Division	NFCE	DAL	NFCE	PHI	NFCS	NO	NFCS	ATL
		NYG		WAS		TB		CAR
Interconference by Division	AFCS	HOU	AFCS	JAC	AFCN	BAL	AFCN	CLE
		IND		TEN		CIN		PIT
Intraconference by Position	NFCW		NFCS		NFCW		NFCE	

MINNESOTA VIKINGS

	2002				2003			
	Home		*Away*		*Home*		*Away*	
Intraconference by Division	NFCS	ATL	NFCS	NO	NFCW	SF	NFCW	ARI
		CAR		TB		SEA		STL
Interconference by Division	AFCE	BUF	AFCE	NE	AFCW	DEN	AFCW	OAK
		MIA		NYJ		KC		SD
Intraconference by Position	NFCE	NYG	NFCW	SEA	NFCE	NYG	NFCS	ATL

	2004				2005			
	Home		*Away*		*Home*		*Away*	
Intraconference by Division	NFCE	DAL NYG	NFCE	PHI WAS	NFCS	NO TB	NFCS	ATL CAR
Interconference by Division	AFCS	JAC TEN	AFCS	HOU IND	AFCN	CLE PIT	AFCN	BAL CIN
Intraconference by Position	NFCW	SEA	NFCS	NO	NFCW	STL	NFCE	NYG

	2006				2007			
	Home		*Away*		*Home*		*Away*	
Intraconference by Division	NFCW	ARI STL	NFCW	SF SEA	NFCE	PHI WAS	NFCE	DAL NYG
Interconference by Division	AFCE	NE NYJ	AFCE	BUF MIA	AFCW	OAK SD	AFCW	DEN KC
Intraconference by Position	NFCS	CAR	NFCE	WAS	NFCS	ATL	NFCW	SF

	2008				2009			
	Home		*Away*		*Home*		*Away*	
Intraconference by Division	NFCS	ATL CAR	NFCS	NO TB	NFCW	SF SEA	NFCW	ARI STL
Interconference by Division	AFCS	HOU IND	AFCS	JAC TEN	AFCN	BAL CIN	AFCN	CLE PIT
Intraconference by Position	NFCE	NYG	NFCW	ARI	NFCE	NYG	NFCS	CAR

	2010				2011			
	Home		*Away*		*Home*		*Away*	
Intraconference by Division	NFCE	DAL NYG[1]	NFCE	PHI WAS	NFCS	NO TB	NFCS	ATL CAR
Interconference by Division	AFCE	BUF MIA	AFCE	NE NYJ	AFCW	DEN OAK	AFCW	KC SD
Intraconference by Position	NFCW	ARI	NFCS	NO	NFCW	ARI	NFCE	WAS

	2012				2013			
	Home		*Away*		*Home*		*Away*	
Intraconference by Division	NFCW	ARI SF	NFCW	STL SEA	NFCE	PHI WAS	NFCE	DAL NYG
Interconference by Division	AFCS	JAC TEN	AFCS	HOU IND	AFCN	CLE PIT[2]	AFCN	BAL CIN
Intraconference by Position	NFCS	TB	NFCE	WAS	NFCS	CAR	NFCW	SEA

	2014				2015			
	Home		*Away*		*Home*		*Away*	
Intraconference by Division	NFCS	ATL CAR	NFCS	NO TB	NFCW	STL SEA	NFCW	ARI SF
Interconference by Division	AFCE	NE NYJ	AFCE	BUF MIA	AFCW	KC SD	AFCW	DEN OAK
Intraconference by Position	NFCE		NFCW		NFCE		NFCS	

	2016				2017			
	Home		*Away*		*Home*		*Away*	
Intraconference by Division	NFCE	DAL NYG	NFCE	PHI WAS	NFCS	NO TB	NFCS	ATL CAR
Interconference by Division	AFCS	HOU IND	AFCS	JAC TEN	AFCN	BAL CIN	AFCN	CLE PIT
Intraconference by Position	NFCW		NFCS		NFCW		NFCE	

[1] Game moved to Detroit due to Minneapolis blizzard.

[2] Game played at London, England.

2002–2017 NON-DIVISIONAL OPPONENTS (By Team)
NFC South
ATLANTA FALCONS

	2002				2003			
	Home		*Away*		*Home*		*Away*	
Intraconference by Division	NFCN	CHI	NFCN	GB	NFCE	PHI	NFCE	DAL
		DET		MIN		WAS		NYG
Interconference by Division	AFCN	BAL	AFCN	CLE	AFCS	JAC	AFCS	HOU
		CIN		PIT		TEN		IND
Intraconference by Position	NFCW	SEA	NFCE	NYG	NFCN	MIN	NFCW	STL

	2004				2005			
	Home		*Away*		*Home*		*Away*	
Intraconference by Division	NFCW	ARI	NFCW	SF	NFCN	GB	NFCN	CHI
		STL		SEA		MIN		DET
Interconference by Division	AFCW	OAK	AFCW	DEN	AFCE	NE	AFCE	BUF
		SD		KC		NYJ		MIA
Intraconference by Position	NFCN	DET	NFCE	NYG	NFCE	PHI	NFCW	SEA

	2006				2007			
	Home		*Away*		*Home*		*Away*	
Intraconference by Division	NFCE	DAL	NFCE	PHI	NFCW	SF	NFCW	ARI
		NYG		WAS		SEA		STL
Interconference by Division	AFCN	CLE	AFCN	BAL	AFCS	HOU	AFCS	JAC
		PIT		CIN		IND		TEN
Intraconference by Position	NFCW	ARI	NFCN	DET	NFCE	NYG	NFCN	MIN

	2008				2009			
	Home		*Away*		*Home*		*Away*	
Intraconference by Division	NFCN	CHI	NFCN	GB	NFCE	PHI	NFCE	DAL
		DET		MIN		WAS		NYG
Interconference by Division	AFCW	DEN	AFCW	OAK	AFCE	BUF	AFCE	NE
		KC		SD		MIA		NYJ
Intraconference by Position	NFCW	STL	NFCE	PHI	NFCN	CHI	NFCW	SF

	2010				2011			
	Home		*Away*		*Home*		*Away*	
Intraconference by Division	NFCW	ARI	NFCW	STL	NFCN	GB	NFCN	CHI
		SF		SEA		MIN		DET
Interconference by Division	AFCN	BAL	AFCN	CLE	AFCS	JAC	AFCS	HOU
		CIN		PIT		TEN		IND
Intraconference by Position	NFCN	GB	NFCE	PHI	NFCE	PHI	NFCW	SEA

	2012				2013			
	Home		*Away*		*Home*		*Away*	
Intraconference by Division	NFCE	DAL	NFCE	PHI	NFCW	STL	NFCW	ARI
		NYG		WAS		SEA		SF
Interconference by Division	AFCW	DEN	AFCW	KC	AFCE	NE	AFCE	BUF[1]
		OAK		SD		NYJ		MIA
Intraconference by Position	NFCW	ARI	NFCN	DET	NFCE	WAS	NFCN	GB

	2014				2015			
	Home		*Away*		*Home*		*Away*	
Intraconference by Division	NFCN	CHI	NFCN	GB	NFCE	PHI	NFCE	DAL
		DET		MIN		WAS		NYG
Interconference by Division	AFCN	CLE	AFCN	BAL	AFCS	HOU	AFCS	JAC
		PIT		CIN		IND		TEN
Intraconference by Position	NFCW		NFCE		NFCN		NFCW	

	2016		2017	
	Home	*Away*	*Home*	*Away*
Intraconference by Division	NFCW ARI	NFCW STL	NFCN GB	NFCN CHI
	SF	SEA	MIN	DET
Interconference by Division	AFCW KC	AFCW DEN	AFCE BUF	AFCE NE
	SD	OAK	MIA	NYJ
Intraconference by Position	NFCN	NFCE	NFCE	NFCW

[1] Game played at Toronto.

CAROLINA PANTHERS

	2002		2003	
	Home	*Away*	*Home*	*Away*
Intraconference by Division	NFCN CHI	NFCN GB	NFCE PHI	NFCE DAL
	DET	MIN	WAS	NYG
Interconference by Division	AFCN BAL	AFCN CLE	AFCS JAC	AFCS HOU
	CIN	PIT	TEN	IND
Intraconference by Position	NFCW ARI	NFCE DAL	NFCN DET	NFCW ARI

	2004		2005	
	Home	*Away*	*Home*	*Away*
Intraconference by Division	NFCW ARI	NFCW SF	NFCN GB	NFCN CHI
	STL	SEA	MIN	DET
Interconference by Division	AFCW OAK	AFCW DEN	AFCE NE	AFCE BUF
	SD	KC	NYJ	MIA
Intraconference by Position	NFCN GB	NFCE PHI	NFCE DAL	NFCW ARI

	2006		2007	
	Home	*Away*	*Home*	*Away*
Intraconference by Division	NFCE DAL	NFCE PHI	NFCW SF	NFCW ARI
	NYG	WAS	SEA	STL
Interconference by Division	AFCN CLE	AFCN BAL	AFCS HOU	AFCS JAC
	PIT	CIN	IND	TEN
Intraconference by Position	NFCW STL	NFCN MIN	NFCE DAL	NFCN GB

	2008		2009	
	Home	*Away*	*Home*	*Away*
Intraconference by Division	NFCN CHI	NFCN GB	NFCE PHI	NFCE DAL
	DET	MIN	WAS	NYG
Interconference by Division	AFCW DEN	AFCW OAK	AFCE BUF	AFCE NE
	KC	SD	MIA	NYJ
Intraconference by Position	NFCW ARI	NFCE NYG	NFCN MIN	NFCW ARI

	2010		2011	
	Home	*Away*	*Home*	*Away*
Intraconference by Division	NFCW ARI	NFCW STL	NFCN GB	NFCN CHI
	SF	SEA	MIN	DET
Interconference by Division	AFCN BAL	AFCN CLE	AFCS JAC	AFCS HOU
	CIN	PIT	TEN	IND
Intraconference by Position	NFCN CHI	NFCE NYG	NFCE WAS	NFCW ARI

	2012		2013	
	Home	*Away*	*Home*	*Away*
Intraconference by Division	NFCE DAL	NFCE PHI	NFCW STL	NFCW ARI
	NYG	WAS	SEA	SF
Interconference by Division	AFCW DEN	AFCW KC	AFCE NE	AFCE BUF
	OAK	SD	NYJ	MIA
Intraconference by Position	NFCW SEA	NFCN CHI	NFCE NYG	NFCN MIN

· 205 ·   2002–2017

	2014		2015	
	Home	*Away*	*Home*	*Away*
Intraconference by Division	NFCN CHI DET	NFCN GB MIN	NFCE PHI WAS	NFCE DAL NYG
Interconference by Division	AFCN CLE PIT	AFCN BAL CIN	AFCS HOU IND	AFCS JAC TEN
Intraconference by Position	NFCW	NFCE	NFCN	NFCW

	2016		2017	
	Home	*Away*	*Home*	*Away*
Intraconference by Division	NFCW ARI SF	NFCW STL SEA	NFCN GB MIN	NFCN CHI DET
Interconference by Division	AFCW KC SD	AFCW DEN OAK	AFCE BUF MIA	AFCE NE NYJ
Intraconference by Position	NFCN	NFCE	NFCE	NFCW

NEW ORLEANS SAINTS

	2002		2003	
	Home	*Away*	*Home*	*Away*
Intraconference by Division	NFCN GB MIN	NFCN CHI[a] DET	NFCE DAL NYG	NFCE PHI WAS
Interconference by Division	AFCN CLE PIT	AFCN BAL CIN	AFCS HOU IND	AFCS JAC TEN
Intraconference by Position	NFCW SF	NFCE WAS	NFCN CHI	NFCW SEA

	2004		2005	
	Home	*Away*	*Home*	*Away*
Intraconference by Division	NFCW SF SEA	NFCW ARI STL	NFCN CHI[1] DET[2]	NFCN GB MIN
Interconference by Division	AFCW DEN KC	AFCW OAK SD	AFCE BUF[2] MIA[1]	AFCE NE NYJ
Intraconference by Position	NFCN MIN	NFCE DAL	NFCE NYG[3]	NFCW STL

	2006		2007	
	Home	*Away*	*Home*	*Away*
Intraconference by Division	NFCE PHI WAS	NFCE DAL NYG	NFCW ARI STL	NFCW SF SEA
Interconference by Division	AFCN BAL CIN	AFCN CLE PIT	AFCS JAC TEN	AFCS HOU IND
Intraconference by Position	NFCW SF	NFCN GB	NFCE PHI	NFCN CHI

	2008		2009	
	Home	*Away*	*Home*	*Away*
Intraconference by Division	NFCN GB MIN	NFCN CHI DET	NFCE DAL NYG	NFCE PHI WAS
Interconference by Division	AFCW OAK SD[b]	AFCW DEN KC	AFCE NE NYJ	AFCE BUF MIA
Intraconference by Position	NFCW SF	NFCE WAS	NFCN DET	NFCW STL

	2010		2011	
	Home	*Away*	*Home*	*Away*
Intraconference by Division	NFCW STL SEA	NFCW ARI SF	NFCN CHI DET	NFCN GB MIN
Interconference by Division	AFCN CLE PIT	AFCN BAL CIN	AFCS HOU IND	AFCS JAC TEN
Intraconference by Position	NFCN MIN	NFCE DAL	NFCE NYG	NFCW STL

	2012				2013			
	Home		*Away*		*Home*		*Away*	
Intraconference by Division	NFCE	PHI	NFCE	DAL	NFCW	ARI	NFCW	STL
		WAS		NYG		SF		SEA
Interconference by Division	AFCW	KC	AFCW	DEN	AFCE	BUF	AFCE	NE
		SD		OAK		MIA		NYJ
Intraconference by Position	NFCW	SF	NFCN	GB	NFCE	DAL	NFCN	CHI

	2014				2015			
	Home		*Away*		*Home*		*Away*	
Intraconference by Division	NFCN	GB	NFCN	CHI	NFCE	DAL	NFCE	PHI
		MIN		DET		NYG		WAS
Interconference by Division	AFCN	BAL	AFCN	CLE	AFCS	JAC	AFCS	HOU
		CIN		PIT		TEN		IND
Intraconference by Position	NFCW		NFCE		NFCN		NFCW	

	2016				2017			
	Home		*Away*		*Home*		*Away*	
Intraconference by Division	NFCW	STL	NFCW	ARI	NFCN	CHI	NFCN	GB
		SEA		SF		DET		MIN
Interconference by Division	AFCW	DEN	AFCW	KC	AFCE	NE	AFCE	BUF
		OAK		SD		NYJ		MIA
Intraconference by Position	NFCN		NFCE		NFCE		NFCW	

In 2005, due to Hurricane Katrina, game was played at:
[1]Baton Rouge, LA; [2]San Antonio, TX; [3]Giants Stadium, East Rutherford, NJ.
[a]Played at Champaign, IL.
[b]Played at London, England.

TAMPA BAY BUCCANEERS

	2002				2003			
	Home		*Away*		*Home*		*Away*	
Intraconference by Division	NFCN	GB	NFCN	CHI[1]	NFCE	DAL	NFCE	PHI
		MIN		DET		NYG		WAS
Interconference by Division	AFCN	CLE	AFCN	BAL	AFCS	HOU	AFCS	JAC
		PIT		CIN		IND		TEN
Intraconference by Position	NFCW	STL	NFCE	PHI	NFCN	GB	NFCW	SF

	2004				2005			
	Home		*Away*		*Home*		*Away*	
Intraconference by Division	NFCW	SF	NFCW	ARI	NFCN	CHI	NFCN	GB
		SEA		STL		DET		MIN
Interconference by Division	AFCW	DEN	AFCW	OAK	AFCE	BUF	AFCE	NE
		KC		SD		MIA		NYJ
Intraconference by Position	NFCN	CHI	NFCE	WAS	NFCE	WAS	NFCW	SF

	2006				2007			
	Home		*Away*		*Home*		*Away*	
Intraconference by Division	NFCE	PHI	NFCE	DAL	NFCW	ARI	NFCW	SF
		WAS		NYG		STL		SEA
Interconference by Division	AFCN	BAL	AFCN	CLE	AFCS	JAC	AFCS	HOU
		CIN		PIT		TEN		IND
Intraconference by Position	NFCW	SEA	NFCN	CHI	NFCE	WAS	NFCN	DET

	2008			2009		
	Home		*Away*	*Home*		*Away*
Intraconference by Division	NFCN GB MIN		NFCN CHI DET	NFCE DAL NYG		NFCE PHI WAS
Interconference by Division	AFCW OAK SD		AFCW DEN KC	AFCE NE[2] NYJ		AFCE BUF MIA
Intraconference by Position	NFCW SEA		NFCE DAL	NFCN GB		NFCW SEA

	2010			2011		
	Home		*Away*	*Home*		*Away*
Intraconference by Division	NFCW STL SEA		NFCW ARI SF	NFCN CHI[2] DET		NFCN GB MIN
Interconference by Division	AFCN CLE PIT		AFCN BAL CIN	AFCS HOU IND		AFCS JAC TEN
Intraconference by Position	NFCN DET		NFCE WAS	NFCE DAL		NFCW SF

	2012			2013		
	Home		*Away*	*Home*		*Away*
Intraconference by Division	NFCE PHI WAS		NFCE DAL NYG	NFCW ARI SF		NFCW STL SEA
Interconference by Division	AFCW KC SD		AFCW DEN OAK	AFCE BUF MIA		AFCE NE NYJ
Intraconference by Position	NFCW STL		NFCN MIN	NFCE PHI		NFCN DET

	2014			2015		
	Home		*Away*	*Home*		*Away*
Intraconference by Division	NFCN GB MIN		NFCN CHI DET	NFCE DAL NYG		NFCE PHI WAS
Interconference by Division	AFCN BAL CIN		AFCN CLE PIT	AFCS JAC TEN		AFCS HOU IND
Intraconference by Position	NFCW		NFCE	NFCN		NFCW

	2016			2017		
	Home		*Away*	*Home*		*Away*
Intraconference by Division	NFCW STL SEA		NFCW ARI SF	NFCN CHI DET		NFCN GB MIN
Interconference by Division	AFCW DEN OAK		AFCW KC SD	AFCE NE NYJ		AFCE BUF MIA
Intraconference by Position	NFCN		NFCE	NFCE		NFCW

[1] Game played at Champaign, IL.
[2] Game played at London, England.

2002–2017 NON-DIVISIONAL OPPONENTS (By Team)

NFC West

ARIZONA CARDINALS

	2002			2003		
	Home		*Away*	*Home*		*Away*
Intraconference by Division	NFCE DAL NYG		NFCE PHI WAS	NFCN GB MIN		NFCN CHI DET
Interconference by Division	AFCW OAK SD		AFCW DEN KC	AFCN BAL CIN		AFCN CLE PIT
Intraconference by Position	NFCN DET		NFCS CAR	NFCS CAR		NFCE DAL

	2004				2005		
	Home		**Away**		**Home**		**Away**
Intraconference by Division	NFCS	NO	NFCS	ATL	NFCE	PHI	NFCE	DAL
		TB		CAR		WAS		NYG
Interconference by Division	AFCE	NE	AFCE	BUF	AFCS	JAC	AFCS	HOU
		NYJ		MIA		TEN		IND
Intraconference by Position	NFCE	NYG	NFCN	DET	NFCS	CAR	NFCN	DET

	2006				2007		
	Home		**Away**		**Home**		**Away**
Intraconference by Division	NFCN	CHI	NFCN	GB	NFCS	ATL	NFCS	NO
		DET		MIN		CAR		TB
Interconference by Division	AFCW	DEN	AFCW	OAK	AFCN	CLE	AFCN	BAL
		KC		SD		PIT		CIN
Intraconference by Position	NFCE	DAL	NFCS	ATL	NFCN	DET	NFCE	WAS

	2008				2009		
	Home		**Away**		**Home**		**Away**
Intraconference by Division	NFCE	DAL	NFCE	PHI	NFCN	GB	NFCN	CHI
		NYG		WAS		MIN		DET
Interconference by Division	AFCE	BUF	AFCE	NE	AFCS	HOU	AFCS	JAC
		MIA		NYJ		IND		TEN
Intraconference by Position	NFCN	MIN	NFCS	CAR	NFCS	CAR	NFCE	NYG

	2010				2011		
	Home		**Away**		**Home**		**Away**
Intraconference by Division	NFCS	NO	NFCS	ATL	NFCE	DAL	NFCE	PHI
		TB		CAR		NYG		WAS
Interconference by Division	AFCW	DEN	AFCW	KC	AFCN	CLE	AFCN	BAL
		OAK		SD		PIT		CIN
Intraconference by Position	NFCE	DAL	NFCN	MIN	NFCS	CAR	NFCN	MIN

	2012				2013		
	Home		**Away**		**Home**		**Away**
Intraconference by Division	NFCN	CHI	NFCN	GB	NFCS	ATL	NFCS	NO
		DET		MIN		CAR		TB
Interconference by Division	AFCE	BUF	AFCE	NE	AFCS	HOU	AFCS	JAC
		MIA		NYJ		IND		TEN
Intraconference by Position	NFCE	PHI	NFCS	ATL	NFCN	DET	NFCE	PHI

	2014				2015		
	Home		**Away**		**Home**		**Away**
Intraconference by Division	NFCE	PHI	NFCE	DAL	NFCN	GB	NFCN	CHI
		WAS		NYG		MIN		DET
Interconference by Division	AFCW	KC	AFCW	DEN	AFCN	BAL	AFCN	CLE
		SD		OAK		CIN		PIT
Intraconference by Position	NFCN		NFCS		NFCS		NFCE	

	2016				2017		
	Home		**Away**		**Home**		**Away**
Intraconference by Division	NFCS	NO	NFCS	ATL	NFCE	DAL	NFCE	PHI
		TB		CAR		NYG		WAS
Interconference by Division	AFCE	NE	AFCE	BUF	AFCS	JAC	AFCS	HOU
		NYJ		MIA		TEN		IND
Intraconference by Position	NFCE		NFCN		NFCS		NFCN	

ST. LOUIS RAMS

2002

	Home		Away	
Intraconference by Division	NFCE	DAL NYG	NFCE	PHI WAS
Interconference by Division	AFCW	OAK SD	AFCW	DEN KC
Intraconference by Position	NFCN	CHI	NFCS	TB

2003

	Home		Away	
Intraconference by Division	NFCN	GB MIN	NFCN	CHI DET
Interconference by Division	AFCN	BAL CIN	AFCN	CLE PIT
Intraconference by Position	NFCS	ATL	NFCE	NYG

2004

	Home		Away	
Intraconference by Division	NFCS	NO TB	NFCS	ATL CAR
Interconference by Division	AFCE	NE NYJ	AFCE	BUF MIA
Intraconference by Position	NFCE	PHI	NFCN	GB

2005

	Home		Away	
Intraconference by Division	NFCE	PHI WAS	NFCE	DAL NYG
Interconference by Division	AFCS	JAC TEN	AFCS	HOU IND
Intraconference by Position	NFCS	NO	NFCN	MIN

2006

	Home		Away	
Intraconference by Division	NFCN	CHI DET	NFCN	GB MIN
Interconference by Division	AFCW	DEN KC	AFCW	OAK SD
Intraconference by Position	NFCE	WAS	NFCS	CAR

2007

	Home		Away	
Intraconference by Division	NFCS	ATL CAR	NFCS	NO TB
Interconference by Division	AFCN	CLE PIT	AFCN	BAL CIN
Intraconference by Position	NFCN	GB	NFCE	DAL

2008

	Home		Away	
Intraconference by Division	NFCE	DAL NYG	NFCE	PHI WAS
Interconference by Division	AFCE	BUF MIA	AFCE	NE NYJ
Intraconference by Position	NFCN	CHI	NFCS	ATL

2009

	Home		Away	
Intraconference by Division	NFCN	GB MIN	NFCN	CHI DET
Interconference by Division	AFCS	HOU IND	AFCS	JAC TEN
Intraconference by Position	NFCS	NO	NFCE	WAS

2010

	Home		Away	
Intraconference by Division	NFCS	ATL CAR	NFCS	NO TB
Interconference by Division	AFCW	KC SD	AFCW	DEN OAK
Intraconference by Position	NFCE	WAS	NFCN	DET

2011

	Home		Away	
Intraconference by Division	NFCE	PHI WAS	NFCE	DAL NYG
Interconference by Division	AFCN	BAL CIN	AFCN	CLE PIT
Intraconference by Position	NFCS	NO	NFCN	GB

2012

	Home		Away	
Intraconference by Division	NFCN	GB MIN	NFCN	CHI DET
Interconference by Division	AFCE	NE[1] NYJ	AFCE	BUF MIA
Intraconference by Position	NFCE	WAS	NFCS	TB

2013

	Home		Away	
Intraconference by Division	NFCS	NO TB	NFCS	ATL CAR
Interconference by Division	AFCS	JAC TEN	AFCS	HOU IND
Intraconference by Position	NFCN	CHI	NFCE	DAL

2014

	Home		Away	
Intraconference by Division	NFCE	DAL NYG	NFCE	PHI WAS
Interconference by Division	AFCW	DEN OAK	AFCW	KC SD
Intraconference by Position	NFCN		NFCS	

2015

	Home		Away	
Intraconference by Division	NFCN	CHI DET	NFCN	GB MIN
Interconference by Division	AFCN	CLE PIT	AFCN	BAL CIN
Intraconference by Position	NFCS		NFCE	

	2016			2017		
	Home		*Away*	*Home*		*Away*
Intraconference by Division	NFCS	ATL	NFCS NO	NFCE	PHI	NFCE DAL
		CAR	TB		WAS	NYG
Interconference by Division	AFCE	BUF	AFCE NE	AFCS	HOU	AFCS JAC
		MIA	NYJ		IND	TEN
Intraconference by Position	NFCE		NFCN	NFCS		NFCN

[1]Game played at London, England.

SAN FRANCISCO 49ERS

	2002			2003		
	Home		*Away*	*Home*		*Away*
Intraconference by Division	NFCE	PHI	NFCE DAL	NFCN	CHI	NFCN GB
		WAS	NYG		DET	MIN
Interconference by Division	AFCW	DEN	AFCW OAK	AFCN	CLE	AFCN BAL
		KC	SD		PIT	CIN
Intraconference by Position	NFCN	GB	NFCS NO	NFCS	TB	NFCE PHI

	2004			2005		
	Home		*Away*	*Home*		*Away*
Intraconference by Division	NFCS	ATL	NFCS NO	NFCE	DAL	NFCE PHI
		CAR	TB		NYG	WAS
Interconference by Division	AFCE	BUF	AFCE NE	AFCS	HOU	AFCS JAC
		MIA	NYJ		IND	TEN
Intraconference by Position	NFCE	WAS	NFCN CHI	NFCS	TB	NFCN CHI

	2006			2007		
	Home		*Away*	*Home*		*Away*
Intraconference by Division	NFCN	GB	NFCN CHI	NFCS	NO	NFCS ATL
		MIN	DET		TB	CAR
Interconference by Division	AFCW	OAK	AFCW DEN	AFCN	BAL	AFCN CLE
		SD	KC		CIN	PIT
Intraconference by Position	NFCE	PHI	NFCS NO	NFCN	MIN	NFCE NYG

	2008			2009		
	Home		*Away*	*Home*		*Away*
Intraconference by Division	NFCE	PHI	NFCE DAL	NFCN	CHI	NFCN GB
		WAS	NYG		DET	MIN
Interconference by Division	AFCE	NE	AFCE BUF	AFCS	JAC	AFCS HOU
		NYJ	MIA		TEN	IND
Intraconference by Position	NFCN	DET	NFCS NO	NFCS	ATL	NFCE PHI

	2010			2011		
	Home		*Away*	*Home*		*Away*
Intraconference by Division	NFCS	NO	NFCS ATL	NFCE	DAL	NFCE PHI
		TB	CAR		NYG	WAS
Interconference by Division	AFCW	DEN[1]	AFCW KC	AFCN	CLE	AFCN BAL
		OAK	SD		PIT	CIN
Intraconference by Position	NFCE	PHI	NFCN GB	NFCS	TB	NFCN DET

	2012			2013		
	Home		*Away*	*Home*		*Away*
Intraconference by Division	NFCN	CHI	NFCN GB	NFCS	ATL	NFCS NO
		DET	MIN		CAR	TB
Interconference by Division	AFCE	BUF	AFCE NE	AFCS	HOU	AFCS JAC[1]
		MIA	NYJ		IND	TEN
Intraconference by Position	NFCE	NYG	NFCS NO	NFCN	GB	NFCE WAS

	2014		2015	
	Home	*Away*	*Home*	*Away*
Intraconference by Division	NFCE PHI WAS	NFCE DAL NYG	NFCN GB MIN	NFCN CHI DET
Interconference by Division	AFCW KC SD	AFCW DEN OAK	AFCN BAL CIN	AFCN CLE PIT
Intraconference by Position	NFCN	NFCS	NFCS	NFCE

	2016		2017	
	Home	*Away*	*Home*	*Away*
Intraconference by Division	NFCS NO TB	NFCS ATL CAR	NFCE DAL NYG	NFCE PHI WAS
Interconference by Division	AFCE NE NYJ	AFCE BUF MIA	AFCS JAC TEN	AFCS HOU IND
Intraconference by Position	NFCE	NFCN	NFCS	NFCN

[1]Game played at London, England.

SEATTLE SEAHAWKS

	2002		2003	
	Home	*Away*	*Home*	*Away*
Intraconference by Division	NFCE PHI WAS	NFCE DAL NYG	NFCN CHI DET	NFCN GB MIN
Interconference by Division	AFCW DEN KC	AFCW OAK SD	AFCN CLE PIT	AFCN BAL CIN
Intraconference by Position	NFCN MIN	NFCS ATL	NFCS NO	NFCE WAS

	2004		2005	
	Home	*Away*	*Home*	*Away*
Intraconference by Division	NFCS ATL CAR	NFCS NO TB	NFCE DAL NYG	NFCE PHI WAS
Interconference by Division	AFCE BUF MIA	AFCE NE NYJ	AFCS HOU IND	AFCS JAC TEN
Intraconference by Position	NFCE DAL	NFCN MIN	NFCS ATL	NFCN GB

	2006		2007	
	Home	*Away*	*Home*	*Away*
Intraconference by Division	NFCN GB MIN	NFCN CHI DET	NFCS NO TB	NFCS ATL CAR
Interconference by Division	AFCW OAK SD	AFCW DEN KC	AFCN BAL CIN	AFCN CLE PIT
Intraconference by Position	NFCE NYG	NFCS TB	NFCN CHI	NFCE PHI

	2008		2009	
	Home	*Away*	*Home*	*Away*
Intraconference by Division	NFCE PHI WAS	NFCE DAL NYG	NFCN CHI DET	NFCN GB MIN
Interconference by Division	AFCE NE NYJ	AFCE BUF MIA	AFCS JAC TEN	AFCS HOU IND
Intraconference by Position	NFCN GB	NFCS TB	NFCS TB	NFCE DAL

	2010		2011	
	Home	*Away*	*Home*	*Away*
Intraconference by Division	NFCS ATL CAR	NFCS NO TB	NFCE PHI WAS	NFCE DAL NYG
Interconference by Division	AFCW KC SD	AFCW DEN OAK	AFCN BAL CIN	AFCN CLE PIT
Intraconference by Position	NFCE NYG	NFCN CHI	NFCS ATL	NFCN CHI

	2012				2013			
	Home		*Away*		*Home*		*Away*	
Intraconference by Division	NFCN	GB	NFCN	CHI	NFCS	NO	NFCS	ATL
		MIN		DET		TB		CAR
Interconference by Division	AFCE	NE	AFCE	BUF[1]	AFCS	JAC	AFCS	HOU
		NYJ		MIA		TEN		IND
Intraconference by Position	NFCE	DAL	NFCS	CAR	NFCN	MIN	NFCE	NYG

	2014				2015			
	Home		*Away*		*Home*		*Away*	
Intraconference by Division	NFCE	DAL	NFCE	PHI	NFCN	CHI	NFCN	GB
		NYG		WAS		DET		MIN
Interconference by Division	AFCW	DEN	AFCW	KC	AFCN	CLE	AFCN	BAL
		OAK		SD		PIT		CIN
Intraconference by Position	NFCN		NFCS		NFCS		NFCE	

	2016				2017			
	Home		*Away*		*Home*		*Away*	
Intraconference by Division	NFCS	ATL	NFCS	NO	NFCE	PHI	NFCE	DAL
		CAR		TB		WAS		NYG
Interconference by Division	AFCE	BUF	AFCE	NE	AFCS	HOU	AFCS	JAC
		MIA		NYJ		IND		TEN
Intraconference by Position	NFCE		NFCN		NFCS		NFCN	

[1] Game played at Toronto.

Appendix A: Schedule Release Dates (1933–2013)[1]

Thu. April 18, 2013, 8 P.M. ET
Tue. April 17, 2012, 7 P.M. ET
Tue. April 19, 2011, 7 P.M. ET
Tue. April 20, 2010, 7 P.M. ET
Tue. April 14, 2009, 7 P.M. ET
Tue. April 15, 2008, 2 P.M. ET
Wed. April 11, 2007, 1 P.M. ET
Thu. April 6, 2006, 2 P.M. ET
Wed. April 13, 2005, 2 P.M. ET
Wed. April 14, 2004, 5 P.M. ET
Thu. April 3, 2003
Thu. March 28, 2002
Thu. April 12, 2001
Tue. April 4, 2000
Thu. April 1, 1999
Thu. April 2, 1998
Wed. March 26, 1997
Wed. April 24, 1996
Tue. April 25, 1995
Thu. April 28, 1994
Wed. April 28, 1993
Wed. May 6, 1992
Thu. April 18, 1991
Thu. April 26, 1990
Fri. April 7, 1989
Tue. April 5, 1988
Tue. April 7, 1987
Wed. April 2, 1986
Wed. April 10, 1985
Thu. April 12, 1984
Wed. April 20, 1983
Thu. April 8, 1982
Tue. April 7, 1981
Thu. April 10, 1980

Thu. April 5, 1979
Sat. April 8, 1978
Wed. April 27, 1977
Wed. April 21, 1976
Sat. April 12, 1975
Tue. April 16, 1974
Mon. April 30, 1973
Sat. April 22, 1972
Tue. April 13, 1971
Mon. April 20, 1970
Sat. May 17, 1969
Thu. April 18, 1968
Tue. April 18, 1967
Mon. April 4, 1966
Thu. April 1, 1965
Thu. April 23, 1964
Sat. March 23, 1963
Tue. April 3, 1962
Wed. April 12, 1961
Tue. June 21, 1960
Thu. June 25, 1959
Mon. June 16, 1958
Tue. June 25, 1957
Wed. June 27, 1956
Tue. July 12, 1955
Mon. June 28, 1954
Thu. Aug. 13, 1953
Wed. June 25, 1952
Wed. July 11, 1951
Tue. June 27, 1950
Thu. Aug. 18, 1949
Tue. Sept. 14, 1948
Wed. Sept. 10, 1947
Mon. April 29, 1946

Wed. April 11, 1945
Sun. April 23, 1944
Mon. June 21, 1943
Sun. March 29, 1942
Sat. June 28, 1941
Mon. July 22, 1940
Sun. April 2, 1939
Thu. July 7, 1938
Thu. July 8, 1937
Mon. Aug. 10, 1936
Fri. July 19, 1935
Fri. Aug. 24, 1934
Sun. July 9, 1933

AAFC schedule release dates:
Mon. June 27, 1949
Mon. July 26, 1948
Sat. May 31, 1947
Sat. July 6, 1946

AFL schedule release dates:
Sat. May 24, 1969
Mon. April 29, 1968
Fri. May 5, 1967
Thu. April 28, 1966
Sun. April 11, 1965
Wed. May 6, 1964
Fri. May 24, 1963
Mon. April 23, 1962
Mon. May 1, 1961
Mon. April 25, 1960

Note: Prior to 1960, individual teams announced their tentative home dates earlier in the year. The dates listed above indicate when the NFL, AFL and AAFC released their official schedule. From 1947 to 1949, the NFL released their official schedule just prior to the start of the season to prevent the rival All-America Football Conference from rearranging dates in cities where both leagues had teams.[2]

Appendix B: Number of Teams and Games Played by Season (1933–2012)

	Number of Teams	Games Per Team	Regular Season Games
2002–2012	32	16	256
1999–2001	31	16	248
1995–1998	30	16	240
[a]1987	28	15	210
[b]1982	28	9	126
[c]1978–1994	28	16	224
1976–1977	28	14	196
1970–1975	26	14	182
1967–1969 (NFL)	16	14	112
1966 (NFL)	15	14	105
1961–1965 (NFL)	14	14	98
1960 (NFL)	13	12	78
1968–1969 (AFL)	10	14	70
1966–1967 (AFL)	9	14	63
1960–1965 (AFL)	8	14	56
1951–1959	12	12	72
1950	13	12	78
1947–1949 (NFL)	10	12	60
1946 (NFL)	10	11	55
1949 (AAFC)	7	12	42
1946–1948 (AAFC)	8	14	56
1944–1945	10	10	50
1943	8	10	40
1937–1942	10	11	55
1936	9	12	54
1935	9	12	53[d]
1934	11[e]	11 to 13	60
1933	10	9 to 14	57

[a]The 224-game schedule was reduced to 210 games due to the Players' strike.
[b]The 224-game schedule was reduced to 126 games due to the Players' strike.
[c]Excluding 1982 and 1987.
[d]One game between Boston and Philadelphia was canceled.
[e]After Cincinnati Reds were suspended after first eight games, the St. Louis Gunners assumed last three games of Reds' schedule.

Appendix C: Divisional, Conference and Interconference Games Per Team/Season (1933-2012)

1933	Division Games	Games vs. Other Div.	Total
BOS	5	7	12
BKN	5	5	10
NYG	8	6	14
PHI	3	6	9
PIT	7	4	11
ChiB	7	6	13
ChiC	6	5	11
CIN	4	6	10
GB	6	7	13
POR	7	4	11
League total	29	28	57
1934			
BOS, PIT	8	4	12
BKN, PHI	8	3	11
NYG	8	5	13
ChiB, DET	8	5	13
ChiC	9	2	11
GB	9	4	13
CIN	6	2	8
STL	2	1	3
League total	41	19	60
1935			
BKN, NYG, PIT	8	4	12
BOS, PHI	7[a]	4	11[a]
ChiB	6	6	12
ChiC, DET	7	5	12
GB	8	4	12
League total	33[a]	20	53[a]

[a]One game between Boston and Philadelphia was canceled.

1936			
BOS, BKN, PHI	8	4	12
NYG, PIT	7	5	12
ChiB, DET	6	6	12

	Division Games	Games vs. Other Div.	Total
ChiC, GB	7	5	12
League total	32	22	54
1937-1942			
All 10 teams	8	3	11
League total	40	15	55
1943			
All 8 teams	6	4	10
League total	24	16	40
1944			
All 10 teams	8	2	10
League total	40	10	50
1945			
NYG, PHI	7	3	10
PIT, WAS	8	2	10
Bos. Yanks	6	4	10
ChiB	8	2	10
ChiC, CleR, Det, GB	7	3	10
League total	36	14	50
1946			
All 10 teams	8	3	11
League total	40	15	55
1947-1949			
All 10 teams	8	4	12
League total	40	20	60

1950	Conference Games	Interconf. Games	Total
CLE, NYG, PHI, PIT	10	2	12
ChiC, WAS	9	3	12
DET, GB, LA,			

Appendix C

1950	Conference Games	Interconf. Games	Total
NYY, SF	11	1	12
ChiB	10	2	12
BAL	5	7	12
League Total	64	14	78

1951			
CLE, PHI, PIT, WAS	9	3	12
ChiC	8	4	12
NYG	10	2	12
ChiB, SF	8	4	12
DET, NYY	10	2	12
GB, LA	9	3	12
League Total	54	18	72

1952			
ChiC, CLE, PHI, WAS	10	2	12
NYG, PIT	9	3	12
ChiB, DAL, DET, LA	10	2	12
GB, SF	9	3	12
League Total	58	14	72

1953-1959			
All 12 teams	10	2	12
League total	60	12	72

1960			
All East teams	10	2	12
All West teams, (except DAL)	11	1	12
DAL	6	6	12
League total	66	12	78

1961-1965			
All 14 teams	12	2	14
League total	84	14	98

1966	Conference Games	Interconf. Games	Total
All East teams, (except ATL)	13	1	14
ATL	7	7	14
All West teams	12	2	14
League total	91	14	105

AAFC (1946–1949)

1946-1948	Division Games	Games vs. Other Div.	Total
All 8 teams	6	8	14
League total	24	32	56

1949			
All 7 teams	12	-	12
League total	42	-	42

AFL (1960-1969)

1960-1965	Division Games	Games vs. Other Div.	Total
All 8 teams	6	8	14
League total	24	32	56

1966			
BUF, HOU, NYJ	8	6	14
BOS, MIA	7	7	14
All West teams	6	8	14
League total	31	32	63

1967			
BOS, BUF, MIA	8	6	14
HOU, NYJ	7	7	14
All West teams	6	8	14
League total	31	32	63

1968-1969			
All 10 teams	8	6	14
League total	40	30	70

1967-1969	Division Games	Non-division Conf. Games	Conference Games	Interconf. Games	Total
All 16 teams	6	4	10	4	14
League total	48	32	80	32	112

1970-1975					
Teams in a five-team division	8	3	11	3	14
Teams in a four-team division	6	5	11	3	14
DEN and one club from the NFC Central or NFC West[a]	6	4	10	4	14
League total	88	54	142	40	182

[a] Please see 1970-1975 section for further details. In 1975, CLE was the assigned AFC team.

1976					
AFC East and NFC East	8	4	12	2	14
AFC Central and NFC Central	6	6	12	2	14
AFC West and NFC West					

Appendix C

1976	Division Games	Non-division Conf. Games	Conference Games	Interconf. Games	Total
(except OAK, NO, SEA, TB)	7	5	12	2	14
OAK and NO	7	4	11	3	14
SEA and TB	4	9	13	1	14
League total	96	72	168	28	196
1977					
AFC East and NFC East	8	4	12	2	14
AFC Central (except CIN)	6	6	12	2	14
AFC West and NFC Central (except GB, SEA, TB)	7	5	12	2	14
NFC West	6	6	12	2	14
CIN	6	5	11	3	14
GB	7	4	11	3	14
SEA and TB	4	9	13	1	14
League total	96	72	168	28	196
1978-1994 (except 1982, 1987)					
Teams that finish 1-4 in a five-team division[a]	8	4	12	4	16
Teams in a four-team division[b]	6	6	12	4	16
Fifth-place teams[a]	8	6	14	2	16
League total	104	68	172	52	224

[a]Refers to where teams finished in the standings the previous season.
[b]AFC Central and NFC West.

1982	Division Games	Non-division Conf. Games	Conference Games	Interconf. Games	Total
DAL, KC, LARm, GB, TB	3	3	6	3	9
ATL, CHI, CLE	4	3	7	2	9
CIN, PIT, NE	4	4	8	1	9
MIN, NYJ, SF	4	1	5	4	9
BUF, HOU	4	2	6	3	9
DEN, PHI	6	0	6	3	9
NO, SEA	3	5	8	1	9
NYG, SD	5	3	8	1	9
BAL	5	2	7	2	9
DET	6	2	8	1	9
LARd	5	1	6	3	9
MIA	7	0	7	2	9
STL	5	4	9	0	9
WAS	7	2	9	0	9
League total	61	35	96	30	126
1987					
BUF, MIA, NE, KC, DAL, NYG, WAS, MIN	8	4	12	3	15
NYJ, DEN, LARd, PHI	8	3	11	4	15
CHI, DET, GB, SEA	7	4	11	4	15
CLE, HOU, PIT, SF	6	5	11	4	15
CIN, LARm	6	6	12	3	15
ATL, NO	5	6	11	4	15
IND, STL	8	6	14	1	15
SD, TB	7	6	13	2	15
League total	100	64	164	46	210

1995–1998	Division Games	Non-division Conf. Games	Conference Games	Interconf. Games	Total
All 30 teams	8	4	12	4	16
League total	120	60	180	60	240
1999–2001					
All teams (except AFC Central)	8	4	12	4	16
AFC Central teams 1 and 2	10	2	12	4	16
AFC Central teams 3 through 6	10	3	13	3	16
League total	130	58	188	60	248
2002–Current					
All 32 teams	6	6	12	4	16
League total	96	96	192	64	256

Appendix D: Number of Regular Season Games in Pro Football History (1920–2012)

Includes the American Professional Football Association (APFA) 1920–1921, National Football League (NFL) 1922–2012, American Football League (AFL) 1960–1969, and the All-America Football Conference (AAFC) 1946–1949. AAFC totals are listed separately.

Year	SUN	MON	TUE	WED	THU	FRI	SAT	TOTAL
1920 (APFA)	78	0	0	0	8	0	3	89
1921 (APFA)	61	1	0	0	2	0	2	66
1922	67	0	0	0	6	0	1	74
1923	80	0	0	0	5	0	3	88
1924	64	0	1	0	5	0	10	80
1925	80	0	1	3	7	0	13	104
1926	88	0	1	0	10	0	17	116
1927	51	0	2	1	4	1	13	72
1928	42	0	1	0	4	0	9	56
1929	54	0	3	1	3	0	10	71
1930	50	0	1	8	6	0	8	73
1931	43	0	0	5	4	2	5	59
1932	44	0	0	0	4	0	0	48
1933	50	0	0	5	2	0	0	57
1934	50	1	2	4	3	0	0	60
1935	44	0	2	2	3	2	0	53
1936	47	1	0	3	3	0	0	54
1937	47	1	1	0	3	3	0	55

Year	SUN	MON	TUE	WED	THU	FRI	SAT	TOTAL
1938	46	1	0	2	2	3	1	55
1939	49	2	0	1	2	1	0	55
1940	49	0	0	1	1	1	3	55
1941	51	0	1	0	0	0	3	55
1942	55	0	0	0	0	0	0	55
1943	39	0	0	0	0	0	1	40
1944	49	0	1	0	0	0	0	50
1945	48	0	1	0	1	0	0	50
1946	51	1	1	0	1	1	0	55
1947	57	2	0	0	1	0	0	60
1948	53	1	0	1	2	2	1	60
1949	50	3	0	0	2	3	2	60
1950	68	1	0	0	4	2	3	78
1951	67	2	0	0	1	1	1	72
1952	64	1	0	0	2	1	4	72
1953	60	0	0	0	1	1	10	72
1954	60	0	0	0	1	0	11	72
1955	62	1	0	0	1	0	8	72
1956	66	0	0	0	1	0	5	72
1957	66	0	0	0	1	0	5	72
1958	67	0	0	0	1	0	4	72
1959	66	0	0	0	1	0	5	72
1960 (AFL)	39	0	0	0	1	11	5	56
1960 (NFL)	72	0	0	0	1	2	3	78
1961 (AFL)	44	0	0	0	1	3	8	56
1961 (NFL)	93	0	0	0	2	0	3	98
1962 (AFL)	38	0	0	0	1	8	9	56
1962 (NFL)	94	0	0	0	1	0	3	98
1963 (AFL)	37	0	0	0	1	4	14	56
1963 (NFL)	91	0	0	0	1	0	6	98
1964 (AFL)	40	0	0	0	1	5	10	56
1964 (NFL)	89	2	0	0	1	1	5	98
1965 (AFL)	46	0	0	0	1	2	7	56
1965 (NFL)	91	1	0	0	1	0	5	98
1966 (AFL)	52	0	0	0	1	2	8	63
1966 (NFL)	96	1	0	0	2	2	4	105
1967 (AFL)	55	0	0	0	2	0	6	63
1967 (NFL)	105	1	0	0	2	1	3	112
1968 (AFL)	57	1	0	0	2	1	9	70
1968 (NFL)	104	2	0	0	2	0	4	112
1969 (AFL)	60	1	0	0	2	0	7	70
1969 (NFL)	106	2	0	0	2	0	2	112
1970	158	13	0	0	2	1	8	182
1971	162	13	0	0	2	0	5	182
1972	163	13	0	0	2	0	4	182
1973	163	13	0	0	2	0	4	182
1974	162	13	0	0	2	0	5	182
1975	160	13	0	0	2	0	7	182
1976	175	13	0	0	2	0	6	196
1977	175	13	0	0	2	0	6	196
1978	199	16	0	0	3	0	6	224
1979	198	16	0	0	5	0	5	224
1980	199	16	0	0	5	0	4	224
1981	198	16	0	0	5	0	5	224
1982	109	9	0	0	4	0	4	126
1983	197	16	0	0	5	1	5	224

Year	SUN	MON	TUE	WED	THU	FRI	SAT	TOTAL
1984	198	17	0	0	4	1	4	224
1985	199	16	0	0	4	1	4	224
1986	198	16	0	0	5	1	4	224
1987	188	16	0	0	2	0	4	210
1988	202	16	0	0	2	0	4	224
1989	201	16	0	0	2	0	5	224
1990	198	16	0	0	3	0	7	224
1991	200	17	0	0	3	0	4	224
1992	197	17	0	0	4	0	6	224
1993	198	17	0	0	3	1	5	224
1994	186	17	0	0	5	0	16	224
1995	211	17	0	0	5	0	7	240
1996	215	17	0	0	4	0	4	240
1997	214	18	0	0	4	0	4	240
1998	215	17	0	0	4	0	4	240
1999	222	17	0	0	5	1	3	248
2000	222	17	0	0	4	0	5	248
2001	222	15	0	0	5	0	6	248
2002	231	17	0	0	3	0	5	256
2003	232	16	0	0	3	0	5	256
2004	230	16	0	0	3	1	6	256
2005	220	15	0	0	3	1	17	256
2006	227	18	0	0	8	0	3	256
2007	228	17	0	0	8	0	3	256
2008	229	17	0	0	10	0	0	256
2009	228	17	0	0	9	1	1	256
2010	227	18	1	0	10	0	0	256
2011	215	17	0	0	10	0	14	256
2012	222	16	0	1	16	0	1	256
TOTAL	12285	706	20	38	330	76	507	13962

All-America Football Conference (1946–1949)

Year	SUN	MON	TUE	WED	THU	FRI	SAT	TOTAL
1946 (AAFC)	28	4	2	1	1	11	9	56
1947 (AAFC)	40	0	0	0	2	14	0	56
1948 (AAFC)	39	1	1	1	3	10	1	56
1949 (AAFC)	30	1	0	0	3	8	0	42
TOTAL	137	6	3	2	9	43	10	210

Combined APFA, NFL, AFL and AAFC

Year	SUN	MON	TUE	WED	THU	FRI	SAT	TOTAL
1920–2012	12422	712	23	40	339	119	517	14172

Appendix E: Scheduling Facts and Figures

Most Head-to-Head Regular-Season Games Between Two Clubs (1920–2012)

184	Chicago vs. Green Bay
166	Chicago vs. Detroit
165	Detroit vs. Green Bay
160	N.Y. Giants vs. Washington
156	N.Y. Giants vs. Philadelphia
155	Philadelphia vs. Washington

Instances in Which Two Teams from the Same Conference Went at Least Seven Seasons Between Meetings (Since 1970)

Number of Seasons Between Meetings/Conference Matchups		Prior Meeting	Subsequent Meeting
13	Buffalo vs. San Diego	1985	1998
	Denver vs. Miami	1985	1998
	Green Bay vs. Washington	1988	2001
	Indianapolis (Baltimore Colts) vs. Seattle	1978	1991
11	Cleveland[a] vs. Miami	1993	2004
	New England vs. San Diego	1983	1994
10	Atlanta vs. N.Y. Giants	1988	1998
	Chicago vs. N.Y. Giants	1977	1987
	Cincinnati vs. Kansas City	1993	2003
	Dallas vs. St. Louis (L.A. Rams)	1992	2002
	Dallas vs. Tampa Bay	1990	2000
	Denver vs. Miami	1975	1985
	Detroit vs. Philadelphia	1986	1996
	Minnesota vs. N.Y. Giants	1976	1986
9	Arizona (St. Louis-Phoenix Cardinals) vs. Detroit	1980	1989
	Arizona (Phoenix Cardinals) vs. Green Bay	1990	1999
	Atlanta vs. Dallas	1976	1985
	Atlanta vs. Washington	1994	2003
	Chicago vs. San Francisco	1991	2000
	Denver vs. Tennessee (Houston Oilers)	1995	2004
	Indianapolis (Baltimore Colts) vs. Oakland (L.A. Raiders)	1975	1984
	Kansas City vs. New England	1981	1990
8	Arizona (St. Louis Cardinals) vs. Green Bay	1976	1984

	Number of Seasons Between Meetings/Conference Matchups	Prior Meeting	Subsequent Meeting
	Arizona (St. Louis-Phoenix Cardinals) vs. Minnesota	1983	1991
	Cleveland[a] vs. N.Y. Jets	1994	2002
	Denver vs. Indianapolis	1993	2001
	Detroit vs. New Orleans	1980	1988
	Green Bay vs. Philadelphia	1979	1987
	Indianapolis vs. Tennessee (Houston Oilers)	1994	2002
	Miami vs. Seattle	1979	1987
	New England vs. Oakland (L.A. Raiders)	1994	2002
	N.Y. Jets vs. Pittsburgh	1992	2000
	N.Y. Jets vs. San Diego	1975	1983
	N.Y. Jets vs. San Diego	1994	2002
	Philadelphia vs. San Francisco	1975	1983
7	Arizona vs. Tampa Bay	1997	2004
	Atlanta vs. Green Bay	1994	2001
	Buffalo vs. Seattle	1977	1984
	Carolina vs. N.Y. Giants	1996	2003
	Cleveland[a] vs. Kansas City	1995	2002
	Cleveland vs. Miami	1979	1986
	Cleveland[a] vs. Oakland (L.A. Raiders)	1993	2000
	Cleveland[a] vs. Seattle	1994	2001
	Dallas vs. Detroit	1994	2001
	Dallas vs. Tampa Bay	1983	1990
	Green Bay vs. New Orleans	1995	2002
	Kansas City vs. N.Y. Jets	1975	1982
	New Orleans vs. Washington	1994	2001
	Philadelphia vs. Tampa Bay	1981	1988
	Tampa Bay vs. Washington	1982	1989

[a]Cleveland inactive from 1996 to 1998.

Note: Does not include Seattle vs. New England (both teams met in 1993 and did not play again until 2004) or Seattle vs. Tennessee (met in 1998, played again in 2005), since the Seahawks moved to the NFC in 2002.

Instances Where Two Interconference Teams Went at Least 10 Seasons Between Meetings (Since 1970)

	Number of Seasons Between Meetings/Interconference Matchups	Prior Meeting	Subsequent Meeting
20	Kansas City vs. Philadelphia	1972	1992
18	Arizona (St. Louis-Phoenix Cardinals) vs. N.Y. Jets	1978	1996
	Miami vs. N.Y. Giants	1972	1990
17	Seattle vs. Tampa Bay	1977	1994
14	Indianapolis (Baltimore Colts) vs. San Francisco	1972	1986
13	Atlanta vs. Kansas City	1972	1985
	Cincinnati vs. Washington	1991	2004
	Cleveland[a] vs. Washington	1991	2004
	Indianapolis (Baltimore Colts) vs. New Orleans	1973	1986
	New England vs. N.Y. Giants	1974	1987
12	Arizona (St. Louis-Phoenix Cardinals) vs. Denver	1977	1989
	Atlanta vs. Indianapolis (Baltimore Colts)	1974	1986
	Buffalo vs. Detroit	1979	1991
	Denver vs. Tampa Bay	1981	1993
	Detroit vs. San Diego	1984	1996
	Minnesota vs. N.Y. Jets	1982	1994

Number of Seasons Between Meetings/Interconference Matchups	Prior Meeting	Subsequent Meeting
Oakland (L.A. Raiders) vs. Tampa Bay	1981	1993
11 Indianapolis (Baltimore Colts) vs. Minnesota	1971	1982
Indianapolis (Baltimore Colts) vs. N.Y. Giants	1979	1990
Indianapolis (Baltimore Colts) vs. St. Louis (L.A. Rams)	1975	1986
10 Arizona (St. Louis Cardinals) vs. Oakland (L.A. Raiders)	1973	1983
Cleveland[a] vs. Dallas	1994	2004
Cleveland[a] vs. Minnesota	1995	2005
Cleveland[a] vs. San Francisco	1993	2003
Detroit vs. Pittsburgh	1973	1983
Green Bay vs. Kansas City	1977	1987

[a]Cleveland inactive from 1996 to 1998

Most Consecutive Seasons Playing a Non-Divisional Opponent in the Regular Season (Since 1970)

- 12 New Orleans vs. Tampa Bay, 1981–1992
- 10 Green Bay vs. St. Louis (L.A. Rams), 1988–1997
-     Indianapolis vs. New England, 2003–2012
-     Pittsburgh vs. San Diego, 1987–1996
- 9 Atlanta vs. Dallas, 1985–1993
-     Cleveland vs. Seattle, 1977–1985
-     Denver vs. New England, 1995–2003
-     Kansas City vs. Tennessee (Houston Oilers), 1988–1996

Most Consecutive Regular Season Meetings Between Two Teams at the Same Site (Since 1970)

	Visiting Team	Home Team	
9	New England	Pittsburgh	1981–1995
8	Buffalo	Tampa Bay[a]	1976–2005
	Denver	Buffalo	1979–1994
7	Pittsburgh	Kansas City	1992–2003
6	Dallas	Detroit	1981–1992
	Pittsburgh	N.Y. Jets	1983–1990
	San Francisco	Green Bay	1976–1987
	Seattle	Cincinnati[a]	1977–1986
	Seattle	New England	1986–1993
	Tampa Bay	San Francisco[a]	1977–1984
5	Arizona (St. Louis Cardinals)	Tampa Bay[a]	1977–1986
	Carolina	Minnesota[a]	1996–2002
	Chicago	San Francisco	1975–1981
	Cincinnati	Denver	1983–1994
	Cleveland	Indianapolis	1989–1994
	Cleveland	Oakland (L.A. Raiders)	1986–2000
	Dallas	N.Y. Jets	1975–1993
	Denver	Pittsburgh	1979–1988
	Detroit	St. Louis (L.A. Rams)	1980–1986
	Detroit	Washington	1981–1987
	Indianapolis	Cincinnati	1989–1994
	Minnesota	Buffalo	1982–1997
	Minnesota	N.Y. Giants	1989–1999
	N.Y. Jets	Oakland[b]	1999–2003
	New Orleans	N.Y. Giants	1995–2001
	Oakland (L.A. Raiders)	Tennessee (Hou. Oilers)	1984–1991
	Philadelphia	Atlanta	1990–1998

Visiting Team	Home Team	
Pittsburgh	Oakland (L.A. Raiders)	1981–1995
St. Louis	Philadelphia	1995–2002
St. Louis (L.A. Rams)	Philadelphia	1978–1988
Tampa Bay	Dallas[a]	1977–1990
Tampa Bay	New Orleans[b]	1984–1988
Washington	Green Bay	1983–2002
Washington	St. Louis (L.A. Rams)	1991–1996

[a]These games were also the first ever meetings between the two teams.
[b]The five games were played in consecutive seasons (Tampa Bay at New Orleans, 1984–1988; N.Y. Jets at Oakland, 1999–2003).

Most Head-to-Head Regular Season Games Between Two Interconference Teams (1970–2001)

11	Chicago vs. Denver
10	Arizona (St. Louis-Phoenix Cardinals) vs. New England
	Atlanta vs. Denver
	Atlanta vs. New England
	Atlanta vs. Oakland (L.A. Raiders)
	Atlanta vs. Pittsburgh
	Atlanta vs. Tennessee (Houston Oilers)
	Chicago vs. Oakland (L.A. Raiders)
	Dallas vs. Tennessee (Houston Oilers)
	Denver vs. Minnesota
	Green Bay vs. Miami
	Indianapolis (Baltimore Colts) vs. Philadelphia
	Indianapolis (Baltimore Colts) vs. Washington
	Kansas City vs. N.Y. Giants
	Miami vs. Philadelphia
	Minnesota vs. Oakland (L.A. Raiders)
	New England vs. New Orleans
	New Orleans vs. Tennessee (Houston Oilers)
	N.Y. Jets vs. St. Louis (L.A. Rams)
	Pittsburgh vs. San Francisco
	San Francisco vs. Tennessee (Houston Oilers)
	Seattle[a] vs. Washington

[a]Seattle was a member of the AFC from 1977 to 2001; includes 1976 meeting when Seattle was in the NFC.

Most Head-to-Head Regular Season Games Between Two Interconference Teams (2002–2012)

3	many[a]

[a]Beginning in 2002, each team plays each interconference opponent once every four years. By the end of the 2013 regular season, each team would have played every team from the opposite conference three times.

Most Head-to-Head Regular Season Games Between Two Interconference Teams (1970–2012)

Note: Does not include Seattle vs. AFC teams as the Seahawks were a member of the AFC from 1977 to 2001.

14	Chicago vs. Denver
13	Arizona (St. Louis-Phoenix Cardinals) vs. New England
	Atlanta vs. Denver
	Atlanta vs. Oakland (L.A. Raiders)

Atlanta vs. Pittsburgh
Atlanta vs. Tennessee (Houston Oilers)
Chicago vs. Oakland (L.A. Raiders)
Dallas vs. Tennessee (Houston Oilers)
Denver vs. Minnesota
Green Bay vs. Miami
Indianapolis (Baltimore Colts) vs. Philadelphia
Indianapolis (Baltimore Colts) vs. Washington
Miami vs. Philadelphia
Minnesota vs. Oakland (L.A. Raiders)
New Orleans vs. Tennessee (Houston Oilers)
N.Y. Jets vs. St. Louis (L.A. Rams)
Pittsburgh vs. San Francisco

Fewest Head-to-Head Regular Season Meetings Between Two Interconference Teams (1970–2001)

Note: Does not include the following four teams that entered the league most recently: Carolina (1995), Jacksonville (1995), Baltimore (1996), and Houston (2002).

4   Kansas City vs. Philadelphia
    Miami vs. N.Y. Giants
5   Arizona (St. Louis-Phoenix Cardinals) vs. N.Y. Jets
    Arizona (St. Louis-Phoenix Cardinals) vs. Oakland (L.A. Raiders)
    Atlanta vs. Indianapolis (Baltimore Colts)
    Atlanta vs. Kansas City
    Cleveland vs. Tampa Bay[a]
    Denver vs. Tampa Bay[a]
    Indianapolis (Baltimore Colts) vs. Minnesota
    New England vs. Tampa Bay[a]
    Oakland (L.A. Raiders) vs. Tampa Bay[a]
    Seattle vs. Tampa Bay

[a]Includes 1976 meeting when Tampa Bay was a member of the AFC.

Fewest Head-to-Head Regular Season Meetings Between Two Interconference Teams (2002–2012)

2   many[a]

[a]Beginning in 2002, each team plays each interconference opponent once every four years. By the end of the 2013 regular season, each team would have played every team from the opposite conference three times since realignment in 2002.

Fewest Head-to-Head Regular Season Meetings Between Interconference Teams (1970–2012)

Note: Does not include the following four teams that entered the league most recently: Carolina (1995), Jacksonville (1995), Baltimore (1996), and Houston (2002).

6   Kansas City vs. Philadelphia
7   Miami vs. N.Y. Giants
    New England vs. Tampa Bay[a]
8   Arizona (St. Louis-Phoenix Cardinals) vs. N.Y. Jets
    Arizona (St. Louis-Phoenix Cardinals) vs. Oakland (L.A. Raiders)
    Atlanta vs. Indianapolis (Baltimore Colts)
    Atlanta vs. Kansas City
    Chicago vs. Cleveland
    Cleveland vs. Tampa Bay[a]
    Denver vs. Tampa Bay[a]
    Indianapolis (Baltimore Colts) vs. Minnesota

Indianapolis (Baltimore Colts) vs. St. Louis (L.A. Rams)
Indianapolis (Baltimore Colts) vs. San Francisco
Kansas City vs. Washington
Oakland (L.A. Raiders) vs. Tampa Bay[a]

[a]Includes 1976 meeting when Tampa Bay was a member of the AFC.

Most Head-to-Head Regular Season Games Between Two Non-Division Teams from the Same Conference (1970–2001)

24	Atlanta vs. Detroit
	Kansas City vs. Tennessee (Houston Oilers)
23	Green Bay vs. St. Louis (L.A. Rams)
	Kansas City vs. Pittsburgh
22	Chicago vs. St. Louis (L.A. Rams)
	Pittsburgh vs. San Diego
21	Cincinnati vs. San Diego
	N.Y. Giants vs. St. Louis (L.A. Rams)
20	Detroit vs. San Francisco
	Minnesota vs. New Orleans
	Minnesota vs. San Francisco
	New Orleans vs. Tampa Bay

Most Head-to-Head Regular Season Games Between Two Non-Division Teams from the Same Conference (2002–2012)

10	Indianapolis vs. New England
9	Arizona vs. Carolina
8	Arizona vs. Detroit
	Atlanta vs. Philadelphia
	Buffalo vs. Jacksonville
	Buffalo vs. Kansas City
	Dallas vs. Detroit
	Denver vs. New England
	Minnesota vs. N.Y. Giants
	Philadelphia vs. San Francisco
	Pittsburgh vs. Tennessee
	St. Louis vs. Washington
	Tampa Bay vs. Washington

Most Head-to-Head Regular Season Games Between Two Non-Division Teams from the Same Conference (1970–2012)

Note: Does not include matchups between teams that played in the same division from 1970 to 2001.

31	Atlanta vs. Detroit
30	Green Bay vs. St. Louis (L.A. Rams)
28	Chicago vs. St. Louis (L.A. Rams)
	Kansas City vs. Pittsburgh
	Kansas City vs. Tennessee (Houston Oilers)
	Pittsburgh vs. San Diego
27	Cincinnati vs. San Diego
26	Detroit vs. San Francisco
	Miami vs. Oakland (L.A. Raiders)
	Minnesota vs. New Orleans
	N.Y. Giants vs. St. Louis (L.A. Rams)

25	Atlanta vs. Philadelphia
	Cincinnati vs. Indianapolis (Baltimore Colts)
	Denver vs. New England
	Miami vs. Tennessee (Houston Oilers)
	Minnesota vs. San Francisco
	Oakland (L.A. Raiders) vs. Tennessee (Houston Oilers)

Fewest Head-to-Head Regular Season Meetings Between Two Non-Division Teams from the Same Conference (1970–2001)

Note: Does not include the following four teams that entered the league most recently: Carolina (1995), Jacksonville (1995), Baltimore (1996), and Houston (2002).

6	Denver vs. Miami
7	Philadelphia vs. Tampa Bay
8	Dallas vs. Tampa Bay
	Detroit vs. Philadelphia
	Green Bay vs. Washington
	Indianapolis (Baltimore Colts) vs. Seattle[a]
	Miami vs. Seattle[a]
9	Arizona (St. Louis-Phoenix Cardinals) vs. Green Bay
	Buffalo vs. Seattle[a]
	Chicago vs. N.Y. Giants
	Indianapolis (Baltimore Colts) vs. Oakland (L.A. Raiders)
	New England vs. Oakland (L.A. Raiders)
	N.Y. Jets vs. San Diego

[a]Seattle was a member of the AFC from 1977 to 2001.

Fewest Head-to-Head Regular Season Meetings Between Two Non-Division Teams from the Same Conference (2002–2012)

3[a]	Arizona vs. New Orleans
	Arizona vs. Tampa Bay
	Buffalo vs. Pittsburgh
	Carolina vs. San Francisco
	Dallas vs. Minnesota
	Detroit vs. N.Y. Giants
	Indianapolis vs. Oakland
	Minnesota vs. Philadelphia
4	Arizona vs. Chicago
	Arizona vs. Green Bay
	Atlanta vs. Dallas
	Atlanta vs. San Francisco
	Atlanta vs. Washington
	Baltimore vs. Buffalo
	Buffalo vs. Indianapolis
	Carolina vs. St. Louis
	Carolina vs. Seattle
	Chicago vs. Dallas
	Chicago vs. N.Y. Giants
	Cincinnati vs. Miami
	Cincinnati vs. New England
	Cincinnati vs. Oakland
	Cleveland vs. New England

Cleveland vs. Tennessee
Dallas vs. San Francisco
Denver vs. Houston
Denver vs. Tennessee
Detroit vs. Philadelphia
Detroit vs. Seattle
Green Bay vs. Washington
Houston vs. New England
Houston vs. Pittsburgh
Houston vs. San Diego
Indianapolis vs. N.Y. Jets
Indianapolis vs. Pittsburgh
Jacksonville vs. Miami
Jacksonville vs. New England
Jacksonville vs. Oakland
Kansas City vs. Tennessee
N.Y. Giants vs. Tampa Bay
New England vs. Oakland
New Orleans vs. Seattle

ᵃBeginning in 2002, each team plays every non-division conference opponent at least once every three years. By the end of the 2013 regular season, each team would have played every team in their conference at least four times since realignment in 2002.

Fewest Head-to-Head Regular Season Meetings Between Two Non-Division Teams from the Same Conference (1970–2012)

Note: Does not include the following four teams that entered the league most recently: Carolina (1995), Jacksonville (1995), Baltimore (1996), Houston (2002); and Seattle which moved from the AFC to NFC in 2002.

11	Denver vs. Miami
12	Detroit vs. Philadelphia
	Green Bay vs. Washington
	Indianapolis (Baltimore Colts) vs. Oakland (L.A. Raiders)
	Philadelphia vs. Tampa Bay
13	Arizona (St. Louis-Phoenix Cardinals) vs. Green Bay
	Chicago vs. N.Y. Giants
	New England vs. Oakland (L.A. Raiders)
14	Dallas vs. Tampa Bay
15	Arizona (St. Louis-Phoenix Cardinals) vs. Chicago
	Cleveland vs. Miami
	Kansas City vs. New England
	N.Y. Jets vs. San Diego

Regular Season Games Played Against Conference Opponents

AFC EAST
Buffalo Bills

| YEARS | AFC EAST | | | AFC NORTH | | | | AFC SOUTH | | | | AFC WEST | | | |
	MIA	NE	NYJ	BAL	CIN	CLE	PIT	HOU	IND	JAC	TEN	DEN	KC	OAK	SD
1960–69	8	20	20	-	2	-	-	-	-	-	20	17	18	18	17
1970–01	64	63	62	1	16	11	17	-	63	3	16	13	15	13	11
2002–12	22	22	22	4	7	6	3	6	4	8	5	5	8	5	5
TOTAL	94	105	104	5	25	17	20	6	67	11	41	35	41	36	33

Miami Dolphins

YEARS	AFC EAST			AFC NORTH				AFC SOUTH				AFC WEST			
	BUF	NE	NYJ	BAL	CIN	CLE	PIT	HOU	IND	JAC	TEN	DEN	KC	OAK	SD
1966–69	8	7	8	–	3	–	–	–	–	–	8	5	6	6	5
1970–01	64	63	64	2	12	10	16	–	64	1	18	6	14	19	13
2002–12	22	22	22	6	4	5	5	7	5	4	7	5	5	7	6
TOTAL	94	92	94	8	19	15	21	7	69	5	33	16	25	32	24

New England Patriots

YEARS	AFC EAST			AFC NORTH				AFC SOUTH				AFC WEST			
	BUF	MIA	NYJ	BAL	CIN	CLE	PIT	HOU	IND	JAC	TEN	DEN	KC	OAK	SD
1960–69	20	7	20	–	2	–	–	–	–	–	20	18	17	17	19
1970–01	63	63	63	2	16	17	15	–	63	2	13	17	10	9	11
2002–12	22	22	22	5	4	4	7	4	10	4	5	8	5	4	6
TOTAL	105	92	105	7	22	21	22	4	73	6	38	43	32	30	36

New York Jets

YEARS	AFC EAST			AFC NORTH				AFC SOUTH				AFC WEST			
	BUF	MIA	NE	BAL	CIN	CLE	PIT	HOU	IND	JAC	TEN	DEN	KC	OAK	SD
1960–69	20	8	20	–	3	–	–	–	–	–	19	17	17	18	18
1970–01	62	64	63	3	14	15	15	–	63	3	15	11	12	13	9
2002–12	22	22	22	5	5	5	5	6	4	7	6	5	5	7	6
TOTAL	104	94	105	8	22	20	20	6	67	10	40	33	34	38	33

AFC NORTH

Baltimore Ravens

YEARS	AFC EAST				AFC NORTH			AFC SOUTH				AFC WEST			
	BUF	MIA	NE	NYJ	CIN	CLE	PIT	HOU	IND	JAC	TEN	DEN	KC	OAK	SD
1996–01	1	2	2	3	12	6	12	–	3	12	12	2	1	2	3
2002–12	4	6	5	5	22	22	22	6	7	5	5	7	5	5	6
TOTAL	5	8	7	8	34	28	34	6	10	17	17	9	6	7	9

Cincinnati Bengals

YEARS	AFC EAST				AFC NORTH			AFC SOUTH				AFC WEST			
	BUF	MIA	NE	NYJ	BAL	CLE	PIT	HOU	IND	JAC	TEN	DEN	KC	OAK	SD
1968–69	2	3	2	3	–	–	–	–	–	–	2	4	4	4	4
1970–01	16	12	16	14	12	57	63	–	19	14	64	17	16	19	21
2002–12	7	4	4	5	22	22	22	6	6	5	6	6	7	4	6
TOTAL	25	19	22	22	34	79	85	6	25	19	72	27	27	27	31

Cleveland Browns

YEARS	AFC EAST				AFC NORTH			AFC SOUTH				AFC WEST			
	BUF	MIA	NE	NYJ	BAL	CIN	PIT	HOU	IND	JAC	TEN	DEN	KC	OAK	SD
1950–69	–	–	–	–	–	–	40	–	4	–	–	–	–	–	–
1970–01	11	10	17	15	6	57	58	–	17	8	57	19	17	13	18
2002–12	6	5	4	5	22	22	22	7	6	6	4	5	6	7	5
TOTAL	17	15	21	20	28	79	120	7	27	14	61	24	23	20	23

Pittsburgh Steelers

YEARS	AFC EAST				AFC NORTH			AFC SOUTH				AFC WEST			
	BUF	MIA	NE	NYJ	BAL	CIN	CLE	HOU	IND	JAC	TEN	DEN	KC	OAK	SD
1933–69	–	–	–	–	–	–	40	–	2	–	–	–	–	–	–
1970–01	17	16	15	15	12	63	58	–	14	14	63	17	23	13	22
2002–12	3	5	7	5	22	22	22	4	4	7	8	5	5	7	6
TOTAL	20	21	22	20	34	85	120	4	20	21	71	22	28	20	28

AFC SOUTH

Houston Texans

YEARS	AFC EAST				AFC NORTH				AFC SOUTH			AFC WEST			
	BUF	MIA	NE	NYJ	BAL	CIN	CLE	PIT	IND	JAC	TEN	DEN	KC	OAK	SD
2002–12	6	7	4	6	6	6	7	4	22	22	22	4	5	7	4
TOTAL	6	7	4	6	6	6	7	4	22	22	22	4	5	7	4

Indianapolis Colts

YEARS	AFC EAST				AFC NORTH				AFC SOUTH			AFC WEST			
	BUF	MIA	NE	NYJ	BAL	CIN	CLE	PIT	HOU	JAC	TEN	DEN	KC	OAK	SD
1953–69	-	-	-	-	-	-	4	2	-	-	-	-	-	-	-
1970–01	63	64	63	63	3	19	17	14	-	2	14	12	14	9	19
2002–12	4	5	10	4	7	6	6	4	22	22	22	7	5	3	5
TOTAL	67	69	73	67	10	25	27	20	22	24	36	19	19	12	24

Jacksonville Jaguars

YEARS	AFC EAST				AFC NORTH				AFC SOUTH			AFC WEST			
	BUF	MIA	NE	NYJ	BAL	CIN	CLE	PIT	HOU	IND	TEN	DEN	KC	OAK	SD
1995–01	3	1	2	3	12	14	8	14	-	2	14	3	3	2	0
2002–12	8	4	4	7	5	5	6	7	22	22	22	5	6	4	5
TOTAL	11	5	6	10	17	19	14	21	22	24	36	8	9	6	5

Tennessee Titans

YEARS	AFC EAST				AFC NORTH				AFC SOUTH			AFC WEST			
	BUF	MIA	NE	NYJ	BAL	CIN	CLE	PIT	HOU	IND	JAC	DEN	KC	OAK	SD
1960–69	20	8	20	19	-	2	-	-	-	-	-	19	18	17	17
1970–01	16	18	13	15	12	64	57	63	-	14	14	13	24	19	16
2002–12	5	7	5	6	5	6	4	8	22	22	22	4	4	6	6
TOTAL	41	33	38	40	17	72	61	71	22	36	36	36	46	42	39

AFC WEST

Denver Broncos

YEARS	AFC EAST				AFC NORTH				AFC SOUTH				AFC WEST		
	BUF	MIA	NE	NYJ	BAL	CIN	CLE	PIT	HOU	IND	JAC	TEN	KC	OAK	SD
1960–69	17	5	18	17	-	4	-	-	-	-	-	19	20	20	20
1970–01	13	6	17	11	2	17	19	17	-	12	3	13	63	63	64
2002–12	5	5	8	5	7	6	5	5	4	7	5	4	22	22	22
TOTAL	35	16	43	33	9	27	24	22	4	19	8	36	105	105	106

Kansas City Chiefs

YEARS	AFC EAST				AFC NORTH				AFC SOUTH				AFC WEST		
	BUF	MIA	NE	NYJ	BAL	CIN	CLE	PIT	HOU	IND	JAC	TEN	DEN	OAK	SD
1960–69	18	6	17	17	-	4	-	-	-	-	-	18	20	20	20
1970–01	15	14	10	12	1	16	17	23	-	14	3	24	63	63	63
2002–12	8	5	5	5	5	7	6	5	5	5	6	4	22	22	22
TOTAL	41	25	32	34	6	27	23	28	5	19	9	46	105	105	105

Oakland Raiders

YEARS	AFC EAST				AFC NORTH				AFC SOUTH				AFC WEST		
	BUF	MIA	NE	NYJ	BAL	CIN	CLE	PIT	HOU	IND	JAC	TEN	DEN	KC	SD
1960–69	18	6	17	18	-	4	-	-	-	-	-	17	20	20	20
1970–01	13	19	9	13	2	19	13	13	-	9	2	19	63	63	64
2002–12	5	7	4	7	5	4	7	7	7	3	4	6	22	22	22
TOTAL	36	32	30	38	7	27	20	20	7	12	6	42	105	105	106

San Diego Chargers

YEARS	AFC EAST BUF	MIA	NE	NYJ	AFC NORTH BAL	CIN	CLE	PIT	AFC SOUTH HOU	IND	JAC	TEN	AFC WEST DEN	KC	OAK
1960–69	17	5	19	18	–	4	–	–	–	–	–	17	20	20	20
1970–01	11	13	11	9	3	21	18	22	–	19	0	16	64	63	64
2002–12	5	6	6	6	6	6	5	6	4	5	5	6	22	22	22
TOTAL	33	24	36	33	9	31	23	28	4	24	5	39	106	105	106

NFC EAST

Dallas Cowboys

YEARS	NFC EAST NYG	PHI	WAS	NFC NORTH CHI	DET	GB	MIN	NFC SOUTH ATL	CAR	NO	TB	NFC WEST ARI	STL	SF	SEA
1960–69	17	19	19	4	3	4	4	3	–	5	–	16	4	5	–
1970–01	62	63	63	13	11	15	14	16	3	14	8	63	13	17	7
2002–12	22	22	22	4	8	5	3	4	7	6	6	7	5	4	7
TOTAL	101	104	104	21	22	24	21	23	10	25	14	86	22	26	14

New York Giants

YEARS	NFC EAST DAL	PHI	WAS	NFC NORTH CHI	DET	GB	MIN	NFC SOUTH ATL	CAR	NO	TB	NFC WEST ARI	STL	SF	SEA
1925–69	17	70	74	35	24	31	4	2	–	3	–	55	13	6	–
1970–01	62	64	64	9	13	15	10	12	1	18	14	63	21	17	9
2002–12	22	22	22	4	3	5	8	7	6	6	4	6	5	6	6
TOTAL	101	156	160	48	40	51	22	21	7	27	18	124	39	29	15

Philadelphia Eagles

YEARS	NFC EAST DAL	NYG	WAS	NFC NORTH CHI	DET	GB	MIN	NFC SOUTH ATL	CAR	NO	TB	NFC WEST ARI	STL	SF	SEA
1933–69	19	70	69	17	17	16	3	3	–	5	–	45	18	9	–
1970–01	63	64	64	14	8	15	15	17	2	16	7	63	13	13	8
2002–12	22	22	22	7	4	6	3	8	5	5	5	5	5	8	5
TOTAL	104	156	155	38	29	37	21	28	7	26	12	113	36	30	13

Washington Redskins

YEARS	NFC EAST DAL	NYG	PHI	NFC NORTH CHI	DET	GB	MIN	NFC SOUTH ATL	CAR	NO	TB	NFC WEST ARI	STL	SF	SEA
1932–69	19	74	69	20	17	19	1	3	–	5	–	51	12	6	–
1970–01	63	64	64	15	17	8	10	15	6	13	10	64	13	14	10
2002–12	22	22	22	5	5	4	6	4	5	6	8	5	8	5	5
TOTAL	104	160	155	40	39	31	17	22	11	24	18	120	33	25	15

NFC NORTH

Chicago Bears

YEARS	NFC EAST DAL	NYG	PHI	WAS	NFC NORTH DET	GB	MIN	NFC SOUTH ATL	CAR	NO	TB	NFC WEST ARI	STL	SF	SEA
1920–69	4	35	17	20	81	100	18	4	–	1	–	74	60	36	–
1970–01	13	9	14	15	63	62	63	16	1	18	48	11	22	17	7
2002–12	4	4	7	5	22	22	22	5	6	6	6	4	6	6	7
TOTAL	21	48	38	40	166	184	103	25	7	25	54	89	88	59	14

Detroit Lions

YEARS	NFC EAST DAL	NYG	PHI	WAS	NFC NORTH CHI	GB	MIN	NFC SOUTH ATL	CAR	NO	TB	NFC WEST ARI	STL	SF	SEA
1930–69	3	24	17	17	81	79	18	4	–	1	–	40	60	37	–
1970–01	11	13	8	17	63	64	63	24	1	15	48	13	17	20	8

Appendix E

	NFC EAST				NFC NORTH			NFC SOUTH				NFC WEST			
YEARS	DAL	NYG	PHI	WAS	CHI	GB	MIN	ATL	CAR	NO	TB	ARI	STL	SF	SEA
2002–12	8	3	4	5	22	22	22	7	5	5	6	8	5	6	4
TOTAL	22	40	29	39	166	165	103	35	6	21	54	61	82	63	12

Green Bay Packers

	NFC EAST				NFC NORTH			NFC SOUTH				NFC WEST			
YEARS	DAL	NYG	PHI	WAS	CHI	DET	MIN	ATL	CAR	NO	TB	ARI	STL	SF	SEA
1921–69	4	31	16	19	100	79	18	4	-	1	-	57	61	35	-
1970–01	15	15	15	8	62	64	63	16	5	16	46	9	23	16	8
2002–12	5	5	6	4	22	22	22	5	6	6	6	4	7	6	6
TOTAL	24	51	37	31	184	165	103	25	11	23	52	70	91	57	14

Minnesota Vikings

	NFC EAST				NFC NORTH			NFC SOUTH				NFC WEST			
YEARS	DAL	NYG	PHI	WAS	CHI	DET	GB	ATL	CAR	NO	TB	ARI	STL	SF	SEA
1961–69	4	4	3	1	18	18	18	4	-	1	-	3	15	15	-
1970–01	14	10	15	10	63	63	63	15	4	20	48	13	15	20	6
2002–12	3	8	3	6	22	22	22	6	6	6	5	7	5	5	6
TOTAL	21	22	21	17	103	103	103	25	10	27	53	23	35	40	12

NFC SOUTH

Atlanta Falcons

	NFC EAST				NFC NORTH				NFC SOUTH			NFC WEST			
YEARS	DAL	NYG	PHI	WAS	CHI	DET	GB	MIN	CAR	NO	TB	ARI	STL	SF	SEA
1966–69	3	2	3	3	4	4	4	4	-	2	-	2	7	7	-
1970–01	16	12	17	15	16	24	16	15	14	63	17	19	63	63	7
2002–12	4	7	8	4	5	7	5	6	22	22	22	5	5	4	6
TOTAL	23	21	28	22	25	35	25	25	36	87	39	26	75	74	13

Carolina Panthers

	NFC EAST				NFC NORTH				NFC SOUTH			NFC WEST			
YEARS	DAL	NYG	PHI	WAS	CHI	DET	GB	MIN	ATL	NO	TB	ARI	STL	SF	SEA
1995–01	3	1	2	6	1	1	5	4	14	14	3	2	14	14	1
2002–12	7	6	5	5	6	5	6	6	22	22	22	9	4	3	4
TOTAL	10	7	7	11	7	6	11	10	36	36	25	11	18	17	5

New Orleans Saints

	NFC EAST				NFC NORTH				NFC SOUTH			NFC WEST			
YEARS	DAL	NYG	PHI	WAS	CHI	DET	GB	MIN	ATL	CAR	TB	ARI	STL	SF	SEA
1967–69	5	3	5	5	1	1	1	1	2	-	-	4	2	2	-
1970–01	14	18	16	13	18	15	16	20	63	14	20	19	62	63	7
2002–12	6	6	5	6	6	5	6	6	22	22	22	3	6	7	4
TOTAL	25	27	26	24	25	21	23	27	87	36	42	26	70	72	11

Tampa Bay Buccaneers

	NFC EAST				NFC NORTH				NFC SOUTH			NFC WEST			
YEARS	DAL	NYG	PHI	WAS	CHI	DET	GB	MIN	ATL	CAR	NO	ARI	STL	SF	SEA
1976–01	8	14	7	10	48	48	46	48	17	3	20	14	13	14	5
2002–12	6	4	5	8	6	6	6	5	22	22	22	3	5	6	6
TOTAL	14	18	12	18	54	54	52	53	39	25	42	17	18	20	11

NFC WEST

Arizona Cardinals

YEARS	NFC EAST DAL	NYG	PHI	WAS	NFC NORTH CHI	DET	GB	MIN	NFC SOUTH ATL	CAR	NO	TB	NFC WEST STL	SF	SEA
1920–69	16	55	45	51	74	40	57	3	2	–	4	–	29	5	–
1970–01	63	63	63	64	11	13	9	13	19	2	19	14	17	16	6
2002–12	7	6	5	5	4	8	4	7	5	9	3	3	22	22	22
TOTAL	86	124	113	120	89	61	70	23	26	11	26	17	68	43	28

St. Louis Rams

YEARS	NFC EAST DAL	NYG	PHI	WAS	NFC NORTH CHI	DET	GB	MIN	NFC SOUTH ATL	CAR	NO	TB	NFC WEST ARI	SF	SEA
1937–69	4	13	18	12	60	60	61	15	7	–	2	–	29	40	–
1970–01	13	21	13	13	22	17	23	15	63	14	62	13	17	64	7
2002–12	5	5	5	8	6	5	7	5	5	4	6	5	22	22	22
TOTAL	22	39	36	33	88	82	91	35	75	18	70	18	68	126	29

San Francisco 49ers

YEARS	NFC EAST DAL	NYG	PHI	WAS	NFC NORTH CHI	DET	GB	MIN	NFC SOUTH ATL	CAR	NO	TB	NFC WEST ARI	STL	SEA
1950–69	5	6	9	6	36	37	35	15	7	–	2	–	5	40	–
1970–01	17	17	13	14	17	20	16	20	63	14	63	14	16	64	6
2002–12	4	6	8	5	6	6	6	5	4	3	7	6	22	22	22
TOTAL	26	29	30	25	59	63	57	40	74	17	72	20	43	126	28

Seattle Seahawks

YEARS	NFC EAST DAL	NYG	PHI	WAS	NFC NORTH CHI	DET	GB	MIN	NFC SOUTH ATL	CAR	NO	TB	NFC WEST ARI	STL	SF
1976–01	7	9	8	10	7	8	8	6	7	1	7	5	6	7	6
2002–12	7	6	5	5	7	4	6	6	6	4	4	6	22	22	22
TOTAL	14	15	13	15	14	12	14	12	13	5	11	11	28	29	28

Regular Season Games Played Against Interconference Opponents

Read left to right for number of games played by any AFC team vs. all NFC clubs. Read top to bottom for number of games played by any NFC team vs. all AFC clubs. Note: Cleveland and San Francisco were members of the AAFC from 1946 to 1949; Cleveland, Indianapolis (Baltimore Colts), and Pittsburgh were members of the NFL prior to 1970; Tampa Bay was a member of the AFC in 1976 and also Seattle from 1977 to 2001.

AFC EAST

BUF	NFC EAST DAL	NYG	PHI	WAS	NFC NORTH CHI	DET	GB	MIN	NFC SOUTH ATL	CAR	NO	TB	NFC WEST ARI	STL	SF	SEA
1970–01	6	8	9	9	8	6	8	9	8	3	7	7	7	8	8	9
2002–12	3	3	3	3	3	3	3	3	2	2	2	2	3	3	3	3
TOTAL	9	11	12	12	11	9	11	12	10	5	9	9	10	11	11	12
MIA	DAL	NYG	PHI	WAS	CHI	DET	GB	MIN	ATL	CAR	NO	TB	ARI	STL	SF	SEA
1970–01	9	4	10	8	8	7	10	7	9	2	8	7	8	9	8	8
2002–12	3	3	3	3	3	3	3	3	2	2	2	2	3	3	3	3
TOTAL	12	7	13	11	11	10	13	10	11	4	10	9	11	12	11	11
NE	DAL	NYG	PHI	WAS	CHI	DET	GB	MIN	ATL	CAR	NO	TB	ARI	STL	SF	SEA
1970–01	8	6	8	6	8	7	6	8	10	2	10	5	10	8	9	13
2002–12	3	3	3	3	3	3	3	3	2	2	2	2	3	3	3	3
TOTAL	11	9	11	9	11	10	9	11	12	4	12	7	13	11	12	16

Appendix E

NYJ	NFC EAST				NFC NORTH				NFC SOUTH				NFC WEST			
	DAL	NYG	PHI	WAS	CHI	DET	GB	MIN	ATL	CAR	NO	TB	ARI	STL	SF	SEA
1970–01	7	9	6	7	7	9	8	6	8	3	9	8	5	10	9	15
2002–12	3	3	3	3	3	3	3	3	2	2	2	2	3	3	3	3
TOTAL	10	12	9	10	10	12	11	9	10	5	11	10	8	13	12	18

AFC NORTH

BAL	NFC EAST				NFC NORTH				NFC SOUTH				NFC WEST			
	DAL	NYG	PHI	WAS	CHI	DET	GB	MIN	ATL	CAR	NO	TB	ARI	STL	SF	SEA
1996–01	1	1	1	2	2	1	2	2	1	1	2	1	2	2	1	1
2002–12	3	3	3	3	2	2	2	2	3	3	3	3	3	3	3	3
TOTAL	4	4	4	5	4	3	4	4	4	4	5	4	5	5	4	4
CIN	DAL	NYG	PHI	WAS	CHI	DET	GB	MIN	ATL	CAR	NO	TB	ARI	STL	SF	SEA
1970–01	8	6	9	6	7	8	9	9	9	1	9	7	7	9	9	15
2002–12	3	3	3	3	2	2	2	2	3	3	3	3	3	3	3	3
TOTAL	11	9	12	9	9	10	11	11	12	4	12	10	10	12	12	18
CLE	DAL	NYG	PHI	WAS	CHI	DET	GB	MIN	ATL	CAR	NO	TB	ARI	STL	SF	SEA
1946–49	-	-	-	-	-	-	-	-	-	-	-	-	-	-	8	-
1950–69	16	39	37	36	6	8	8	3	2	-	4	-	40	7	7	-
1970–01	8	6	8	6	6	8	7	8	8	1	9	5	6	9	8	14
2002–12	3	3	3	3	2	2	2	2	3	3	3	3	3	3	3	3
TOTAL	27	48	48	45	14	18	17	13	13	4	16	8	49	19	26	17
PIT	DAL	NYG	PHI	WAS	CHI	DET	GB	MIN	ATL	CAR	NO	TB	ARI	STL	SF	SEA
1933–69	16	67	66	67	15	20	22	4	2	-	4	-	49	12	7	-
1970–01	9	6	8	7	8	8	8	9	10	2	7	6	6	9	10	13
2002–12	3	3	3	3	2	2	2	2	3	3	3	3	3	3	3	3
TOTAL	28	76	77	77	25	30	32	15	15	5	14	9	58	24	20	16

AFC SOUTH

HOU	NFC EAST				NFC NORTH				NFC SOUTH				NFC WEST			
	DAL	NYG	PHI	WAS	CHI	DET	GB	MIN	ATL	CAR	NO	TB	ARI	STL	SF	SEA
2002–12	3	3	3	3	3	3	3	3	3	3	3	3	2	2	2	2
TOTAL	3	3	3	3	3	3	3	3	3	3	3	3	2	2	2	2
IND	DAL	NYG	PHI	WAS	CHI	DET	GB	MIN	ATL	CAR	NO	TB	ARI	STL	SF	SEA
1953–69	3	5	4	16	31	31	31	15	7	-	2	-	3	34	34	-
1970–01	8	6	10	10	7	7	8	5	5	2	6	9	9	6	6	8
2002–12	3	3	3	3	3	3	3	3	3	3	3	3	2	2	2	2
TOTAL	14	14	17	29	41	41	42	23	15	5	11	12	14	42	42	10
JAC	DAL	NYG	PHI	WAS	CHI	DET	GB	MIN	ATL	CAR	NO	TB	ARI	STL	SF	SEA
1995–01	2	2	1	2	3	2	2	2	2	2	2	2	1	1	1	4
2002–12	3	3	3	3	3	3	3	3	3	3	3	3	2	2	2	2
TOTAL	5	5	4	5	6	5	5	5	5	5	5	5	3	3	3	6
TEN	DAL	NYG	PHI	WAS	CHI	DET	GB	MIN	ATL	CAR	NO	TB	ARI	STL	SF	SEA
1970–01	10	7	7	8	8	8	8	9	10	1	10	7	7	8	10	12
2002–12	3	3	3	3	3	3	3	3	3	3	3	3	2	2	2	2
TOTAL	13	10	10	11	11	11	11	12	13	4	13	10	9	10	12	14

AFC WEST

DEN	NFC EAST				NFC NORTH				NFC SOUTH				NFC WEST			
	DAL	NYG	PHI	WAS	CHI	DET	GB	MIN	ATL	CAR	NO	TB	ARI	STL	SF	SEA
1970–01	8	8	9	9	11	8	9	10	10	1	7	5	6	9	9	49
2002–12	2	2	2	2	3	3	3	3	3	3	3	3	3	3	3	3
TOTAL	10	10	11	11	14	11	12	13	13	4	10	8	9	12	12	52

	NFC EAST				NFC NORTH				NFC SOUTH				NFC WEST			
KC	DAL	NYG	PHI	WAS	CHI	DET	GB	MIN	ATL	CAR	NO	TB	ARI	STL	SF	SEA
1970–01	7	10	4	6	8	9	7	7	5	2	7	8	8	7	8	47
2002–12	2	2	2	2	3	3	3	3	3	3	3	3	3	3	3	3
TOTAL	9	12	6	8	11	12	10	10	8	5	10	11	11	10	11	50
OAK	DAL	NYG	PHI	WAS	CHI	DET	GB	MIN	ATL	CAR	NO	TB	ARI	STL	SF	SEA
1970–01	8	9	8	9	10	8	8	10	10	2	9	5	5	9	9	48
2002–12	2	2	2	2	3	3	3	3	3	3	3	3	3	3	3	3
TOTAL	10	11	10	11	13	11	11	13	13	5	12	8	8	12	12	51
SD	DAL	NYG	PHI	WAS	CHI	DET	GB	MIN	ATL	CAR	NO	TB	ARI	STL	SF	SEA
1970–01	7	8	8	7	8	7	7	8	6	2	8	7	9	7	9	46
2002–12	2	2	2	2	3	3	3	3	3	3	3	3	3	3	3	3
TOTAL	9	10	10	9	11	10	10	11	9	5	11	10	12	10	12	49

Appendix F: Site Priorities for Postseason Games (1933–2012)

In 1933, the NFL divided its ten teams into two divisions with the Eastern and Western division champions meeting in the championship game. Prior to the final week of the season, NFL President Joe F. Carr announced that the NFL championship game would take place at the site of the division champion with the highest winning percentage.[1] On December 10, the Chicago Bears, who had already clinched the Western division title, defeated the Green Bay Packers 7–6 to assure themselves of homefield advantage against the Eastern division champion New York Giants. The Bears then defeated the Giants, 23–17 at Wrigley Field to win the first NFL championship game scheduled before the season. The following year, club owners decided "that beginning with the 1934 season the game for the League Championship between the Eastern and Western be played in the Eastern section, the following year in the Western, and alternate each year."[2] The NFL continued to alternate the site of the title game between the East and West each year through the 1966 season.

The All-America Football Conference adopted a similar policy as the NFL in determining home playoff sites. The AAFC alternated the site of its championship game from 1946 to 1948, rotating between divisions. The Western division champion hosted the title game after the 1946 and 1948 seasons, while the Eastern division winner hosted the game in 1947. In 1949, with the AAFC realigned into one division, the top four teams would make the playoffs with homefield advantage being awarded to the two teams with the best records. In the first round, the team with the fourth best record would play at the team with the best overall record and the second-place team would host the third-place team in the other matchup. The two winners would then compete for the AAFC championship.

From 1960 to 1968, the American Football League would also follow the same format as the NFL. The Eastern and Western division winners would meet at the homefield of the Eastern division champion in even-numbered years, while the Western division champion would host the AFL championship in odd-numbered years. The AFL then instituted a four-team playoff format for 1969 in which the two division winners would play the runner-up of the opposite division in the interdivisional playoffs. The two winners would then meet for the AFL championship at the homefield of the Western division champion.[3]

When the NFL divided its 16 teams into four divisions of four teams each in 1967, a new playoff format was instituted with the four division winners advancing to the playoffs. The two division champions in each conference would play in the conference championships. The Capitol division winner would host the Century division champion in the Eastern conference, and in the West the winner of the Coastal division would play at the Central division champion with the home sites rotating each year by division. The two winners would then meet for the NFL championship. The league, continuing its policy that began in 1934, rotated the site of the title game each year by conference. The Western conference champion would host in 1967 and 1969, while the East hosted the championship game in 1968.

With the merger in 1970, the playoff field expanded to eight teams which included the three division champions and the best second place finisher in each conference. At NFL owners' meetings in 1970, a new postseason site rotation for 1970–1972 was adopted unanimously by member clubs. The new divisional rotation that would begin with the 1970 season was determined in drawings conducted by AFC President Lamar Hunt of the Kansas City Chiefs and NFC President George Halas of the Chicago Bears. Slips of paper, which were labeled "Eastern," "Central," and "Western," were drawn out of a hat one at a time. The first division selected was designated as "A," the second division "B," and the third "C." The wildcard club would automatically be designated as "D." The results of the drawing were as follows for the Divisional playoffs:[4]

	A	B	C
AFC	Eastern	Western	Central
NFC	Eastern	Central	Western

For the AFC playoffs in 1970, the Eastern and Western division winners (the first two divisions selected by draw), would host the two divisional playoff games, and in the NFC, the Eastern and Central divisions would be hosts. For example, in 1970 the matchups in the AFC would have "C" at "A," the Central champion at the Eastern champion and "D" at "B," the Wildcard team at the Western division winner. The matchups for the divisional playoff round would then rotate in 1971 and 1972.[5] The owners had also decided that two teams from the same division could not meet in the divisional playoffs so the Wildcard club could not meet a team from their division in the first round.[6] Therefore, in the 1970 AFC example above, if the Wildcard "D," came from the Western division, the pairings would then switch. In that event the Wildcard would then play at the other division champion due to host a divisional playoff game, in this case "A," the Eastern champion. The Central would then play at the West. This would occur only twice from 1970 to 1974 — both times in the NFC. In 1970, Detroit could not meet Minnesota in the first round of the Divisional playoffs, so the Lions played at Dallas and San Francisco went to Minnesota. In the 1972 NFC playoffs, although the Wildcard was assigned to play at the East winner, Dallas could not play Washington since both teams could not meet prior to the championship game. Instead, Dallas played at San Francisco and Green Bay at Washington in the Divisional Playoffs.

As for the conference championships, in a separate draw the AFC order of selection was A, B, and C (Eastern, Western, and Central), and in the NFC the results were C, A, and B (Western, Eastern and Central), with the divisions rotating in 1971 and 1972. The first division chosen would have first priority to host the conference championship. For example, in 1972 the undefeated Miami Dolphins had to play the AFC Championship at Pittsburgh since the Central division champion was scheduled to host the game. However, if the team with first priority lost in the divisional playoffs, then the second division in priority would host the game. In 1973, the NFC title game between the Vikings and Cowboys was played at Dallas since the Western champion, Los Angeles, lost in the first round. The NFC East winner was then next in line to host the championship game. Similarly, the Rams-Vikings NFC title game was played in Minnesota in 1974, after Washington, the Eastern champions, were ousted in the Divisional Playoffs. The third division could only host if they and the wildcard team would advance to the championship game. This would occur in the AFC in 1971 when Baltimore played at Miami, and also in 1972 when Dallas played at Washington in the NFC championship game.[7]

In 1973, a proposal which would have based the sites of playoff games at the home of teams with the best regular-season records was defeated by a vote of 16–10. Instead, the owners, by a 26–0 vote, opted to retain the same divisional rotation formula that was utilized in 1970, 1971 and 1972 for the 1973, 1974, and 1975 seasons.[8] The three year rotation was recycled as 1973 would use the same format as 1970, 1974 the same as 1971, etc.

The divisional site rotation system, however, would only last through the 1974 playoffs. In 1975, NFL clubs decided to reverse their decision made two years earlier and voted 23–3 to abolish assigning home sites of playoff games by rotation and instead reward teams that had the best records during the regular season with homefield advantage.[9] The Wildcard team would play at the division champion with the best won-lost-tied percentage and the division champion with the second-best record would host the division winner with the third-best record in each conference. In the event that the Wildcard club and the division winner with the best record were from the same division, then the divisional playoff matchups would change. The Wildcard would then play the division champion with the second-best record and the top division winner would host the third division champion.

The owners then voted unanimously to add a second wildcard team in each conference in 1978 to expand the playoff field to ten teams.[10] This resulted in an extra round of playoffs. The two Wildcard teams in each conference would play each other in the first round. The winner of the Wildcard contest would then play at the division champion with the best record and the third division winner would play at the division champion with the second-best record. As with the 1975–1977 format, if the Wildcard team and the top seed in the conference came from the same division, the pairings would switch as two teams from the same division could not meet in the Divisional Playoffs.

In 1990, the league adopted by 28–0 vote, the addition of a third wildcard in each conference to increase the number of postseason teams to 12.[11] In the Wild Card round, the top two seeds would receive byes. The division champion with the third-best record (3rd seed) would host the third Wild Card (6th seed) and the Wild Card with the best record (4th seed) would host the Wild Card club with the second-best record (5th seed). Beginning in 1990, there would no longer be any restrictions on intradivisional matchups prior to the championship game. The winners in the Wild Card round would then play the top two seeds in the divisional playoff round. The top seed would be guaranteed of facing the lowest remaining seed.

When the NFL realigned in 2002, member clubs voted unanimously to modify the playoff format to include the four division champions and two wildcards in each conference.[12] In the Wildcard Playoffs, the second-best Wild Card (6th seed) would visit the division champion with the third-best record (3rd seed) and the fourth-best division winner (4th seed) would host the Wild Card with the best record (5th seed) in each conference. The division champions with the two best records would have a bye. In the Divisional Playoffs, the top seed would host the lowest remaining seed while the division champion with the second-best record would host the highest remaining seed.

Here is a summary of playoff formats used in the NFL, AFL and AAFC and how the sites of postseason games were determined.

1933–1966 (NFL)

NFL Championship

1933: at homefield of division champion with best winning percentage:
N.Y. Giants (11–3–0 .786) at Chicago Bears (10–2–1 .833)

1934–1949: at Eastern division champion (even numbered years)[a]
at Western division champion (odd numbered years)

[a] 1936 NFL Championship, Green Bay vs. Boston Redskins played at Polo Grounds, NY.

1950–1952: at American Conference Champion (1950, 1952)
at National Conference Champion (1951)

1953–1966: at Western Conference Champion (odd numbered years)
at Eastern Conference Champion (even numbered years)

Note: If two teams ended the regular season tied for first place, the site of the divisional or conference playoff game would be determined by coin flip.

1946–1948 (AAFC)

AAFC Championship

at Western division champion (1946, 1948)
at Eastern division champion (1947)

Note: If two teams ended the regular season tied for first place, the site of the divisional playoff game would be determined by coin flip.

1949 (AAFC)

First Round

The team with the best record would host the team with the fourth-best record and the team with the second-best record would host the team with the third-best record:

(4) Buffalo at (1) Cleveland
(3) Brooklyn-New York Yankees at (2) San Francisco

AAFC Championship

The home team would be the surviving playoff winner with the best won-lost percentage during the regular season:

(2) San Francisco at (1) Cleveland

1960–1968 (AFL)

AFL Championship

at Eastern division champion (even numbered years)
at Western division champion (odd numbered years)

Note: If two teams ended the regular season tied for first place, the site of the divisional playoff game would be determined by coin flip.

1969 (AFL)

AFL Divisional Playoffs

The two division champions would host the runner-up from the other division:

Eastern division runner-up (**Houston**) at Western division champion (**Oakland**)
Western division runner-up (**Kansas City**) at Eastern division champion (**NY Jets**)

AFL Championship

The championship game would be at the site of the Western division winner, however, if both teams from the Eastern division advanced to the title game then the Eastern division champion would host the game. The following scenarios existed as possible matchups in the AFL Championship Game depending on results of the interdivisional playoff games:[13]

AFC Divisional Playoffs		AFL Championship Game
KC at NYJ	Hou at Oak	(actual matchup in bold)
KC win	+ HOU win	→ Houston at Kansas City
KC win	+ **OAK win**	→ **Kansas City at Oakland**
NYJ win	+ HOU win	→ Houston at NY Jets
NYJ win	+ OAK win	→ NY Jets at Oakland

1967–1969 (NFL)

NFL Conference Championships

1967
EAST — Century Division Champion (**Cleveland**) at Capitol Division Champion (**Dallas**)
WEST — Coastal Division Champion (**Los Angeles**) at Central Division Champion (**Green Bay**)

1968
EAST — Capitol Division Champion (**Dallas**) at Century Division Champion (**Cleveland**)
WEST — Central Division Champion (**Minnesota**) at Coastal Division Champion (**Baltimore**)

1969
EAST — Century Division Champion (**Cleveland**) at Capitol Division Champion (**Dallas**)
WEST — Coastal Division Champion (**Los Angeles**) at Central Division Champion (**Minnesota**)

NFL Championship
at Western Conference Champion (1967, 1969)
at Eastern Conference Champion (1968)

1970–1974

The four postseason participants from each conference are as follows:

- The three division champions.
- The Wild Card club (second-place team with the best record). In no case would the wildcard team play at home in either the Divisional Playoffs or Conference Championship game.

Note: From 1970 to 1989, two teams from the same division could not meet in the Divisional Playoffs.

Divisional Playoffs

Below is the rotation that was established in 1970 to determine game sites for the Divisional Playoffs. In each conference, the division champion listed under the heading "Home Team 1" would host the division champion scheduled to play on the road, i.e. the division winner noted as "Road Team 1." The Wild Card team, "Road Team 2," would play at the division champion listed as "Home Team 2." However, if the Wild Card club is from the same division as "Home Team 2," the Wild Card would instead play at "Home Team 1" and the division winner "Road Team 1" would play at "Home Team 2."[14]

	AFC				NFC			
	Home Team 1	Home Team 2	Road Team 1	Road Team 2	Home Team 1	Home Team 2	Road Team 1	Road Team 2
	A	B	C	D	A	B	C	D
1970	East	West	Central	Wildcard	East	Central	West	Wildcard
	B	C	A	D	B	C	A	D
1971	West	Central	East	Wildcard	Central	West	East	Wildcard
	C	A	B	D	C	A	B	D
1972	Central	East	West	Wildcard	West	East	Central	Wildcard
	A	B	C	D	A	B	C	D
1973	East	West	Central	Wildcard	East	Central	West	Wildcard
	B	C	A	D	B	C	A	D
1974	West	Central	East	Wildcard	Central	West	East	Wildcard

1970

AFC Central at East → **CINCINNATI AT BALTIMORE**
       Wildcard at West → **MIAMI AT OAKLAND**

NFC Wildcard at East → **DETROIT AT DALLAS**
       West at Central → **SAN FRANCISCO AT MINNESOTA**

Detroit did not play Minnesota in the Divisional Playoffs because two teams from the same division could not meet prior to the championship game.

Appendix F • 240 •

1971

AFC East at West → **MIAMI AT KANSAS CITY**
     Wildcard at Central → **BALTIMORE AT CLEVELAND**

NFC East at Central → **DALLAS AT MINNESOTA**
     Wildcard at West → **WASHINGTON AT SAN FRANCISCO**

1972

AFC West at Central → **OAKLAND AT PITTSBURGH**
     Wildcard at East → **CLEVELAND AT MIAMI**

NFC Wildcard at West → **DALLAS AT SAN FRANCISCO**
     Central at East → **GREEN BAY AT WASHINGTON**

Dallas did not play Washington in the Divisional Playoffs because two teams from the same division could not meet prior to the championship game.

1973

AFC Central at East → **CINCINNATI AT MIAMI**
     Wildcard at West → **PITTSBURGH AT OAKLAND**

NFC West at East → **LOS ANGELES AT DALLAS**
     Wildcard at Central → **WASHINGTON AT MINNESOTA**

1974

AFC East at West → **MIAMI AT OAKLAND**
     Wildcard at Central → **BUFFALO AT PITTSBURGH**

NFC East at Central → **ST. LOUIS AT MINNESOTA**
     Wildcard at West → **WASHINGTON AT LOS ANGELES**

Conference Championship Games

The following is the rotation established in 1970 to determine game sites for conference championship games. Listed below is the order of priority. Actual host division and matchups depicted in **bold**.

	AFC			NFC		
	1	*2*	*3*	*1*	*2*	*3*
	A	B	C	C	A	B
1970	**East**	West	Central	**West**	East	Central
	B	C	A	A	B	C
1971	**West**	Central	East	**East**	Central	West
	C	A	B	B	C	A
1972	**Central**	East	West	Central	West	**East**
	A	B	C	C	A	B
1973	**East**	West	Central	West	**East**	Central
	B	C	A	A	B	C
1974	**West**	Central	East	East	**Central**	West

1970

AFC At East. → **OAKLAND AT BALTIMORE**
NFC At West. → **DALLAS AT SAN FRANCISCO**

1971

AFC At East. → **BALTIMORE AT MIAMI**

The AFC Championship game was played at the Eastern division champion because both the Western and Central division champions lost in the Divisional Playoffs.

NFC At East. → **SAN FRANCISCO AT DALLAS**

1972

AFC At Central. → **MIAMI AT PITTSBURGH**
NFC At East. → **DALLAS AT WASHINGTON**

The NFC Championship game was played at the Eastern division champion because both the Central and Western division champions lost in the Divisional Playoffs.

1973

AFC At East. → **OAKLAND AT MIAMI**
NFC At East. → **MINNESOTA AT DALLAS**

The NFC Championship game was played at the Eastern division champion because the Western division champion lost in the Divisional Playoffs.

1974

AFC At West. → **PITTSBURGH AT OAKLAND**
NFC At Central. → **LOS ANGELES AT MINNESOTA**

The NFC Championship game was played at the Central division champion because the Eastern division champion lost in the Divisional Playoffs.

1975–1977

Beginning with the 1975 season, playoff teams are seeded based on best won-lost-tied percentage during the regular season. Any ties are broken based on the tiebreaking procedures in effect for that particular season.

The four postseason participants from each conference are seeded as follows:

1. The division champion with the best record.
2. The division champion with the second-best record.
3. The division champion with the third-best record.
4. The Wild Card club (second-place team with the best record).

In each conference, the playoff matchups will be as follows:

Divisional Playoffs

(4) the Wild Card club at (1) the division champion with the best record; and
(3) the division champion with the third-best record at (2) the division champion with the second-best record

If the Wild Card club is from the same division as the team with the highest winning percentage, then:

(3) the division champion with the third-best record at (1) the division champion with the best record; and
(4) the Wild Card club at (2) the division champion with the second-best record

Conference Championship Games

The divisional playoff winners with the highest seeds in each conference will have homefield advantage.[15]

1978–1989 (except 1982)

The five postseason participants from each conference are seeded as follows:

1. The division champion with the best record.
2. The division champion with the second-best record.
3. The division champion with the third-best record.

4. The Wild Card club with the best record.
5. The Wild Card club with the second-best record.

In each conference, the playoff matchups will be as follows:

First Round Playoff Games

(5) the Wild Card club with the second-best record at (4) the Wild Card club with the best record.

Divisional Playoff Games

(4) or (5) the Wild Card winner at (1) the division champion with the best record; and

(3) the division champion with the third-best record at (2) the division champion with the second-best record

If the Wild Card winner is from the same division as the team with the highest winning percentage, then:

(3) the division champion with the third-best record at (1) the division champion with the best record; and (4) or (5) the Wild Card winner at (2) the division champion with the second-best record

Conference Championship Games

The divisional playoff winners with the highest seeds in each conference will have homefield advantage.[16]

1982

Due to the 57-day players' strike, a 16-team postseason Super Bowl Tournament was conducted with teams being seeded 1–8 in each conference based on regular season records:

First Round

In each conference, the 1st-seed would host the 8th seed, the 2nd seed would host the 7th seed, the 3rd seed would host the 6th seed, and the 4th seed would host the 5th seed.

AFC	NFC
(8) Cleveland at (1) LA Raiders	(8) Detroit at (1) Washington
(7) New England at (2) Miami	(7) Tampa Bay at (2) Dallas
(6) NY Jets at (3) Cincinnati	(6) St. Louis at (3) Green Bay
(5) San Diego at (4) Pittsburgh	(5) Atlanta at (4) Minnesota

Second Round

The two highest remaining seeds in each conference would be the home teams. The highest remaining seed would host the lowest seed; and the second highest seed would host the second lowest seed.

AFC	NFC
(6) NY Jets at (1) LA Raiders	(4) Minnesota at (1) Washington
(5) San Diego at (2) Miami	(3) Green Bay at (2) Dallas

Conference Championship Games

The two second round winners in each conference would play in the conference championship game. The home teams would be the surviving second round winners with the highest seeds.

AFC	NFC
(6) NY Jets at (2) Miami	(2) Dallas at (1) Washington

1990–2001

The six postseason participants from each conference are seeded as follows:

1. The division champion with the best record.
2. The division champion with the second-best record.
3. The division champion with the third-best record.
4. The Wild Card club with the best record.
5. The Wild Card club with the second-best record.
6. The Wild Card club with the third-best record.

Note: Beginning with the 1990 season, there would no longer be any restrictions on intra-divisional matchups prior to the conference championship game.

In each conference, the playoff matchups will be as follows:

Wild Card Playoff Games

(6) the Wild Card club with the third-best record at (3) the division champion with the third-best record; and (5) the Wild Card club with the second-best record at (4) the Wild Card club with the best record

Divisional Playoff Games

(6), (4), or (5) lowest seeded Wild Card survivor at (1) the division champion with the best record; and

(3), (4), or (5) highest seeded Wild Card survivor at (2) the division champion with the second-best record

Conference Championship Games

The divisional playoff winners with the highest seeds in each conference will have homefield advantage.[17]

2002–Current

The six postseason participants from each conference are seeded as follows:

1. The division champion with the best record.
2. The division champion with the second-best record.
3. The division champion with the third-best record.
4. The division champion with the fourth-best record.
5. The Wild Card club with the best record.
6. The Wild Card club with the second-best record.

In each conference, the playoff matchups will be as follows:

Wild Card Playoff Games

(6) the Wild Card club with the second-best record at (3) the division champion with the third-best record; and (5) the Wild Card club with the best record at (4) the division champion with the fourth-best record

Divisional Playoff Games

(6), (4), or (5) lowest seeded Wild Card survivor at (1) the division champion with the best record; and

(3), (4), or (5) highest seeded Wild Card survivor at (2) the division champion with the second-best record

Conference Championship Games

The divisional playoff winners with the highest seeds in each conference will have homefield advantage.[18]

Chapter Notes

Preface

1. *1980 NFL Record Manual*, p. 396.

Introduction

1. Chris Willis, *The Man Who Built the National Football League: Joe F. Carr* (Lanham, MD: Scarecrow Press, 2010), pp. 275–76.
2. Carl Becker, *The Coffin Corner*, vol. 19, no. 6 (1997).
3. PFRA, "Three-Peat! The 1931 Season."
4. *1938 National Football League Constitution & Bylaws*, article VIII, section 15.
5. Robert S. Lyons, *On Any Given Sunday: A Life of Bert Bell* (Philadelphia: Temple University Press, 2009), p. 141.
6. Michael MacCambridge, *America's Game: The Epic Story of How Pro Football Captured a Nation* (New York: Anchor Books, 2005), p. 40.
7. *Chicago Daily Tribune*, July 7, 1946.
8. *New York Times*, May 31, 1947; *1947 All-America Football Conference Record Manual*, p. 7.
9. Lyons, pp. 193–94.
10. "Washington will play Baltimore each year one game at home or one game at Baltimore home field ... the Bears will play the Cardinals each year one game at home or one game at Cardinals' home field."—*1953 National Football League Constitution & Bylaws*, Article VII, Section 7, pp. 17–18. The Colts and Redskins would continue to play each other once each season until 1967.
11. Ed Bouchette, *Pittsburgh Post-Gazette*, April 13, 2001; George Strickler, *Chicago Daily Tribune*, April 4, 1962; Joseph M. Sheehan, *New York Times*, April 4, 1962; *Elyria (OH) Chronicle Telegram*, April 4, 1962; *Cumberland (MD) Evening Times*, March 19, 1963.
12. George Strickler, *Chicago Tribune*, December 1, 1966; *Los Angeles Times*, December 1, 1966; *1968 National Football League Constitution & Bylaws*, article N–IV, pp. 81–82.
13. *1970 National Football League Constitution & Bylaws*, article VIII, p. 46; *1970 NFL Record Manual*, pp. 11–12; Norm Miller, *New York Daily News*, May 12, 1969.
14. Dave Nelson, *Rocky Mountain News*, May 12, 1969; William N. Wallace, *New York Times*, May 12, 1969.
15. Ted Brock, *Pro!*, November 13, 1977, Cincinnati vs. Minnesota edition, pp. 7B, 15B.
16. Bob Oates, *Los Angeles Times*, May 29, 1970; Dave Brady, *Washington Post*, May 29, 1970; Dave Anderson, *New York Times*, April 21, 1970.
17. Dave Anderson, *New York Times*, May 29, 1970.
18. Jay Zahn, *The Coffin Corner*, vol. 32, no. 6 (2010).
19. "NFL Meeting Minutes," March 29, 1977.
20. *Pro!*, November 13, 1977, Cincinnati vs. Minnesota edition, pp. 3B, 5B.
21. *1978 National Football League Media Information Book*, p. 8.
22. MacCambridge, *America's Game*, pp. 330–31.
23. Aaron Sharockman, *St. Petersburg Times*, March 9, 2004.
24. Carolyn Braff, "Val Pinchbeck," December 2, 2008, accessed July 31, 2012, http://www.sportsvideo.org/halloffame/league/val-pinchbeck.
25. Pete Rozelle, "New Look For '78," *1977 NFL Record Manual*, pp. 360–61.
26. "NFL Meeting Minutes," March 13, 1986.
27. Ibid., March 15, 1990.
28. "NFL Meeting Minutes," March 18, 1987; *1990 NFL Record & Fact Book*, p. 16.

29. "NFL Meeting Minutes," March 20, 1991; "NFL Meeting Minutes," March 23, 1993.
30. *Houston Chronicle,* December 22, 1994; *1995 NFL Record & Fact Book,* p. 14; *1997 NFL Record & Fact Book,* p. 14.
31. NFL press release, October 28, 1998.
32. "Ask Tiebreaker Expert Joe Ferreira," CBSSports.com, December 21, 2008, accessed on December 22, 2008, http://www.cbssports.com/mcc/messages/chrono/11532891/0/L (page no longer online).
33. "NFL Meeting Minutes," May 22, 2001; *2001 NFL Record & Fact Book,* p. 15.
34. "NFL Meeting Minutes," October 31, 2000.
35. "Ask Tiebreaker Expert Joe Ferreira," CBSSports.com, December 21, 2008.
36. NFL press release, August 15, 2001.
37. *2002 NFL Record & Fact Book,* p. 16.
38. *2009 NFL Record & Fact Book,* p. 16.
39. "NFL modifies West Coast formula," ESPN.com, March 23, 2009, accessed March 24, 2010, http://sports.espn.go.com/nfl/news/story?id=4009230.
40. NFL Annual Meeting news conference transcript, NFLcommunications.com, March 26, 2010, accessed April 1, 2010, http://nflcommunications.com/2010/03/26/commissioner-goodell-league-meeting-press-conferences/#more-1049.
41. Judy Battista, *New York Times,* April 19, 2012.
42. Paul Domowitch, *Philadelphia Daily News,* April 14, 2009.
43. *SportsBusiness Daily,* April 26, 2010.
44. Judy Battista, *New York Times,* April 19, 2012.
45. Thomas Wailgum, "NFL Schedule, Rivalries and Potential TV Ratings Optimized by Packaged Software," CIO.com, September 5, 2008, accessed March 12, 2010, http://www.cio.com/article/447683/NFL_Schedule_Rivalries_and_Potential_TV_Ratings_Optimized_by_Packaged_Software.
46. John Ourand, *SportsBusiness Daily,* January 17, 2011.
47. NFL press release, January 5, 2012; NFL press release, May 24, 2012.

1967–1969 (NFL)

1. *1968 National Football League Constitution & Bylaws,* Article N–XI, pp. 92–93.

1970–1975

1. *1970 National Football League Constitution & Bylaws,* Article XIII, pp. 45–47.
2. Ibid., p. 47.

1976–1977

1. "NFL Meeting Minutes," November 4, 1975.

1978–1987

1. *1978 NFL Media Information Book,* p. 8.
2. "NFL Meeting Minutes," March 29, 1977.
3. *1978 National Football League Constitution & Bylaws,* Article XIII, pp. 48–49.
4. 1982 Games Canceled by Strike: Original 1982 NFL Schedule Week 3 through 10 is from *1982 NFL Media Information Book,* pp. 178–80.
5. 1987 Games Canceled by Strike: Original 1987 Week 3 Schedule is from *1987 NFL Record & Fact Book,* p. 5.

1988–1994

1. *1987 NFL Record & Fact Book,* p. 14.

1995–1998

1. *1997 NFL Record & Fact Book,* p. 14.

1999–2001

1. *1999 NFL Record & Fact Book*, p. 14; NFL press release, October 28, 1998.

2002–Current

1. *2002 NFL Record & Fact Book*, p. 16.

Appendix A: Schedule Release Dates (1933–2012)

1. NFL: *Chicago Tribune*, July 10, 1933; *New York Times*, August 25, 1934; *Christian Science Monitor*, July 19, 1935; *New York Times*, August 11, 1936; *New York Times*, July 9, 1937; *New York Times*, July 8, 1938; *New York Times*, April 3, 1939; *New York Times*, July 23, 1940; *New York Times*, June 29, 1941; *New York Times*, March 30, 1942; *New York Times*, June 22, 1943; *New York Times*, April 24, 1944; *New York Times*, April 12, 1945; *New York Times*, April 30, 1946; *Washington Post*, September 11, 1947; *Christian Science Monitor*, September 15, 1948; *New York Times*, August 19, 1949; *New York Times*, June 28, 1950; *New York Times*, July 12, 1951; *New York Times*, June 26, 1952; *New York Times*, August 14, 1953; *Los Angeles Times*, June 29, 1954; *New York Times*, July 13, 1955; *New York Times*, June 28, 1956; *Chicago Tribune*, June 26, 1957; *Los Angeles Times*, June 17, 1958; *New York Times*, June 26, 1959; *New York Times*, June 22, 1960; *Los Angeles Times*, April 13, 1961; *New York Times*, April 4, 1962; *Chicago Tribune*, March 24, 1963; *Hartford Courant*, April 24, 1964; *Chicago Tribune*, April 2, 1965; *New York Times*, April 5, 1966; *Chicago Tribune*, April 19, 1967; *New York Times*, April 19, 1968; *Hartford Courant*, May 18, 1969; *Los Angeles Times*, April 21, 1970; *Los Angeles Times*, April 14, 1971; *Los Angeles Times*, April 23, 1972; *New York Times*, May 1, 1973; *New York Times*, April 17, 1974; *New York Times*, April 13, 1975; *Chicago Tribune*, April 22, 1976; *New York Times*, April 28, 1977; *Chicago Tribune*, April 9, 1978; *Chicago Tribune*, April 6, 1979; *Boston Globe*, April 11, 1980; *Los Angeles Times*, April 8, 1981; *Chicago Tribune*, April 9, 1982; *Miami Herald*, April 21, 1983; *Miami Herald*, April 13, 1984; *Miami Herald*, April 11, 1985; *Philadelphia Inquirer*, April 3, 1986; *Dallas Morning News*, April 8, 1987; *Fresno Bee*, April 6, 1988; *Dallas Morning News*, April 8, 1989; *Philadelphia Daily News*, April 27, 1990; *Milwaukee Journal Sentinel*, April 19, 1991; *Miami Herald*, May 7, 1992; *Dallas Morning News*, April 29, 1993; *San Antonio Express-News*, April 29, 1994; *Miami Herald*, April 26, 1995; *Sacramento Bee*, April 25, 1996; *Sacramento Bee*, March 27, 1997; *Miami Herald*, April 3, 1998; *Sacramento Bee*, April 2, 1999; *St. Louis Post-Dispatch*, April 5, 2000; *Philadelphia Inquirer*, April 13, 2001; *Miami Herald*, March 29, 2002; *Philadelphia Inquirer*, April 4, 2003; *Philadelphia Inquirer*, April 15, 2004; *USA Today*, April 15, 2004; *Buffalo News*, April 14, 2005; *USA Today*, April 14, 2005; *Boston Globe*, April 7, 2006; *USA Today*, April 7, 2006; *New York Times*, April 12, 2007; *USA Today*, April 12, 2007; *Pittsburgh Post-Gazette*, April 16, 2008; *USA Today*, April 16, 2008; *Boston Globe*, April 15, 2009; *USA Today*, April 15, 2009; *Pittsburgh Post-Gazette*, April 21, 2010; *USA Today*, April 21, 2010; *Los Angeles Times*, April 20, 2011; *USA Today*, April 20, 2011; *New York Times*, April 18, 2012; *USA Today*, April 18, 2012. AAFC: *Chicago Daily Tribune*, July 7, 1946; *New York Times*, June 1, 1947; *New York Times*, July 27, 1948; *New York Times*, June 28, 1949. AFL: *New York Times*, April 26, 1960; *Washington Post*, May 2, 1961; *Christian Science Monitor*, April 24, 1962; *Christian Science Monitor*, May 25, 1963; *New York Times*, May 7, 1964; *New York Times*, April 12, 1965; *Chicago Tribune*, April 29, 1966; *New York Times*, May 6, 1967; *Chicago Tribune*, April 30, 1968; *New York Times*, May 25, 1969.

2. *Washington Post*, September 11, 1947; *Christian Science Monitor*, September 15, 1948; *New York Times*, August 19, 1949.

Appendix F: Site Priorities for Postseason Games

1. Chris Willis, *The Man Who Built the National Football League: Joe F. Carr* (Lanham, MD: Scarecrow Press, 2010), p. 316; *Chicago Daily Tribune*, December 5, 1933; *New York Times*, December 7, 1933; *Los Angeles Times*, December 12, 1933.
2. Willis, *The Man Who Built*, p. 326; *Hartford Courant*, July 2, 1934.
3. "AFL Meeting Minutes," January 11, 1969.
4. "NFL Meeting Minutes," March 20, 1970; NFL press release, March 30, 1970.
5. *1970 NFL Record Manual*, pp. 12–14.
6. "NFL Meeting Minutes," May 28, 1970.
7. *1973 National Football League Constitution & Bylaws*, Article XXI, pp. 80–81.
8. "NFL Meeting Minutes," April 3, 1973.
9. Ibid., June 24, 1975.
10. Ibid., March 29, 1977.
11. Ibid., March 11–15, 1990.
12. Ibid., March 19, 2002.
13. 1969 AFL Playoffs: "AFL Meeting Minutes," April 30, 1969; William N. Wallace, *New York Times*, December 20, 1969.

14. 1970–1974 Playoffs: *1970 NFL Record Manual*, pp. 12–14; *1971 NFL Record Manual*, pp. 9–10; *1973 National Football League Constitution & Bylaws*, Article XX, p. 78 and Article XXI, pp. 80–81.
15. 1975–1977 Playoffs: *1975 National Football League Constitution & Bylaws*, Article XX, p. 81.
16. 1978–1989 Playoffs (except 1982): *1978 NFL Media Information Book*, p. 176.
17. 1990–2001 Playoffs: *1994 NFL Record & Fact Book*, p. 9.
18. 2002–Present Playoffs: *2002 NFL Record & Fact Book*, pp. 9–10.

Bibliography

The information compiled for this book was derived from various sources including NFL, AFL and AAFC team and league media guides, league press releases, the official minutes of NFL owners' meetings as well as the following publications.

Newspapers and Periodicals

Baltimore Sun
Boston Globe
Buffalo News
Chicago Tribune
Christian Science Monitor
The Coffin Corner: The Official Magazine of the Professional Football Researchers Association
Dallas Morning News
Fresno Bee
Green Bay Press Gazette
Hartford Courant
Houston Chronicle
Los Angeles Times
Miami Herald
Milwaukee Journal Sentinel
New York Daily News
New York Times
Philadelphia Daily News
Philadelphia Inquirer
Pittsburgh Post-Gazette
Portsmouth Times
Pro!
Rocky Mountain News
Sacramento Bee
St. Louis Post-Dispatch
St. Petersburg Times
San Antonio Express-News
San Francisco Chronicle
USA Today
Washington Post

Books

1947 All-America Football Conference Record Manual: All-America Football Conference, 1947.
1970 NFL Record Manual: National Football League, 1970.
1971 NFL Record Manual: National Football League, 1971.
1977 NFL Record Manual: National Football League, 1977.
1978 NFL Media Information Book: National Football League, 1978.
1980 NFL Record Manual. New York: Dell, 1980.
1982 NFL Media Information Book. New York: Workman, 1982.

1987 NFL Record & Fact Book. New York: Workman, 1987.
1990 NFL Record & Fact Book. New York: Workman, 1990.
1994 NFL Record & Fact Book. New York: Workman, 1994.
1995 NFL Record & Fact Book. New York: Workman, 1995.
1997 NFL Record & Fact Book. New York: Workman, 1997.
1999 NFL Record & Fact Book. New York: Workman, 1999.
2001 NFL Record & Fact Book. New York: Workman, 2001.
2002 NFL Record & Fact Book. New York: Workman, 2002.
2009 NFL Record & Fact Book. New York: Time Inc. Home Entertainment, 2009.
2012 NFL Record & Fact Book. New York: Time Inc. Home Entertainment, 2012.
Lyons, Robert S. *On Any Given Sunday: A Life of Bert Bell*. Philadelphia: Temple University Press, 2009.
MacCambridge, Michael. *America's Game: The Epic Story of How Pro Football Captured a Nation*. New York: Anchor Books, 2005.
Palmer, Pete, Ken Pullis, Sean Lahman, Tod Maher, Matthew Silverman, Christina Kahrl, Gary Gillette. *The ESPN Pro Football Encyclopedia, Second Edition*. New York: Sterling, 2007.
Willis, Chris. *The Man Who Built the National Football League: Joe F. Carr*. Lanham, MD: Scarecrow, 2010.

Other Official League Sources

1938 National Football League Constitution & Bylaws: National Football League, 1938.
1953 National Football League Constitution & Bylaws: National Football League, 1953.
1964 National Football League Constitution & Bylaws: National Football League, 1964.
1968 AFL & NFL Constitution & Bylaws: American and National Football Leagues, 1968.
1969 AFL & NFL Constitution & Bylaws: American and National Football Leagues, 1969.
1970 National Football League Constitution & Bylaws: National Football League, 1970.
1973 National Football League Constitution & Bylaws: National Football League, 1973.
1975 National Football League Constitution & Bylaws: National Football League, 1975.
1978 National Football League Constitution & Bylaws: National Football League, 1978.

Websites

CBSSports.com
CIO.com
ESPN.com
FICO.com
Newspaperarchive.com
NFL.com
NFLcommunications.com
NFLmedia.com
OptimalPlanning.com
Profootballarchives.com
Profootballresearchers.org
Shrpsports.com
SportsBusinessDaily.com
Sportsvideo.org
The506.com
Timeanddate.com

Index

alignment: (1933) 23; (1934) 25; (1935) 27; (1936) 28; (1937–1942) 30; (1943) 32; (1944) 32; (1945) 33; (1946; NFL) 35; (1946–1948; AAFC) 37; (1947–1949; NFL) 35–36; (1949; AAFC) 38; (1950) 39; (1951) 40; (1952) 42; (1953–1959) 44; (1960–1965; AFL) 53; (1960; NFL) 45; (1961–1965; NFL) 47; (1966; NFL) 49; (1966–1967; AFL) 54; (1967–1969; NFL) 50–51; (1968–1969; AFL) 55; (1970–1975) 56; (1976) 71–72; (1977) 80; (1978–1987) 84; (1988–1994) 116; (1995–1998) 135; (1999–2001) 145; (2002–2017) 154; *see also* realignment
All-America Football Conference 7, 9
American Football League 8–9
American Professional Football Association 3
America's Game: The Epic Story of How Pro Football Captured a Nation 11
Arizona Cardinals 18; Chicago Cardinals 5–7; St. Louis Cardinals 10, 17
Atlanta Falcons 8, 10

Baltimore Colts (AAFC) 7
Baltimore Colts (NFL) 7, 9–10, 17
Bell, Bert 6–8, 19, 22
Bell, Bert, Jr. 6, 8
Bell, Upton 6
Brooklyn Dodgers (AAFC) 7
Brooklyn Dodgers (NFL) 4
Buffalo Bills (AAFC) 7
Buffalo Bills (NFL) 17–18
Buffalo Bisons (AAFC) 7
Buffalo Bisons (NFL) 3

Canton Bulldogs 3
Card-Pitt 5

Carolina Panthers 13
Carr, Joe F. 4, 235
Chicago Bears 4–7, 235
Chicago Cardinals *see* Arizona Cardinals
Chicago Rockets 7
Chicago Stadium 5
Cincinnati Bengals 9, 11
Cincinnati Reds 5
Cleveland Browns 7–10, 13, 18
Cleveland Rams *see* St. Louis Rams
Columbus Panhandles 3
common opponent scheduling 11–13; *see also* modified common opponent formula
comparison intraconference chart: 1978–1994 117; 1978–1998 137
Competition Committee 13
Crowley, James H. 7

Dallas Cowboys 8, 10, 14
Dallas Texans (NFL) 7
Dayton Triangles 3
Denver Broncos 9, 17–18
Detroit Lions 6, 13; Portsmouth Spartans 4, 5
division games in Week 17 18–19
divisional, conference, interconference games per team/season 215–218
divisions, league divided into two 5, 235

Ewbank, Weeb 10

Ferreira, Joe 14
fewest head-to-head regular-season meetings: interconference teams (1970–2001) 225; (1970–2012) 225–226; (2002–2012) 225; intraconference teams (non-division) (1970–2001) 227; (1970–2012) 228; (2002–2012) 227–228
"flexible scheduling" 18

games canceled by strike: (1982) 99–103; (1987) 115
games removed from 1976–1977 rotation 75–78
Goodell, Roger 18
Green Bay Packers 4–6, 8, 11, 13, 17, 235

Halas, George 5, 236
Hooey, Robert 4
Houston Oilers *see* Tennessee Titans
Houston Texans 14
Hunt, Lamar 236

Ingram, Admiral Jones H. 7
"instant" scheduling 12
interconference rotation 9–10, 14; (1967–1969) 51; (1970–1975) 60–62; (1976–1977) 73–75; (1978–2001) 88; (1999–2001) 146; (2002–2017) 155
intraconference rotation 9, 14; (1970–1975) 58–60; (1976–1977) 75–78; (1978–1987) 85; (1988–1994) 116–117; (1995–1998) 136; (1999–2001) 145–146; (2002–2017) 155

Jacksonville Jaguars 13

Kansas City Chiefs 10, 17–18
Katz, Howard 19–21
Kensil, Jim 9, 11, 22
Kiesling, Walt 8

Lambeau, Curly 4
Lewin, Dennis 12
Los Angeles Dons 7
Los Angeles Rams *see* St. Louis Rams
Louisville Brecks 3
Lyons, Robert S. 5

MacCambridge, Michael 11
Marshall, George Preston 5–6

Index

matchups between former division rivals 14–15
Miami Dolphins 9–10, 17
Miami Seahawks 7
Minnesota Vikings 8, 10–11, 18
modified common opponent formula 13; *see also* common opponent scheduling
Monday Night Football 10, 11, 21
most consecutive regular-season meetings at same site 17, 223–224
most consecutive seasons playing a non-division opponent 223
most head-to-head regular season meetings: (1920–2012) 221; between interconference teams (1970–2001) 224; (1970–2012) 224–225; (2002–2012) 224; between intraconference teams (non-division) (1970–2001) 226; (1970–2012) 226–227; (2002–2012) 226

The Neilsen Company 21
New England Patriots 17–18
New Orleans Saints 8, 10
New York Giants 3, 5–6, 10–11, 14, 17, 235
New York Jets 10–11, 17–18
New York Yankees (AAFC) 7
New York Yanks (NFL) 7
NFL Media Information Book 11–12
NFL Record & Fact Book 12
NFL Record Manual 12
NFL Total Access 21
1931 scheduling controversy 4
1932 Bears–Spartans playoff 4–5
1933 rule changes 5
non-divisional opponent breakdown charts *see* opponent breakdown charts
North, Michael 19–20
number of games played against: conference opponents 228–233; interconference opponents 233–235
number of regular-season games played 218–220
number of teams and games played by season 214

Oakland Raiders 10, 18
Ohio State Journal 4
O'Malley, Kevin 12
On Any Given Sunday: A Life of Bert Bell 5–6
opponent breakdown charts: (1933) 24; (1934) 26; (1935) 28; (1936) 29; (1937–1942) 30–31; (1943) 32; (1944) 33; (1945) 34; (1946; NFL) 35; (1946–1948; AAFC) 37–38; (1947–1949; NFL) 36–37; (1949; AAFC) 38; (1950) 40; (1951) 42; (1952) 43; (1953–1959) 44–45; (1960; NFL) 46; (1960–1965; AFL) 54; (1961–1965; NFL) 47–49; (1966; NFL) 49–50; (1966–1967; AFL) 54–55; (1967–1969; NFL) 51–53; (1968–1969; AFL) 56; (1970–1975) 62–71; (1976) 78–80; (1977) 82–84; (1978–1987) 89–115; (1988–1994) 119–134; (1995–1998) 137–144; (1999–2001) 148–153; (2002–2013; yearly) 156–174; (2002–2017; team-by-team) 174–212
Optimal Planning Solutions 19
owners' meetings 5–7, 11–14, 18, 75, 236

Phil-Pitt "Steagles" 5
Philadelphia Eagles 5–6, 18
Pinchbeck, Val, Jr. 11, 19
Pittsburgh Pirates *see* Pittsburgh Steelers
Pittsburgh Steelers 8–9, 12, 17; Pittsburgh Pirates 5
playoff formats 235–243; *see also* postseason game sites
Portsmouth Spartans *see* Detroit Lions
"position games" 155–156; *see also* standings-based matchups
postseason game sites 235–243; *see also* playoff formats
Pro! 12

rare meetings: between interconference teams 17–18, 222–223; between intraconference teams 17, 221–222; *see also* teams not meeting for many seasons
realignment: (1967) 8, 50–51; (2002) 14, 154; *see also* alignment
Rock Island Independents 3
Rooney, Art 5, 8
Rooney, Dan 8
Rosenbloom, Carroll 7
rotation scheduling 9–11
Rozelle, Pete 8, 12

St. Louis Cardinals *see* Arizona Cardinals
St. Louis Rams 18; Cleveland Rams 5–6; Los Angeles Rams 10
St. Paul Ideals 3
San Diego Chargers 10, 17–18
San Francisco 49ers 7, 10, 13, 18
schedule release dates 213
"Schedule Release Show" 21
scheduling formula by position: (1978–1987) 86–87; (1988–1994) 117–119
scheduling formulas: (1933) 23–24; (1934) 25–26; (1935) 27–28; (1936) 28–29; (1937–1942) 5, 30; (1943) 32; (1944) 33; (1945) 33–34; (1946; NFL) 35; (1946–1948; AAFC) 7, 37; (1947–1949; NFL) 5, 36; (1949; AAFC) 7, 38; (1950) 39–40; (1951) 40–42; (1952) 42–43; (1953–1959) 7, 44; (1960; NFL) 46; (1961–1965) (NFL) 8, 47; 1966 (NFL) 49; 1967–1969 (NFL) 8, 51; 1960–1965 (AFL) 8, 53–54; (1966–1967; AFL) 9, 54; (1968–1969; AFL) 9, 55; (1970–1975) 9, 57; (1976) 72–73; (1977) 80–82; (1978–1987) 12, 84–85; (1988–1994) 116–117; (1995–1998) 13, 136; (1999–2001) 13, 145–147; (2002–2017) 14, 154
Seattle Seahawks 10, 17–18, 75
Shea Stadium 12
site locations: interconference games 12–13; for intraconference games 13
standings-based matchups 155–156; *see also* "position games"
Stone, Rick 19–20
Sunday Night Football 18, 21

Tagliabue, Paul 15
Tampa Bay Buccaneers 10, 17–18, 75
teams not meeting for many seasons: interconference 17–18, 222–223; intraconference 17, 221–222; *see also* rare meetings
teams not visiting another team for many seasons 15–17
teams required to play same number of games 5
Tennessee Titans 14; Houston Oilers 10
Three Rivers Stadium 12
Thursday Night Football 21
2012–2013 yearly non-divisional opponents 156–174; *see also* opponent breakdown charts
2012–2017 team-by-team non-divisional opponents 174–212; *see also* opponent breakdown charts

Washington Redskins 6–7, 13–14
West Coast rotation modified 18, 154
Wrigley Field 4, 235

Yankee Stadium 8